True Stories
from the American Past

Volume II: Since 1865

SECOND EDITION

TRUE STORIES FROM THE AMERICAN PAST

VOLUME II: SINCE 1865

EDITED BY

William Graebner
State University of New York
College at Fredonia

THE McGRAW-HILL COMPANIES, INC.

New York St. Louis San Francisco Auckland Bogotá Caracas Lisbon
London Madrid Mexico City Milan Montreal New Delhi
San Juan Singapore Sydney Tokyo Toronto

McGraw-Hill

A Division of The **McGraw·Hill** Companies

TRUE STORIES FROM THE AMERICAN PAST
VOLUME II: SINCE 1865

Copyright © 1997 by The McGraw-Hill Companies, Inc. All rights reserved.
Previously published under the title of *True Stories from the American Past*.
Copyright © 1993 by The McGraw-Hill Companies, Inc. All rights reserved.
Printed in the United States of America. Except as permitted under the United
States Copyright Act of 1976, no part of this publication may be reproduced or
distributed in any form or by any means, or stored in a data base or retrieval
system, without the prior written permission of the publisher.

This book is printed on acid-free paper.

1 2 3 4 5 6 7 8 9 0 FGR FGR 9 0 9 8 7 6

ISBN 0-07-023015-3

This book was set in Plantin by ComCom, Inc.
The editors were Lyn Uhl and Monica Freedman;
the production supervisor was Diane Ficarra.
The cover was designed by Joseph A. Piliero.
The photo editor was Anne Manning.
Project supervision was done by The Total Book.
Quebecor Printing/Fairfield was printer and binder.

Library of Congress Cataloging-in-Publication Data

Graebner, William.
  True stories from the American past / edited by
William Graebner. -- 2nd ed.
    p. cm.

  Contents: v.   1. To 1865 -- v.   2. Since 1865
  --ISBN 0-07-023015-3 (v.   2) ISBN 0-07-067954-1 (v.   1).
  1. United States--History.   I. Graebner, William.   II. Title.
E178.W265   1997
973--dc20   96-9569

About the Authors

BETH BAILEY is associate professor of history at Barnard College, Columbia University. She is the author of *From Front Porch to Back Seat: Courtship in 20th Century America* and, with David Farber, *The First Strange Place: Race and Sex in World War II Hawaii*. She is currently working on a new book, *Sex in the Heartland*, about the sexual revolution in Kansas.

PAUL BOYER is Merle Curti Professor of History at the University of Wisconsin-Madison and editor-in-chief of the forthcoming *Oxford Companion to American History*. Particularly relevant to the Waco essay in this volume is his 1992 book *When Time Shall Be No More: Prophecy Belief in Modern American Culture* (Cambridge, Mass., Harvard University Press).

LEONARD DINNERSTEIN is professor of history and Director of Judaic Studies at the University of Arizona. He specializes in American ethnic history. Among his books are *The Leo Frank Case* (New York: Columbia University Press, 1968), *America and the Survivors of the Holocaust* (New York: Columbia University Press, 1982), and *Antisemitism in America* (New York: Oxford University Press, 1994). He has also coauthored *Ethnic Americans*, with David Reimers (New York: Harper and Row, 1988) and *Natives and Strangers: A Multicultural History of Americans*, with Roger L. Nichols and David Reimers (New York: Oxford University Press, 1996). He is currently doing research for a book on the holocaust, the survivors, and the memories.

DAVID FARBER is assistant professor of history at Barnard College, Columbia University. He is the author of *Chicago '68* (Chicago: The University of Chicago Press, 1988), and *The Age of Great Dreams: America in the 1960s* (New York: Hill and Wang, 1994), editor of *The Sixties: From Memory to History* (Chapel Hill: The University of North Carolina Press, (1994) and co-author, with Beth Bailey, of *The First Strange Place: Race and Sex in World War II Hawaii* (New York: The Free

Press, 1992). He is currently working on a book about the public life of Alfred Sloan of General Motors.

MICHAEL FRISCH is an American social historian who had recently completed graduate school when he joined the throng at the Woodstock Festival in 1969. Since then, he has been teaching history and American studies at SUNY Buffalo. He is the author of *A Shared Authority: Essays on the Craft and Meaning of Oral and Public History* (Albany: State University of New York Press, 1990). His most recent book is *Portraits in Steel* (Ithaca: Cornell University Press, 1993), an oral history of ex-steelworkers prepared in collaboration with documentary photographer Milton Rogovin.

WILLIAM GRAEBNER is professor of history at the State University of New York, College at Fredonia. He has written on a variety of aspects of twentieth-century American history. His books include *A History of Retirement* (New Haven: Yale University Press, 1980), *The Engineering of Consent: Democracy and Authority in Twentieth-Century America* (Madison: University of Wisconsin Press, 1987), *Coming of Age in Buffalo* (Philadelphia: Temple University Press, 1990), and *The Age of Doubt: American Thought and Culture in the 1940s* (Boston: Twayne, 1991). He is Associate Editor of *American Studies.*

WALTER LAFEBER is Noll Professor of History at Cornell University. His recent books are *The American Age: U.S. Foreign Relations At Home and Abroad Since 1750* (New York, 1989), and *America, Russia, and the Cold War, 1945–1990,* 6th edition (New York, 1990). He currently serves on the editorial boards of *Political Science Review* and *International History Review.*

GEORGE LIPSITZ is professor of ethnic studies at the University of California, San Diego and the author of *Rainbow at Midnight* (Urbana: University of Illinois Press, 1994), *Dangerous Crossroads* (London and New York: Verso, 1994), *Sidewalks of St. Louis* (Columbia: University of Missouri Press, 1991), *Time Passages* (Minneapolis: University of Minnesota Press, 1990), and *A Life in the Struggle: Ivory Perry and the Culture of Opposition* (Philadelphia: Temple University Press, 1988 and 1995).

GERALD MARKOWITZ is professor of history and chair of the interdepartment of thematic studies at John Jay College of Criminal Justice, City University of New York. He is author of numerous articles on twentieth-century politics and culture in America. He has authored a number of books and collections including *Democratic Vistas: Post Offices and Public Art During the New Deal* (Philadelphia: Temple University Press, 1984). With David Rosner he has edited *Dying for Work: Workers' Safety and Health in Twentieth-Century America* (Bloomington, IN: Indiana University Press, 1987) and *"Slaves of the Depression": Workers' Letters about Life on the Job* (Ithaca, NY: Cornell University Press, 1987).

ELAINE TYLER MAY is professor of American studies and history at the University of Minnesota. She is the author of *Great Expectations: Marriage and Divorce in*

Post-Victorian America (Chicago: University of Chicago, 1980), *Homeward Bound: American Families in the Cold War Era* (New York: Basic Books, 1988), *Pushing the Limits: American Women, 1940–1961* (New York: Oxford University Press, 1994), and *Barren in the Promised Land: Childless Americans and the Pursuit of Happiness* (Basic Books, 1995).

STUART CREIGHTON MILLER is emeritus professor of social science and history and director of the social science program at San Francisco State University. He is the author of *The Unwelcome Immigrant: The American Image of the Chinese, 1785–1882* (Berkeley: University of California Press, 1969), the runner-up for the 1970 Bancroft Prize, and *"Benevolent Assimilation": The American Conquest of the Philippines, 1899–1903* (New Haven: Yale University Press, 1982). His current research is on immigration history, focusing on cultural pluralism as a romantic quest.

STEPHEN NISSENBAUM teaches history at the University of Massachusetts at Amherst. His most recent book is *The Battle for Christmas* (Knopf 1996) He has also written *Salem Possessed: Social Origins of Witchcraft* (with Paul S. Boyer, 1974), *Sex, Diet, and Debility in Jacksonian America* (1980), *The Pursuit of Liberty* (third edition 1996; a multi-authored textbook), and *All Over the Map: Rethinking American Regions* (1996, with Edward L. Ayers, Patricia Nelson Limerick, and Peter Onuf). Active in the public humanities, he has served as member and president of the Massachusetts Foundation for the Humanities. He holds degrees from Harvard College, Columbia University, and the University of Wisconsin.

DAVID ROSNER is professor of history at Baruch College and the Graduate Center of the City University of New York. He is also adjunct professor of community medicine at Mt. Sinai Medical School. He has written extensively on the history of public health and medicine in America and is the author of *A Once Charitable Enterprise: Hospitals and Health Care in Brooklyn and New York, 1885–1915* (Princeton, NJ: Princeton University Press, 1986) and most recently, with Gerald Markowitz, *Deadly Dust: Silicosis and the Politics of Occupational Disease in Twentieth-Century America* (Princeton, NJ: Princeton University Press, 1991).

CARLOS A. SCHWANTES is professor of history at the University of Idaho. He is the author of twelve books including *Coxey's Army: An American Odyssey* (Lincoln: University of Nebraska Press, 1985) and *Railroad Signatures Across the Pacific Northwest* (Seattle: University of Washington Press, 1993). He is currently writing a book on the stagecoach and steamboat era in the northern West.

RONALD STORY is professor of history at the University of Massachusetts at Amherst. Story's work includes *Generations of Americans* (New York: St. Martins, 1976), *The Forging of an Aristocracy* (Middletown: Wesleyan University Press, 1980), *Sports in Massachusetts* (Westfield: Institute for Massachusetts Studies, 1991), *Five Colleges, Five Histories* (Amherst: Five Colleges, Inc., 1992), and *A More Perfect Union*, 4th edition (Boston: Houghton-Mifflin, 1995). He is currently working on a set of ten CD-ROMs on the wars of the United States for Infobase Corporation.

ALAN TRACHTENBERG is Neil Gray, Jr. Professor of English and American Studies at Yale University. He is the author of *Brooklyn Bridge: Fact and Symbol* (New York: Oxford University Press, 1965), *The Incorporation of America: Culture and Society in the Gilded Age* (New York: Hill & Wang, 1982), and *Reading American Photographs: Images as History, Matthew Brady to Walker Evans* (New York: Hill & Wang, 1989). He is currently working on the relationship between Native Americans and ideas of national identity.

ALTINA L. WALLER is professor of history at the University of Connecticut. She received her doctorate from the University of Massachusetts at Amherst and has taught at West Virginia University and Rhodes College in Memphis, Tennessee. Her first book was *Reverend Beecher and Mrs. Tilton: Sex and Class in Victorian America* (Amherst, MA: University of Massachusetts Press, 1982). Her second book, *Feud: Hatfields, McCoys and Social Change in Appalachia, 1860–1900* (Chapel Hill, NC: University of North Carolina Press, 1988) is the basis for her story about the feud.

Contents

Preface

True Stories is a special kind of reader. It consists of fifteen stories, each thoroughly researched and impeccably crafted by scholars who are authorities in their respective fields. Each story deals with a significant and compelling episode in the history of the United States since the Civil War. Every decade of that history is represented by at least one story.

In selecting the stories, I have been moved by the sense that the American past is too rich and varied to be bound and contained by the traditional and comfortable narratives with which most historians are conversant. Nonetheless, some of our stories—the story of the nation's imperial adventure in the Philippines, or the account of Francis Townsend's confrontation with Franklin D. Roosevelt's New Dealers over pensions for the aged—will be generally familiar to instructors, if not students. Other episodes, including the opening of Disneyland and the rock concerts at Woodstock and Altamont, will have resonance for many Americans, yet received their first serious historical treatment in the first edition of *True Stories*. Still others, including the story of the debate over an early artificial insemination, concern issues and incidents that are not even mentioned in survey textbooks. After surveying readers of the first edition, I have added stories on the nineteenth-century West, the South, World War II, and the late-twentieth-century religious right. The Reconstruction era is represented by a new story on the "Christmas Riots" of 1865. I hope readers will appreciate the remarkable diversity of *True Stories*.

Together, the stories cover a wide variety of fields of historical inquiry, many of them new to the study of history in the last two or three decades. These include popular culture; the history of medicine; sexuality; rural life; youth culture; women's history; the history of African-Americans; crime and violence; the aged; urban history; and the history of science and technology. Most important, each episode was selected because it promised to make, well, a good *story*.

Why use stories to study and learn history? The idea is not as unusual as it might seem. We live in a culture steeped in stories: the myths of ancient Greece,

Biblical narratives, bedtime stories, fairy tales, newspaper accounts, Hollywood epics, neighborhood rumors, one's personal account of the day's events after a hard day at school or at the office. Even the standard history textbooks are essentially stories—longer, more general, more familiar, and more generally accepted stories than the ones found in this book—but stories, just the same.

The accounts that make up *True Stories* are obviously not myths, or fairy tales, or rumors. They are a certain kind of story that we easily recognize as "history." Indeed, history might be understood as a set of analytical stories about the past whose authors think are "true." When we read an historical account, we expect it to be balanced, to be based on historical research and "facts," and to show respect for the past; by these standards, the stories in *True Stories* certainly qualify as history. But it is not quite the history one finds in a history textbook. *True Stories* features people who live and act in specific places and times and in precise historical circumstances. Its flesh and blood protagonists—some of them resembling mythic heroes or anti-heroes—build bridges, march on nation's capitol, take money to throw baseball games, justify the marketing of hazardous substances, speak from the big stage at the Woodstock Music & Art Fair, engage in armed combat with the federal government, or confront the nation's racist heritage on the sidewalks of World War II Hawaii. In short, one function of any story—and one purpose of *True Stories*—is to put people, and people's deeds, back into history.

There is another lesson to be learned from these stories, one that has to do with what a story is. Although the stories presented here often involve individuals acting in specific situations, they have significance that goes far beyond the setting or the actors. The people in *True Stories* (indeed, all of us) inevitably live their lives on the stage of history. The things that they do—even the odd, eccentric, or criminal things—are ultimately historical deeds, carried out within the economic, political, social, and cultural frameworks of a particular historical era. Therefore, a good story provides the insights of the traditional textbook, though in a very different form.

Sometimes it can be difficult to see the connections between a story and history, between the text and its context. When one sees a movie, or watches the 11 o'clock television news, one does not easily or automatically think of these "stories" as part of history; and making the connections between a specific event and the larger past can be more difficult when the event occurred decades ago. To help students make these connections, and to see the need for making them, each episode concludes with an interpretive section that pulls together the themes in the story and links the story proper with some larger and familiar historical context. For example, the epic hill-country feud between the Hatfields and the Mc-Coys in the 1880s emerges as a product of industrialization and urbanization; and the Iranian hostage crisis that began in 1979 is shaped as a moment in America's decline as a world economic and political power.

Each episode, then, has two distinct parts. The first part is the narrated story. Our goal was to keep this story section as free as possible from analysis and interpretation, in the hope that students would fashion their own perspectives once freed, if only relatively and momentarily, from the learned authority of the historian. The second part of the episode is a shorter interpretive conclusion, where the authors have been given free reign to bring their considerable analytical skills to bear on the body of the story.

As students and instructors will discover, the attempt to separate narrative and interpretation has been only moderately successful. Even the most rudimentary collections of "facts" and the simplest narratives begin with preconceptions, proceed from moral and ethical premises, and imply interpretive frameworks. So do our "true stories." Despite our efforts to put these elements in the background, they inevitably appear in the stories. Indeed, one purpose of the collection is to draw attention to the inescapable subjectivity of historians. Nonetheless, we also believe that the effort made here to separate narrative and analysis can assist students in generating their own readings of the past and, by doing so, in becoming active participants in the complex process of understanding and creating their own history.

ACKNOWLEDGMENTS

The authors wish to thank Andrea Balis, Hunter College; E.H. Beardsley, University of South Carolina, Columbia; Russ Huebel, Texas A&M University; and Kenneth Lyftogt, Northern Iowa, for their helpful reviews.

William Graebner

True Stories
from the American Past

Volume II: Since 1865

1

AN INSURRECTION THAT NEVER HAPPENED: THE "CHRISTMAS RIOTS" OF 1865

STEPHEN NISSENBAUM

At the end of the Civil War there remained the unresolved question of what was to be done about the more than three million African-Americans who had been freed from slavery. While Southerners were fearful about their own economic futures, to say nothing of fears for their physical safety if their former slaves united in retribution. Freed slaves had every reason to expect that a government which had been willing to sacrifice over 300,000 lives to end the slave system would also be willing to provide them with the essential economic means—land—to allow them to become contributing members of society. Yet the fate of both white Southerners and freedmen and freedwomen was in the hands of Northern politicians who had never been able to agree that the rights of freedpeople were a high priority in the war. What was universally celebrated at war's end was the subjugation of the South and the preservation of the Union. Considering that so many lives had been sacrificed, it was almost inevitable that the Union had become a "holy" cause, couched, by the President himself, in terms of a religious cleansing that would lead to a sanctified nation.

This emphasis on the preservation of the Union rather than the rights of African-Americans was clear from the beginning of the war right through to the end. Lincoln's Emancipation Proclamation, for example, was a very controversial, politically sensitive document. The President stood to lose much of his support for the war if he were to issue it in the early stages; such a proclamation only became feasible when the Union was in a militarily strong position after the bloody battle of Antietam. Even then the proclamation did not free slaves in slave states that had sided with the Union—Delaware, Maryland, Kentucky, and Missouri. In the South, of course, with the Confederacy in control, the proclamation had no effect until the military situation changed. Another example is the decision to use African-American troops in the Northern army. Northerners demonstrated their racism by initially denying the right of free blacks in the North to fight for the Union cause. Even when it became clear that enthusiasm for the war was waning and conscription was necessary to fill the ranks of the army, there was resistance to allowing African-Americans to fight. Only because of that shortage of men combined with extensive politicking and lobbying on the part of African-American leaders such as Frederick Douglas did black regiments become

1

grudgingly acceptable to Northerners. Despite the not inconsiderable accomplishment of ending slavery as an institution, the still rampant racist attitudes in the North made the future of African-American freedpeople in the South very precarious.

Stephen Nissenbaum's story of the rumored Christmas insurrection reveals much about the immediate aftermath of the Civil War, when the hopes of freedpeople soared and white Southerners' fears reached almost hysterical proportions—emotions that were exacerbated by contested and ambiguous Northern policies. But this story also explores the nature of human relations in the plantation South before the war, the human give-and-take that was impossible to avoid, even though whites attempted to deny the essential humanity of their slaves. Embedded in the rituals of Christmas was reinforcement of the unequal and oppressive power hierarchy juxtaposed with the potential for resistance and the ultimate destruction of that hierarchy. What we know now is that despite the sacrifices of the Civil War, the Reconstruction era was not to overturn the hierarchy at all; that would have to wait another hundred years.

This is the story of an insurrection that never happened—a revolt that was never even planned. It is a story that would never have taken place at all except for the convergence of three elements, each involving a different kind of "history." The first element, one of *military history*, was the defeat of the South at the end of the Civil War. The second element, one of *political and economic history*, was the liberation of slaves and a new federal policy that promised them their own land. The third and final element, one of *social and cultural history*, was Christmas.

It is that final element, Christmas, which requires the most explanation. The Christmas season had long been a special occasion in the American South for both white and black people. And for the most part the season did not involve what we might expect—church services, or elegant balls, or Santa Claus. Instead, this was a season of hard drinking, noisemaking, and generally rowdy behavior. (It can best be considered as a New Year's Eve, Mardi Gras, and Halloween, all rolled into one.) Christmas was a time when the ordinary rules that governed social behavior simply ceased to operate, or when those rules were actually turned upside down. Children were allowed to demand gifts from grown-ups, women from men, and the poor from the rich. This was an occasion when "the world turned upside down." And those who really controlled Southern society—wealthy adult males—were generally willing to go along with this topsy-turvy state of affairs: they knew it would only last a short time.

As early as 1773, one visitor recorded in his diary on Christmas day that "I was waked this morning by Guns fired all around the House." In 1823, a rural white Southerner attacked the Christmas season for being a "general scene of dissipation and idleness." Some folks spent the time making "rough jokes." "Apprentice boys and little negroes" fired guns and crackers. And everyone—"parents, children, servants, old, young, white, black, and yellow"—drank hard. "And if you inquire what it is all for, no earthly reason is assigned . . . , except this, 'Why man! It is Christmas.'" More than three decades later, a teenage Virginia girl named Amanda Edmonds was awakened "by the repeated blows of the firecrackers, and the merry voices shouting 'hurr[a]y for Christmas,' and then the nog was on the wing until the eggs were foaming, in went the milk and all ingredients poured together; lastly it was foaming in our glasses, till they were drained of the contents."

Everybody commented at the time about how much Southerners drank during the Christmas season. It is clear that people—women and even children among them—commonly began drinking at breakfast. Teenager Amanda Edmonds began Christmas day in 1857 drinking "glass after glass" of spiked eggnog. Once again, in 1861, the first thing Edmonds did in the morning was to have "a joyful eggnog drink—I really got tight. The first signs of Christmas that I've seen."

The American South was not unique in celebrating the Christmas season in such a fashion. In much of the North, and in Europe, too—in most early agricultural societies—late December was taken as a time of carnival. Here was the one time of the year in which there was fresh food and drink aplenty from the recently completed harvest and an extended period of leisure in which to consume it— leisure that followed hard upon months of grueling and intensive labor. (In a way, it was much like the same holiday season in modern college communities, in which the conclusion of final examinations is similarly celebrated with boisterous drinking and letting off steam.)

But in one important particular, Christmas in the antebellum South was unique. For, in that society, all those carnivalesque holiday rituals extended across the color line—they encompassed black slaves as well as their white masters. If Southern society was "turned upside down" at Christmas, that inversion involved not simply age, class, and gender (as it did in other places); above all, it involved race.

First of all, Christmas in the slave quarters meant *freedom*—for a little while. Christmas was the one time of year when slaves were released from the obligation to work, usually for several days in a row. Slaves became, in a sense, free— free from labor, free to do whatever they wished, free even to travel off their masters' property. One Northerner, living on a plantation as a tutor to the owner's children, reported that "[t]hroughout the state of South Carolina, Christmas is a holiday, together with 2 of the succeeding days . . . especially for the negroes. On these days the chains of slavery . . . are loosed. A smile is seen on every countenance."

Slaves employed their freedom in a variety of ways, from visiting friends and family members to participating in religious meetings. But perhaps the activities that were most often reported involved revelry: eating, drinking, dancing, making noise, and making love. Solomon Northup, a free black who was kidnapped into slavery in Louisiana, later wrote of Christmas as "the times of feasting, and frolicking, and fiddling—the carnival season with the children of bondage . . . the only days when they are allowed a little restricted liberty, and heartily indeed do they enjoy it." A white Southerner used the same term, calling Christmas "the time of the blacks' high carnival," while another white man described the period as "times of cramming, truly awful. [T]hey stuffed and drank, and sang and danced." The wife of ex-U.S. President John Tyler wrote in 1845 that the family's slaves "have from now a four days' holiday and have given themselves up completely to *their* kind of happiness—drinking, with nothing on earth to do."

It seems clear that sex was involved in all this, too. More than one visitor explicitly described the slave Christmas as a modern version of the old Roman Saturnalia, an orgiastic occasion. One writer who did so employed language whose euphemisms were not intended to conceal the author's meaning: "From three to four days *and* nights are given as holiday, during which every indulgence and license consistent with any subordination and safety are allowed."

Christmas misrule entailed even more than leisure and "liberty." It also meant a symbolic turning of the tables between masters and slaves. Christmas was the one occasion of the year when slaves were actually allowed to demand gifts from their masters, even to do so in an aggressive fashion that might have led to a whipping at any other time of the year. One common seasonal ritual was termed "Christmas Gift." "Christmas Gift!" usually amounted to a boisterous wake-up call combined with a demand for presents. A former slave described one version of the ritual: "The cock crowing for sunrise is scarcely over when the servants steal into the Big House on tiptoe so they can catch everybody there with a shouted 'Christmas Gift!' before the kitchen fire is even started or the water put on to boil for the early morning coffee." In response, each member of the white family who is thus "captured" must hand over a gift to the slave who has "caught" her. Years later, a planter's daughter, Susan Dabney Smedes, described the game with nostalgic affection:

> On Christmas mornings the servants delighted in catching the family [i.e., the owner's family] with "Christmas giff!" "Christmas giff!" betimes in the morning. They would spring out of unexpected corners and from behind doors on the young masters and mistresses. At such times [she adds in explanation] there was an affectionate throwing off of the reserve and decorum of every-day life.

Young Amanda Edmonds, the same teenager who got tight on eggnog at breakfast, wrote to her diary in 1857 that " 'Christmas Gift' was heard from every tongue this morning before we hardly saw the first gleam of morning in the far east." The recollections of a one-time slave, a Georgia field hand named James Bolton, suggest that the custom was not always limited to house servants: "We runned up to the big house early Christmas morning and holler out, 'Morning, Christmas Gif!' Then they gave us plenty of Santy Claus, and we would go back to our cabins to have fun till New Year's Day."

Christmas was the one occassion of the year on which plantation owners would formally offer presents to their chattel slaves. It was a rare planter who did not give something to his slaves at Christmas. At a minimum, the gifts were small—the kinds of things we might dismiss today as "trinkets" but which the slaves had good reason to value: sugar, tobacco, or hats, along with ribbons, bandannas, and other decorative items for the women. Some slaveholders distributed money. An especially lavish (and ostentatious) example of this practice was reported by Richard Jones, a former slave from South Carolina, whose account also reminds us how demeaning such ritualized generosity could be:

> Marse allus carried a roll of money as big as my arm. He would come up to de Quarter on Christmas, July 4th and Thanksgiving, and get up on a stump and call all the chilluns out. Den he would throw money to 'em. De chilluns got dimes, nickels, quarters, half-dollars and dollars. At Christmas he would throw ten-dollar bills. De parents would take de five and ten dollar bills in change, but Marse made dem let de chilluns keep de small change. I ain't never seed so much money since my marster been gone.

Dressing for the Carnival (1877). The great American artist Winslow Homer painted this large oil canvas while traveling in southern Virginia at the very end of Reconstruction. An immensely respectful and dignified portrayal, it shows a man being dressed for the John Canoe Christmas ritual by his wife and another women as the children watch in fascination. (Metropolitan Museum of Art Amelia B. Lazarus Fund, 1922).

On many plantations slaves were asked to approach the Big House to receive their gifts in person from their master and his family (along with the family's best wishes). More often, it was masters and their families who visited the slave quarters to attend the slaves' own party there. But wherever these scenes took place, in the quarters or the Big House, some planters and their families used the occasion to make elaborate gestures of deference to their slaves. Oftentimes they joined in the festivities themselves, at least symbolically. Just as often, they prepared the party meal themselves, or they personally superintended its preparation. Occasionally, a master even made the ostentatious gesture of serving part of the meal to the slaves himself. One North Carolina slaveholder centered his version of the ritual on the preparation and distribution of eggnog: after the drink was "pronounced right," it was ceremoniously placed out on the piazza (on a beautiful mahogany table that came from the Big House). At this point the slaves assembled and were ceremoniously handed one glass apiece:

> My grandfather knew every one of his negroes, big and little, by name; and his greeting was always personal to each. They came up in couples, according to age and dignity, and the unvarying formula was: "Sarvant, Master; merry Christmas to you, an' all de fambly, sir!" "Thank you, Jack; merry Christmas to you and yours!"

Whites were aware of the symbolic significance of these gestures of deference, gestures that demonstrated that they were playing their part in the expected seasonal ritual in which the world was briefly and symbolically "turned upside down." They would refer to the unprecedented degree of "familiarity" between masters and slaves on this occasion. One Tennessee slaveowner claimed that at Christmas his "people" were "as happy as Lords." Another man wrote: "Here all authority and all distinction of colour ceases; black and white, overseer and bookkeeper, mingle together in the dance." Another planter stressed how different Christmas was from the only other holiday he permitted his sixty slaves—the Fourth of July: "The one in July is celebrated with a dinner and whiskey. The Christmas holiday is a very different thing. It lasts from four to six days, and during this *jubilee* it is difficult to say who is master. The servants are allowed the largest liberty."

"It is difficult to say who is master." That was surely an exaggeration. But it was also the very point at which the meaning of Christmas in the slave South became potentially *political*—the point at which, under certain circumstances, slaves might think about becoming their own masters for real. In fact, some black people used Christmas to take *permanent* control of their lives. For example, the season offered unique opportunities for escaping slavery altogether by running away, taking advantage of the common Christmas privilege of freedom to travel (and along roads that might now be crowded with unfamiliar black faces). Christmas also presented a tempting occasion for more aggressive forms of resistance. Sanctioned disorders could always step across the bounds and edge over into violence, riot, or even revolt. A striking number of actual or rumored slave revolts were planned to take place at Christmas—nearly one-third the known total, according to one historian. Reports of Christmas insurrection were especially rampant in 1856; in that year revolts were reported in almost every one of the Southern states.

That was in slavery times. But the most serious rumors of planned insurrection at Christmas (rumors that amounted, in the end, to very little) came just *after* the slaves were finally emancipated, with the end of the Civil War, in December 1865. Here was the point at which the memory of the traditional rituals of the Southern Christmas converged with a moment of serious political crisis in the lives of both black and white Southerners.

Some political history, then. If ever there was a time when the hopes of African-Americans were at fever pitch, it was in 1865. Those hopes had been raised by a set of executive orders and congressional acts, passed during the war itself and for essentially military purposes. The Union army of General William Tecumseh Sherman had marched irresistibly through Georgia late in 1864, finally taking Savannah in late December. (Sherman telegraphed President Lincoln a famous message, offering him Savannah as a "Christmas present.") Sherman's march had created a refugee army of slaves, tens of thousands of newly liberated slaves who were now impoverished and homeless and who turned for assistance to the Northern troops. To deal with the army of refugees, in January 1865, General Sherman issued a proclamation that would have important consequences: Special Field Order No. 15. This proclamation set aside for the freedmen any lands (in the area of his recent march) that had been confiscated by the Union army or abandoned by their white owners. These lands, to be divided into 40-acre lots, included some of the best real estate in Georgia and South Carolina.

A few months later, in March 1865, the U.S. Congress established a new federal agency, the Freedmen's Bureau, designed to deal more systematically with the difficult but imminent transition to freedom. The Freedmen's Bureau adopted Sherman's policy and extended it to the entire Confederacy. In late July, the head of the Freedmen's Bureau, General Oliver O. Howard, issued to his staff Circular No. 13 (a circular was a memorandum designed to circulate to all agents of an organization). Circular No. 13 contained a set of procedures that would divide abandoned or confiscated Southern plantations into 40-acre lots and distribute them to black families. Each of these families would receive a written certificate of possession. (The policy became associated with the catchphrase *forty acres and a mule*).

But in the summer of 1865, with the war over and Andrew Johnson in the White House, federal priorities in Washington underwent a significant change. President Johnson decided that the most important task facing the United States was not that of dealing with the freed slaves but rather that of reestablishing the loyalty of white Southerners. To do so would involve "restoring" abandoned lands to their former owners. The President now instructed General Howard to reverse his policy and to withdraw Circular No. 13. The Freedmen's Bureau was ordered to persuade the former slaves to abandon their hopes for land—and to sign labor contracts for the coming year with their former masters.

Both blacks and whites knew this was a crucial issue. Each side knew that the key to the future lay not just in legal freedom from slavery but also in the linked questions of land and labor. Whoever was able to own the one would also be able to control the other. Without working on land that belonged to them (or that they could later purchase), the freedmen and their families would be at the mercy of their former owners. And both sides knew that plantation owners would never voluntarily sell their land to blacks. Without land reform, the freedmen could never control their own labor. They would be working under conditions almost identical to those imposed by slavery itself.

The situation was profoundly muddled during the fall of 1865. Most agents of the Freedmen's Bureau (but not all of them) dutifully spent the fall of 1865 trying to extinguish the very hopes they had earlier helped to spread. In reality the cause of land reform was lost. But many freedmen could not bring themselves to believe that they were being betrayed by the very people who had just liberated them.

At this time of mixed and confusing messages, large numbers of Southern blacks came to pin their lingering hopes on the coming Christmas season. Word passed through the African-American community, often spread by Union soldiers, that when Christmas arrived in 1865, the government would provide them with land and the other necessities of economic independence. An ex-slaveholder from Greensboro, Alabama, wrote to his daughter that the Union troops who were stationed near his plantation had assured his former slaves "that our lands were to be divided among them at Christmas," and he added in frustration that they had already ceased doing any work. "Almost all are living along thoughtless of the future" and paying no attention to "what they will do after Christmas, when all will be turned adrift."

Black Refugees Crossing the Rappahannock River, 1862. Even relatively early in the Civil War, before emancipation, many African-American slaves fled their legal places of residence, especially in areas such as this one in northeastern Virginia, where Union troops were located nearby. Note the heavily laden cart drawn by oxen in this photograph. (Library of Congress).

It should not be surprising that the freedmen chose to hold such high hopes for the Christmas season, since for African-Americans Christmas had long been associated with the symbolic inversion of the social hierarchy—with grand gestures of paternalistic generosity by the white patrons who had always governed their lives. In 1865 those white patrons happened to be the government of the United States. To intensify black hopes still further, the Thirteenth Amendment to the U.S. Constitution (abolishing slavery) was due to take effect on December 18, one week to the day before Christmas.

By mid-November 1865, Southern newspapers were publishing stories about these Christmas dreams. One story (titled "The Negroes at Christmas Time") reported that blacks throughout the South entertained expectations of "being furnished, about Christmas, by the Government, with the necessaries of 'housekeeping' . . . waiting in a life of ease and idleness, for the jubilee. . . ." A newspaper in Mississippi reported that "wildly credulous and wildly hopeful of men are . . . awaiting the millennium of the 25th of December, who expect a big division of land and plunder on that day." And the *New Orleans Daily Picayune* editorialized that "it has seemed to be impossible to eradicate from their minds the belief that about Christmas they were to have lands partitioned among them; and their imaginations have been heated with the expectation of becoming landholders, and living as their old masters used to do without personal labor."

Without personal labor. . . . a life of ease and idleness . . . awaiting the millennium . . . waiting for the jubilee. For white Southerners these were also code words. What they meant was that many blacks had not returned to work for their old masters at war's end (in fact, the crops of the 1865 season had gone mostly unharvested) and that they were refusing to sign degrading labor contracts with their former masters for the coming season. Alabama landowner Henry Watson reported that "Not a solitary negro in the country has made a contract for next year. The soldiers told them not to make them, that if they did they would be branded and become slaves again!" Their refusal posed a serious threat to the regional economy and especially to the well-being of the planter class.

It also indicated that the freedmen might be politically organized. Whites tended to interpret the hopes of the freedmen as aggressive and threatening, a sign that they were ready to turn to violence. And whites, like blacks, looked to the Christmas season as the time when matters would finally come to a head. Interpretations varied as to precisely how, and for what reason, violence would break out. Some whites thought it would happen spontaneously. An Atlanta newspaper warned that the holiday might start out as a "frolic" but that it would soon turn into something considerably more menacing. Emboldened by alcohol and encouraged by "bad white men," the blacks could be easily "persuaded to . . . commit outrage and violence." A planter from South Carolina told a visiting reporter that "some families will be murdered and some property destroyed," and he concluded ominously, *"It will begin the work of extermination."*

The fears of the one race were commingling in volatile fashion with the hopes of the other. As December approached, an increasing number of Southern whites became convinced that the freedmen were actively plotting an organized insurrection. All across the South, "apprehensions" of such a planned insurrection during the Christmas holidays were reported (and spread) by newspapers. In mid-November a Louisiana newspaper reported that "there is an increasing dread of what may turn up in the future. The negroes are, by some means, procuring arms, and are daily becoming more insolent." Toward the end of the month the *Cincinnati Daily Enquirer* headlined a story "A Negro Conspiracy Discovered in Mississippi" and explained that "a conspiracy had been organized among the blacks, extending from the Mississippi River to South Carolina, and that an insurrection was contemplated about Christmas." Such stories were printed and reprinted by newspapers throughout the South. Some of the rumors were quite detailed. A letter printed in the *New Orleans True Delta* cited a "reliable" report that blacks would collectively revolt "on the night before Christmas" and "wreak their vengeance" on whites whose names had already been chosen. The victims were to be identified to their attackers "by signs and marks placed on each house and place of business"—these marks would consist of coded numbers, as well as the letters X and O "set in chalk marks."

It was largely to the Freedmen's Bureau that there fell the task of persuading the freedmen that Christmas would not be ushering in the "jubilee," that further disruption of the Southern economy would harm them as well as whites, that the signing of labor contracts was now their best available recourse—and that insurrection would be futile. Under orders from President Johnson himself, the head of the Freedmen's Bureau, General O. O. Howard, spent the late fall touring the South in order to communicate these points. On November 12, General Howard sent a policy statement to his staff:

> It is constantly reported to the Commissioner and his agents that the free[d]men have been deceived as to the intentions of the Government. It is said that lands will be taken from the present holders and be divided among them on next Christmas or New Year's. This impression, wherever it exists, is wrong. All officers and agents of the Bureau are hereby directed to take every possible means to remove so erroneous and injurious an impression. They will further endeavor to overcome other false reports that have been industriously spread abroad, with a purpose to unsettle labor and give rise to disorder and suffering. Every proper means will be taken to secure fair written agreements or contracts for the coming year, and the freedmen instructed that it is for their best interests to look to the property-holders for employment. . . .

On another occasion, General Howard warned the freedmen directly that there would be "no division of lands, that nothing is going to happen at Christmas, that . . . [you] must go to work [and] make contracts for next year. . . . [I]nsurrection will lead to nothing but [your] destruction." Most agents of the bureau dutifully (if reluctantly) passed along the word that the freedmen's Christmas hopes were nothing but a pipe dream—or, as a Memphis newspaper put it, "a la mode Santa Claus." Colonel William E. Strong, the bureau's inspector general, addressed a group of Texas freedmen in plain language:

> I have been sent here from Washington, to make a speech to the colored people. I have little to say, and that is in plain words. Winter is coming on—go back to your former masters, work, be obedient, and show that you are worthy of freedom. You expect the Government to divide your late master's lands out to you, and about the first of January you will get buggies and carriages; but you are mistaken. You

will not get a cent. It all belongs to the former owners, and you will not get anything unless you work for it. It is true that rations have been given to some of you,
but you will not get any more. You have had good masters, I know. I have been
through here long enough to find out for myself.

But white Southerners were skeptical about whether such a cautionary message would be heeded by the black community. What was needed, one newspaper argued (in a sarcastic reference to the abolitionist leanings and the New
England background of many Freedmen's Bureau officials), was straight talk
from "imposing" men "who were born at least one thousand miles distant from
Cape Cod." Of course the planters themselves reiterated the message to their
ex-slaves. But the slaves would not heed *their* warnings, either. As one Mississippi newspaper conceded, "It amounts to nothing for former masters and mis-
tresses to read these orders to negroes. . . . They do not believe anything we can
tell them."

Some whites consciously manipulated the fear of an insurrection as a way
of convincing state and federal authorities to allow Southern whites to rearm
themselves—and to disarm (and harass) the freedmen. An Alabama official used
just such an argument in a letter to the governor of that state: "I am anxious to
organize the local company. It is feared the negroes will be troublesome about
Christmas unless there is some organization that can keep them in subjection."

But many whites were truly fearful. The mistress of one plantation near Columbia, South Carolina, later recalled how she was terrified by the nocturnal
singing that came from what until recently had been her slave cabins—singing that
evoked "expectations of a horde pouring into our houses to cut our throats and
dance like fiends over our remains."

It is possible that some African-Americans were indeed harboring thoughts
of (if not making plans for) a Christmas revolt. But those plans could hardly have
amounted to a coordinated conspiracy. What is far more likely is an explanation
that places both white fears and black hopes in the context of the intense expectations that normally surrounded Christmas on the slave plantation. For if Christmas was a time when slaves expected gestures of paternalist largesse, it was also
a time when slaves were used to acting up. (In that sense, the Atlanta paper may
have been shrewd in suggesting that the Christmas insurrection might begin as a
"frolic.")

What was happening in late 1865 was that a serious, contested set of political and economic issues—issues involving the radical redistribution of property
and the radical realignment of power—chanced to converge with a holiday season whose ordinary rituals had always pointed, however symbolically, to just such
a redistribution of property and just such a realignment of power. On both sides
of the color line there was a shared mythos about Christmas that made the holiday loom with ominous weight in the watershed year of white defeat and black
emancipation.

There was no insurrection. Confrontations, yes—even, in a number of cities, violent riots. The most serious of these was in Alexandria, Virginia, where two people were killed. But it soon transpired that the Alexandria riot was actually initiated by whites and that both victims were black. By December 28 or 29, it was

clear that the danger had subsided. "The *ides* of Christmas are past," one Southern paper proclaimed, "without any insurrection of the colored population of the late slave holding states. There is no probability of any combination of freedmen for hostile purposes; neither are they likely to combine, at present, for political or industrial objects." Another paper simply reported that "some cases of collision between blacks and whites occurred on Christmas, but there was no organized demonstration on the part of the former."

It was now possible to reinterpret the events of December 25, to put them back into the old, familiar antebellum categories. Newspapers reassured their readers that such "collisions" as did occur were "isolated" events and that they were not even political in nature but merely a function of old-fashioned Christmas rowdiness— occasioned by alcohol, not ideology. The Virginia correspondent of a Washington newspaper reported with relief that "a few brawls in Norfolk and Portsmouth were the result of whiskey, and had no political significance whatever." "Too much whiskey," claimed one paper; "much bad whiskey," added another; "some colored men, very much under the influence of bad whiskey," chimed in a third. And the newspapers now reported arrests for drunkenness and disorderly conduct by placing their notices in the police log, not the political columns. The racial identity of the offenders now hardly mattered. The *Richmond Daily Whig* reported on December 27 that "Christmas was celebrated in this city with unprecedented hilarity."

> It was more a street than a home celebration. "King Alcohol" asserted his sway and held possession of the town from Christmas eve until yesterday morning. Liquor and fire-crackers had everything their own way. A disposition was manifested to make up for lost time. This was the first real old fashioned Christmas frolic that has been enjoyed in the South for four years. The pent up dissipations and festivities of four Christmas days were crowded into this one day. . . .

By December 29, the *New Orleans Daily Picayune* even chose to use humor as a way of marginalizing the racial content of the violence that had indeed erupted in that city on Christmas day. Under the heading "Every one ought to be eloquent in his own defense," the paper reported that one white man, arrested on Christmas for rowdy behavior, testified in his defense: " 'Your honor, I am charged with being a disturber of the peace. It is a mistake, your honor. I have kept more than a hundred niggers off the streets these Christmas times. May it please your honor, I have a bad cold.' " The man's case was dismissed.

The crisis passed, it was now possible for white Southerners to return to the underlying problem—the collective refusal of the freedmen to work for their old masters. That would take care of itself, the *New Orleans Daily Picayune* explained, as the freedmen came to understand that their "true friends" were the Southern planter class, not the Northern demagogues who had falsely promised them land. When that truth at last dawns upon them—as it inevitably will—"they will learn where to learn their own true interest and duty."

The same editorial went on to explain bluntly just what that would mean:

> As the season passes by, without bringing them the possessions they coveted, and the license to be idle, which they expected with them, and they learn that they must look for support to themselves—for the government will decline to help those who do not help themselves—the relations of labor to capital will begin to be freed

from one of the most perplexing of the elements that have kept them unsettled; and to adjust themselves upon the natural basis of the mutual dependence of planter and freedmen on justice to each other for their mutual prosperity.

In other words, the freedmen would soon be forced back into virtual slavery. A newspaper in Richmond even resorted to a nostalgic evocation of the old interracial Christmas rituals, along with a rueful acknowledgment that the planters were unable to perform the part of patrons in the gift exchange. Not only would the freedmen fail to receive their masters' land, but they might even have to do without the "usual presents" they customarily received on this occasion. However, that was an aberration, indicating only that the planters were temporarily impoverished, not that race relations had changed:

> Heretofore every one of these four millions of beings expected and received a Christmas present, and partook of the master's good cheer. Now, alas, that former master is penniless, and he who depended upon his bounty is a homeless wanderer. The warm blanket, the cheerful fire, the substantial fare, the affectionate greetings, and the gifts they have been accustomed to receive at the hands of old and young will, we fear, be sadly missed.

Emancipated Negroes Celebrating the Emancipation Proclamation of President Lincoln. Like the bleak illustration on page 8, this woodcut-it appeared in March, 1863, in a French magazine, *Le Monde Illustre.* It shows African-American refugees accompanying an ox-drawn wagon (there were also two horses behind the oxen). But the few months that had passed since that earlier photograph made all the difference in the world to these refugees: they were now legally free. (*Le Monde Illustre,* March 21, 1863).

14

Nissenbaum

The Richmond editor summed up the prospect by referring to the eclipse of an old tradition—a tradition we have already encountered at the beginning of this story: "The familiar salutation of 'Christmas gift, master,' will not be heard." (That was the ritual in which slaves awakened their masters' families with a demand for gifts.) But the real object of nostalgia here was the *master's* loss, not the disappointment of his former slaves. That point came across clearly enough in the editor's concluding shot, an expression of hope that in another year or so things would be back to normal for the freedmen—"that their future condition may be better than their condition is at present, and that the next Christmas may dawn upon a thrifty, contented and well regulated negro peasantry."

Even now, with the Civil War lost and the black population legally free, the capital city of the Confederacy was continuing to link rituals of Christmas misrule with the maintenance of the antebellum racial hierarchy. A "contented and well regulated negro peasantry" was, after all, just what was needed to sustain a prosperous class of white planters. The cry of "Christmas gift!" would be music to their ears.

AN INTERPRETATION

The story of the "Christmas Riots" of 1865 is a microcosm of the entire period that became known as Reconstruction, the years between 1865 and 1877. It was a period of great hopes for the freedmen, hopes that were dashed, then raised, and then dashed once again.

As we have seen, with the war over, President Johnson quickly placed his highest priority on restoring the states of the late Confederacy to their former place in the federal Union. The new President rescinded Field Order No. 15. With his tacit encouragement, the Confederate states attempted to act as if little had been changed by their military defeat. They passed "Black Codes," requiring freedmen to sign annual contracts (those who refused were subject to arrest by any white man) or stipulating that unemployed blacks had to pay a "vagrancy" fine—and if they were unable to pay the fine, they could be bound out to work for anyone who paid it for them.

The South seemed to be reestablishing slavery in all but name. The defiance of a few states was especially brazen: Mississippi and Texas would not recognize the Thirteenth Amendment, and South Carolina actually refused to nullify its secession ordinance. When the South held elections at the end of 1865 to choose men who would go to Washington to serve in Congress (once again, with President Johnson's approval), the men they chose included former Confederate leaders: more than fifty members of the old Confederate legislature, nine Confederate generals, six members of Jefferson Davis's cabinet, and even the vice president of the Confederacy, Alexander Stephens!

This time they had gone too far, and there was a Northern backlash. To begin with, the Republican-dominated Congress simply refused to seat the newly elected representatives of the ex-Confederacy. Soon President Johnson completely lost control of the process, and Congress itself took charge. Beginning in 1866 it embarked on a program that became known as "Congressional Reconstruction" (to distinguish it from the brief preceding period of "Presidential Reconstruction"). The President vetoed several of the bills that reached his desk, but Congress passed them over his veto. By 1868, Johnson's authority was so low that he was actually impeached by the House of Representatives, and the Senate fell only a single vote shy of the two-thirds majority necessary to convict him, and thereby remove him from office!

The first three years of Congressional Reconstruction, from 1866 to 1869, were the most militant. Bolstered by the 1866 elections, which brought large majorities in both houses for the Republicans (majorities that were, of course, enhanced by the absence of representatives from the Confederate states), Congress embarked on a program designed to make certain that the states of the Confederacy would have to make radical changes before they were readmitted to the Union. Over President Johnson's veto, it passed a Civil Rights Bill and a law granting broader power to the Freedmen's Bureau. The following year, 1867, Congress passed the Fourteenth Amendment, which guaranteed the right of American citizenship to the former slaves and barred states from depriving any citizen of "life, liberty, or property without due process of law." In 1867, too, Congress passed a series of new laws designed to rein in the defiant South. The Old Confederacy was now divided up into five military districts, each overseen by a U.S. general. This military occupation was to be the cornerstone of the new process by which the individual states would be readmitted to the Union. First, the occupying armies were given the task of registering all eligible voters—adult white males who had not been disenfranchised by the Fourteenth Amendment, together with all adult black males. Next, those voters would choose delegates to constitutional conventions, conventions that would draft new state constitutions (those constitutions would be required to ratify the Fourteenth Amendment and to guarantee blacks the right to vote). Third, the new constitutions would be ratified by popular vote. Finally, then—and only then—could regular elections be held for representatives and senators who would at last be admitted as members of the U.S. Congress.

This was the process by which, one by one, the states of the Confederacy actually reentered the Union. By 1869, with black voters playing a central role, every one of the Confederate states had been readmitted—all with Republican majorities. That same year Congress passed the Fifteenth Amendment, which explicitly granted the right to vote to all adult black males. For the first time in Southern history (and, as it happened, the last time for another century), black people were exercising real political power. The African-American community greeted the suffrage with as much fervor as they had earlier greeted emancipation itself. They voted in large numbers, and many of them were elected to office. All in all, fourteen black men were elected to the U.S. House of Representatives and two to the Senate. (On the state level, though, the situation was different: not a single state had a black governor during the Reconstruction years, and only in South Carolina was there ever a black legislative majority.) Still, even this degree of black political power represented a startling change in Southern—and American—life.

Such radical change came about in part because many Northern Republicans were truly concerned with the rights of African-Americans. But it also depended on the support of *other* Northern Republicans, so-called moderates whose support for black suffrage came chiefly from the desire to punish the South for the terrible war it had waged or to make sure that when the Southern states finally *were* readmitted to the Union, the political power of the national Republican party would not be weakened by the election of Southern Democrats. These moderates knew that almost 80 percent of the Republican voters in the South were African-Americans.

In part for this reason, Congressional Reconstruction had its limits. Above all, it addressed not at all the one issue that had been responsible for rumors of the "Christmas Riots" of 1865: the confiscation and redistribution of lands formerly belonging to wealthy white slaveowners. Instead, the legislation of the period of Congressional Reconstruction was focused on black political equality. Despite the efforts of more radical Republicans, it ignored the need for black economic rights. No laws like Field Order No. 15 or Circular No. 13 were ever passed—even though one proposal that would have provided the freedmen with rights in land nearly managed to make it through Congress, only to be dropped at the very end.

In any case, Reconstruction was not to last or even to generate much enduring change. In one state after another during the 1870s, political power fell back into the hands of the Democratic party—into the control of "unreconstructed" Southern whites. The term used by Southern whites to name this process was *redemption* (a word ordinarily used to refer to the ransoming of hostages or, alternatively, to the salvation of souls). But the "redemption" of the South meant the restoration of power to wealthy ex-slaveholders and the subsequent denial of political rights to the black community.

Reconstruction ended for a variety of reasons. In most Southern states, blacks did not amount to a majority of the population. Three of these states—Tennessee, North Carolina, and Virginia—were "redeemed" as early as 1870. And where blacks were more numerous, they were systematically intimidated, notably by the Ku Klux Klan. The Klan (founded in 1866) directed terror attacks against black schools and churches and also against black economic and political leaders. The Ku Klux Klan was responsible for many hundreds of political murders across the South. These attacks were not random; instead, they were part of an attempt to undermine black autonomy and to destroy the infrastructure of the Republican party in the South.

In several states, election times regularly produced something approaching civil war. In Mississippi, the situation in 1875 was so tense that the state's Republican governor asked for federal military help. But by now most Northern Republicans had wearied of the battle. Former Union general Ulysses Grant (who had succeeded Andrew Johnson as President) refused to intervene in Mississippi, declaring that "the whole public are tired of these annual autumnal outbreaks in the South." The result was that the Democrats regained control of Mississippi. By the beginning of 1876 only South Carolina, Florida, and Louisiana remained in Republican control.

The presidential election of 1876 put a final end to Reconstruction. The two major candidates, Republican Rutherford B. Hayes and Democrat Samuel J. Tilden, ended up in an electoral deadlock (Tilden actually won the popular vote). Hayes finally managed to win the election by agreeing to remove all the remaining federal troops from the South—in exchange for the disputed electoral votes of three crucial Southern states. With the implementation of that bargain in 1877, the South was at last fully "redeemed."

Let this story end on a personal note. When I myself was in graduate school, during the 1960s, one of the first books I was assigned to read was about the end of Reconstruction. It was a well-known and respected book with an inspiring title, *The Road to Reunion*. On the front cover of this book was a picture that showed two hands entwined in a mutual handshake. The hands represented, of course, the two sections of the United States that had so recently been at war with each other: the North and the South. What I failed to notice, until a classmate pointed it out, was the color of those two hands. They were both white.

Sources: There is no full-fledged study of the "Christmas Riots"; this story was written mostly from contemporary newspapers. The one article on the subject is Dan T. Carter, "The Anatomy of Fear: The Christmas Day Insurrection Scare of 1865," in *Journal of Southern History,* vol. 42, 1976, pp. 345–364. Useful books include William McFeely, *Yankee Stepfather: General O. O. Howard and the Freedmen* (New Haven: Yale University Press, 1968), and Claude F. Oubre, *Forty Acres and a Mule: The Freedmen's Bureau and Black Land Ownership* (Baton Rouge: Louisiana State University Press, 1978), especially pp. 1–89. The Civil War origins of a potential land-reform policy are discussed in LaWanda Cox, "The Promise of Land for the Freedmen," *Mississippi Valley Historical Review,* vol. 45, 1958, pp. 413–440. A splendid study of the entire period is Eric Foner, *Reconstruction: America's Unfinished Revolution, 1863–1877* (New York. Harper & Row, 1988).

2

BUILDING THE BROOKLYN BRIDGE

ALAN TRACHTENBERG

It took 15 years to build, but when the bridge spanning 1,600 feet of East River between Brooklyn and Manhattan was opened in 1883, it was undeniably one of the great engineering and scientific feats of the age—the equivalent, perhaps, of the development of the atomic bomb in the 1940s, the construction of the nation's system of interstate highways in the 1950s, or the drive to place a man on the moon in the 1960s. But, although these were all entirely public projects, carried out by the national government with public funds, the Brooklyn Bridge was begun and partially built by a private company—chartered, to be sure, by the state government, as nearly all corporations were—but for the most part beyond the purview of the public. Even after the mid-1870s, when legislation recognized that the people deserved a larger role in the project, key decisions were made by corporations and politicians who paid only lip service to the public trust. And so it was altogether appropriate that the opening of the bridge involved bestowing the structure on the public—that is, granting it not to equals but to supposed inferiors. In this and other ways, as Alan Trachtenberg's story reveals, the bridge was a product of a transitional era in American history. It was an era in which large corporations and big factories were still the exception rather than the rule, millions of ordinary Americans worked in the skilled trades, and government played a limited role in encouraging and policing the economy.

But in other ways the bridge looked toward the future, and shunned the past. After generations of sectional conflict, culminating in a traumatic Civil War, many Americans longed for an end to division and discord. They built bridges across the Ohio and the Mississippi. In 1869, they celebrated the joining of the Union Pacific and the Central Pacific railroads at Provo, Utah, and with it the linking of the coasts. And in the aftermath of the disputed national election of 1876, the major parties laid aside the ideological politics and disagreements on questions of race that had helped bring on the Civil War and fostered the bitterness of Reconstruction, and agreed to a historic compromise—the Compromise of 1877—that gave the election to Republican Rutherford B. Hayes and signaled a final end to the involvement of the federal government in helping black people in the South secure their legal and political rights. (Among those who had a hand in this process was Abram S. Hewitt, the campaign manager of the Democratic candidate, Samuel J. Tilden; a few years later, Hewitt would be a featured speaker at the opening of the bridge.) Uniting two land masses in one giant span, the Brooklyn Bridge stood as a symbol of a desire for unity that went well beyond the two cities that stood to gain the most from its construction. The unity embodied in the bridge was not just geographical, but social and economic: the unity of rich and poor, haves and have nots; and the unity of the unified and uniform national market being created not just by bridges across the Ohio, Mississippi, and East rivers, but by the proliferation of giant corporations.

The story of the bridge is also the story of corruption so far-reaching that even the structure's enormous cables were braided with defective wire. Despite this sordid reality, contemporaries did not succumb to the cynicism that marks the present. Unlike the current generation of Americans, who believe themselves to be at the mercy of dark forces beyond their control, the generation of Americans who built the Brooklyn Bridge saw their creation as a wondrous sign that the world would yield— surely and inevitably—to their knowledge, their expertise, and their desire.

Before the Brooklyn Bridge, which opened to the public on May 24, 1883, ferry boats provided the sole means of crossing the East River between the boroughs of Manhattan and Brooklyn. A leisurely ride, open to fresh breezes as it moved diagonally upstream from the foot of Fulton Street in Brooklyn to its landing near South Street in Manhattan, the ferry offered thrilling vistas of the two shorelines. By the 1850s lower New York had already become a crowded commercial and manufacturing center, its shorelines hemmed with tall-masted ships. While Manhattan had expanded rapidly into a world center of trade, a center of wealth with an increasingly visible population of wage-laborers without personal wealth or property, Brooklyn enlarged at a slower pace. Even at mid-century it retained the look of a village, its residential hills and open spaces tempting many middle-class New Yorkers to seek homes there. The ferry ride seemed to many people, such as the poet Walt Whitman, a native of Long Island and Brooklyn who loved the streets of Manhattan, a perfect way to make the transition from village to metropolis. Whitman's poem, "Crossing Brooklyn Ferry," written in 1856, sang of the beauty of the views, of the sun sparkling on the water, and the pleasure of mingling with the crowds of working people passing to and fro across the river.

But the ferry had its shortcomings. It did not always provide so pleasant and relaxing a ride. Really a tidal strait rather than a true river, the lower East River is often shrouded in fog and churns with treacherous currents, and in winter it can be gorged with jagged chunks of ice. The winter of 1851 to 1852 was notably severe, and voices of exasperation arose demanding relief. Why not throw a bridge over the river, a quicker, surer, more reliable method of getting from one shore to the other? The idea was not new; an East River bridge had been proposed as early as 1811. By the 1840s and 1850s, when the idea revived, Brooklyn businessmen became increasingly serious about the prospect of more reliable and efficient connections with the financial and commercial markets of Manhattan; the growing numbers of people commuting to jobs in New York concurred. But would such a bridge, spanning about a mile between the shores, be feasible? No bridge of such magnitude had yet been constructed anywhere in the world. Most commonly bridges in America and Europe still employed the time-honored materials of wood and stone carved into arches. Recently, engineers had applied iron in the making of trusses, a rigid framework formed of separate members such as bars or rods, to build trestles for railroads. Chain links were employed in America and Europe to suspend roadways from stone towers, as in the Clifton Bridge (1859) at Bristol, England, by I. K. Brunel. But metal had not yet been tested in structures of the magnitude necessary to span the East River.

During that frigid winter of 1852, a German-born engineer, who placed great value on promptness, sat fuming at the inconvenience of being stuck on an ice-bound ferry boat in midstream. John Augustus Roebling began at once to imagine how a bridge might be built to replace or supplement the inefficient ferry. He had been trained as a civil engineer at the Royal Polytechnical Institute of Berlin; blocked in his career by the Prussian bureaucracy, he emigrated to Western Pennsylvania in 1831 with a group who shared utopian ideals. They founded the agricultural community of Saxonburg. With the increase in commerce the construction of canals, railroads, aqueducts, and bridges soon became a necessity in the region. Roebling eventually found opportunities to put his training to practical use. By 1849 he had built a few aqueducts and small bridges in cities such as Pittsburgh. He added the manufacture of wire rope to the activities of Saxonburg, and then established a plant near Trenton, New Jersey, for the production of wire to be used in spinning cables for suspension bridges, the form to which he particularly applied himself.

From the beginning of his career Roebling pioneered in developing techniques for building suspension bridges. The form appealed to him for its simplicity and beauty. Combining several distinct elements, the suspension bridge embodied a philosophical principle especially attractive to Roebling. Along with engineering he had studied philosophy in Berlin with G. W. F. Hegel, who taught that opposition or contradiction lay at the base of nature, society, and mind. In a suspension bridge a cable is hung over two piers or towers and then anchored at each shore. The towers and anchorage represent force in compression, solid masses planted firmly on a solid base or ground; the cable, meanwhile, hangs in extension, approximating a catenary curve (the curve formed when you hold, say, a cord at each end and allow it to hang loosely). The entire structure represents, then, opposite forces, compression and extension, in harmonious balance. Using this form bridge builders are able to suspend upwardly curving central spans between the two towers, thus allowing for unhindered river traffic beneath the bridge. With the additional possibility of making such a bridge rigid enough to carry railroad trains, the suspension form seemed to Roebling an ideal solution to America's bridge-building needs.

At the time he was stranded in the ice-bound river, Roebling was at work on just such a railroad bridge over Niagara Falls, completed in 1855. In 1857 he wrote to Horace Greeley, editor of the New York *Tribune,* proposing "a wire suspension bridge crossing the East River by one single span at such an elevation as will not impede the navigation." Greeley responded enthusiastically and the engineer began to sketch his plans. But the time was not yet ripe. After the dramatic success of the Niagara bridge, Roebling was called on to build what would then be the world's longest suspension bridge, between Cincinnati and Covington over the Ohio River, a project that kept him occupied through the years of the Civil War. The bridge opened in 1867. Roebling then turned all his energy to the task of persuading people of wealth and influence in New York and Brooklyn that an East River bridge was both necessary and feasible.

In 1865, just after the Civil War in which his son Washington, also an engineer, served as a Union colonel, Roebling approached several Brooklyn businessmen to see if a private company might be established to recruit public support and money for such a bridge. Roebling preferred to deal directly with private capitalists rather than approach elected municipal officials. His experiences during the 1840s and 1850s taught him that public financing of construction projects often proved inefficient and expensive; politicians, he learned, tended to offer costly contracts in exchange for bribes. As early as 1860 Roebling anticipated similar problems in dealing with the city halls of New York and Brooklyn, and wrote that it was not "desirable to add to the complication and corruption of the governmental machinery of these cities" by seeking their official sponsorship for his proposed bridge.

In fact the problem of financing public projects had proved a complicated matter throughout the "internal improvements" period in the decades before the Civil War. One especially troubling issue concerned the respective roles of private capital and public funds raised by the sale of bonds. The issue centered on the question of ownership and control: Should private people or corporations, for example, be entitled to collect tolls on roads or bridges serving the public interest? The New York–Brooklyn situation was further complicated by the fact that the state government at Albany held final authority over the financing of public projects in both cities. The situation opened room for irregularities and corruption, exactly what Roebling feared.

In 1865 Roebling met with a dynamic Brooklyn contractor, William C. Kingsley, who in turn persuaded State Senator Henry C. Murphy to introduce a bill to charter the New York Bridge Company. The fact that the winter of 1866 to 1867 was one of the severest yet on record aroused popular support for the bill. Passed in April of 1867, the law fixed the capital of the Company at $5,000,000 and endowed it with the power to raise more funds. It also authorized the cities of New York and Brooklyn to subscribe to the capital stock of the Company to the extent of 60 percent. The arrangement thus resulted in a "mixed" enterprise, joining private and public funds in a project too large and costly to be undertaken alone by either the private or public spheres. Yet the Company was chartered as a *private* enterprise, with unlimited control over public funds. The charter allowed the cities to "guarantee the payment of the principal and interest" of Company bonds; yet only by an amendment in 1869 were city officials assured seats on the board of directors, and then only as a small minority. To be sure, the charter gave the cities the right to take full control of the project if they wished, for a price: the full value of "the said bridge and appurtenances," plus $33\frac{1}{3}$ percent of that value, to be paid directly to the Company.

No wonder suspicions arose. They appeared initially because the cities of New York and Brooklyn, and indeed the legislature in Albany, were then under the control of a group known as the Tweed Ring, after its leader, William Marcy "Boss" Tweed. Although not himself a holder of high office, Tweed, like other big city bosses in the post-Civil War era, exercised vast power through a system of graft and favoritism. Elected officials loyal to Tweed or indebted to him for their office, frequently through rigged elections, awarded contracts for public buildings and utilities to contractors willing to "kick back" a certain amount of cash. Tweed came to power in the late 1860s through the local New York Democratic Party club known as Tammany Hall. When the Ring was disbanded and Tweed indicted in 1871, it was estimated that his crew had stolen as much as $30 million. One of the Ring's typical devices for tapping the public purse was to arrange for delays in construction of public projects, resulting in higher expenses padded to include kick backs. The Chamber Street Courthouse was one of their most notorious schemes.

Was Brooklyn Bridge another? Doubts surfaced periodically throughout the lengthy 16-year interval between the approval of the charter in 1867 and the opening of the bridge in 1883. One newspaper listed the bridge among "the seven fraudulent wonders of the New World," and wrote: "Conceived in inequity and begun in fraud, it has been continued in corruption." And indeed, in 1878 Tweed confessed that in 1867 he took a bribe of $60,000 from Kingsley to help push the chartering bill through the legislature, and, further, that the deal allowed Tweed himself to buy shares at an 80 percent reduction, and gave Kingsley a 15 percent cut on all purchases of construction materials. Overpayment to Kingsley, the principal shareholder, had been publicly revealed as early as 1872, at which time the contractor promised to make repayment.

Was the problem merely the greed of evil people, or was the charter itself at fault for allowing a private corporation full control over a public enterprise? The

John Augustus Roebling (1806–1869). Roebling's piercing eyes were perhaps his most memorable physical feature.

legislative act set no controls over the decisions of the Company, no process of public review. It was an act "to incorporate the New York Bridge Company, for the purpose of constructing and maintaining a bridge over the East River, between the cities of New York and Brooklyn." The law empowered the Company "to purchase, acquire and hold as much real estate as may be necessary for the site of the said bridge," and to fix rates of toll. It also set a handsome limit of 15 percent per annum as allowable net profits for investors. Typical of such private corporations contrived to fund public projects in the antebellum era, the Bridge Company was free of accountability to the public whose funds it solicited. Only the federal government required obedience to any regulation; Congress in 1869 granted that the proposed bridge might receive status as a lawful post road, provided it met standards of height appropriate to river traffic as recommended by a commission of the Army Engineers.

In May of 1867, the Company appointed John A. Roebling as Chief Engineer. Given his role in initiating the project, his reputation as the world's masterbuilder of the modern suspension bridge, and his known doggedness in seeing his projects through to the finish, the choice was inevitable. The 61-year-old engineer, industrialist, inventor, and philosopher applied himself at once to surveying the site and drawing up plans. By September his report to the New York Bridge Company was ready.

Roebling wrote the report not only as a plan but an argument to meet any possible objection to his design. In the preface he set the tone of cold, irrefutable logic mixed with appeals to civic pride.

> The contemplated work, when constructed in accordance with my designs, will not only be the greatest Bridge in existence, but it will also be the greatest engineering work of this continent, and of the age. Its most conspicuous features, the great towers, will serve as landmarks to the adjoining cities, and they will be entitled to be ranked as national monuments.

Roebling's report addressed an audience primarily of businessmen, shareholders in the New York Bridge Company who wanted to know if the bridge would pay in the short and long run. Most telling were his strategic comments about a change about to occur on completion of the Union Pacific Railroad (which occurred 2 years later, in 1869) in America's commercial relations with the world, a change of vast significance for business, especially for the commercial interests of New York:

> This change will at first be very slow, but the breadth and depth of the commercial channell will increase with every coming year, until at last the city of New York will have become the great commercial emporium, not of this continent only, but of the world.

The East River bridge, he argued, would be a major link within a national and eventually international system of transportation, communication, and trade, and would enhance the flow of wealth into the coffers of New York. One use of the spaces within the approaches to the bridge, he suggested, might be as vaults for accumulated gold and silver.

The public was more concerned with safety than profits, and justifiably so, given the unprecedented length of the bridge and its several novel features. Roeb–

ling's report envisioned a bridge almost 1,600 feet in length, one half again as long
as the Cincinnati bridge. It would replace that bridge as the longest in the world.
The roadway of the new bridge, to be held in place by four cables 16 inches in di-
ameter, would bear 18,700 tons. A multipurpose roadway, it would allow for cable
car traffic and horse-drawn traffic in side-by-side lanes in each direction, and an
elevated promenade for pedestrians above the noise and dirt of the vehicular traffic; with benches and lamps and balconies around the base of each tower, the
promenade was Roebling's particular pride. The granite towers, each pierced with
two immense Gothic arches, would rise 276 feet and compete with the spire of
Trinity Church on Wall Street as the tallest structures in New York at the time.

Roebling explained that theoretically "any span inside of three thousand feet
is practicable." The only vital question was safety, and this was simply a question
of cost. At this point Roebling estimated a cost of $7,000,000 exclusive of the
amount necessary to acquire the land, about $3,800,000; the final cost (includ-
ing the land) was closer to $15,500,000, largely a result of modifications such as
raising the height of the bridge and increasing its width. Roebling explained the
system of supports he had devised which, if followed according to his plan, would
guarantee complete peace of mind about the stability of the structure:

> To guard against vertical and horizontal oscillations, and to insure that degree of
> stiffness in the flooring which is absolutely necessary to meet the effects of violent
> gales in such an exposed situation, I have provided six lines of iron trusses which
> run the whole length of the suspended floor from anchor wall to anchor wall. . . . I
> am not disposed to underrate the great force of a severe gale. . . . But my system of
> construction differs radically from that formerly practiced, and I have planned the
> East River Bridge with a special view to fully meet these destructive forces. It is for
> the same reason that, in my calculation of the requisite supporting strength, so
> large a proportion has been assigned to stays [diagonal wire supports, like the stays
> on sailing vessels] in place of cables. . . . The supporting power of the stays alone
> will be 15,000 tons; ample to hold up the floor. If the cables were removed, the
> Bridge would sink in the center but would not fall.

The confidence that speaks here, that the bridge would survive all imaginable
traumas, persuaded the Company. But in order to obliterate all remaining doubts
(absolute thoroughness being his style), Roebling convened a select board of eminent engineers to review his plans in meticulous detail, and to examine his other
bridges on site. Their unanimous confirmation of his design and calculations in
May, 1869, signalled that work could then commence.

Within 3 weeks there occurred a trauma Roebling's report did not antici-
pate: his own sudden death, the result of injuries when a boat crushed his right
foot on the Brooklyn wharf as he surveyed the position of the main piers. He died
horribly, of lockjaw, on July 22, 1869. The bridge had taken its first and most tragic
toll.

Responsibility for the project now passed to Roebling's 32-year-old son,
Colonel Washington A. Roebling, appointed in August to supervise construction
of the bridge according to his father's design. A graduate of Rensselaer Polytechnic Institute and an engineer with the Union Army of the Potomac during the Civil
War, Colonel Roebling's main experience had been as assistant to his father on

the Cincinnati Bridge. In October, presumably to free his mind from all distractions but actual construction, the Executive Committee of the Company relieved Roebling of all responsibility for the awarding of contracts—and indeed of attending meetings unless specifically requested to—and appointed William Kingsley as General Superintendent precisely to perform that function. Colonel Roebling assembled his own youthful staff of assistants, whose age averaged 31 years in that year. E. F. Farrington, who had worked on the Cincinnati Bridge, was later named Master Mechanic. Among Colonel Roebling's responsibilities was the presentation in writing of exhaustive periodic reports on progress in construction to the Executive Committee of the Bridge Company.

Roebling's first dramatic step as Chief Engineer was the launching of the pneumatic caisson for the Brooklyn tower. While on a European tour after the Civil War, directed by his father to learn as much as he could about new building techniques, the younger Roebling studied closely the use of caissons for laying firm foundations for weight-carrying piers. Caissons are essentially large airtight boxes tapered into an open cutting edge on the bottom. For excavating the floor of the East River Roebling contrived a caisson with a timber roof 15 feet thick. Weighing 3,000 tons and measuring 168 feet long and 102 feet wide, his caissons would be the largest ever used. An enormous chamber using compressed air, the caisson was designed to provide breathing space for the workers known as "sandhogs." They dug away at the mud and clay on the river bottom while masons laid the granite of the tower on the roof of the caisson. The weight of the stone combined with the digging sunk the caisson through the river bed to bedrock, where the finished tower would find absolutely solid support.

An intricate construction balancing a number of elements—an airlock into the work area, supply shafts, water shafts to make possible the removal of debris without loss of air pressure—the caisson was as hazardous as it was essential. If the water shafts were not kept tightly sealed, blowouts could shower stone and mud into the air. There was the constant threat of fire; explosives were often used to break up compacted materials on the river floor, and because electric lighting was not yet available, lighted candles served as illumination. One newspaper account described them as "submarine giants [which] delve and dig and ditch and drill and blast." They performed their work around the clock.

For the sand-hogs the work was often unbearable. "The work of the buried bridge-builder," wrote one newspaper, "is like the onward flow of eternity; it does not cease for the sun at noonday or the silent stars at night. Gangs are relieved and replaced, and swart, perspiring companies of men follow each other up and down the iron locks, with a dim quiet purpose." The interior was hot, the air foul, and sickness quite common. Work shifts were reduced to 4 hours or less, at $2 a day for ordinary labor, increased to $2.25 a day as the caisson reached deeper below the river floor. The work crew for the Brooklyn caisson numbered 112 during each of the day shifts, and 40 at night; the New York caisson crew ranged from 50 to 125 during the day and 15 to 30 at night. Work crews for this relatively unskilled but extremely punishing labor were recruited mainly from Irish, German, and Italian immigrants, many undernourished and desperate for work. The turnover was enormous: 2,500 different workers for the Brooklyn caisson alone. In 1872, the entire New York caisson crew walked off the job, insisting on higher pay for such hazardous, fatiguing work: $3 for a 4-hour day. The strike lasted several days before the men settled for less of an increase than they demanded.

No serious accident occurred until December 2, 1870, when a burning candle ignited the oakum caulking lining the inside of the caisson; the fire was driven by air pressure deep into the caisson, but out of sight. Colonel Roebling rushed to the scene and helped fight the fire for 7 hours, until he lost consciousness. The caisson was finally flooded, and the water expelled some days later. The "Great Fire" caused no deaths but delayed work for 3 months. By March, 1871, excavation for the foundation was finally complete, the caisson filled with concrete, and the Brooklyn tower began to rise layer by layer, the first above-water sign that a monumental bridge was in the making. In October of 1871, the New York caisson was launched and reached bedrock in May of 1872.

Just at this time, in 1871, Tweed's empire began to unravel. Spearheaded by upper-class figures like Abram Hewitt, son-in-law of the revered Peter Cooper, and partner in his iron business, and Samuel Tilden, who would be the Democratic candidate for president in the controversial election of 1876, a movement developed against the corruption and fraud that was draining the city's resources. Campaigns in the press and public meetings led to Tweed's downfall and arrest. Called "reformers," such upper-class figures sought to replace corrupt party politicians with qualified political figures drawn from the class of "the best men," the rich, the cultivated, the socially respectable. Investigative committees appeared in both cities, and in June of 1872, the old Tammany representatives on the Bridge Company were replaced by figures with names like Vanderbilt, Aspinwall, Appleton, Hewitt, names of older wealthy and propertied families who viewed themselves as responsible for the civic health of the cities. Hewitt himself led an internal investigation on behalf of the Bridge Company, which resulted in exacting Kingsley's promise for repayment of funds, redefining his responsibilities, and essentially exonerating him and the Company of any fundamental wrong-doing. A report by Colonel Roebling assured the directors of the Company that all contract awards had resulted in the finest materials at the lowest costs; this proved decisive in dispelling the suspicion that the physical integrity of the bridge had been compromised.

The issue of accountability remained unresolved. Was the Company truly a *private* corporation, like a railroad company, free to do its business however it wished? Or, considering that the cities of New York and Brooklyn were both large stockholders, did the Company not have a special responsibility to the publicly elected bodies of those cities? These more critical views were advanced by Demas Barnes, chairman of the Committee of Investigation appointed by the board of the Company, who issued a separate report calling for board meetings open to the public. Hewitt and others agreed the charter should be amended to dispel ambiguities in the original document that made it seem an invitation to theft, but no changes were made at this time. After 3 years of construction, the jailing of Tweed, the chiding of Kingsley, the Bridge Company remained under a cloud of suspicion.

Then another sudden event profoundly affected the project. At the end of May, 1872, after spending long hours in the depths of the New York caisson, Colonel Roebling collapsed. Mysterious symptoms of paralysis had already attacked a number of the workers, and Roebling had asked a medical specialist to investigate. Little was then known about the sudden onset of caisson disease or "the bends," an affliction of the nervous system caused by living and working too long under atmospheric pressure much greater than normal. By 1883 the surgeon of the Bridge Company reported 110 cases of the disease, three of which were fatal, at that point. Roebling himself remained paralyzed the rest of his life, perhaps the result as much of a nervous disorder exacerbated by the strain of his position as of the bends. He never returned to the construction site, although he retained his position, making detailed drawings and writing out meticulous instructions that his wife Emily delivered to his staff, and following progress at the site through binoculars from his home nearby.

In June of 1874, the state legislature passed an amendment urged by Barnes requiring that the Bridge Company accept membership on its board of a signifi-cant number of representatives of the cities of New York and Brooklyn. The fol-lowing year the legislature dissolved the original New York Bridge Company al-together; the bridge was now understood to be "a public work, to be constructed by the two cities for the accommodation, convenience and safe travel of the in-habitants." The change made a difference in the public's relation to the still ghostly structure slowly materializing into the shape of a bridge before their eyes—although the personnel of the actual day-by-day management remained the same.

What remained of the construction tasks were the completion of the towers and the two anchorages on each shore to which the four central cables would be attached. The Brooklyn tower reached its full height in May of 1875, and the New York tower in July of 1876. Then the real artistry of labor would commence—the spinning of the four main wire cables. By August of 1876, with the saddles de-signed to carry each cable over the top of each tower in place, the spinning itself began.

Apart from the drama of scandal and injury, the building of the bridge had provided another kind of daily spectacle: sheer physical work of the most de-manding kind among new, odd-shaped pieces of machinery such as caissons, hoisting machines, cable saddles, the intricately arranged anchor plates. Through the press and firsthand observation, the public witnessed the skilled work of car-penters, machinists, masons, blacksmiths, sand-hogs, iron-workers, and seamen engaged to lash the diagonal stays to the vertical suspenders attaching the road-way to the main cables. At one time as many as 600 men worked together at the site, making this perhaps the largest outdoor concentration of a multiple-craft work force yet assembled in one site in the United States. It is impossible to say exactly how many workers lost their lives; estimates range from 20 to 40. Others suffered lasting effects from caisson disease.

None of the skilled tasks attracted as much attention as the spinning and wrapping of the four main cables. On August 14, 1876, a scow ran a rope across the river, which was then hoisted into position over and between the towers. Not until then could the structure be called a bridge. Now two cities were joined, or as a newspaper headline put it, "wedded." The next dramatic step would be for someone to cross the structure on the rope, and the Master Mechanic E. F. Far-rington was selected to make the historic venture in a boatswain's chair. The date was Friday, August 25, 1876, and to the cheers of workers swarming on the towers, crowds on both shores and on boats in the river, Farrington made the first trip via bridge from Brooklyn to New York; it took 22 minutes. A footbridge of slatted wood was soon added for less adventuresome passage by workers and occasional visitors.

Just when the end of construction seemed in sight, further delays caused by charges of corruption and recrimination among the principals almost brought the entire project to a permanent standstill. By September of 1876, with the actual spinning of the cables ready to proceed, Roebling submitted his detailed specifications for cable wire to the Executive Committee, as required, for their approval. Abram Hewitt, vice president of the board and himself a dealer in wire, judged the specifications "eminently wise," but insisted that no bids for the wire contract be accepted from any person or firm with a direct interest in the bridge. He declared that he himself would refrain from bidding, and he insisted that Colonel Roebling, an owner along with his brothers of the cable wire manufactory his father had founded near Trenton, be especially forbidden from entering a bid.

Washington Roebling became an increasingly remote and mysterious figure after his illness. He is depicted here, on the occasion of the opening of the bridge, as a somewhat grim but thoughtful Victorian gentleman, restraining his emotions of pride as his father's bridge nears completion. (*Frank Leslie's Illustrated Newspaper,* May 26, 1883)

Indignant, the incapacitated Chief Engineer instantly penned an angry letter of resignation. In his reply to the board's refusal of the resignation, Roebling wrote:

> I was publicly and specifically singled out by name by Mr. Hewitt, as if I had spent my whole life in concocting a specification which I alone could fill or as if I were a thief trying to rob the bridge in some underhanded manner and against whom every precaution should be taken.

Then he added:

> As you seem to be deeply impressed with Mr. Hewitt's action in declining to become a competitor for this wire, I desire to say that his magnanimity is all a show, as the firm of Cooper and Hewitt have no facilities for making the steel wire, and if you receive a bid from Mr. Haigh of South Brooklyn, it will be well for you to investigate a little.

And to be sure, the award was made to a Mr. Haigh of South Brooklyn.

Roebling's suspicion of venality on the part of Hewitt deepened as a result of another disastrous event. In July, 1877, spinning of the cables began by means of a huge mechanical device that travelled from anchorage to anchorage, taking about 10 minutes each way. In November a wire snapped, and on examining the broken pieces, Roebling judged the wire, supplied by Haigh, to be defective. The following June two men were killed when another wire rope snapped, raising even more public anxiety about the safety of the bridge into which some $9 million had already been poured. Among New York Democrats who wished to distance themselves as far as possible from the lingering taint of Boss Tweed, a number agitated to cut off all further money to the bridge. On July 22, 1878, Roebling presented board president Henry Murphy with physical proof that Haigh had been supplying the bridge with consistently defective wire, fraudulently returning rolls of wire that had been already rejected on regular inspection. Roebling informed Murphy that "the distressing point of this affair is that all the rejected wire which has come to the Bridge has been worked into the cables, and cannot be removed." The Executive Committee chose to hush up a scandal potentially fatal to the completion of the bridge; it may be, though no certain evidence exists, that Haigh's friends, including Hewitt, insisted on the cover-up. The board was relieved to hear from Roebling, however, that because the cables had been designed with a sufficient margin of safety (six times beyond the tensile strength actually required), the damage was inconsequential—although the Chief Engineer did require that each cable be strengthened by 150 more strands of tested wire. On October 5, 1878, the spinning of the cables was completed—"this desirable event," remarked Master Mechanic E. F. Farrington, "was marked by no demonstrations, save the sounding of a steam whistle, and the raising of a United States flag on the Brooklyn tower." In later years Haigh was imprisoned in Sing Sing for passing bad checks.

The tasks that remained consisted chiefly of assembling the complex roadway, tieing it into place by the diagonal stays John A. Roebling had designed to guarantee the security of the span, and the construction of the terminals at either end of the bridge. But in the face of continuing threats from New York to close out its funding of the project and rapidly deteriorating relations between an increasingly impatient and snappish Roebling and the board of directors, almost 5 more years would elapse before these relatively undemanding objectives could be accomplished. As late as 1882 a move was launched to replace the Chief Engineer because of his physical disability; his position was saved partly by the eloquence of his wife in pleading with the board against such a move. When Abram Hewitt, now a congressman and future mayor of New York, wrote to Colonel Roebling requesting information he might use in his Opening Ceremonies oration, the blunt-speaking engineer replied: "It took Cheops twenty years to build his pyramid, but if he had had a lot of Trustees, contractors and newspaper reporters to worry him, he might not have finished by this time. The advantages of modern engineering are in many ways overbalanced by the disadvantages of modern civilization."

On May 24, 1883, the Hon. J. S. T. Stranhahan, a "leading citizen" of Brooklyn, and a trusted trustee of the New York and Brooklyn Bridge Company from the start, presided over the Opening Ceremonies of The Great Bridge—a public drama the central act of which would be performed by officials: the bestowing of the bridge directly to the people. As the souvenir publication of the Opening Cer-

The Brooklyn anchorage in the process of construction. Note the bundles of wire which comprise each of the four central cables, yet to be wrapped in this image, and the footbridge to the left. The picture conveys the awesome power of the cables and the security of their attachment to the anchor plates (not themselves visible in the print). Note, too the artist's rendering of the great height of the Brooklyn tower against the low skyline of 1870s Manhattan. (*Harper's New Monthly Magazine,* May 1883)

emonies put it, "It was a holiday for high and low, rich and poor; it was, in fact, the People's Day."

It was a day of great local pride, in Brooklyn especially. One store window displayed a sign that became a kind of motto of the day: "Babylon had her hanging gardens, Egypt her pyramid, Athens her Acropolis, Rome her Athenaeum; so Brooklyn has her Bridge." Crowds in the tens of thousands—crowds of local citizens swelled by visitors from nearby towns, cities, and countryside, arriving by train, boat, and wagon—thronged along the thoroughfares in both cities leading to the bridge.

Local as the immediate meanings were for the participants, the day was also national in significance, as the red, white, and blue flags and banners everywhere, including at the summits of each of the bridge's two towers, indicated. As Brooklyn Mayor Seth Low himself said, "it is distinctly an American triumph. American genius designed it, American skill built it, and American workshops made it." Thus the meaning of the presence of the chief of state himself, President Chester A. Arthur—a New Yorker, as it happened, the dapper former head of the New York Custom House and a great favorite among the crowds. The president played a role strictly symbolic—he had no speeches to make, no awards to present—only to be there in recognition of the national import of such a bridge. As the New York *Sun*'s reporter quipped: "the climax of fourteen years' suspense seemed to have been reached, since the President of the United States of America had walked dry shod to Brooklyn from New York."

Above all else it was a festive day—happy crowds scouting the celebrities, buying souvenirs, and awaiting with mounting excitement the evening's promised climaxes of the day's public drama. At midnight the bridge was to be thrown open to pedestrians, and many positioned themselves for that unique experience: their first walk "dry shod" across the East River. But first, as darkness fell, came the moment that thrilled the crowd beyond all description—the contours of the bridge suddenly illuminated by strings of electric lights! And as the lights just as suddenly went out there followed the most spectacular display of fireworks (as it was described) ever witnessed on the continent—bursts of color which cast an eerie, many-hued glow on the bridge that was destined, even from its start 14 years earlier, to hold a special place in the life and the imagination of the wedded cities, of the nation, and of the world. The age of steel and electricity had begun.

AN INTERPRETATION

A week later, on Memorial Day, the entire roadway was thrown open to pedestrians. Someone shouted, "The bridge is falling!" and twelve people were trampled or crushed to death in the ensuing panic.

That event provides another reminder, bloodier than others, of the entire ambiguous history of this bridge, in which the idealism of visionary engineers collided with the sordid realities of everyday political life in American cities of the Gilded Age. The meaning of the building of the Brooklyn Bridge in just these years, 1869 to 1883, must include recognition of such ambiguities, the complexities of motive, the many-dimensioned facets of behavior that comprise the larger truths of all historical "stories." It must also include the implicit threat to life and limb of modern construction projects based on new technologies.

In the case of the Brooklyn Bridge one is tempted to celebrate the creative acts of the Roeblings, their staffs, and the nameless corps of skilled and unskilled workers responsible for the actual building of the bridge, and to push aside the parallel story of Tweed and Kingsley and Haigh. Yet the two stories are not simply parallel; they are intertwined as tightly as the wire strands of each of the main cables. To interpret the building of the bridge in historical perspective, all aspects of the related stories must be taken into account.

One lesson of the bridge lies in the contradictions within the age's definitions of private and public, between profit and the common good, which the story of its construction brings to the surface. The scandals themselves, whether substantiated or merely suspected, reveal a period of great uncertainty, of public distrust of the hierarchy of political and social figures above them, a deep suspicion of wealth and power. Writing in 1883 in the month before the opening of the bridge, the radical social critic and future opponent of Abram Hewitt in the mayoralty election in 1886, Henry George, described the bridge as an emblem of the underlying contradiction in modern America between wealth and poverty, private profit and public good:

Someone shouted, "The bridge is falling," and a catastrophe followed. The rendering here emphasizes the great crush of an urban crowd in panic, an image calling to mind other mass scenes of the period, including those of soldiers firing at fleeing strikers during the 1877 Great Railroad Strike. Certainly such images helped plant the thought that city crowds held the menace of turning into fearsome mobs. (*Frank Leslie's Illustrated Newspaper*, June 9, 1883)

We have brought machinery to a pitch of perfection that, fifty years ago could not have been imagined; but in the presence of political corruption, we seem as helpless as idiots. The East River Bridge is a crowning triumph of mechanical skill; but to get it built a leading citizen of Brooklyn had to carry to New York sixty thousand dollars in a carpetbag to bribe a New York alderman. The human soul that thought out the great bridge is prisoned in a crazed and broken body that lies bedfast, and could only watch it grow by peering through a telescope. Nevertheless, the weight of the immense mass is estimated and adjusted for every inch. But the skill of the engineer could not prevent condemned wire from being smuggled into the cable.

The building of Brooklyn Bridge represented a historical transition, though what the future would hold was not at all clear at the time. John A. Roebling envisioned the bridge as a monument to the commercial and civic greatness of the cities. The story of corruption attending the making of the bridge certainly seems to sully that vision. But perhaps, in the face of the confused relations between private and public interest during this era, there was no other means of achieving Roebling's vision. The period of construction was dominated by the ruthless conviction on the part of the wealthy and powerful that they deserved whatever rewards they could achieve for themselves, whatever the social consequences. As it did for Henry George, the venality and mismanagement implied by the full story of the building of the Brooklyn Bridge would provide a useful lesson for progressive reformers in the following two decades, who proposed a more positive, direct, and responsible role by government in serving the collective interests of the public.

The Bridge in 1883 represented an initiation into a significantly different way of life. Consider its contrast with the old ferry boats. With their tempo keyed to currents and weather, the ferries belonged to a relatively simple era ending throughout the United States; their replacement by Brooklyn Bridge in the 1880s would dramatically signal the arrival of modern metropolitan and industrial life. By its size and scale, Brooklyn Bridge stood for something radically new in scale—and in danger, as the Memorial Day disaster vividly proclaims. Yet the bridge also represents a transitional moment, one that still retains a connection with the craft traditions of earlier, preindustrial modes and systems of labor. The abilities of the workers at the site of construction represented highly skilled crafts in working with stone, wood, and metal, and also collective coordination, willingness to take risks for the sake of performing a job, feats of personal courage. The mechanics, masons, sand-hogs, carpenters, surveyors, and the unskilled as well, all remind us that the built world was made by the refined and intricate manual efforts of human labor. The human features of the story of the bridge bring that great structure to life as a lesson in the coordination of mental and physical abilities.

Finally, we can interpret the building of the Brooklyn Bridge as the manifestation of a conception, originally conceived by John A. Roebling and adapted by many others, of a harmonious metropolitan culture. Roebling thought of the bridge as a symbol of civic greatness, the towers standing as thresholds to the centers of each city. The elevated promenade was a special pride of the elder Roebling, signifying amenity; a respect for pauses in busy days, for the pleasures of open-air walks; and the unequalled visual excitement of the views of New York harbor. The least practical or profitable of the features of the bridge from the point

A panoramic view of the completed bridge, including its cable railroad trains, from the New York side. Note the variety of traffic: horse and wagon, electric-powered cable car, and pedestrian. (*Harper's Weekly*, June 2, 1883)

of commercial utility, the promenade remains one of the bridge's most eloquent gifts to the cities it joins. To the future it offered an ideal of urban experience tied into, shaped and formed by, and yet not overwhelmed by modern technology. Brooklyn Bridge emerges from an age steeped in corruption and greed, as a hope for the possibility of community. It is for this that later generations have most valued Roebling's masterpiece. We can interpret the building of the bridge, then, as a story of a clash of values reshaping America as the nation entered the modern era.

Sources: The most convenient source of information about the building of the bridge, the personalities of the figures involved, the delays and scandals, is David McCullough, *The Great Bridge* (New York: Simon & Schuster, 1972). An interpretation of Brooklyn Bridge, including the art and literature it inspired, can be found in Alan Trachtenberg, *Brooklyn Bridge: Fact and Symbol* (New York: Oxford University Press, 1965). Most important among contemporary documents is John Roebling's initial plan, published as *Report of John A. Roebling, C. E., to the President and Directors of the New York Bridge Company, on the Proposed East River Bridge* (Brooklyn, N.Y.: Eagle Book and Job Printing Department, 1870). Other contemporary sources useful in reconstructing the story of Brooklyn Bridge include: William C. Conant, "The Brooklyn Bridge," *Harper's New Monthly Magazine* (May 1883); E. F. Farrington, *Concise Description of the East River Bridge* (New York: C. D. Wynkoop, 1881); and Montgomery Schuyler, "The Bridge as a Monument," *Harper's Weekly* (24 May 1883). The Roebling Collections at the Library of Rensselaer Polytechnic Institute include an indispensable collection of manuscripts and drawings by both John A. and Washington Roebling. The Special Collections of the Library at Rutgers University include a rich collection of personal manuscript materials and drawings by John A. Roebling, including his philosophical writings. Lewis Mumford sensitively places the Roeblings and the bridge in *The Brown Decades* (New York: Harcourt, Brace, & Company, 1931). Alan Trachtenberg's *The Incorporation of America: Culture and Society in the Gilded Age* (New York: Hill & Wang, 1982), provides an overview of the post-Civil War period.

3

THE HATFIELD–McCOY FEUD

ALTINA L. WALLER

Most Americans first heard about the Hatfields and the McCoys in early 1888, while reading newspaper accounts of the New Year's Day midnight raid of eight Hatfields on the home of Old Ranel McCoy, deep in the Appalachian hills of Pike County, Kentucky. Old Ranel had escaped, but 2 of his 16 children were dead. When big-city reporters discovered that this was only the latest in a series of incidents dating back at least a decade, an interpretation of the feud emerged: Two almost barbaric backwoods families, remote from the institutions, restraints, and refinements of civilization, were locked in a petty, senseless, and deadly vendetta.

Altina Waller's story of the Hatfield–McCoy feud has a very different message. The events she describes take place in a region already undergoing economic modernization and laced with legal institutions that the Hatfields and the McCoys often used to resolve their differences. Neither were the principals in the struggle— whether Old Ranel McCoy, Devil Anse Hatfield, or Perry Cline—the rustic hillbillies depicted in the popular press of the day. Even the families involved were not the monolithic blocs inscribed in the legend of the Hatfields and the McCoys.

The Hatfields and the McCoys were feuding, then, not because they were too isolated, but because they were not isolated enough. Rendered in these terms, the tale seems less like a rural curiosity and more like other stories that might be told of the same period: the story of the Sioux Indians on the Great Plains "reservations," fleeing before the new railroads, the mining companies, and the white man's unquenchable thirst for land; the story of the central Illinois farmer, selling his wheat in world markets and in competition with the newly opened granaries of the Dakotas; or the story of the proprietor of the general store in Kearney, Nebraska, who in 1890 is about to find out that his customers have direct access to the goods he sells through the Sears & Roebuck mail-order catalogue. These stories are all stories of penetration: the penetration of railroads onto the Plains; of the Sears company into rural homes; and— in the case of the Hatfields and the McCoys—of the penetration, first of timbering companies and then of railroads and coal-mining operations, into the Tug River Valley. The story of the Hatfields and the McCoys is very much a part of the central phenomenon of the age: the rise of big business.

But simply because we have a new way of understanding the feud does not mean that the old way has nothing to teach us. Indeed, the mythic perspective on the conflict, embodied in the photograph on p. 53, must have been especially compelling to have lasted so long and to have been fashioned in apparent defiance of the evidence. What, then, might account for the origin and persistence of the older view? One possibility is that the myth was fashioned by sophisticated eastern city dwellers, for whom the primitives of rural Kentucky and West Virginia functioned as an "Other"—defining what they were not and did not want to be. But it is also possible that a nation engaged in a headlong rush toward the urban, industrialized, and bureaucratic world of the twentieth century relished the image of the gun-toting mountaineer as a sign that something still remained of the unfettered, intuitive freedom of the American frontiersman. Like Bonnie and Clyde in the 1930s, and Butch Cassidy and the Sundance Kid in the cinematic myth of the 1960s, the Hatfields and the McCoys were the objects of our collective desire.

In the 1870s Randolph and Sally McCoy lived on the Blackberry Fork of Pond Creek in Pike County, Kentucky. Randolph and Sally were in their 50s and presided over a family of 16 children. Their log home was typical of this mountainous region; called a "dog-trot" house, it consisted of two log houses connected by a kind of passageway or breezeway. In other external circumstances as well the McCoys were not very different from other families living in this remote region. Their log house was built on the side of a mountain with beautiful vistas on every side but little land that was level enough for cultivation. However, by supplementing farming with hunting and fishing, they managed to support themselves well enough.

Randolph and his wife Sally were the third generation of white settlers in this little community nestled along the tributaries of the Tug River. Despite the fact that the Tug River was the boundary between the states of West Virginia and Kentucky, Randolph and Sally, like most residents, considered *both* sides of the river their "neighborhood." Randolph—or "Old Ranel," as he was commonly known—had grown up just across the Tug in Logan County, Virginia (which became Logan County, West Virginia, when the new state was created in 1863). Only after he married Sally did the two move to the Kentucky side, so many family members and friends still lived on the West Virginia side. The river was not an obstacle to this sense of community; it was shallow and could be forded easily on horseback and often on foot as well.

On a fall day in 1878, Old Ranel McCoy made his way down the steep mountain trail that traversed the ridge between the headwaters of Blackberry Creek and then followed the road down Pond Creek. Near the banks of the Tug River the road passed the home of Floyd Hatfield. Despite the Hatfield name, Floyd was also related to the McCoys—he was married to Old Ranel's niece. Passing by Hatfield's barnyard, McCoy noticed to his chagrin that the hog pen contained a sow and her pigs that Old Ranel was sure belonged to him—they had been missing for weeks. Enraged, Old Ranel hurried off to the nearest Justice of the Peace where he lodged an official complaint. Despite the fact that the Justice of the Peace was also a Hatfield—a common name (as common as Smith in other parts of the country) on both sides of the Tug River—Old Ranel did not worry about getting fair treatment. The judge, William Anderson Hatfield or "Anse," was also the minister of the local church, universally liked and trusted by everyone in the community; Even in his judicial capacity he was respectfully referred to as "Preacher" Anse.

Having listened to Old Ranel's tirade against Floyd Hatfield, Preacher Anse now faced a dilemma. He had known Old Ranel McCoy all his life so he was well aware that the old man had developed quite a reputation for malicious gossip. In one instance many years before, Old Ranel's own cousin filed a suit against him for a slander; apparently Old Ranel had spread rumors about this cousin's sodomy with a cow. However, this official complaint was unusual; over the years, most Valley residents simply tried to avoid or ignore Old Ranel as his loose tongue rarely caused any real harm. The name by which he was familiarly known, "Old Ranel," conveyed something of the affectionate tolerance with which he was regarded. But now, Old Ranel's accusation of theft could not be easily dismissed. Hog theft, or indeed, any kind of theft in this small, isolated, closely knit community was a very rare and thus a very serious crime.

Worse, by accusing Floyd Hatfield of hog theft, Old Ranel was also indirectly challenging not only Floyd himself but the powerful figure of yet another Hatfield who lived across the Tug River in West Virginia. This Hatfield was, in fact, a second cousin of Preacher Anse who bore exactly the same name, William Anderson Hatfield. Although this repetition of names may sound confusing to outsiders, people who lived in the Tug Valley never had any problem distinguishing between the two. Although both were about the same age, tall and commanding in appearance with prominent noses, piercing dark eyes, and black beards, they had distinct personalities and played entirely different roles in the community. If "Preacher" conveyed the strong yet essentially gentle nature of the William Anderson Hatfield who lived on the Kentucky side, then his namesake who resided in West Virginia had a sobriquet that encapsulated *his* history and reputation. The West Virginia Hatfield was known as "Devil" Anse. Some in the community claimed he earned the sobriquet as a precocious child; others insisted it was a result of his brave, if sometimes foolhardy behavior as the leader of a guerrilla band during the Civil War; still others pointed to his accomplishments as the best marksman and horseman in the Valley or even his open contempt for religion in a community that took religious values very seriously. But wherever he got the name, he acquired it long before the feud began.

Old Ranel McCoy must have been just as conscious as was Preacher Anse that his tale of hog stealing would be considered not just an accusation of Floyd Hatfield but of Devil Anse Hatfield as well. This was not so much because Floyd shared the same surname (remember that Hatfield was as common a name as Smith or Jones) but because he was known as a loyal employee in Devil Anse's logging business. Because Old Ranel talked so much, everyone in the community was aware of his long simmering animosity toward Devil Anse and his timbering business. And, given Old Ranel's record of slander and gossip, local residents could be expected to be skeptical about the accusation. Yet local judicial traditions were strong and could not be easily ignored; Preacher Anse would not, indeed could not, dismiss Old Ranel without a hearing.

True to his reputation for fairness, Preacher Anse came up with a diplomatic solution. Calling for an immediate trial, he chose an evenly balanced jury; six Hatfields and six McCoys. In a clever maneuver on his part, one of the McCoys he

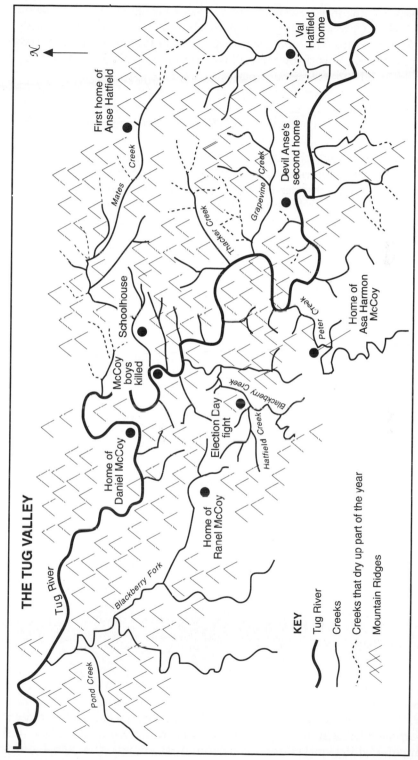

The Tug Valley. (Reprinted, by permission of the publisher, from *Feud: Hatfields, McCoys, and Social Change in Appalachia,* by Altina L. Waller. Copyright © 1988 by The University of North Carolina Press.)

39

chose to serve on the jury—Selkirk McCoy—was a nephew of Old Ranel's but, like Floyd Hatfield, was a member of Devil Anse's timber crew. With such divided loyalties, Preacher Anse hoped, Selkirk would vote on the side of truth and who could complain? And Selkirk did, indeed, vote with the Hatfields; Old Ranel lost the case and Floyd kept the sow and pigs.

Although Preacher Anse's strategy was initially successful, in the long term it was this court case that began the escalation of a long simmering animosity between Devil Anse Hatfield and Old Ranel McCoy from the realm of neighborhood name calling into a bizarre series of murders, ambushes, and pitched battles. These events not only shocked the community but gripped the attention of a nationwide audience, contributing in no small way to stereotypes of mountaineer lawlessness and violence that persist even to the present. Yet there was more to it than petty family grievances. America's most famous feud occurred at the very moment that economic modernization was about to destroy forever the rural isolation of the southern mountains. The history of the feud also reveals something of the capitalist transformation of Appalachia.

In the 1870s the Tug River community was still completely rural; it had no towns, no market center, no newspaper, not even a county seat. This meant that when-

This photograph of Devil Anse Hatfield probably was taken about the time of the feud. The jacket, tie, and Confederate medals indicate Devil Anse's pride in his role in the Civil War and his respected status in the community. (Courtesy West Virginia and Regional History Collection, West Virginia University Library)

ever a land transaction needed to be registered, a marriage license applied for, or taxes paid, a long and arduous journey was required. It was approximately a 30-mile trip by foot or horseback over rough mountain trails, either south to Pikeville, the county seat of Pike County, Kentucky, or north to Logan, the county seat of Logan County, West Virginia. The trip was physically exhausting and time-consuming and most people avoided it; they raised most of their own food—corn, potatoes, vegetables, cows, and pigs, voted in their own election districts within the valley, took their boundary disputes or other legal problems to the local Justice of the Peace and attended church only once a month when the circuit preacher made his rounds. For help in times of distress or sickness and for entertainment they depended on each other. It was a community more normally characterized by the stability of cooperation than by the divisiveness of conflict.

For the Tug Valley, even the Civil War—so divisive in many communities—reinforced community solidarity. During that conflict, despite its location straddling the boundary of two Union states, the people inhabitating the Tug Valley were almost unanimously loyal to the Confederacy. Ruled by state governments loyal to the Union and surrounded by Yankees (especially to the south in Kentucky, where the county seat of Pikeville was Yankee dominated) the Tug River was not spared the violence of war. A Union force under James Garfield (later president of the United States) invaded the Valley and burned the county court house in Logan, not because of any hostile actions taken by the residents, but simply because they were known Confederate sympathizers. When Devil Anse Hatfield formed a guerrilla band known as the "Logan Wildcats" as a defense against the Union Army and Yankee guerrillas who raided the Valley from places like Pikeville, almost every young man in the community served. Randolph McCoy, later Hatfield's nemesis in the feud, collaborated with the Logan Wildcats. Even when Randolph's brother, Asa Harmon McCoy, one of the very few Union sympathizers in the Valley, was killed, presumably by the Logan Wildcats, there was no legal action taken nor is there any legendary evidence that Old Ranel attempted any retaliation. The absence of conflict over this incident suggests community solidarity against Yankee traitors. Devil Anse and all those who served in the Logan Wildcats, were universally regarded as heroes.

If the Tug River community weathered the Civil War without serious internal conflict, it was not so harmonious in the post-war era when a very different set of problems emerged. One was the land itself. The terrain was so rugged that only one-third could be cultivated. This fixed supply of land severely limited economic opportunity for the younger generation. Tug Valley families were large, six to eight children on average. Devil Anse Hatfield, for example, had 13 children while Old Ranel McCoy had 16. When these children grew to adulthood and required land, farms became smaller and located in more remote hollows. Indeed, the census schedules indicate that many young people could never hope to acquire farms. Between 1850 and 1880 the percentage of landless families rose dramatically from 35 to 50 percent. In a traditional culture in which land was essential not only for economic survival but for self-esteem and social status, this change had profound implications. But despite this declining economic opportunity, family ties remained strong, so much so that they constituted the second problem. Children expected to settle down near their families and were extremely reluctant to move out of the region. Changing economic circumstances had transformed a cultural asset—strong family bonds—into an economic liability.

In the 1870s and 1880s the hardship created by this demographic crisis had the potential of being partially offset by a new economic opportunity—one that did not require leaving home and family—the demand of industrialized America for timber. Although large-scale timbering was not feasible because of a lack of efficient transportation, the farmers of the Tug Valley, soon after the Civil War, had begun to supplement family farming by cutting small amounts of timber and floating it to market in the nearest urban centers of Cincinnati and Cattlettsburg.

Both Old Ranel McCoy and Devil Anse Hatfield engaged in the timbering business with very different consequences. McCoy's involvement in marketing timber was to cause such serious family conflict that his parents lost their farm and were eventually divorced. In a court deposition, Old Ranel's mother explained how this came about:

> . . . about eleven years ago [1867] as near as she recollects, said plaintiff [Daniel McCoy, Randolph's father] went into what is generally termed the timber business, that is cutting and hauling saw-logs for market, and . . . cut a huge quantity of timber upon lands . . . other than his own, and when remonstrated with by this respondent [Margaret McCoy, Randolph's mother] for doing so great a wrong and one that would involve him in a law-suit and eventually break him up, he became very angry with said respondent and has ever since acted towards her with a coolness and indifference that he never manifested before that time.

Unfortunately for Margaret McCoy's family, her prediction about the lawsuit and the "breakup" came true. Paying off the court ordered damages led to loss of the farm and the destruction of the family; Old Ranel's parents were divorced in 1871. Old Ranel himself escaped relatively unscathed economically because his wife had inherited a farm from her father. Yet he did not fare so well socially or psychologically. Old Ranel became notorious as a gossip and a complainer.

Devil Anse Hatfield, on the other hand, thrived on timbering. Undaunted by his lack of resources, Devil Anse, in a bold move, borrowed money and organized a company—a company rooted in family and neighborhood relationships. Of the approximately 30 men he hired, about half were kin, including his brothers Valentine, Ellison, and Elias, his brothers-in-law, John, Moses, and Tom Chafin, his sons, William Anderson (or "Cap") and Johnson (or Johnse), and assorted nephews and cousins (like Floyd Hatfield). Not all Devil Anse's relatives approved of Devil Anse or the timbering business; his youngest brother, Pat, refused to become involved in timbering or the later feud. Needing more men than the family could or would provide, Devil Anse hired more than half of the timber crew from neighboring families, not necessarily related, men such as Selkirk McCoy and his two sons, Lorenzo and Albert, the Whitt brothers, Dan and Jeff, the Christian brothers, Dan and Moses, and the Staton brothers, Bill and John.

However, despite Hatfield's enterprising spirit, he still lacked the large amounts of forested land required for success. That obstacle was overcome when, as the result of a lawsuit against his nearest neighbor Perry Cline, Hatfield gained possession of a large tract of prime timber land. Although some aspects of the case remain puzzling because of incomplete court records, the broad outlines are clear. In 1872, Devil Anse sued Perry Cline, claiming that Cline and others had cut timber from Hatfield's land. Settling out of court 5 years later, Cline turned over to Devil Anse 5,000 acres of land—his sole inheritance from his father. In a startling reversal of social roles, Cline had been impoverished while Devil Anse became one of the wealthiest men in the Tug Valley. Cline, now without farmland to sustain himself or his family, moved south across the mountain ridge to the town of Pikeville, Kentucky.

Devil Anse, entrenched with an unusually large parcel of land and a prosperous timber company, embraced the role of entrepreneur. He made contracts with local merchants, boldly sued them when disagreements arose, and instituted numerous lawsuits against his own neighbors when they dared trespass on his land. In an environment in which freedom to hunt, walk, or ride wherever one wished had been assumed, residents were shocked to discover that cutting one tree or trespassing on Hatfield land could land them in court where they stood to lose their own farms or animals. Although Hatfield certainly did not win most of these cases, the 5,000 acres of the "Cline tract" kept his timber crew busy. Hatfield had succeeded where Old Ranel McCoy had failed. But what Devil Anse won in profits and economic power he lost in friendship and good will. Worse, he angered his neighbors by demonstrating contempt for community values—values that associated such worldly pursuits as self-interest and profit with the Devil. "You can say,"

Before the railroads and the mechanization of timbering, oxen, horses, or mules were used by family-based logging crews to cut timber in the mountains. (West Virginia State Archives, West Virginia Division of Culture and History, Charleston, West Virginia, 25305)

Devil Anse once declared, "that I belong to no church except the church of the world. You can say . . . I belong to the Devil's church."

Paradoxically, the opportunities provided by the timber market had accomplished what even the Civil War had not done: set neighbor against neighbor and seriously disrupted community and family harmony. In this newly competitive context, Devil Anse with his entrepreneurial maneuvering and flaunting of his success, towered like a lightning rod, attracting the ill feelings of his neighbors. He seemed to be the most obvious example of just what happened when selfish competition replaced cooperation. Ironically, it was Old Ranel McCoy, whose family had been so severely scarred by greed and dishonesty in the timber business, who was the first to openly challenge the Hatfields. Old Ranel's accusation of Floyd Hatfield for theft was that challenge. The hog trial, then, was more than simply an argument over the possession of a sow and pigs. It threatened to expose community fault lines of such depth that most residents instinctively recoiled from the prospect.

At first, Preacher Anse's strategy worked; although Old Ranel vociferously complained and attempted to persuade some of his kinsmen (there were many who lived nearby) to take some action against Devil Anse and his family, none would. When even his wife urged acceptance of the verdict, Old Ranel, grumbling, agreed. But in the long term the matter was far from settled. The younger generation—a few of Old Ranel's nephews and sons and some of Devil Anse's timber employees—continued to insult and harass each other, sometimes engaging in out and out brawls. Finally, two of Old Ranel's nephews killed a Hatfield timber employee. Arrested and tried in a West Virginia court, where Devil Anse Hatfield's older brother was the Judge, the two McCoys were acquitted on grounds of self-defense. It was an unexpected verdict favorable to the McCoys but it did not cool the feud.

In the summer of 1880, McCoy hostility was refueled when Roseanna McCoy, the dark-eyed, 21-year-old daughter of Old Ranel McCoy, and Johnse Hatfield, Devil Anse's son, fell in love. Disowned by her father, Roseanna moved in with the Hatfield family and was soon pregnant. However, Johnse was not a faithful lover; he spent most of his time away, flirting openly with other women. Hurt and angry, Roseanna fled to the household of her Aunt Betty. Although Old Ranel was furious and, despite tearful appeals from his wife, would not allow his daughter to return home, he did not instigate any violence against the Hatfields.

It was Old Ranel's son, 26-year-old Tolbert, who seized the leadership in pursuing a vendetta against the Hatfields. Tolbert had spent most of his life subjected to Old Ranel's repeated tirades on the subject of Hatfield knavery. He had watched as his cousin Perry Cline lost his land to Devil Anse. He harbored vivid memories of the family humiliation at the hog trial. Now his sister had been "stolen" and then abandoned by Johnse Hatfield. Yet the Hatfields' arrogance seemed to bring them prosperity, admiration, and respect, while Tolbert himself faced a bleak future. Although he was 26 years old, a husband, and soon to be father, Tolbert McCoy was hired out as a farm laborer with negligible prospects of obtaining his own farm.

Tolbert formulated a plot to have himself deputized by the Pike County sheriff so that he could arrest Johnse for some trumped up charge like carrying a concealed weapon or violating the liquor tax law. He ambushed Johnse on the Kentucky side of the river and would have hauled him off to the Pikeville jail had not

Roseanna, still in love with Johnse, discovered the plan and informed Devil Anse. Devil Anse surprised Tolbert escorting Johnse, at gunpoint, toward Pikeville and retrieved his son without violence. In the process, however, Devil Anse treated Tolbert like a bad boy who needed spanking—taking away his gun and administering a tongue lashing that was profoundly humiliating. Tolbert never forgot it.

On election day in August of 1882, Tolbert McCoy, according to his friends, was drunk and "looking for trouble." At first his hostility seemed unfocused. Badgering a neighbor for repayment of an old debt, he disregarded repeated warnings from the local constable and Preacher Anse to cease his belligerent behavior. Finally, Ellison Hatfield, a brother of Devil Anse and partner in the timber business, intervened. Ellison Hatfield was a big man, a Confederate war hero much admired by the young women of the Tug Valley and full of his own importance. Challenging Tolbert's drunken antics, he is reputed to have shouted, "I'm the best goddammed man on earth!" Electioneering festivities came to a sudden halt in stunned silence. Enraged, Tolbert seized a knife and lunged at Ellison even while screaming at his brothers for help. Two of them rushed to his side and the three McCoys attacked the powerful, massively built, but unarmed, Ellison Hatfield. Before the bystanders could untangle the feudists, the McCoys had stabbed Ellison Hatfield more than two dozen times as well as fired several shots into him. And although he was not dead, it was difficult to imagine that Ellison would survive for very long.

A strange drama followed. Devil Anse Hatfield had not been present that day so a shocked community seemed to hold its breath until Ellison's brothers were notified. What would they do—especially if Ellison died, as he was likely to do, of his severe wounds? Once again, as in the hog dispute, Preacher Anse Hatfield took charge of the situation. He began by urging Tolbert McCoy and his brothers to submit to arrest and go quietly to jail in Pikeville. When Tolbert protested, saying they would rather fight, Preacher Anse painted such a graphic picture of what was likely to happen when Devil Anse arrived on the scene that the three McCoys meekly submitted.

But it was not Devil Anse who came after the McCoys. It was his older brother, Valentine, who took the initiative. Valentine Hatfield was a Justice of the Peace in West Virginia and, like Preacher Anse, his counterpart in Kentucky, he was a respected elder statesman. The next morning it was the venerable Judge Valentine Hatfield who crossed the river into Kentucky in pursuit of the three McCoy sons and the constables. He finally caught up with the party only a few miles down the rugged trail to Pikeville. At the trial, one of the constables described the scene that ensued:

> I was one of the guards, guarding the McCoy boys when Wall [Valentine's nickname] came to us he said that all he wanted was that the boys should stand the civil law. That he had not slept any the night before and was tired and worn out and that he wanted them to go down to the mouth of the creek to have a trial. That he wanted to be near his brother [Devil Anse] and wanted to get the evidence of Dr. Rutherford and old Uncle Wall Hatfield. [Dr. Rutherford was the local physician and Uncle Wall was one of the oldest, most respected members of the community.]

Without apparent resistence the constables capitulated and agreed to return to the Tug Valley with their charges. Once there Preacher Anse made another effort to mediate the explosive situation. He invited Valentine and Devil Anse (who had finally appeared on the Kentucky side of the Tug River) along with the Mc-

Coys and the constables to have dinner with him. Apparently he tried to persuade the Hatfields to allow the McCoys to face trial in Pikeville, that justice would indeed be accomplished there. Needless to say, both Hatfield brothers were skeptical, for Pikeville was not part of their world; they had long memories going back to Civil War days when Pikeville was the center of Union loyalty, a headquarters for the Union Army and the place where Union guerrillas were outfitted to raid the Tug Valley. Moreover, Devil Anse's old enemy, Perry Cline, had become a powerful figure in Pikeville politics; he certainly could not be counted on to see that the McCoys faced justice for their crime. Still, Valentine seemed more inclined to consider this alternative than Devil Anse who, growing impatient, stomped out into the front yard and ordered "all Hatfields to line up." It was his way of announcing that the argument was over; he intended to take the McCoys back to West Virginia and find out whether his brother was still alive before any decisions would be made.

Once in West Virginia, Devil Anse converted an abandoned schoolhouse (near the present Matewan, West Virginia) into a makeshift jail. Here he stationed some of his followers as guards while sending others off to inquire about Ellison's condition. When he learned that Ellison was still alive Devil Anse informed Tolbert and his brothers that if Ellison died, so would they; if Ellison survived, they would be returned to the constables for trial in Pikeville. In the all-night vigil that followed, Devil Anse allowed Tolbert's wife and mother to visit the prisoners while Devil Anse and Valentine questioned witnesses about the fight and debated their next step.

Forty-eight hours after the fight, Ellison Hatfield died. Despite some disagreement in the family about killing the McCoys, Devil Anse could not be dissuaded from his ultimatum. He and about 20 of his followers (including Valentine) took the McCoys back to the Kentucky side of the Tug River, tied them to some pawpaw bushes on the banks of the river, blindfolded them and in an execution ritual, shot all three. It was the first time that Devil Anse Hatfield had engaged in feud violence. By the next day, a horrified community became aware of the gruesome retribution.

In spite of this unusual violence, however, most people in the community seemed unwilling to take any action against Devil Anse. Once again Old Ranel attempted but could not persuade any of his relatives or neighbors to take up arms against the Hatfields. Although Tug Valley residents may not have approved of Devil Anse, many of them had actually seen the three McCoys kill Ellison Hatfield in an unfair fight before dozens of witnesses. Thus, although indictments were issued in Pike County for the 20 Hatfields who had killed the McCoys, no attempt was made to serve the warrants or make arrests. The Sheriff of Pike County made a terse note on the back of the warrant issued for the arrest of Devil Anse and his supporters: "Not found," and no further action was taken for fully 5 years.

Indeed, it is likely that the feud would have ended in 1882, and the world would never have heard of the Hatfields and McCoys, had it not been for the actions, 5 years later, of Devil Anse Hatfield's old nemesis, Perry Cline. Cline's career in Pikeville, after the loss of his inheritance to Devil Anse and his flight from the Tug Valley, had been a successful one. By 1887 he was a lawyer and sheriff of the county and belonged to the small circle of businessmen and politicians who wielded power in Pikeville. Rumor had it that as a friend and political supporter of Kentucky's newly elected Governor, Simon Buckner, Cline's power extended beyond Pikeville to the state capital.

Not only was Cline now in a position of power, but in the intervening 14 years since he had left the Tug Valley, his resentment toward Devil Anse for the loss of his property had grown more acute. In 1886 and 1887 it was obvious that the value of his lost property was about to skyrocket. First, in 1886, the Norfolk and Western Railroad announced its intention to build the "Ohio Extension" from Virginia to the Ohio River. But the building of the railroad was only the beginning; the very next year, 1887, the Kentucky legislature published the results of a geological survey that confirmed discovery of extensive seams of high quality coal in the Tug Valley. The geological survey was more than a routine report; it was also a public relations document through which the legislature signaled its plans to actively recruit investment by eastern capitalists. Cline was only beginning to understand the extent of the economic boom about to engulf the entire region.

It was in this frame of mind, then, that Perry Cline listened to his old Uncle Ranel one cold winter day in the year 1886. Old Ranel had ridden over the mountain ridge to relate, once again, the tale of Hatfield crimes. In the 4 years since the election day fight and the killing of his three sons, Old Ranel had many times brought his complaints to Cline, who listened sympathetically but took no action. This time, however, Cline was more attentive. Although the most recent incident described by Old Ranel was not clearly part of the old feud, Cline perceived his opportunity to strike back at Devil Anse Hatfield. Yes, Perry Cline said to old Uncle Ranel, he would approach his friend the Governor about reinstating the arrest warrants against Devil Anse and the 20 men who had taken part in the execution of the McCoys. For the first time in 4 years Old Ranel rode back across the mountain ridge a happy man, while Cline began to marshal support from his influential friends.

By the following summer, Perry Cline had succeeded in persuading the Governor to revive the 5-year-old indictments against the Hatfields and actively prosecute the case. Just how he accomplished this, what arguments he used, it is impossible to know as no one involved kept any records or directly stated their reasons. All we can do is surmise from the circumstances surrounding the meetings. If the Governor did feel indebted to Cline, his inclination to go along with the request was probably strengthened by a desire to make Kentucky appear to be a law and order state, especially as recent national publicity about several other Kentucky feuds had created a violent image for the state. Newspapers in the state were already lamenting the inhibiting effect that feud violence might have on potential capitalist investment in the rich coal mining region and the Hatfield–McCoy feud, although not active at the moment, was located in the most highly visible region for attracting coal investors. Whatever his reasons, the Governor issued official rewards for the capture of the Hatfields and began legal proceedings to extradite them from West Virginia.

The Governor's action had the effect of reactivating the feud, this time pitting the power of the state of Kentucky against Devil Anse Hatfield and his supporters. Back in Pikeville, armed with the authority of the Governor, Cline recruited a posse to cross the state boundary into West Virginia and, ignoring the extradition process, captured his first Hatfield supporter. Ironically, this first "Hatfield" captive was none other than Selkirk McCoy, who had served on the hog trial jury and voted with the Hatfields. This intervention by the state government was a shocking departure from the local autonomy of county government. The first response of Devil Anse Hatfield, however, was not violence, but bribery. He tried to buy off Perry Cline by offering him $250 to stop the posse raids and rescind the rewards. Cline initially agreed and accepted the bribe but then continued to send his posse across the border.

Next Devil Anse attempted a political solution. He approached the Governor of West Virginia, E. Willis Wilson, through a friend and political crony, John B. Floyd. Floyd had grown up in the Tug Valley and knew Hatfield and his family well. Both Floyd and Wilson were sympathetic to the Hatfields' dilemma because of their politics. Both men belonged to a faction of the Democratic Party that defended the interests of farmers and working people against wealthy businessmen and capitalists. They perceived the mountain farmers of the Appalachian region as victims who were losing their land to railroad and coal companies and rapidly being reduced from independent yeomen to wage laborers. Wilson spent his entire political career fighting big corporations and trying to protect his constituents from such exploitation. He advocated state control of the railroads and reasonable levels of taxation for absentee corporations which controlled West Virginia's valuable mineral resources. An idealist, he was the last of a vanishing breed in late 19th century politics. In fact, he was the last Governor of West Virginia to actively oppose corporate domination of West Virginia's politics and economy. When Wilson heard from John Floyd of the Hatfields' history of legal and economic difficulties with Perry Cline, and Cline's influence with the Governor of Kentucky, he was willing to consider the possibility that the Hatfields, too, were victims. He delayed signing the extradition papers by requesting further information from Governor Buckner of Kentucky.

But for some of Devil Anse's supporters, including his sons Cap and Johnse, none of this was enough. Cap came up with a plan to get rid of the people who had caused their problems—the family of Old Ranel McCoy. He proposed burning down the McCoy home in a midnight raid that would destroy all potential witnesses against them. It was a desperate solution, so shocking to most Hatfield supporters that they refused to be involved.

But Cap Hatfield was so infuriated (and probably frightened) that he ignored all advice to the contrary, even his father's. Just past midnight on January 1st of 1888, accompanied by only eight of the Hatfield group (Devil Anse not among them), he led the attack on Old Ranel's home on the Blackberry Fork of Pond Creek. This was the infamous New Year's Day raid in which two of Old Ranel's children were killed—both shot as they attempted to run from the burning house—and his wife Aunt Sally McCoy beaten when she tried to reach her dying daughter in the snow. Old Ranel and the other children escaped and made their way to Pikeville where Perry Cline took them in. Meanwhile, the Hatfields realized with horror that the whole idea had been a tragic blunder, one that far from resolving anything, would only exacerbate the trouble.

It was this incident that catapulted the feud into national attention as Perry Cline and his friends seized the public relations offensive by circulating press releases to Kentucky newspapers, which were then picked up by papers all over the country. The first newspaper item that focused national attention on the feud was headlined, "A MURDEROUS GANG—A TERRIBLE TRAGEDY PERPETRATED BY DESPERADOES—MOTHER AND SON MURDERED WHILE FATHER AND DAUGHTER ESCAPE A FIERY GRAVE." During the next 6 months, the names Hatfield and McCoy became household words all over America, as newspapers from Maine to California sensationalized every detail and reported every rumor as though it were fact. Reporters from Pittsburgh and New York City arrived on the scene and attempted to interview anyone remotely connected with the two families but received most of their information from Perry Cline. *New York World* reporter T. C. Crawford rushed into print a book on the feud entitled *An American Vendetta: A Story of Barbarism in the United States.* It was only the first of many sensationalized accounts.

Cline was not content with a journalistic war, however. He stepped up his raids into West Virginia during the month of January and managed to capture eight more Hatfield supporters, including Justice of the Peace Valentine Hatfield. In the process, two Hatfield supporters were shot and killed. The final violent confrontation came at the end of January when a Hatfield posse met a Cline posse and engaged in a quasi-military skirmish. It became legendary as the Battle of Grapevine Creek.

Now alarmed by violence in the Tug Valley, Governor E. Willis Wilson of West Virginia was willing to admit that he could have misjudged the situation. If so he was ready to take drastic action by sending in the militia to keep the peace. He even urged Governor Buckner to do the same. Before giving the order, however, Governor Wilson sent a personal emissary to the Tug Valley to investigate. The report returned by the special investigator assured the Governor that the violence was not as severe as had been rumored. It also, however, substantiated his earlier belief that the Hatfields were victims. "I visited all the Hatfields," stated the investigator, "and found them to be good, law-abiding citizens who have the respect and confidence of everyone in the neighborhood."

This information confirmed that of Wilson's trusted political ally, John Floyd, who argued that the trouble had only arisen because Perry Cline had decided "he would stir up the thing again and make some money out of it, knowing that the Hatfields owned some good property." Convinced of Cline's culpability in the affair and infuriated that the state of Kentucky was violating extradition procedures by kidnapping and jailing West Virginia citizens, Governor Wilson went on the offensive. Refusing to sign the extradition request, he issued formal rewards for the arrest and capture of members of Cline's posse who had killed the two Hatfield supporters.

But Governor Wilson was still not satisfied. There were important moral and legal principles involved, he thought, and he intended to pursue them at the highest possible level. Convinced that Governor Buckner and the state of Kentucky had illegally "invaded" West Virginia to capture its citizens, Wilson filed Writs of Habeas Corpus for the Hatfields in the federal district court in Louisville. This meant that the Sheriff of Pikeville had to produce the eight Hatfields in the Louisville court for a determination as to whether they were being illegally held in the Pikeville jail. When the appointed day arrived for the hearing, Governor Wilson himself, accompanied by John B. Floyd, appeared to argue West Virginia's case.

Although the district judges ruled against West Virginia and sent the Hatfields back to Pikeville to stand trial, the case was appealed to the United States Supreme Court where it was heard in May of 1888. However, the Supreme Court also decided in favor of Kentucky, arguing that states possessed only "limited sovereignty" and therefore could not seek redress with habeas corpus to reclaim citizens who had been kidnapped. In effect the Court ruled that it did not matter *how* the accused Hatfield supporters came to be in Kentucky—once there, the authorities could legally arrest them.

While these legal proceedings were in process, actual violence between the Hatfields, McCoys, and Cline had ended with the Battle of Grapevine Creek, but the rewards offered by both states brought into the Valley a number of bounty hunters, usually members of private detective agencies such as Eureka and Baldwin–Felts, intent on scouring the mountains for anyone remotely resembling a feudist. Fear and suspicion of strangers mounted as local residents, who were, after all, most of them related to the Hatfields and McCoys, could expect to be accosted, beaten, or even killed in the manhunt. Newspapers, employing sensational rhetoric, played up the violence and attributed every encounter between a Tug Valley resident and a detective as a feud incident directly caused, not by outside bounty hunters, but by the violent and lawless nature of mountain culture itself.

Ironically, Perry Cline had contributed to this growing national perception that *all* Appalachians were, as he said of the Hatfields in a letter to Governor Wilson, "outlaws" and desperadoes who had been "in arms" since the Civil War, the worst "merauders" [sic] ever who would not live "as citizens ought." Further reinforcing the stereotype, Cline spread the rumor that Valentine Hatfield, Devil Anse's older brother and long time respected county judge, had "five wives and thirty-three . . . children" and had "peculiar ideas of polygamy." Without any evidence other than Cline's word, the *New York Times* repeated this false story, reporting that the "fact" of Hatfield's five wives made it "evident that a strong course of common schools, churches, soap and water . . . is required before these simple children of nature will forbear to kill a man whenever they take a dislike to him." This latest "vendetta," declared the *Times*, ". . . shows the purely savage character of the population." In a strange twist of events, the hillbilly stereotype produced by the feud was to obscure to history the role played by Devil Anse as an ambitious, and typically American, entrepreneur.

As the Hatfields became the target for every private detective in the East, Devil Anse Hatfield decided that enough was enough and retreated. With nine of his supporters lodged in the Pikeville jail, and private detectives waiting to ambush him at every turn, Devil Anse concluded that life on the banks of the Tug had become too dangerous. He sold the hard won 5,000 acres for half of what it was worth to an agent for a group of Philadelphia capitalists. All through the 1880s this agent had been buying up the lands of local farmers in anticipation of the railroad and coal mines that would soon open up. Most farmers were completely unaware of the plans then being made that would soon make their forested slopes much more valuable. But he had not been able to persuade Devil Anse, who was far too independent and stubborn to sell. Now, however, with the threat of arrest by detectives, Devil Anse sold the land for half its value and moved his family back away from the Tug boundary to Main Island Creek near the town of Logan, where he built a virtual fortress on the side of a mountain.

Within a year of his move, at about the same time as Devil Anse's brother Valentine and other supporters were being tried in Pikeville, the railroad was built right through his former land and the town of Matewan sprang up where the three McCoys had been killed in 1882. Although the Pikeville trials led to the deaths of two (Valentine Hatfield died in prison while Ellison Mounts was hanged in February of 1890) and the life imprisonment of the others, Devil Anse was never captured or extradited. Safe on his mountain, Devil Anse outlived Old Ranel McCoy, who died in a fire in 1914 and Perry Cline, who had a heart attack in 1891 at the age of 42. In 1921 Devil Anse's death of old age was overshadowed in the press by the outbreak of a series of bloody wars between mine workers and private police employed by the coal companies. Progress, it seems, had not brought peace to Appalachia.

Ellison Mounts was a Hatfield feudist and the only one to be executed by the state of Kentucky. His hanging on February 18, 1890, was the last such public spectacle in Pike County.

AN INTERPRETATION

The Hatfield–McCoy feud traditionally has invoked images and stereotypes of ignorance, violence, and family loyalty gone berserk. Derogatory stories and jokes about Appalachian mountaineers continue to be acceptable today at a time in which there is sensitivity to insults directed toward blacks, women, Indians, and other minority groups. Even middle-class Americans whose roots are in the southern mountains frequently accept these negative assumptions and feel ashamed of their background.

Yet in many ways the world of the Hatfields and McCoys was not at all unusual. The feuding families were part of a traditional farming community, like farming communities located in New England, upstate New York, Pennsylvania, and small farm areas of the South in the antebellum era. Extensive kin networks defined individual identity and status in the community as well as economic activity and local government. Community self-sufficiency and autonomy predominated, but there was never a complete absence of commerce with surrounding regions or isolation from larger political issues at the state and national levels. The complex family relations manifested in the story of the feud could apply to almost any region before the Civil War. Appalachians, then, initially were not so different from most Americans; why then did the violence of the late nineteenth century erupt and why did it become so well-known?

The initial stage of the feud was brought about because of a demographic and economic crisis within the Tug Valley community itself. Not enough land and too many people with strong family bonds led to declining opportunity, which in turn produced anxiety, tension, and increased competition for scarce resources. To this increased competition for traditional farm occupations was added the "opportunity" to supply industrialized America with timber. Rising land values, competition for trees, and the cash that could be gotten from selling them led to disruption of a traditional subsistence economy based on community cooperation and sharing. More significantly, it led to a breakdown in a spirit of cooperation in the community. The animosity that polarized around those committed to a market economy (timber) versus those still primarily engaged in semisubsistence farming became apparent in the initial stage of the feud when only members of the timber operation were singled out as enemies by the McCoys. Preacher Anse Hatfield as well as many of Devil Anse Hatfield's brothers, uncles, and cousins were not attacked by the McCoys, nor did they rush to the defense of Devil Anse. The feud story also reveals that many of Old Ranel McCoy's relatives refused to become involved or, like Selkirk McCoy, took the Hatfield side. Family bonds were strong in the Tug Valley but apparently not strong enough to overcome emerging economic conflict and the emotional response that went with it.

The story of the feud also reveals that mountain communities were neither chronically lawless nor violent. The local judicial system was strong and functioned effectively. Devil Anse, for example, apparently won his case against Perry Cline on solid legal grounds and when he did not win in court, Devil Anse did not use force or violence or ignore judicial authority. Violence emerged from the threat or the reality of outside infringement on the local system of authority. The first example apparent in the feud was the problem caused because the Tug Valley community was arbitrarily divided by the boundary between West Virginia and Kentucky. When Devil Anse's brother Ellison was killed on the Kentucky side of the river, the Hatfields, who had always before been willing to rely on the courts, could not allow Ellison Hatfield's killers to be taken to Pikeville for trial. Valentine and Devil Anse were reluctant to engage in vigilantism—to take the law into their own hands—but were convinced they had no choice. Significantly, they did not simply kill the three McCoys on the West Virginia side of the river; fearful that West Virginia authorities might take legal action against them, they took the McCoys back to the Kentucky side before executing them. It was a way of keeping themselves law abiding in West Virginia and, at the same time, administering justice. Still, it was not until Perry Cline took his case to the Governor of Kentucky that the local judicial system broke down entirely. When Cline and his Kentucky posse raided West Virginia and the Hatfields retaliated with the New Year's Day raid on the McCoy home, it was obvious that state intervention had completely shattered the local system of authority.

At this point the feud took on much broader political and economic dimensions. Governor Buckner allied Kentucky with capitalists and modernizers both inside and outside the region; he perceived the mountaineers as obstructing

This photograph of the Hatfield family was taken in 1897 by an itinerant photographer well after the feud had made the Hatfields famous. Attempting to exploit that notoriety, the photographer posed the family with guns prominently displayed. This picture has become one of the most famous images associated with the feud. (West Virginia State Archives, West Virginia Division of Culture and History, Charleston, West Virginia, 25305)

the economic development of the region and hoped to make an example of the Hatfields. Governor Wilson of West Virginia represented that strain of late 19th century political thought identified as "agrarian" or "populist," which sought to resist the overweening political and economic power of the eastern industrialists. Wilson's earnestness in defending the Hatfields was part and parcel of his entire career as a defender of small farmers in his state. Thus, when the case went to the Supreme Court at Wilson's instigation, it could be interpreted as a national level dispute over the rights of weaker, powerless people in opposition to the economic and political power of the modernizers. Although this issue was not overt in the arguments before the Supreme Court, put in the larger context of the changes in the federal judiciary toward protecting corporations at the expense of individuals and ruling against minority groups such as blacks and Indians, this case can be interpreted as part of a larger pattern.

Finally, if the worst violence of the feud was brought about by the industrialization process, why was that process so much more violent than in the rest of the country? For the most part, antebellum communities in the North or even other parts of the South did not experience the level of violence during industrialization that Appalachia did. Part of the answer may be that the process was more gradual in other areas, allowing people time to adjust, but the key factor for Appalachians may have been that it was largely imposed on them from outside. Although local boosters collaborated with outside industrialists, local capital was not sufficient to make the process indigenous and thus most mountaineers were exploited in much the same way as the people of Latin America or the Philippines as the United States took on more and more foreign ventures. Thus, the relationship became adversarial and violent as many Appalachians, like the Hatfields after Kentucky's posse raids, realized that they would no longer be allowed to control their own future or benefit from the process of economic development.

Sources: This story is based on extensive research in the County Court Records of Logan County, West Virginia, and Pike County, Kentucky; the Kentucky State Archives in Frankfort, Kentucky, and the West Virginia State Archives in Charleston, West Virginia; newspapers such as the *Louisville Courier–Journal,* the *Logan Banner,* the *Wheeling Intelligencer,* the *New York World,* and the *New York Times;* and books written with firsthand information such as T. C. Crawford's *An American Vendetta: A Story of Barbarism in the United States,* NY: Bedford, Clarke & Co. (1889), and Truda McCoy's *The McCoys: Their Story As Told to the Author by Eyewitnesses and Descendents,* edited by Leonard Roberts, Pikeville, KY: Pikeville College Press (1976) which is based on interviews with many women involved in the feud. The best short narrative treatment of the feud is Otis Rice, *The Hatfields and the McCoys,* Lexington: University Press of KY (1978). For the most detailed examination of the feud and its economic and social implications see Altina L. Waller, *Feud: Hatfields, McCoys, and Social Change in Appalachia 1860–1900,* Chapel Hill: University of North Carolina Press (1988).

4

COXEY'S ARMY: DRAMATIZING THE MALAISE OF THE 1890s

CARLOS A. SCHWANTES

The "army" of about 400 men that massed in the nation's capital in late April 1894 did not in most ways resemble an army at all. In their dark suits, vests, and bowler hats, the unarmed "recruits" seemed more prepared for a dinner party than battle. One of its commanders resembled Buffalo Bill Cody, and the other, "General" Jacob Coxey (who was not a general), could have been mistaken for an accountant. The group referred to itself as the "J. S. Coxey Good Roads Association" or the "Commonweal of Christ," names whose evocations of social reformism and spiritual crusading must have aroused more curiosity than fear. But the press had called it "Coxey's Army," and that was that.

Coxey's legions were from Ohio and West Virginia, Los Angeles and Seattle, Montana and Illinois, Portland and Denver, and dozens of other places. As Carlos A. Schwantes's story reveals, the movement was remarkably strong in the trans-Mississippi West, where a diminishing supply of free land had shed doubt on the ability of the nation's economy to absorb the unemployed. Some supporters had dodged railroad police to hitch a ride on a freight train, others had rafted down the Missouri, and still others—the largest contingent, as it turned out—had followed Coxey's route, traveling by foot from Northeastern Ohio and across the Appalachian Mountains to Washington, D.C., where they hoped to convince the national government to mount a federal jobs program.

Surely something had to be done. Serious economic depressions, of the sort that created widespread unemployment and threatened the social order, had become a regular feature of the American scene. In 1877, a series of strikes that had begun on the railroads produced general strikes and violence in many cities and towns. The economic downturn of the mid-1880s was less severe, but marked nonetheless by violent confrontations over the 8-hour day, culminating in the 1886 "riot" in Chicago's Haymarket Square and the hanging of the "anarchists" who supposedly were responsible for the tumult. Then, in 1893, a financial panic sent the economy into a tailspin and left millions of workers without jobs and millions more with reduced wages. This depression lasted 4 years and produced several memorable events: the great Pullman strike of 1894; a last, failed effort by William Jennings Bryan to *rally workers and farmers under the banner of monetary reform; and Coxey's Army of the unemployed.*

Nearly 40 years later, another "army," this one composed of unemployed veterans of the Great War, would call on the federal government to help its constituents through yet another depression—the Great Depression of the 1930s—and by mid-decade Franklin D. Roosevelt's New Deal had produced just the sort of public works programs that had once seemed so radical. By 1963, when Rev. Martin Luther King, Jr., spoke of freedom—and jobs—to hundreds of thousands from the steps of the Lincoln Memorial, the "march on Washington" had become almost an American tradition.

To the congressmen and senators peering from their office windows at the strange aggregation that moved on Capitol Hill on the morning of May 1, 1894, Coxey's ideas were outrageous, and his army as unpredictably dangerous as the Haymarket troublemakers. There was a price to be paid for pioneering.

By noon an estimated thirty thousand spectators—men, women, and children—waited elbow to elbow under the canvas awnings and shade trees that lined Pennsylvania Avenue. The crowd nearly covered Capitol Hill. Normally only the inauguration of a president attracted so many onlookers, but this was no inauguration: Grover Cleveland occupied the White House, his term not yet half completed. This Tuesday—May 1, 1894—belonged to Jacob Sechler Coxey and his army, a protest as unprecedented in the history of the United States as the massive unemployment that gave it life and purpose.

Coxey's name was on everyone's lips, first as a murmur and then as a shout as his carriage pulled into view. Behind him marched the 400 tatterdemalion veterans of the Commonweal of Christ, the advance guard of America's first national crusade against unemployment, a "petition in boots" that hoped to pressure Congress into financing a program of public works to employ the jobless until the economy could regain its health.

Some called Coxey a revolutionary; others dismissed him as a crank. Slight of build, clean-shaven except for a light brown mustache, wearing wire-rimmed glasses and a dark gray business suit, he looked more like a harmless middle-aged professor than the wild man that newspaper cartoonists typically sketched to represent cranks. Occasionally he rose and bowed to the crowd. His flashing blue eyes suggested a sense of humor.

For the past 6 weeks Americans had read numerous accounts of Coxey, his ragtag army of the unemployed, and the several imitators he inspired. The daily press often carried the story on page 1, and rare was the 4-page country weekly that did not print at least some news of the Commonweal. In fact, since the end of the Civil War in 1865, perhaps only the disputed election of 1876 had generated more intense newspaper coverage.

Readers had pondered, laughed at, or worried about the Coxey movement a great deal. Some regarded it as a national joke, only slightly less humorous than Congress and certainly less expensive. They wondered whether it drew its inspiration from the showman Phineas T. Barnum or from the radical Communards who gained control of Paris in 1871. There were always many questions and few answers.

"General" Coxey's name became a household word, although he personally shunned the military terminology that journalists used to describe the movement. He preferred to style himself simply as president of the J. S. Coxey Good Roads Association of the United States and ex-officio of the Commonweal of Christ, the formal name that organizers gave their protest movement. Like the odd name itself, much about the Coxey movement defied conventional logic; and that, together with the hard times that began in mid-1893, helped to account for the seemingly insatiable popular interest in its progress.

Coxey was a wealthy man, the owner of a quarry in northern Ohio that produced a special type of white sand needed by the steel, glass, and pottery industries that until recently had enjoyed boom times. By the early 1890s he had expanded his holdings to include a stock farm located outside his hometown of Massillon (south of Cleveland) and ranches near Lexington, Kentucky, and Guthrie, Oklahoma, where he raised several dozen blooded race horses. Most horses in the march down Pennsylvania Avenue were his: for a single stallion he reportedly paid $40,000, enough money in the 1890s to hire 80 laborers for a year.

When in late March Coxey's thinly clad Commonwealers tramped out of Massillon in a snowstorm, it seemed impossible that they would survive to parade

A portrait of Jacob Coxey at the age of 40 at the time of his famous march. Afterward, he often campaigned for public office—primarily as a monetary reformer—and lost, the sole exception being his election as mayor of Massillon in 1931. Coxey died on May 18, 1951, his life having spanned the administrations of 19 presidents—from Franklin Pierce to Harry S. Truman. [Henry Vincent, *The Story of the Commonweal* (Chicago: W. B. Conkey Company, 1894)]

through the streets of Washington. Could they live off the land for more than 400 miles? Not since William Tecumseh Sherman and his Union soldiers marched 300 miles through Georgia 30 years before had anything like it been attempted. But when Coxey's marchers crossed the Appalachian Mountains and descended into the valley of the Potomac, disbelief and derision turned to amazement and alarm. No one knew how large or dangerous the Commonweal might become by the time it reached Capitol Hill.

Turning from Fourteenth Street onto Pennsylvania Avenue, marchers glimpsed the White House off to their right. Except for the extra guards, life there appeared normal. A routine cabinet meeting was reportedly in progress. Outwardly the president was calm, stolid as the Rock of Gibraltar, to which the heavyset chief executive bore a slight resemblance. But those around him were clearly nervous. They scanned the minute-by-minute dispatches forwarded by special agents who shadowed the procession. Guarding the president was the largest detail of Secret Service agents, District of Columbia police, and watchdogs assembled since Civil War days. Special telephone lines had been strung to call in police reserves if necessary. Throughout the city 200 extra policemen were on duty, and detectives from several large cities of the Northeast quietly mingled with the spectators.

Many of the president's men feared that Coxey's army would attract violent individuals, possibly not as marchers but certainly as sympathizers. Within living memory, men of this description had assassinated two presidents; and just 6 months ago another had gunned down the popular mayor of Chicago. During the past winter a "Jack the Ripper" had slipped unnoticed into the White House, slashed the curtains in the Green Room, and stabbed his knife through several elegant sofas and chairs. All this, combined with the many threatening letters the president had received of late, lay behind the effort to "crank proof" the White House. "The air seems to breed cranks and the demon of destruction is abroad in the land," fretted the *Chicago Herald*.

As Commonwealers continued slowly down Pennsylvania Avenue, spectators who had waited peaceably for hours rushed out to greet Coxey. Some seemed so determined to climb into his carriage that journalists formed a cordon of special guards to keep off intruders. At several locations sympathizers nearly blocked the broad thoroughfare until a vanguard of 25 mounted policemen pushed them aside.

The procession took nearly an hour to pass. Coxey's troops, mostly veterans of the long march from Massillon, stepped along smartly in dilapidated shoes yellow with the dust of country roads, threadbare shirts and jackets, and battered but functional hats that shielded their well-tanned faces from the noonday sun. Each man carried a long oaken stave of peace bearing a white flag with the slogan "Peace on earth, good will toward men, but death to interest on bonds." A Commonweal band of six pieces, mostly bass drums and cymbals, pounded out a rendition of "Marching Through Georgia."

Two black trotters pulled a carriage bearing Coxey, his wife, and their 2-month-old son, Legal Tender—"Leeg" for short. The baby's odd name was a reflection of his father's lifelong obsession with monetary reform. As a young man Coxey had spent countless hours reading and thinking about the money question that so agitated post-Civil War America, arguing endlessly about interest rates, paper money, and bank credit with fellow workers in the iron-rolling mill where he was once employed. A Good Roads Bill, which combined Coxey's highway-building proposal, fiat-money ideas, and desire to help the unemployed, had been introduced in Congress in 1892 but got nowhere. Two years later Coxey added a proposal for non-interest-bearing bonds, a complicated plan that would provide federal loans to enable local governments to construct schools, courthouses, libraries, museums, and other public buildings in addition to streets and highways, all of which would provide jobs for the unemployed.

"Coxey! Coxey!" The roar continued along the length of Pennsylvania Avenue. Although Coxey gave his name to the movement and used it to publicize his public works program, the man who actually conceived the march on Capitol Hill was Carl Browne, a Californian who served as the Commonweal's chief marshal. Riding astride a magnificent gray stallion at the head of the procession, he sported a large white sombrero tilted rakishly over his right eye and long hair that cascaded over his shoulders. Buttons fashioned from silver dollars decorated his fringed buckskin jacket and caused Browne to resemble Buffalo Bill Cody, the pop-

Members of Coxey's Army encamped on the outskirts of Washington to prepare for their historic rendezvous on Capitol Hill. "The money lenders tremble now," their leader Jacob Coxey asserted. "Congress takes two years to vote on anything if left to itself. Twenty-millions of people are hungry and cannot wait two years to eat." (Library of Congress)

ular showman of the Wild West. An eccentric, energetic, and flamboyant man with a genius for self-promotion that anticipated Hollywood, he originated the marchers' many bizarre banners and catch phrases.

Road-weary wagons decorated with Browne's cartoon-like artwork and slogans creaked along at intervals. One banner read "Co-Operation, the cerebellum of the Commonweal," and another, "The medulla oblongata and all other parts of the reincarnated Christ in the whole people." The juxtaposition of mysticism with a call for jobs made sense to Browne and certainly helped to attract the eye of the press, but it also brought forth guffaws and derisive words from skeptics who refused to accept the Commonweal as a legitimate reform movement. For Browne the money question was both personal and visceral: his slogans, lurid artwork, and speeches denounced Wall Street bankers as heartless and blasted the gold standard as an "old vampire."

On Capitol Hill the Senate convened at noon and remained in session for 12 minutes; members adjourned as custom dictated when they received news of the unexpected death of a colleague, Francis Stockbridge of Michigan. Members of the House spent the morning discussing bills pertaining to the accounting offices of the Treasury Department and protection of birds and game in Yellowstone Park. Congressmen wanted to remain in session until after the Commonweal arrived to avoid creating the unseemly impression that they had adjourned early out of fear. Even so, extra guards were on duty in the building, and heavy pine gates, such as were used to control inauguration crowds, were in place on each side of the main rotunda.

At the other end of Pennsylvania Avenue more dispatches reached the White House. "House reports there is large crowd all about the Capitol but everything quiet." "Coxey army just reached Peace Monument and going up hill to B Street and Delaware." After weeks of protest and posturing, Coxey's Army halted in the shadow of the Capitol. Lawmen nearly surrounded the building, and more were hidden inside. If the Ohioan still expected to deliver his speech from the Capitol steps, he needed somehow to push through the sea of blue-jacketed officers. But would he? Would club-wielding policemen beat back Coxey and his followers in an effort to discourage others still on the road? The nation held its collective breath and waited.

An important question that no one could answer that May Day was how many troops Coxey actually commanded. Not even Coxey knew. His crusade had produced such a sudden and spontaneous outpouring of support across the United States that he had no way to keep track of every local division and regiment that claimed to be part of "Coxey's Army." The ranks filled most rapidly in cities of the Far West, where the daily drumbeat of newspaper publicity inspired unemployed workmen to form a dozen additional contingents. To Coxey's jobs program they added a peculiarly regional demand that Uncle Sam hire the unemployed to dig irrigation ditches to bring water to the nation's vast arid domain: "When the ditches are dug and the lands reclaimed we can register homestead claims and be self-supporting ever after." Motivated both by desperation and dreams of a bright future through irrigation, western armies pledged to conquer both distance and desert terrain to rendezvous with Coxey on Capitol Hill.

Underscoring the challenges they faced was an incident at the crest of the Cascade Mountains in remote Washington, the state which contributed more recruits per capita than any other. At the 2-mile-long Stampede Pass tunnel, where driving winter winds piled snow nearly 30 feet high, marchers found federal marshals blocking the west portal. Lawmen gave Commonwealers the cruel choice of scaling the pass high above the railway line or returning home. There were no alternatives. Though ill-fed, lightly clad, and without snowshoes, most crusaders defied the odds and struggled over the mountains, courting pneumonia all the way. Driving them on was a passionate desire to join the great protest on Capitol Hill. Ahead lay an uncertain future, but one of hope; behind lay the assured misery of joblessness and a hand-to-mouth existence.

At times the Coxey protest was so varied and complex that it resembled a 20-ring circus with half a dozen sideshows. In addition to Coxey's own band, which captured the most national and international attention, large armies converged on the nation's capital from the urban West, and not just one contingent from each major city but two or three from Los Angeles and Denver. A Polish Coxey's Army organized in Chicago and marched across America's industrial heartland.

One newspaper counted 13 contingents numbering more than 5,000 troops on the road, and that guess was probably as good as any. Of equal worry to opponents of the movement were the unknown thousands who joined Coxey in spirit. These included supporters who fed and sheltered marchers along the way, as well as those who turned out with brass bands and banners to cheer them on or to intimidate the federal marshals and other lawmen who attempted to halt their progress.

Especially for crusaders from the Far West, the aid of sympathizers was vital. Those Commonwealers, too poor to charter passenger coaches to take them to Capitol Hill, stole rides east on railway cars and walked only when unsympathetic lawmen barred them from the trains. When this happened they sometimes stole the trains themselves. That happened on at least 50 separate occasions, with the most celebrated incident occurring in Montana, where a trainload of federal marshals raced after Coxeyites in the most dramatic locomotive chase since the Civil War. The westerners' struggles across high mountain passes and seemingly endless miles of empty desert made Coxey's journey from Massillon seem almost like a Sunday School picnic by comparison.

This was a war—a curious one to be sure—but a war nonetheless. Newspapermen who covered the protest called themselves "war correspondents" and addressed Coxey as "general." Federal authorities dispatched regular Army troops on several occasions and confined captured Coxeyites in hastily constructed prisoner-of-war camps. The battle line ran nowhere in particular, sometimes through the rolling hills of western Pennsylvania and sometimes through the plains of Kansas or Montana.

From the beginning most newspapers tended to belittle the Commonweal as nothing more than a collection of tramps; but the sheer volume of press coverage contradicted that simplistic view. Americans would not walk around the corner to see tramps. They preferred to "vag" them—that is, to sentence vagrants to the local workhouse, where they could spend 30 days breaking stones, chopping

wood, and learning the value of the American work ethic. Before the advent of
the Commonweal, armies of tramps rode freight trains to seasonal jobs across the
West and seldom received any attention.

On one level the Coxey movement was engaging melodrama, complete with
heroes like the swashbuckling John Sherman Sanders and his men, who stole a
train in Colorado and dashed east across the prairies in a locomotive chase that
appealed to anyone who had ever read a dime novel. Many of the Montana Coxeyites, thwarted in their efforts to run a stolen train all the way to Capitol Hill,
built rafts instead and sailed down the Missouri River in a great American adventure straight from the pages of *Huckleberry Finn*. Perhaps even Jack London's
tales of struggle for survival owed something to the Coxey crusade: well before he
achieved fame for *White Fang* and other best-selling novels, London accompanied
a California contingent of Coxey's Army halfway across the continent.

No one did more to foster the press's melodramatic treatment of the movement than the outrageous Carl Browne. In many ways Browne was a parody of
the Gilded Age promoter, forever dabbling in patent medicine, panoramic art,

Commonwealers on the Chesapeake and Ohio Canal west of Washington.
After the long hike overland from Massillon to Cumberland, Maryland, weary
marchers welcomed the chance to ride in two boats. A third boat, a coal barge
christened the *Flying Demon,* was commandeered by the accompanying journalists. The name was a response to Commonweal marshal Carl Browne, who had
once berated the press as "lying demons." Browne himself stands by the Flag. (Library of Congress)

journalism, and political nostrums. But it would be a mistake to treat him as a simple-minded charlatan. A sometimes journalist himself, Browne recognized that the movement's bizarre trappings attracted the attention of a jaded press and excited more publicity than any reformer could ever dream of purchasing. Even Samuel Gompers, the founder and longtime head of the American Federation of Labor, who had only harsh words for "reformers" who treated American workers as pawns, called Browne "a big-hearted lover of men, a dreamer and an idealist."

Often obscured by the emphasis on melodrama was the fact that Browne, Coxey, and other guiding spirits of the movement managed to illuminate the economic ills besetting America in the late nineteenth century as few had done before. During those years the nation experienced a disturbing and poorly understood transformation from a rural-agrarian to an urban-industrial economy. One result was a roller-coaster business cycle. Hard times in the 1870s had been accompanied by a series of major railway strikes and urban disturbances. During a less severe slump in the mid-1880s, white workingmen on the West Coast rioted against Chinese who they feared would displace them by working for less money.

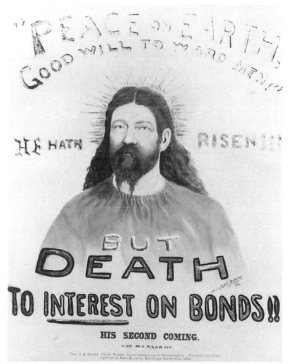

"Peace on Earth, Good Will Toward Men! He Hath Risen!!! But Death to Interest on Bonds." This legend appeared on a popular Commonweal banner prepared by Carl Browne, a religious mystic who believed in reincarnation and used the language of religious mysticism in his reform manifestos. Some cynics noted a striking similarity between the images of Christ on the banners and Browne himself. (Courtesy the Massillon Museum)

In 1893, with the coming of the worst downturn yet, normally confident and optimistic Americans shuddered at the thought of what the future might bring. Already during the winter of 1893–94 the ominous cry "Bread or Blood" had been heard in several of the nation's cities, and the rise of Coxeyism suggested that worse was yet to come.

The season of economic despair began in mid-1893, when panic on Wall Street signaled the start of a depression that would last 4 years. Within 6 months nearly 500 banks and 16,000 businesses failed. No matter what the industry, people fortunate enough to retain jobs frequently saw their wages slashed by one-fifth—or even by one-half. Every month thousands more involuntarily joined the ranks of the unemployed, although no one could be certain of the exact number. The federal government did not keep such statistics then, and neither did most states. Any estimate of the number of jobless Americans was crude and not always meaningful. One report claimed that as of January 1, 1894, 25 percent of the bread-winners of Montana and Utah were without work. Fifty thousand were jobless in California and a hundred thousand in Chicago, while in New York City the number fell somewhere between one and two hundred thousand, depending on who was guessing.

Newspapers added a human face to the unemployment statistics when they told of hopeless, penniless old men wandering the streets of Saint Paul, or men in the prime of life without jobs in the timber country of Wisconsin and Oregon. The annual convention of casket manufacturers reported that business was off because of the depression, and one member tried to make light of the situation by quipping that times were so bad that the sick could not afford to call a doctor and thus improve their chances for recovery. But unemployment was no joke. The blow was psychological as well as economic.

The main alternative to joblessness and starvation was private charity, which took a bewildering variety of forms. The *New York World* gave away more than a million loaves of bread, and the rival *New York Herald* distributed thousands of dollars worth of clothing. A cheap and efficient method of relief favored by both private and municipal charities was the soup kitchen. Great caldrons filled with donated meat and vegetables provided mulligan stew to all comers, though in some locales an able-bodied man might first be required to earn his meal by chopping firewood, which was then distributed to heat the homes of the poor. Destitute women were occasionally assigned jobs in a municipal laundry in exchange for a meal. In some places the poverty was so overwhelming and the confusion so great that city officials were reduced to throwing loaves of bread at crowds of the unemployed.

In cities of the East the jobless congregated outside newspaper offices every morning, scrambling to be first to scan the help-wanted ads. Occasionally they also participated in public protest demonstrations and signed petitions that were forwarded to Congress. That was probably the most ineffective thing an unemployed person could have done in 1893.

It was not that congressmen were insensitive to the plight of the jobless. Most were charitable men, but in their politics they nonetheless reflected the survival-of-the-fittest ethic that then prevailed in America. When asked what the government could do to help, the nation's leaders typically answered, "Nothing." They argued that "economic laws are a part of the machinery of the universe as much as the laws of gravitation." Unemployment was a natural phenomenon like an earthquake or cyclone, a product of forces beyond human control. Each bout of economic depression in the nineteenth century yielded its crop of platitudes about the need for the jobless to bear their suffering and privation with patience.

That advice was not without irony. In Chicago in 1893 the World's Columbian Exposition opened in May to celebrate four centuries of American achievement. Until the exposition closed in October, Chicago was the meeting place of America's past and future, where replicas of Christopher Columbus's three caravels competed for attention with the transformers and dynamos of General Electric and Westinghouse. It was also where the accomplishments of industrial civilization stood in greatest contrast to its failures. Surrounding the White City of the exposition were filth and squalor, disease-ridden slums, and air heavy with stench. Who could give meaning to such vivid examples of the contradiction haunting late nineteenth-century America? Why was progress so clearly juxtaposed with poverty?

Not all the excitement of the great Chicago fair was confined to the exhibition halls, where visitors could view a map of the United States in pickles or a Krupp cannon weighing 130 tons, or to the Midway Plaisance, where the sinuous and much-talked-about Little Egypt danced the Hootchy-Kootchy. Chicago was equally alive with ideas. Churchmen and academics gathered for international congresses. One such gathering attracted monetary reformers who in speech after impassioned speech suggested how to resolve the contradiction between poverty and progress. Here the odd friendship between Coxey and Browne had its chance origin.

After a heated dispute between Browne and another delegate over a section of the platform, Coxey walked over to congratulate the Californian. Browne was grateful for any support. "I felt immediately drawn toward Mr. Coxey and among all the men I had met he impressed me the most." Coxey was similarly impressed by Browne and invited him home to Massillon to discuss further his good roads program. However, except for their common interest in monetary reform, the two men were studies in contrast. The shy and retiring Coxey scarcely uttered a word publicly during the Chicago money congress. The tall and powerfully built Browne reveled in the sensation he created when he appeared on the floor of the gathering sporting his Buffalo Bill garb. The Californian was only too glad to speak at length to anyone willing to listen.

The march, as distinct from Coxey's message, was largely a product of Browne's frontier activism. His cartoons lampooning wealthy San Francisco citizens first attracted notice in the late 1870s when they appeared in a radical newspaper called *The Open Letter*. Browne's lurid caricatures so amused Denis Kearney, leader of a white workingmen's movement to rid California of competing Chinese laborers, that he made the artist his personal secretary. The two crossed the continent together in 1878 to take the cause of Chinese exclusion to Boston's workingmen in historic Faneuil Hall, and they even claimed to have instructed President Rutherford B. Hayes during an interview at the White House. Some contemporaries suggested that Browne was the real brains behind the Kearney movement, but that claim was surely an exaggeration. It is true that during the Kearney agitation Browne toyed with the idea of organizing a march of the unemployed to demand jobs from California lawmakers. He also polished his skills as a stump orator for a variety of West Coast causes before discovering Coxey's crusade.

It was during the 1893 Christmas season in Massillon that Browne formally proposed to organize a march on Washington to publicize Coxey's reforms. The Ohioan was appalled at first—fearful that thousands of destitute people would descend on his farm—and warned Browne that "he could not afford to feed all the hungry men in the country." Coxey soon changed his mind, but left most of the organizing work to Browne.

The Californian devoted every waking hour to the "petition in boots." Browne was a prolific writer and promulgated so many manifestos that Coxey worried about the cost of having them all printed. One bulletin in late March contained Browne's order to the troops and several anthems composed especially for the crusade. When the weather warmed enough to permit Browne to work outside, he turned his attention to painting slogans on the panorama wagon that he insisted must accompany the march. He fashioned dozens of Commonweal banners to be carried in the procession. At its head was a huge oil painting of Christ, which bore a suspiciously close likeness to Browne, or "Humble Carl" as he preferred to style himself.

Popular interest in the Commonweal remained almost nonexistent until early March 1894 when suddenly it attracted the attention of the nation's press. It was Coxey's good fortune that a local newspaper, the *Massillon Independent,* had an energetic young reporter who saw in the bizarre crusade an opportunity to grab plenty of space and recognition for himself in the big city dailies. This young man's dispatches over the wires of the Associated Press began to familiarize newspaper readers everywhere with the name of Coxey. By mid-March many of the country's best-known daily papers had sent reporters of their own to investigate the developing curiosity.

The more news the press carried about the Commonweal, the more people and mail poured into Massillon. Many people sent poetry and checks. A Chicago man requested permission to join the march with 150 baseball players and raise money for it by offering an ongoing tournament in towns along the way. Each day the freight trains passing through Massillon dropped off new recruits; and each day the telegraph wires leading out of town pulsed with millions of dots and dashes that when translated into newspaper stories, introduced a nation to the unemployed barbers, cooks, miners, and laborers who were the main actors in the unfolding drama.

All the excitement and publicity did not please Coxey's neighbors. Many only shook their heads in wonder. They could not understand why one of the wealthiest and shrewdest men in the county wanted to head such a dubious enterprise. "Browne is a deep dyed villain, and he is working for Coxey's money and nothing more," fumed the leader's divorced first wife, who held a second mortgage on his sandstone quarry. "The idea of bringing the name of the Savior into this movement and displaying banners inscribed with His name and decorated with His picture is an outrage. Browne is to blame for all this, and he is a wretch, but Coxey is sincere."

For all the excitement, only 122 crusaders marched with Coxey out of Massillon on Easter Sunday in late March, and of those an unknown number were undercover officers sent by the chief of police of Pittsburgh to join the ranks, watch the movement, and get acquainted with the marchers. Most significant for the future of the Commonweal was its unofficial honor guard of 44 journalists, a number greater than covered many major party Presidential conventions. Whenever Browne appeared in public he was immediately surrounded by eager reporters. "Carl is a friend to the reporter. He gives them all the news," gushed one.

People who dismissed the Commonweal as a bubble that had burst because so few recruits set out from Massillon missed its true significance. What Coxey and Browne essentially did was to create an unemployment adventure story that the press found irresistible. With characters sufficiently colorful and the perils of the journey sufficiently great, curiosity alone drew to the drama readers who cared little or nothing about complex economic issues or what it all portended. Whether by accident or design, the originator of the Commonweal march applied to social protest a few of the lessons he had learned in art. Browne knew from having exhibited his gargantuan panoramas in California that no matter how bad a work of art might be, it would elicit comment and attract wide attention if it were sufficiently outrageous.

For some newspaper commentators, particularly those from the Far West, anything the Coxey phenomenon revealed about unemployment was less significant than what it portended for the region and the nation. The *Seattle Telegraph*, which worried a great deal about the supposed closing of the frontier in 1890 and the end of an era of free western lands, observed, "The Anglo-Saxon race has hitherto gained its triumphs through individual self-reliance. It is something new that from all points along the Pacific Coast between Canada and Mexico, organized troops of men have set their faces toward the East to seek from the government what their fathers would have scorned from the hands of the state."

Scarcely 9 months before Coxey launched his crusade, a young history professor from the University of Wisconsin, Frederick Jackson Turner, spoke to one of the learned gatherings at the same Chicago fair that introduced Coxey and Browne. He called attention to the "democracy born of free land" and wondered what problems would result from the apparent end of the frontier. No longer would a series of frontiers "furnish a new field of opportunity, a gate of escape from the bondage of the past." From the assertions of Turner and others a person might easily conclude that America was used up.

A Seattle newspaper succinctly expressed the popular concern when it editorialized in early 1894, "All social problems solve themselves in the presence of a boundless expanse of vacant fertile land." Free land in the West was perceived by many Americans as their God-given inheritance, distinguishing them from the less richly endowed inhabitants of Old World nations. Especially during periods of hard times, the West had long been seen as having a special quality, its free land mythologized into a kind of safety valve relieving the discontent that arose among dwellers in the nation's densely populated industrial neighborhoods.

Thus Americans had a right to wonder whether the numerous episodes of train stealing by unemployed westerners heralded the end of the free-land era. Certainly the rise of Coxeyism made Turner's pronouncements seem almost prophetic. The fact that Canada, with millions of acres of fertile land still available almost for the asking, was spared the trauma of roving armies of indigents seemingly confirmed the correctness of the popular and long-standing environmental approach to America's unemployment problem.

Regardless of their regional or philosophical perspectives, American newspapers made the most of the inherent ambiguity of the Coxey drama. Part of the suspense lay in speculating whether the Commonwealers would make it to Capitol Hill or what they would do once they got there, but readers also wondered whether a clear meaning for America would finally emerge from all the discordant elements. Each day's press coverage was similar to peeling off one layer of an onion only to find another. What would removal of the final layer reveal?

That was what thousands of spectators on Capitol Hill on May Day had come to learn. "We do not regard the invasion of Coxey's army as a joke," fretted one Treasury Department official. He worried that if the marchers failed to achieve their objectives on Capitol Hill, someone would cry, "Here is the United States Treasury filled with money, while our families are starving." Every clerk

Coxey's Army marches through a small town in eastern Ohio or western Pennsylvania. Local coal miners offered food and moral support to Commonwealers. (Library of Congress)

was supposed to render military duty if necessary, and rifles and carbines rushed from the Springfield arsenal were cached all over the building. The vaults were temporarily closed to the public, and police allowed entrance to the building through one door only.

A few days before the rendezvous on Capitol Hill, Coxey went to the office of the police commissioner to obtain permission to speak from the Capitol steps. The chief lawman looked Coxey in the eye. "Then it is your idea to make a speech from the east front of the Capitol?"

"Yes."

"You can't do that," the commissioner responded. "The law prohibits it."

"Is there any law against making a speech on the streets?"

"Yes, the law prohibits that, too."

"Well," responded Coxey, becoming annoyed, "that's what we propose to attempt. It's a Constitutional right." The commissioner snapped that he would not grant Coxey a permit to speak in public because Coxey intended to violate the law.

"I claim it under the Constitution." The words burst from the Ohioan's lips like rifle shots.

When told that only the presiding officer of the Senate or the Speaker of the House could suspend the law, Coxey set out to find them, but here he again met with frustration. Finally, when Coxey learned that an 1882 act of Congress pro-

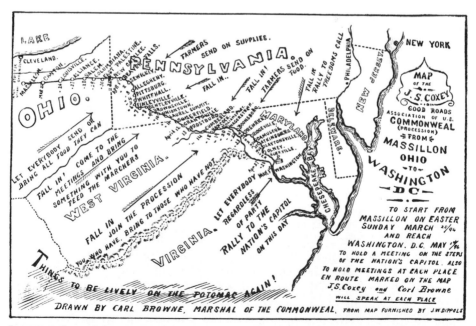

Among the many promotional items prepared by Carl Browne was this hand-drawn map showing the proposed route of the march. It contains numerous exhortations for people living along the way to support the Commonwealers. (Courtesy Ohio Historical Society)

hibited demonstrations on the Capitol grounds, he turned to a reporter for the *Washington Star* and said, "We will keep off the grass around the Capitol. Of course, I appreciate as well as anyone else the fact that the preservation of the grass around the Capitol is of more importance than saving thousands from starvation." Coxey was determined to march and speak from the Capitol steps without a permit.

The saber rattling reminded many people of Civil War days. The parallel was inescapable, and it heightened fears in Washington. On the eve of the confrontation at the Capitol, newsboys on downtown streets shouted out, "Extra! Extra! Bloodshed expected tomorrow! U. S. Troops may be called out to prevent the Coxey army from marching to the Capitol."

As clocks struck one, Coxey's troops made their way up the gentle rise of Capitol Hill and halted just beyond the B Street entrance to the House of Representatives. Waiting for them were an estimated twenty thousand spectators. Three to four hundred policemen blocked access to the building—one for nearly every Coxeyite on the march.

"Attention, Commonweal, Halt!" Browne's booming voice rose above the noise of the restless onlookers. Dismounting, he pushed through the throng to Coxey. "This is the east front," he murmured low. "Are you ready?" Coxey nodded. Rising in his carriage, he stooped low to kiss his wife in a display of affection that brought cheer after cheer from the onlookers. Browne handed his sombrero to Mrs. Coxey. Her husband looked pale as he jumped to the ground.

A mounted policeman blocked Browne's way. "You can't pass here with that flag."

"Why can't I pass?" questioned Browne, who was holding one of the staves of peace. Before the officer could answer, an onlooker cried, "Jump over the wall!" In a moment both Coxey and Browne had cleared the low stone wall and disappeared into the crowd. Small trees, bushes, and flower beds were flattened by the onslaught of mounted officers in pursuit. Browne in his Buffalo Bill suit made an easy target. And that was his plan: to decoy the officers while Coxey made his way unseen through the crowd to the steps where every president since James Monroe had been inaugurated. On this site of new beginnings Coxey planned to deliver his long-promised speech offering a cure for unemployment.

Browne led officers on a wild chase through the shrubbery before a dozen of them finally tackled him at the southeast corner of the building. "I am an American citizen. I stand on my Constitutional rights," he bellowed. Browne spun around suddenly and sent surprised policemen whirling off into the crowd. As officers wrestled Browne into a nearby patrol wagon, bystanders attempted to come to his rescue. Grabbing the bridles of the lawmen's horses, they forced the animals into the low wall and spilled their riders violently to the ground. At this, the police lost their heads. They charged into the crowd, beating everyone within range; people dropped to their knees, dazed by repeated blows from billy clubs.

While this commotion was going on, Coxey slipped unnoticed halfway up the Capitol steps. Then the onlookers spotted him and sent up a great shout. Coxey paused for a moment to catch his breath, turned toward the sea of upturned faces, and tipped his hat. He turned to continue his climb but two officers blocked his way.

"What do you want to do here?" one asked, posing the question on everyone's mind.

"I wish to make an address," Coxey responded in an emotion-choked voice. "But you can't do that."

"Then can I read a protest?" The Ohioan drew a typewritten manuscript from his pocket and proceeded to unfold it. But before he could open his mouth, officers pushed him firmly backwards down the steps. Coxey tossed the document to a nearby reporter, saying, "That is for the press." His message—an appeal for better treatment of the "poor and oppressed"—was published in several newspapers and in the *Congressional Record.*

Bystanders watched as officers escorted Coxey to his carriage. Someone in the crowd shouted his name, and others joined in, louder and louder until everyone was shouting "Coxey!" Police charged into the crowd to disperse it, causing people to fall over one another in a desperate effort to get out of range. The tatterdemalion army remained quiet and orderly at the center of the tempest.

Police cited Coxey for walking on the grass and displaying banners on the Capitol grounds, although Coxey's only "banner" was the small American flag pinned to his lapel. For this crime a judge sentenced Coxey, Browne, and another associate to 20 days in jail. When the leaders emerged from prison they found that the Coxey movement had faded away, having lost both its popular momentum and its ability to interest the press.

If Coxey ever had cause to regret his association with Browne, it was not because the Californian spent too much of his money or caused him to be denounced as a "crank," but because the 47-year-old Browne secretly courted his teenage daughter Mamie. When reporters announced that the couple had been quietly wed in mid-1895, Coxey disowned Mamie and disavowed Browne. That was probably the main reason why Coxey did not lead another march to Washington that year as he had earlier planned to do.

At the turn of the century, the couple was living at Browne's "Commonweal Castle," a modest retreat near Calistoga, California, where Mamie bore a son. They split up a short time thereafter. Browne occasionally mounted a soap box on the streets of San Francisco during the early years of the twentieth century to champion radical causes, primarily those of the Industrial Workers of the World and the Socialist Party. He could be counted on to attend every radical gathering open to the public. Once during a 24-hour anti-capital-punishment rally in San Francisco in 1912, Browne turned up to issue hourly "extras" throughout the day and evening. He reported the speeches, illustrated them with his cartoons, and sold the finished products on the spot. Browne proudly summed up his life by quoting a San Francisco journalist who wrote of him, "Carl Browne has spent his life championing the cause of the underdog."

After his 1894 march, Coxey returned to Ohio where he campaigned often for public office—distinguishing himself primarily as an indefatigable monetary reformer—and lost, with the one exception of being elected mayor of Massillon in 1931 as a Republican. The following year he ran for president as the Farmer-Labor party candidate and received 7,309 votes. Party labels meant little to Coxey, who also ran for office as a Democrat, Greenbacker, and Populist.

Coxey returned to Washington in 1914 and this time spoke legally from the Capitol steps. On May 1, 1944, on the occasion of the fiftieth anniversary of the great march and in the ninetieth year of Coxey's long life, the elder statesman of

American reform once again mounted the Capitol steps and with the permission of Speaker Sam Rayburn and Vice President Henry A. Wallace completed the protest speech he had attempted to deliver there in 1894. Two hundred curious listeners, mostly federal employees and servicemen, heard Coxey repeat his original address, which included this indictment: "Up these steps the lobbyists of trusts and corporations have passed unchallenged on their way to the committee rooms, access to which we, the representatives of the toiling wealth producers, have been denied. We stand here today in behalf of millions of toilers whose petitions have been buried in committee rooms, whose prayers have been unresponded to, and whose opportunities for honest, remunerative, productive labor have been taken away from them by unjust legislation, which protects idlers, speculators, and gamblers."

There was no way to measure accurately the educational impact of the Coxey crusade, yet even hostile observers believed it had one: "These men, after their own fashion are building more wisely than they know of," asserted the *Press-Times* of Seattle. They had made an impression on Americans, "and once the national mind agrees upon the fact that a new direction must be given to affairs, there is no telling to what great and good ends it may lead." The *Rocky Mountain News* of Denver, a supporter of the movement, added that the Commonweal would move the country at the polls. "Better, wiser and more humane laws in the near future must be the outcome." In short, a variety of contemporaries perceived Coxeyism as having chipped away at the popular belief that poverty and unemployment were mainly the result of individual weakness and laziness and promoted the idea that the federal government was responsible for the economic well-being of its citizens.

Although Coxey's jobs and money proposals were never enacted into law, the public-works principle of his crusade was embodied in the New Deal's relief and recovery programs that put the nation's unemployed to work building dams and a host of other projects during the Great Depression of the 1930s. By 1944 his basic ideas were no longer considered radical, and Coxey had attained the status of historical curiosity. Coxey died in Massillon at age 97. Two generations of Americans after 1894 used the epithet "Coxey's Army" to describe any disorganized undertaking, although, in fact, Coxey's followers had generally been well-organized and well-disciplined.

AN INTERPRETATION

The Coxey crusade represented a double-barreled challenge to the economic beliefs cherished by most Americans. It raised troubling questions about the nation's prevailing commitment to laissez-faire, especially when the Commonweal's prominence in the hinterland West undermined the popular conviction that fertile agricultural lands of the frontier represented America's most practical form of social security and offered a wise alternative to governmental paternalism.

In the popular mythology of the West, pioneer residents were self-reliant, rugged individualists, or at least they publicly aspired to that status. But in reality westerners had been quick to turn to the federal government for help. That should not seem so strange, for Uncle Sam's presence was more visible in the West than in any other region. The federal government was (and still is) the most prominent custodian of the region's natural resources. Legislators on Capitol Hill voted to create homesteads on lands most would never see, to encourage private development of remote timber and mineral resources, and to grant the land and loans that helped to finance most of the western transcontinental railroads. Uncle Sam's Army occasionally protected western settlers from Indians (or vice versa).

Why, then, western Coxeyites asked, should not the federal government put the unemployed to work making the desert bloom through irrigation? The jobless of 1894 only wanted Uncle Sam to lend them a helping hand as he had done earlier for the entrepreneurs who built the Pacific railroads or the homesteaders eager to tackle the problems of farming 160 acres of prairie land. Thus for unemployed westerners the call for federal sponsorship of irrigation projects to put the jobless to work building canals in the ultimate hope of resettling them in the new garden marked no real break with the past.

The irrigation scheme was only a way of buying time, however, and finally the mythology of the free-land safety valve proved to be a poor tool to deal with massive unemployment in an urban-industrial society. But it took the hard times of the 1890s and disorders such as the Coxey crusade to hasten the process of exploding the myth. Only when people discarded the environmental approach to unemployment were they able to recognize that the state might deal with the problem without using free land as an intermediary.

Eventually the idea voiced by the Coxey crusaders—that the federal government should provide them with public-works jobs—found its way onto the national political agenda and was finally accepted by the President and Congress during the hard times of the 1930s. In a 1935 radio speech, President Franklin D. Roosevelt observed: "Today we can no longer escape into virgin territory. . . . We have been compelled by stark necessity to unlearn the too comfortable superstition that the American soil was mystically blessed with every kind of immunity to grave economic maladjustments." In sum, the modern welfare state was a response by government to some of the social and economic problems that the supposed free land of the West reputedly solved. If nothing else the Coxey crusade of 1894 vividly revealed that the sparsely populated West's role as a free-land safety valve for the nation's unemployed was a myth.

Sources: This story is drawn primarily from my book *Coxey's Army: An American Odyssey* (Lincoln: University of Nebraska Press, 1985). There is also Donald L. McMurry, *Coxey's Army: A Study of the Industrial Army Movement of 1894* (Seattle: University of Washington Press, 1968 reprint of 1929 edition). Newspapers devoted thousands of column-inches of space to Coxey and his protest crusade in 1894. Probably the best dispatches were filed by Ray Stannard Baker for the *Chicago Record* and are available on microfilm. Henry Vincent, a reform journalist, authored *The Story of the Commonweal* (New York: Arno, 1969 reprint of 1894 edition), a tract sold to raise money for the marchers. A collection of Coxey memorabilia is preserved at the Massillon Museum and also on microfilm at the Ohio Historical Society in Columbus.

5

EMPIRE IN THE PHILIPPINES: AMERICA'S FORGOTTEN WAR OF COLONIAL CONQUEST

STUART CREIGHTON MILLER

The conquest of the Philippines was only one of a series of overseas actions that collectively forged a new American empire and redefined the United States as a formidable world power. Between 1898 and 1917, when the Congress approved Woodrow Wilson's call for a Declaration of War against Germany, the nation took Cuba, Puerto Rico, Guam, and the Philippines from Spain; promoted a rebellion in Panama that paved the way for the canal; dispatched troops to protect American commercial interests in Santo Domingo, Haiti, and Nicaragua; and—under the same General Frederick Funston who appears in the following account—occupied the city of Vera Cruz during the Mexican revolution.

In terms of square miles of territory taken, the American empire was hardly an empire at all—nothing at all like the vast African and Asian colonial empires of Great Britain, France, and Germany. Despite this difference, V. I. Lenin, the Communist leader of the Russian Revolution, lumped the American empire with the European ones, treating them all as an outgrowth of what he called in 1916 "the highest stage of capitalism"—that is, "monopoly" capitalism. The timing of America's imperial escapades roughly fits Lenin's model; a massive merger movement, beginning in 1897 and concluding in 1902, virtually completed the transformation of the economy into a system of oligopolies, with many industries dominated by a few massive corporations. According to this controversial theory, the new American empire reflected the needs of the new, giant corporations and the desires of the men who ran them. American "New Left" historians of the 1960s and 1970s also emphasized the economic origins of empire.

In contrast, not a single businessman appears in Stuart Creighton Miller's account of the American intervention in the Philippine archipelago. Instead, Miller's analysis relies on the behavior and rhetoric of ordinary soldiers and their commanding officers to give us some sense of what Americans were doing in the jungles of the Pacific. It will take some courage to see ourselves in this story, for Miller's portrait is unflaggingly critical, with each character establishing an impressive—and depressing—new standard for racism, bigotry, and truculent nationalism. (In understanding these soldiers, it might help to realize that President Theodore

Roosevelt, who after September 1901 managed the nation's imperial adventures, shared their racist and nationalist sentiments.)

Nonetheless, this story of how Americans fought the Filipinos and talked about their exploits can help reveal the lines of influence that came together to yield an American empire. One of them, surely, was the frontier—officially declared "closed" in the 1890 census when the supply of unsettled land seemed to have been exhausted—yet remarkably alive in the American mind. Another was the exuberant self-confidence of the United States, refracted in the words of thousands of soldiers who went overseas absolutely convinced that they had only to show up to win great victories (Americans would export their products with the same assurance). Racism was another line of influence, running from the Philippines back and forth through turn-of-the-century laws that segregated blacks from whites and disfranchised black voters in the Southern states. American empire was the product, too, of just the sort of confusion over ideals and purposes that made it difficult for even Filipino leader Emilio Aguinaldo to be certain what American troops were doing in his homeland. Was the United States the standard-bearer of civilization and democracy? Or an elitist nation with unfulfilled imperial ambitions? As Americans and Filipinos eyed each other warily in the wake of the siege of Manila, no one—least of all the Americans—knew for sure.

The evening of February 4, 1899, was an ideal moment to begin the war with the fledgling Republic of the Philippines, as most of its leaders were off at a celebration in Malolos, some 30 miles north of Manila. The United States Army had taken Manila the preceding August during the war with Spain, only to be bottled up in the city when the Filipino army, America's erstwhile, de facto ally against the Spanish, re-formed its line of siege around the land side of the city on August 11, 1898. The nationalist leader, General Emilio Aguinaldo y Famy, justified this aggressive action, reasoning that the city could be returned to Spain in the peace negotiations underway in Paris from which his government was excluded. Once the Treaty of Paris was made public in December, converting the Spanish colony into an American one, Aguinaldo continued his siege, insisting that two thirds of the Senate would never consent to a treaty that so violated cherished American principles. That august body heatedly debated an imperial future for America, and finally scheduled a vote on the treaty for February 6, 1899, one that was predicted to be extremely close.

Meanwhile, the two armies facing each other on the outskirts of Manila were ostensibly at peace, but tensions between them escalated daily. Finally, just 2 days before the Senate's scheduled vote, around 8 o'clock that evening, some unarmed, probably drunk, Filipino soldiers refused to heed commands by a sentry of the Nebraska volunteer regiment, and mocked him with their own shouts of "halto! halto!" They were quickly gunned down, and a crescendo of gunfire erupted from both the American and Filipino lines facing each other on the outskirts of Manila. Heavy firing continued until 2 o'clock the next morning, most of it pretty wild in the ensuing darkness, and largely coming from the state volunteer regiments manning the northern sector of Manila's defense perimeter. One regular officer assumed that they must be repulsing a Filipino attack and sent his aide to see if they needed help. He returned to report with disgust that there was no attack, just "green Dakotans wasting ammunition firing away at no discernible targets."

Neither side made a serious effort to advance on the other, and no significant casualties had occurred by the time the firing ceased at 2 A.M. So the skirmish could have easily been dismissed in the sobering light of the next morning as an unfortunate incident caused by the growing tension between the two armies. Instead, land batteries, along with the heavy guns of Admiral George Dewey's warships, began to hammer Filipino positions once the first rays of light had put them in silhouette. At 8 A.M., after several hours of this devastating barrage, the bugles sounded, and the "boys in blue" charged out of Manila with "Montana screams, Tennessee howls, Jayhawk cheers" and fixed bayonets. As Private William Christner described it to his parents: "With a good old Pennsylvania yell we charged up the hill through a hail of bullets," reassuring them that "I hardly think I was born to be killed by a nigger." Actually, the "Pennsy vols" were among the few regiments that received significant fire that day. Most found only dead or wounded in the opposing trenches and continued on for miles past their assigned objectives. Colonel Frederick Funston led his Kansas regiment up the coast so fast that it came under fire from the *U.S.S. Charleston.* Officers of the California regiment even threatened to shoot their own men if they did not halt, but only fatigue ended that charge miles later. Once the Washington and Idaho regiments trapped some retreating Filipinos at midstream in the Pasig River, the slaughter began with a murderous cross fire. "From then on the fun was fast and furious," as the dead "piled up thicker than buffalo chips," one soldier wrote home. Another informed his father that "picking off niggers in the water is more fun than a turkey shoot."

The wild scramble for glory left Filipino stragglers behind American lines to snipe from the rear. The American Commander, General Elwell Otis, ordered a scorched earth tactic to deny cover for them, although he later attributed all the burning to the retreating enemy. The incident also created the widespread belief among American soldiers that wounded Filipinos left on the field were shooting at them. "Because a Filipino is so treacherous even when badly wounded, he has to be killed. When we find one that is not dead, we have our bayonets," one soldier explained to his parents. About 3,000 Filipino soldiers—but only 60 Americans—died that first day.

The American presence in Manila had begun with Admiral George Dewey's stunning victory on May 1, 1898, over Spain's Pacific Squadron anchored in Manila Bay, only days after Congress had declared war. Many Americans were surprised by the action, because the propaganda against Spain leading up to the war had focused on Spanish cruelty in suppressing a rebellion in Cuba, ignoring other Spanish colonies. Indeed, most Americans had never heard of the Philippines. As the character "Mr. Dooley" confessed, in a humorous newspaper column, he "didn't know if they were islands or canned goods." According to legend, the news of Dewey's victory even sent President William McKinley scurrying to a globe to discover the location of "these darned islands."

A small group of dedicated imperialists in government, led by Theodore Roosevelt and Massachusetts Senator Henry Cabot Lodge, knew their precise location, as they had their eyes on the Philippines for potential coaling stations and a naval base to protect America's trade routes to China. As assistant secretary of

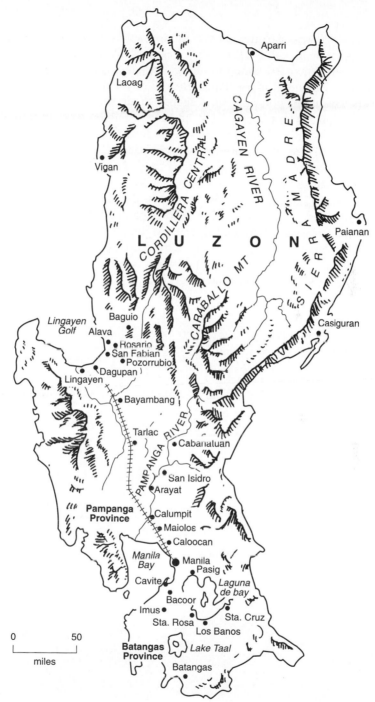

Aparri

Laoag

Vigan

CORDILLERA CENTRAL

CAGAYEN RIVER

SIERRA MADRE

L U Z O N

Paianan

CARABALLO MT

Baguio

Lingayen
Golf

Alava

Casiguran

Rosario
San Fabian
Pozorrubio
Dagupan
Lingayen

Bayambang

PAMPANGA RIVER

Tarlac

Cabanatuan

San Isidro
Arayat

**Pampanga
Province**

Calumpit

Maiolos

Caloocan

*Manila
Bay*

Manila
Pasig

Cavite

*Laguna
de bay*

Bacoor

Imus

Sta. Rosa

Sta. Cruz

Los Banos

0   50

miles

**Batangas
Province**

Lake Taal

Batangas

The island of Luzon is the largest and most populous within the Philippine archipelago. Much of the fighting between Americans and Filipinos occurred in the
immediate vicinity of Manila and in the provinces of Pampanga (just north) and
Batangas (to the south). The hideout of Filipino leader Emilio Aguinaldo was in
the town of Palanan, on the northeast coast.

the navy, Roosevelt was instrumental in stationing a fleet under Dewey's command in Hong Kong to lie in wait for the war to begin. While waiting, the admiral and two American diplomats stationed in Hong Kong and Singapore began negotiations with exiled Filipino leaders of an earlier failed rebellion against Spanish rule in 1896. They would be potential allies against Spain should a war begin. Rebellion in the Philippines had flared anew, and Dewey urged this junta to join him when he sailed for Manila. The Filipinos were in Singapore, however, when America declared war, so Dewey left without them. Following his victory, he dispatched a ship to bring them to Manila. Before departing, Aguinaldo left money with an American diplomat to purchase arms for his cause.

Once back on Luzon, the largest, most populated island in the archipelago, Aguinaldo took charge of the rebellion and began to attack Spanish garrisons throughout the Philippines. He laid siege to Manila on its land side, bottling up the Spanish commanders. He also wrote a formal Declaration of Independence modeled after that of his "ally, the Great North American Nation, the cradle of liberty, and therefore friend to our people." The Declaration was "witnessed by

Filipino dead in their trenches on the first day of combat, victims of deadly American naval and land bombardment that began without warning at dawn of February 5, 1899, after a 3-hour lull in the extensive, but ineffective, exchange of rifle fire that had erupted between the two lines the preceding evening. (National Archives)

the Supreme Judge of the Universe," and was "under the protection of the Mighty and Humane North American Nation." Lieutenant Colonel L. M. Johnson, commanding a small American advance party, signed this document for Aguinaldo as a witness. The nationalist leader then created a government at Malolos, designed a national flag, and ordered his legislative branch to write a constitution, again using the American one as a model. Most of this was accomplished before the American army arrived in significant force, and through it all, Aguinaldo received encouragement from his "good friend," Admiral Dewey.

By mid-June, the steady flow of American soldiers arriving aroused Aguinaldo's suspicions, but he reasoned with his own subordinates that the war in common against Spain, the apparent alliance, plus America's anti-colonial tradition and the fact that the U.S. Constitution made no provision for colonies, would ensure that America would not replace Spain as a new colonial master. Dewey was even able to persuade Aguinaldo to make room for the newly arrived American troops on his line of siege around Manila.

Aguinaldo discovered the extent of America's duplicity on August 11, 1898, when American troops took Manila after a prearranged sham battle with the

Filipino officers posing for a photographer before the Philippine-American War began. Most of these soldiers were shoeless and poorly equipped and trained, however proud and courageous. (Library of Congress)

Spanish that excluded the Filipinos. Aguinaldo's immediate resumption of his line of siege, bottling up the Americans in Manila, enraged American commanders, but Washington refused to give them a green light to attack him.

By December, when the Treaty of Paris officially confirmed Aguinaldo's worst suspicions, the relations between the two armies had already deteriorated to the breaking point. Insults, hostile gestures, and occasional bullets flew in both directions. American soldiers addressed Filipinos of whatever rank as "nigger," and, as one officer warned, "the natives are beginning to understand what 'nigger' means." American sentries took their frustrations out on unarmed Filipino soldiers passing through their lines to visit Manila. Some were knocked down with the butt of a Springfield rifle merely for "looking surly" or "seeming disrespectful." A few were shot for "looking suspicious." Such acts were generally committed by volunteers in the state regiments, already notorious among the regulars for their lack of discipline.

General Otis launched his own diplomatic offensive designed to humiliate the nationalists, ranging from petty refusals to return salutes from an "armed mob," lest it constitute recognition of Aguinaldo's "so-called government," to extraordinarily worded threats if Aguinaldo did not relinquish positions that Otis had quite arbitrarily decreed to be within Manila's municipal boundaries. Otis appears to have undertaken this entirely on his own. Indeed, on September 5th Otis informed Washington that "relations friendly, but require delicate manipulation." Three days later, he ordered Aguinaldo out of one position by September 15th, or he would be "obliged to resort to forcible action." So outrageous was the language of this ultimatum that Aguinaldo asked Otis to withdraw it in favor of a simple request with which he would comply. Otis refused even this face-saving plea. Aguinaldo withdrew, which evoked disgust from Otis's aide that the Filipinos would not fight in the face of such "humiliation." Otis also started a provocative surveillance of Filipino positions under the guise of "recreational activities," and he expressed outraged innocence when Aguinaldo banished back to Manila Americans caught photographing and measuring Filipino fortifications.

When the Spanish garrison at Iloilo on the island of Panay, some 300 miles south of Manila, offered to surrender to the Americans in December, Otis readied a task force under General Marcus Miller to occupy that city, but Dewey refused to transport it without specific orders from Washington. The orders came, but stipulated that the transfer of power must be peaceful. By the time Miller arrived at Iloilo at the end of December, the Spanish had already departed, and he was greeted by the mayor, who informed him that he may "not land foreign troops without express orders from the central government" at Malolos. In spite of Washington's orders, both Miller and Otis wanted to take the city by force, but Dewey vetoed this. Otis ordered Miller to hang on at anchor "until something happened."

Over the next few weeks, Otis made sure that "something" did. In the meantime, he carefully prepared himself for that event, ordering his officers out of dress whites and into "fighting khaki." He moved the Utah Battery up to a more favorable offensive position and coaxed Dewey into maneuvering his warships closer to shore on the flanks of Aguinaldo's semicircular line. On February 2, 1899, he discharged all Filipino civilians in his employ, placed his army on full alert, and tested the waters by ordering sentries posted at a hotly disputed position from which he had earlier forced the Filipinos to retreat. The colonel commanding the Nebraska regiment was personally on hand to post them, and a Filipino lieutenant called him a son of a bitch, whereupon the colonel ordered him arrested. The next day, Otis posted no sentries there, but on February 4th, he did so again, this time with instructions to shoot intruders. It paid off, creating the incident that justified Otis's full scale offensive the following dawn.

America had experienced only easy victories in the war against Spain. It lasted 100 days, leading Roosevelt to complain that "there wasn't war enough to go around." Dewey needed less than 6 hours to destroy the Spanish fleet caught napping at anchor, and the phony Battle of Manila lasted 3 hours. It was easy to assume that Aguinaldo's army had now been shattered in less than 12 hours. As evening approached on February 5th, Otis refused to meet with Aguinaldo's emissary carrying a peace proposal, who was curtly informed by an aide that he "lacked proper credentials," and that an audience with Otis might be construed as "recognition of [his] so-called political organization." Headlines proclaimed a total victory over a thoroughly demoralized enemy:

Aguinaldo Weeps for His Blunder
Sits Crying in His Quarters
Afraid to Surrender to the Americans

In reality, the war had just begun, and it would last another 41 months, claiming the lives of 4,200 American soldiers, while up to 20,000 Filipino troops would perish, along with about 200,000 civilians, most of whom would die of war-related starvation and disease. Nevertheless, to this day Washington maintains the official fiction that it was not a war, but merely an "insurrection."

General Arthur MacArthur, the father of Douglas (then a plebe at West Point), commanded the northern division that continued in pursuit of Aguinaldo. The Filipino commander was much too wise to risk battle with the Americans, who had superior firepower and marksmanship. He settled for delaying actions as he continued his steady retreat northward to a mountain refuge. He abandoned Malolos in flames, and narrowly missed entrapment several times by an American amphibious landing to his rear and "flying columns" of hard riding U.S. cavalry. Meanwhile, Otis, back in Manila, fired off salvos of press releases describing "smashing victories," or "crushing blows" and "final moments," which were dutifully parroted in the nation's press. Editors favored an analogy with former Indian wars, labeling the enemy "Filipino Braves," or even "Apaches" in their headlines.

Actually, the more heavily equipped Americans, prepared for more conventional battle, rarely caught up with their lightly clad adversaries, who moved swiftly on bare feet over familiar terrain. As one soldier complained to his parents, "you have niggers you can't see shoot at you until you get close enough to shoot at them and then Mr. Nigger tears off to another good place and shoots again." One wife in Kansas City sent hometown clippings to her husband, Lieutenant Samuel Lyon, a regular officer, who had fought in the "battles" ballyhooed in the local press. He wrote back: "I hope the idiotic newspapers haven't had you worried to death about those heavy engagements. 'Battles' out here are greatly exaggerated. This rebel is like a flea you can't see."

The war was fought as much in the headlines as it was on the field. It was not just a question of Otis's misleading dispatches, but also of some senior officers engaging in histrionics that had little military value in order to impress correspondents on hand and garner some personal media attention. Colonel Funston, one of the most feted heroes of this war, led a company-size charge into an already abandoned Malolos in flames. He joined three men to swim across a river to take an abandoned fortification when MacArthur had already forded that river elsewhere much closer to the retreating foe. Another publicity hound, General J. Franklin Bell, leapt from a rowboat to reconnoiter enemy defenses while swimming. Lyon pointed out to his wife that "the newspapers featured this, ignoring the fact that from the level of the water his view wasn't nearly as good as it would have been with a good glass on one of the ships or even in the rowboat."

Funston's heroism at Calumpit, however, was quite genuine in carrying out a very daring maneuver to outflank General Antonio Luna's well fortified position on the Rio Grande de Pampanga. Funston had two Kansans swim a line across the river and secure it to the opposite bank. He joined eight men on the first raft propelled across by that line. More trips augmented his force to 41, with which he surprised the enemy, who quickly retreated before discovering how small Funston's contingent was, and before dismantling the railroad bridge so coveted by MacArthur to haul supplies and artillery across the river. Funston was awarded the Congressional Medal of Honor and promoted to brigadier general of volunteers for this brilliant feat.

By May, the rainy season arrived, with the U.S. Army controlling little territory outside of Manila. When towns were taken, they were soon abandoned rather than permanently garrisoned, allowing the nationalists to return and murder any inhabitants suspected of cooperating with Americans during their brief occupation. Otis protected his ludicrously optimistic view of the war by imposing a rigid censorship on the correspondents. It became clear that the censorship was designed less to keep information from the enemy than to cover up Otis's ineptness as a commander. Reporters could bypass the censor by mailing dispatches to Hong Kong for transmission on its cable terminal, but that took time and also risked the general's wrath and possible deportation for "sedition." Finally, these correspondents, including those who were Otis's "favorites," rebelled, mailing a collective protest to their editors. Headlines in response blared that "Situation in the Philippines Is Not 'Well In Hand'," reversing one of Otis's pet phrases. The entire nation had been "snookered" by the "foolish pollyanna" of General Otis, lamented many editors. Oblivious to this reaction, Otis denied that there was any censorship, then announced the appointment of a new censor. He continued to release reports of "final blows" and "crushing victories," until one editor declared that Otis did not "even have enough sense to come in out of the rain."

Under the terms of their enlistment, the state volunteer regiments returned in the summer of 1899 and disbanded. As civilians, these veterans were free to impugn the official view of the war with no reprisal from Otis. They also corroborated the rumors of American atrocities that originated in private letters from soldiers, which were not subjected to censorship. As long as these letters were confined to small, local audiences, they were of little concern to Otis or the government. But sometimes one would fall into the hands of an editor opposed to the war, who would promptly publish it, and it would soon make the rounds of the anti-imperialist press. Then citizens would open their morning paper over coffee to discover a private "report on this nigger fighting business" in the Philippines:

> Last night one of our boys was found shot and his stomach cut open. Immediately orders were received from General [Lloyd] Wheaton to burn the town and kill every native in sight which was done to a finish. About 1,000 men, women and children were reported killed. I am probably growing hard-hearted, for I am in my glory when I can sight my gun on some dark skin and pull the trigger.

Other letters described widespread looting and senseless destruction of property. Captain Albert Otis (no relation to the general) boasted that he "had enough plunder for a family of six. The house I had in Santa Ana had five pianos. I couldn't take them, so I put a big grand piano out of a second story window. You can guess its finish." An Iowa volunteer expressed amazement over such conduct: "You have no idea what a mania for destruction the average man has when the fear of the law is removed. I have seen them . . . knock chandeliers and plate glass mirrors to pieces just because they could not carry them. It is such a pity."

Captain Matthew Batson wisely warned his wife not to let "outsiders" see his complaints to her about the conduct of American soldiers, "as it reflects on the discipline of our Army, and if published would cause me trouble." Batson described barbaric destruction, looting, and the slaughter of innocents. Americans "ransacked churches, private homes, and wantonly destroyed furniture, and not satisfied with this they enter cemeteries, break open the vaults and search the corpses for jewelry." He worried that "these people seem to be devout Catholics, and it will do no good to take their images of Christ and their saints and dress them up in ridiculous garb and generally insult their religion." Some soldiers, he added, "make no distinction between property belonging to insurgents, or the innocent, they simply loot everything they come to." Batson described the total destruction of a pretty village in Pampanga and the slaughter of its inhabitants for no apparent reason, before writing in anguish: "We come here as a Christian people to relieve them from the Spanish yoke and bear ourselves like barbarians."

Once such a letter found its way into print, it could not be ignored, and the War Department would order Otis to investigate. His idea of an investigation was to send a copy of the offending letter to the writer's commanding officer, who had little trouble wringing a retraction from him. It was just "a tall tale to thrill some maiden aunt in Wichita," or some such explanation was proffered. The imperialist press dutifully crowed that "the truth is now made clear," and "another atrocity fable failed the test of time."

On one occasion, however, Private Charles Benner refused to recant his report that Colonel Funston had ordered the Kansas regiment to take no prisoners. This forced Otis to order MacArthur to investigate. Benner confronted that general's advocate general with Private William Putnam, who confessed to shooting two prisoners under orders. Major John Mallory collected a number of corroborative affidavits, including two from officers, suggesting that Benner's original charge was accurate. Private Harris Huskey swore under oath that he had witnessed Major Wilder Metcalf shoot a prisoner on his knees begging for mercy. MacArthur forwarded Mallory's report to Otis, who, amazingly, ordered Benner court-martialed "for writing and conniving at the publication of the article which brought about this investigation," and also Putnam "for assisting by shooting, in the execution of two prisoners." When the judge advocate wisely warned Otis that "if put on trial, it is probable that facts would develop implicating many others," the matter was dropped.

As a civilian, however, Funston was not so easily protected. Charges that he had "commanded, condoned, and rewarded rapine and murder" came from his former officers and seeped into the press. One editor published a letter from a former civilian teamster with the Kansas regiment describing Funston leading a mock mass in a church while wearing stolen ecclesiastical garb to amuse his soldiers from the "Bible belt." A nurse accused him of looting two silver chalices and a lavishly embroidered robe he had removed from a statue of the Madonna to give to his wife.

Under clouds of suspicion, Funston accepted an offer to command a brigade of three new national volunteer regiments. He arrived in Luzon at the end of 1899, when the Filipino nationalists began guerrilla tactics, a mode of warfare not entirely suited to Funston's impetuous personality. He was not back long when he called a press conference to announce that he had just summarily executed two prisoners in retaliation for a successful ambush of his Macabebe scouts. This confirmed the worst rumors that he had left behind, and a headline in the San Francisco *Call* announced that he would be court-martialed. Funston then claimed that he had been misquoted: The prisoners had been killed "while attempting to escape."

A year later, having survived yet another Army inquiry into his past conduct that was more of a cover-up, Funston again became the hero of the hour in the spring of 1901 when he masterminded and led a daring maneuver to capture Aguinaldo in his remote hideaway in Palanan, just off the rugged northeastern coast of Luzon. Soldiers in Funston's command captured a courier from Aguinaldo to his cousin, Baldomero, with a coded message requesting more troops. Once Funston deciphered it and persuaded the courier to reveal Aguinaldo's location, he assembled 80 Tagalog-speaking Macabebe volunteers to pose as the requested reinforcements. Four renegade "insurgent" officers and a former Spanish officer were recruited to play the roles of officers. Naturally, Funston had to get in on the act, so he and four American officers went along as "prisoners" captured en route to Palanan. The Navy dropped them off on the coast far enough away to avoid any detection, and the group trekked over 100 miles to grab Aguinaldo in the midst of a birthday celebration for him. The ruse was carried off so cleverly that the astonished Aguinaldo first thought it was a joke. Funston brought his prize back to the coast for a prearranged rendezvous with the *U.S.S. Vicksburg* on March 25, 1901.

Once again, Funston dominated the headlines. Editors compared his latest feat to Roosevelt's charge up San Juan Hill in Cuba, and even to Dewey's victory on Manila Bay. A year earlier, Republican leaders had thought his heroism at Calumpit would take Funston to Topeka as Governor of Kansas, but now they began to think in terms of a Roosevelt-Funston ticket in 1904. Vice President Roosevelt, long an admirer of Funston, whom he classified as "a perfect corker," pushed the president to reward him with a regular commission at his present rank, the youngest in the Army at age 41. Only weeks earlier McKinley had declared that Funston was "not a man of proper temperament for any rank higher than that of a lieutenant in the regulars." But now that Funston had become a national idol, McKinley, once dubbed "The Emperor of Expediency," capitulated.

As he often did following one of his escapades, Funston rushed into print his own version of this spectacular coup for a popular magazine in order to milk more publicity from it. By entitling the article "The Exploit Which Ended the War," he reinforced the popular view that he had singlehandedly ended this vexatious conflict. In reality, Aguinaldo was little more than figurehead for the nationalist forces during the guerrilla phase of the war. Indeed, the complete autonomy afforded local commanders by Aguinaldo's isolation made the guerrillas much more effective, as quick decisions could be made in response to immediate conditions. Thus the war continued for another 15 months officially, and on September 27, 1901, the Army suffered its worst setback in the war when bolomen,

General Frederick Funston, aboard the *U.S.S. Vicksburg.* (National Archives)

disguised as mourning women, charged out of a church in Balangiga on the island of Samar to massacre the American garrison there.

General Adna Chaffee, a celebrated Indian fighter with hard-line views on how to deal with "savages," had recently relieved MacArthur in command. He was encouraged "to take the most stern measures to pacify Samar" by his new commander-in-chief, Roosevelt, who had succeeded the assassinated McKinley shortly before the Balangiga disaster. Roosevelt made it clear that he did not intend "to repeat [in the Philippines] the folly of which our people were sometimes guilty when they petted hostile Indians." For the "pacification" effort, Chaffee handpicked another famous Indian fighter, General "Hell Roaring" Jacob Smith, already infamous in the anti-imperialist press for violating flags of truce and for having proudly posed for photographs in front of his "tiger cages," in which he crammed Filipino suspects for months with no toilet facilities. Smith's orders to Marine Major Littleton Waller, commanding a brigade on loan to the Army for the Samar campaign, were not subtle: "Kill and Burn! The more you kill and burn the more you will please me." He ordered Waller to make the island "a howling wilderness," and to kill all males 10 years and older found outside of the coastal towns. Actually, Waller had more respect than Smith for the rules of civilized warfare, and informed his men that under no circumstances were they to make war on women and children.

Chaffee had already unleashed General J. Franklin Bell in the province of Batangas in Southern Luzon. Bell, too, was a well known veteran of Indian wars, and like Chaffee, a cavalry hero. While his orders were not as bizarre as Smith's, they were in some ways more sinister. In writing, he gave his officers the "right of retaliation," and directed them "to execute a prisoner of war" for each guerrilla assassination, "one selected by lot from among officers and prominent citizens held [prisoner] . . . chosen when practicable from those who belong to the town where the murder or assassination occurred." Bell also created concentration camps. The Army euphemistically labeled these facilities "models of sanitation" and worried that their inhabitants might not want to leave them following pacification, but an estimated 11,000 Filipinos perished in them, although Bell's tactics merely exacerbated smallpox and cholera epidemics that had preceded him to Batangas.

The year 1902 opened with an investigation into the conduct of the war by Senator Henry Cabot Lodge's Committee on the Philippines, largely due to pressure from the senior senator from Massachusetts, George Frisbee Hoar, a rare anti-imperialist Republican. The first 2 months were spent listening to "safe" witnesses, such as Generals Otis, MacArthur, and Robert Hughes, Admiral Dewey, and Governor of the Philippines William Howard Taft. Even they made some damaging concessions. Hughes, for example, conceded that civilized warfare was not being waged by America, and then tried to justify this by insisting that it was impossible to do otherwise because the enemy was not "civilized." Taft admitted that the "water cure" had been used "on some occasions to extract information." He was referring to a rather mild form of torture in which the victim on his back was forced to swallow huge quantities of water, sometimes salted, until he talked. None died, or was rendered permanently disabled from it, but anti-imperialist propaganda had made it much more draconian in the public mind. As though sensing the enormity of his error, Taft tried to make light of it, recounting that some Filipino suspects actually demanded that they be first subjected to this torture to have an excuse for divulging information. But the damage was done.

Critics on Lodge's committee soon forced the chairman to subpoena more critical witnesses, and by March, the public was being exposed to daily litanies of American atrocities. Ex-Corporal Richard O'Brien, for example, described the senseless destruction of a peaceful village ordered by ex-Captain Fred MacDonald, who spared only the life of a beautiful mestizo mother, whom he and the other officers repeatedly raped before turning her over to the men for their pleasure. Lodge desperately sought more "reliable" veterans, subpoenaing MacDonald to deny O'Brien's charges, which the chair then decreed to be "hearsay." Sometimes this backfired when a carefully selected witness, such as ex-Sergeant Mark Evans, testified that extermination of the natives was the only solution to the problem in the Philippines, and had to be quickly hustled off the stand. To end his investigation on a better note for the administration, Lodge recalled Dewey, Otis, MacArthur, and Taft before abruptly terminating the hearings in June, over anti-imperialist protests.

By then, however, new developments embarrassed the administration. Secretary of War Elihu Root rushed into print a document designed to demonstrate

The *Evening Journal* in New York infuriated apologists for this war of conquest with this cartoon, inspired by General Smith's infamous orders to Marine Major Waller. "Of all the sins of 'yellow journalism,' this is by far the worst," the *New York Times* declared of it. There is some truth to this charge as Waller was much too professional to follow Smith's orders literally. (Newspaper Collection, The New York Public Library, Astor, Lenox and Tilden Foundations)

to the public that in those allegedly "rare instances" in which an American atrocity was committed, the perpetrators were swiftly and severely punished. Forty-four specific crimes committed by Americans were listed along with the punishments meted out. Despite Root's good intentions, the punishments were so ludicrously light that they quickly evoked editorial chortles in the opposition press. Six officers drew nothing more than reprimands for such crimes as rape, murder, and torture. But it was the case of Lieutenant Preston Brown that became the cause célèbre among anti-imperialists. Brown had been appropriately dismissed from the service and sentenced to 5 years at hard labor for murdering a prisoner, only to have President Roosevelt commute that sentence to forfeiture of half his pay for 9 months and a loss of 35 places on the promotion list!

Added to this was a series of devastating leaks to the press of very damaging documents thought to have been safely closeted under lock and key in the War Department. Investigations of Funston and of the rapine of Macabebe scouts against the hated Tagalogs, along with whistle blowing reports on Bell's Batangas campaign suddenly appeared in print. General Wheaton even agreed that "all native troops when they can escape the immediate control of their officers, are liable to commit murders, and they will rob and ravish whenever they have the opportunity." However, the private letters of their commanding officer, Major Batson, the same officer who once complained about similar conduct by American soldiers, reveal that he had encouraged such tactics:

> I am king of the Macabebes and they are terrors. . . . Word reaches a place that the Macabebes are coming and every Tagalog hunts his hole. . . . The time has come when it is necessary to conduct this warfare with the utmost rigor. "With fire and sword" as it were. But the numerous, so styled humane societies, and the poisonous press makes it difficult to follow this policy if reported to the world. . . . At present we are destroying, in this district, everything before us. I have three columns out, and their course is easily traced from the church tower by the smoke of burning houses. . . . Of course no official report will be made of everything.

The individual responsible for these leaks was unquestionably the Army's top commander, General Nelson Miles, who had presidential aspirations. To this end, he had pestered Roosevelt to place him in personal command of the army in the Philippines. When this was denied, Miles went on an inspection tour of the islands, and returned in complete agreement with the anti-imperialists that his Army had routinely committed atrocities, hoping that this issue might open a path for him to the Democratic nomination later that year. The *New York Times* called Miles "one of those birds which fouls its own nest," but Roosevelt refused to make him a martyr for the anti-imperialists, and he served until he reached mandatory retirement age in 1903.

In March, Root got word that Waller had executed eleven prisoners on Samar without benefit of trial. He must have seemed an ideal scapegoat to Root, coming from the rival Navy Department. To Root's chagrin, however, Waller was acquitted by a court-martial in Manila when he revealed the bizarre orders that he had received from Smith. Editors committed entire front-pages to bits and pieces of these orders in extraordinarily large type such as, "KILL ALL!" and "MAKE SAMAR A HOWLING WILDERNESS." One political cartoon depicted little Filipino boys lined up before a firing squad over the caption: "Criminals Because They Were Born Ten Years Before We Took the Philippines." In it, the American eagle was portrayed as a vulture in the national shield. Root simply had no choice but to court-martial Smith. He insisted, however, that Smith's orders were never meant to be taken literally, whereupon Smith declared to reporters that they were, and that this was the only way to fight "savages." Smith was found guilty in May and forced to retire.

As though the administration needed any more embarrassments, the war's greatest hero, "Fighting Fred" Funston, returned to the states early in 1902 to recover from a botched appendectomy. Over the next few months, Root might have wished that Army doctors had sewn up the general's mouth by mistake. Funston soon embarked on a cross country speaking marathon at various banquets in his honor. He was idolized by adoring crowds that blocked his train at whistle-stops until he emerged to say a few words. Headlines greeted "Aguinaldo's Brave Captor" in each city while hordes of reporters dogged him everywhere he went. He rarely disappointed them. Funston scorned the veterans testifying before the Lodge committee as "prattlers" feeding "tall tales" to a few "scoundrelly politicians"—that is, Democratic war critics. Such veterans had "ornamented the inside of a grog house longer than they distinguished themselves in the field," he declared. Funston also mocked Governor Taft's "misguided attempt to establish democracy" in pacified areas: "We believe everything and everybody should have a vote, down to cattle and horses." Instead, "bayonet rule" was needed, as "the only thing a Filipino respects is force." His greatest contempt was aimed at war critics, who "prolonged the war by giving the Filipinos false hopes." The "blood of fallen American boys was on their hands." Such speeches won congratulatory headlines and fawning editorials in the imperialist press: One front-page declared:

Bravo! General Funston
Great Speech By Little Kansan
Silence While Bullets Fly
Ignorant Talk At Home Has Slain Our Soldiers
Got Tremendous Applause
and Prolonged Applause
And Cries of "That's Right!"

Either such headlines went to the general's head, or gin rickeys affected his judgment, as he would later claim, but Funston also bragged about an escalating number of prisoners that he had summarily executed to deter guerrilla activity. At the posh Lotus Club in New York City, this braggadocio took an even more ominous turn when Funston told of hanging two black American deserters, and suggested that it would have been better to string up war critics at home. For starters, he even suggested hanging those who had recently signed a peace petition to Congress. While imperialist editors remained silent, their anti-imperialist counterparts first expressed shock and then rage. "Funston Advises Hanging. Gallows Would Suit Some Americans," announced the *Call*'s front page, while its editor explained how prominent were Funston's proposed victims: "the presidents of nearly all American universities and the leading clergymen of all denominations in the union." The paper advised Funston "to repair his inflated condition and sheath his unruly mouth."

In the middle of his "gallows speech," Funston periodically shouted: "Bully for Waller!" All the way back to San Francisco, he would emerge from his train to shout this and "Hooray for Smith!" at adoring crowds. When he arrived, he insisted to the waiting reporters that he "stood by everything" he had said, although he did claim that his suggestion of hanging Americans was "merely an abstract comparison." He also informed astonished reporters that the president was in complete agreement with his views. That was too much for Roosevelt, who sent a private warning to Funston via their mutual friend, William Allen White, the eminent Kansas journalist, confidant of presidents and Republican leaders, and Funston's fraternity brother at the University of Kansas. Apparently Funston was unable to control self-destructive impulses. At his next duty station in Denver after his long "recuperation" furlough, he mocked "the overheated conscience" of Senator Hoar at a local banquet. This was the proverbial straw that broke the camel's back, and Root ordered him to give no more speeches or press interviews. An official presidential reprimand followed.

Not everybody was satisfied with front-page headlines announcing that "Roosevelt Muzzles Funston." Over the next few weeks, Hoar and fellow war critics denounced Funston for hours on the floor of the Senate. Senator Edward Carmack of Tennessee called him "the mightiest Sampson who ever wielded the jawbone of an ass as a weapon of war." Congressman Samuel McCall informed the Harvard Republican Club that he would push for an indictment, and would not be intimidated "by the threats of some microscopic general [Funston was about 5 feet, 4 inches tall] who knows as much about the rules of civil government as he does about the rules of civilized warfare." But Funston led a charmed life, and he managed to escape relatively unscathed.

In the midst of all this political *sturm and drang,* Roosevelt pulled the rug from under his critics by simply declaring that the war was over in his Fourth of July speech in 1902. Describing it as the most glorious war in the nation's history, he commended "the bravery of American soldiers" fighting "for the triumph of civilization over the black chaos of savagery and barbarism." He did express regret over "the few acts of cruelty in retaliation [for] the hundreds committed by Filipinos against American soldiers."

AN INTERPRETATION

Roosevelt would have been on firmer ground arguing that atrocities on both sides are endemic to guerrilla warfare, enhanced in this case on the American side by the rapid expansion of the Army that spread experienced junior and noncommissioned officers too thin. Senior officers, such as Wheaton, Bell, and Smith, along with the commanders who protected them, Otis, MacArthur, and Chaffee, had spent most of their military careers fighting Indians, which probably hardened them to a certain amount of brutality. Funston did not have the luxury of this excuse. While most soldiers were too young to have fought in Indian wars, they were predominantly Western and Southern descendants of Indian fighters, often alluding to this in letters home. Add to this recipe, the intense nationalism of the era along with the vicious racism that permeated American society at the turn of the century, and one comes up with a formula that made it that much easier for many American soldiers to dehumanize the Filipinos, often ignoring the rules of civilized warfare. Even those who initially criticized such brutality, such as Batson and Lyon, soon capitulated to the view of the majority.

There has been considerable scholarly debate over the causes of an American empire. Some argue that empire was the product of monopoly capitalism. Yet most businessmen opposed the war with Spain; the country had just emerged from a serious depression, and they simply did not want to risk the recovery with new, unpredictable adventures. Other scholars have emphasized the roles of a few well-placed imperialists, including Roosevelt, Lodge, and Dewey. But their imperialistic appetites were severely limited. They wanted strategically located pin-point colonies rather than large, heavily populated ones. Their interest was in coaling stations and naval bases to protect American interests in Asia. They specifically wanted to avoid "England's folly in India," and were initially interested in keeping Manila alone. Aggressive German naval maneuvers in the Philippines plus Japan's colonial interests enhanced the military's argument that Manila alone was indefensible.

Ultimately, the popular appeal of an empire was too strong to resist. The jingoistic fury of the people pushed McKinley into escalating his demands beyond Manila to Luzon and, by summer's end, to the entire archipelago. Having been patriotically aroused to fight Spain, emotional inertia alone made it easier for Americans to conquer the Philippines in the name of "civilization."

There is a related lesson to be learned in the attitudes toward the war that are revealed in the letters that servicemen sent home to family and friends. In our own day, the official ideology of war requires that war at least be talked about as if it were at best an unfortunate event, to be completed as quickly as possible and with as little blood and gore—hopefully, as in the Gulf War of 1990, in a series of "surgical" strikes.

The turn-of-the-century youth who fought in the jungles of the Philippines did not feel that way. They were full of passion for the action and excitement, the shooting and killing, that were part of the conflict. Youth enthusiastically embraced imperialism at the turn of the century, perceiving an empire as a new "frontier" that would both challenge them and provide new opportunities. Above all, the empire offered adventure. As a result, there were no problems getting young men to volunteer to serve in the war, and the morale of the soldiers was extraordinarily high, in spite of the inept and uninspiring leadership of General Otis. Young, swashbuckling, and bumptious leaders, such as Frederick Funston and Theodore Roosevelt, became national idols and spokesmen for the nation's warrior tradition.

American rule was also characterized by ambivalence and limits. As the story reveals, not all Americans approved of the nation's overseas adventures, and criticism in the press and Congress did not end with the war. While the United States was the last of the major powers to acquire an empire, it was also the first to become disillusioned with a formal empire, turning internal control over to Filipino *independistas* by 1907 and pledging future independence in the Jones Act of

1916, when Britain was still jailing Indians calling for independence. At bottom, neo-imperialism—those indirect informal controls over legally independent states—has always been more attractive to Americans. Not only is it more cost effective, but it also protects American innocence with the illusion that the nation can at once have an informal empire, and yet be true to its sacred principle of self-determination.

Sources: Most of the sources for this essay were primary ones, particularly the manuscript collection at the United States Army Military History Research Center at Carlisle Barracks in Pennsylvania. Letters, diaries, unpublished manuscripts and unofficial army newspapers written by hundreds of soldiers from private to general are here. More such records are in the Library of Congress and the National Archives, particularly papers of important leaders, civilian and military, during the war. Other archives, at Harvard, the Boston Atheneum, and the Historical Societies of Massachusetts, Pennsylvania, and California were valuable for the papers of anti-imperialists. Senate and House documents, reports of commanding generals and the War Department were also used along with a carefully balanced, geographically and politically, sample of newspapers and periodicals. Such contemporary publications as *Public Opinion* and *Literary Digest* were valuable in tapping editorial opinion across the nation.

    Related secondary works were also examined, including books written by Teodoro Agoncillo, Bonifacio Salamanca, Reynaldo Ileto, Theodore Friend, Glenn May, Peter Stanley, David Joel Steinberg, E. Berkeley Tomkins, and Richard Welch.

6

ARTIFICIAL INSEMINATION: THE FIRST DEBATE

ELAINE TYLER MAY

The story that follows is really two stories, each with its own context, but curiously inseparable. The first story is from 1884, when a prominent physician artificially inseminated a woman—in front of a class of medical students, and without the woman's permission. The second story Elaine Tyler May tells is from 1909 —in the midst of the period of social reformism known as the Progressive Era—when the earlier event was first revealed and then vigorously debated within the medical community. This story can yield important insights into the society and culture of the early twentieth century. As May's story reveals, the 1909 discussion posed the necessity of scientific and technological "progress" (represented by the insemination) against the requirements of religion and morality. The debate also swirled around questions of genetic breeding that were very much a part of an era when even respectable people—among them Theodore Roosevelt—were concerned that the "racial purity" of the American population was being compromised by high levels of immigration from the "wrong" nations.

The physicians who debated the case also shared a perspective very common among Progressive-Era reformers: They believed that all problems could be solved, and that only experts—experts like themselves—could solve them. This attitude could lead to dramatic social progress. But all too many experts also believed that ordinary people were too stupid or ignorant to have anything important to say, even about their own lives. Thus the physician who impregnated the woman in this story did so with a lack of respect for her wishes. And of those who years later exchanged opinions in the medical journals, few were much concerned with discussing the case from her point of view. Although women actively campaigned for the suffrage throughout the Progressive Era, their claim to equality in the political sphere had not—at least not yet, or for the male physicians who held forth in the pages of the medical journals— spilled over into the area of reproductive rights. Decades later, when birth control, abortion, and surrogate motherhood are regularly discussed in the most public forums, a curious and even bizarre turn-of-the-century case of artificial insemination presents a rare opportunity to look back—back to the future.

In 1909, a brief article in the *Medical World* unleashed a storm of controversy. A physician by the name of Addison Davis Hard wrote that he had witnessed the first human conception by a procedure he called "artificial impregnation." The event he reported had occurred 25 years earlier, in 1884, when he was a student at the Jefferson Medical College in Philadelphia. He claimed that the event he witnessed was performed by his professor, the noted physician Dr. William Pancoast. According to Dr. Hard, a prominent couple living in Philadelphia in the 1880s were distraught over their inability to have children. The 41-year-old husband, whom we shall call Henry Dumont, was a successful merchant; his wife, whom we shall call Margaret, was a wealthy Quaker woman 10 years his junior. They had the means to pursue their goal of parenthood by seeking the best medical assistance available.

The couple sought out the assistance of one of Philadelphia's most prominent physicians, Dr. William Pancoast, who was affiliated with the prestigious Philadelphia Hospital. Dr. Pancoast found their case to be puzzling, as he found no apparent cause for the couple's difficulty. In spite of the knowledge of the function of sperm, it was still widely believed that if a man was not sexually impotent, he was presumed to be fertile. Because Henry did not suffer from impotence, Dr.

Dr. William Henry Pancoast, 1835–1897, is reported to have performed the first artificial insemination by donor on an unconscious female patient in 1884, using the sperm of a medical student. (National Library of Medicine, History of Medicine Division, Prints and Photographs Collection)

Pancoast suspected that the problem resided with his wife. He therefore decided to examine her first. Victorian delicacy did not prevent the doctor and his six students from conducting a thorough investigation. Dr. Hard described the exam as "very complete, almost as perfect as an army examination." The doctor concluded that there were no physiological impediments to impregnation. He went so far as to claim that the examination provided evidence to prove a widely held theory about reproduction: that female orgasm facilitated conception. While it is not clear precisely how the examination proved this theory, Dr. Hard noted that "during this examination was discovered for the first time, as far as I know, the suction function of the uterus, which takes place during orgasm." Whether or not the evidence was valid, it does suggest that the exam went beyond the merely superficial. It also indicates that medical theories at the time were profoundly influenced by ancient folk beliefs, such as the myth of the suction of the uterus during orgasm.

The examination revealed no physiological abnormality. Margaret was therefore spared the common treatments used to correct female sterility, such as bleeding of the cervix with leeches, the application of electricity, and the use of various surgeries and mechanical appliances to rearrange the reproductive organs. She was also spared the typical behavioral prescriptions, such as the regime recommended by one contemporary physician: infrequent coitus, pure air, quietude of mind, temperance in food, drink, and sleep, and the "cultivation of correct habits of mind and body." Having determined that she had no impediment to fertilization, Dr. Pancoast surmised that the problem might reside with Henry. Although he was not impotent, there was the chance that something might be wrong with his semen. The doctor examined him and found no physical defect. But when he studied the semen under the microscope, he found that it contained absolutely no sperm. Dr. Pancoast informed the man of his findings, and suggested that the problem probably resulted from an early bout of gonorrhea, contracted in his youth. Dr. Pancoast then began a course of treatment that he assumed would remedy the problem.

After 2 months of treatment, however, Henry showed no sign of improvement. At this point, one of the students in the class allegedly made a joking remark, suggesting that "the only solution of this problem is to call in the hired man." Although made in jest, the remark gave Dr. Pancoast an idea, which led to an unusual plan of action. In the presence of his six students, he anesthetized Margaret with chloroform. While she was unconscious, Dr. Pancoast selected the "best looking member of the class" to provide semen for the experiment. Using a rubber syringe, he inserted the semen of the student into the uterus of the patient. As it turned out, conception occurred, and Margaret became pregnant.

At this point, according to Dr. Hard, Dr. Pancoast became a bit nervous. He had neither asked permission nor even informed Margaret or Henry of the procedure before doing it, and now they were expecting a child. Reluctantly, Dr. Pancoast decided he must inform the husband (although not the wife) of what he had done. Fortunately for the doctor, Henry was pleased. His only request was for absolute secrecy, so that nobody should ever know what happened, not even his wife. He preferred that she remain ignorant of his early bout of gonorrhea, as well as the method of her impregnation. It was a request Dr. Pancoast was more than happy to grant. Because the procedure was ethically questionable, Dr. Pancoast pledged the six students who witnessed the event to absolute secrecy.

Nine months later, Margaret gave birth to a healthy son, whom she raised according to appropriate middle-class standards. He grew up to follow in his father's footsteps, and by the time he reached the age of 25 years he had moved to New York and become a successful businessman. Nobody ever knew about the peculiar means of his conception. His mother assumed he was the biological child of her husband—indeed, it was said that he resembled his father. But the medical students present at the insemination did not forget, and one in particular—most likely the sperm donor himself—maintained a lifelong interest in the case.

Twenty-five years after the child's birth, when Dr. Pancoast was no longer alive, the most interested of the former medical students finally decided to go public with his story. Dr. Addison Davis Hard, 25 years earlier undoubtedly the "best looking" student in Dr. Pancoast's class, was now a general practitioner in Marshall, Minnesota. To satisfy his curiosity, he traveled to New York in 1909 to see the young man (who in all likelihood he had sired), and there "shook his hand." He then wrote the story.

The insemination was not an isolated event; it took place at a time of medical and scientific ferment. At the time of the experiment, faith in science to bring about progress was increasing. A few decades earlier, Charles Darwin had proclaimed his famous theory of evolution, affirming the "survival of the fittest." At the same time, the crusade for scientific human breeding, known as eugenics, was gaining popularity. Throughout the nineteenth century, several experimental utopian communities developed novel ways to manage sex, reproduction, and family life. One of the most controversial was the Oneida community, which in the 1840s put into place a program of eugenic reproduction that lasted 2 decades, and gained a great deal of attention—mostly negative. The Oneida reproductive experiment was known as stirpiculture, a system in which the founder of this perfectionist religious community, John Humphrey Noyes, determined which individuals could procreate, in order to create a generation of people who were better (that is, more free of sin) than the previous generation. The system prohibited marriage or any exclusive attachments, but established a "free love" environment in which any two individuals could have intercourse, according to certain rules. The man was to make the request through a third party, the woman was expected to consent, and the couple were to avoid pregnancy by "male continence"—a sexual practice based on prolonged intercourse without ejaculation.

Needless to say, contemporaries criticized the community as "promiscuous" and evil, even though it was based on Noyes' notions of the best way to achieve perfect holiness. It attracted the attention of the scientific community, however, because of its experiment in human breeding. As the nineteenth century advanced and the national population became more diverse, the notion of human breeding as a means of social reform became increasingly popular. Eugenicists believed that the "best" human stock (generally defined as white Anglo-Saxon Protestant) should be encouraged to reproduce, while those they defined as inferior (including poor southern European immigrants, people of color, and the "mentally defective") should be discouraged or prevented from procreating. These ideas gained adherents among the American-born white middle class, whose numbers had been declining, relative to the rest of the population, for nearly a century. In this context, childlessness among the "better classes" became a matter of national concern.

By the time the Dumonts turned to the medical profession for help, physicians had been attempting to cure childlessness for decades. Medical knowledge in the area of reproduction was advancing rapidly. Although a full understanding of the female cycle was still decades away, enough was known about female physiology to diagnose the malfunction of certain organs. Medical practitioners also recognized the function of sperm in the process of conception, and by the 1880s the more knowledgeable physicians routinely investigated husbands as well as wives in their efforts to discover the causes of childlessness.

The physician drew on earlier experiments in treating infertility and came up with a novel innovation. Dr. Pancoast was undoubtedly familiar with the work of a physician by the name of J. Marion Sims, who wrote up his notes in 1869 after decades of clinical practice. In his book, *Notes on Uterine Surgery with Specific Reference to the Management of the Sterile Condition,* he recounted several cases of sterility in women treated by surgical and non-surgical means. He was apparently among the first to use an "impregnator" tool, a syringe device, to facilitate conception. In cases where sperm did not travel adequately to fertilize the egg, Dr. Sims used the tool to deposit the semen of the husband directly into the uterus of the wife. The procedure was used when the man's sperm appeared to be viable but some physiological impediment seemed to hinder conception. It was not a very successful form of treatment. Dr. Sims used the syringe 55 times, with only one pregnancy resulting, and ultimately gave up the practice.

Dr. Sims also used anesthesia to render his female patients unconscious in order to perform procedures without their discomfort. He related some infertility cases in which anesthesia was used to facilitate conception without the aid of the syringe. He termed the procedure "ethereal copulation." One patient in particular suffered extreme pain with sexual intercourse, rendering conception impossible. Dr. Sims described the case as it developed under the care of another physician, before the couple came to him for assistance. "Suffice it to say that it became the business of the physician to repair regularly to the residence of this couple two or three times a week to etherize the poor wife. . . . They persevered, hoping that she would become pregnant. . . . This etherization was continued for a year, when conception occurred. . . . At the end of another year of ethereal copulation, there was another conception, which resulted in [a miscarriage] at the third month. After this she was etherized constantly for nearly another year, when at last they saw no hope of a cure, and becoming alarmed at the frequent repetition of the anaesthesia, they concluded to give it up altogether. And when they consulted me there had been no effort at copulation for three or four years." The woman's two conceptions "took place while she was in a state of complete anaesthesia," which was apparently the only way she could tolerate intercourse. Eventually, Dr. Sims performed surgery. Dr. Pancoast must have been aware of this use of anaesthesia, as well as the experiments with the syringe. But he utilized these tools in a new way. His novel innovation was the use of a sperm donor.

It was the introduction of the sperm donor into the process of reproduction that was most intriguing to eugenicists and most appalling to moralists. To understand the impact of the story, it is critical to keep in mind the historical setting in which the story unfolded. Although the actual event took place in 1884, it was not reported until 1909, when Dr. Hard described it in the *Medical World.* By this time, the Progressive Era was in full swing, and social reforms backed by scientific theories gained the support of much of the middle class. While many reformist impulses of the era were humanitarian and forward-looking, such as concerns over working conditions in factories and regulation of big business, others were backward-looking efforts to preserve the status quo in the face of social change, such as immigration restriction. One of the features of the new century that most worried some of the more conservative reformers was the declining birthrate of the white American-born population. Although the downward trend had prevailed for over a century, it caused increasing alarm in the early years of the twentieth century because of what appeared to be the relatively high birthrate of the immigrants, ethnic minorities and non-white peoples. Many feared the rapid population growth of what they believed to be inferior people. Some even argued that

What Kind of Children?

By courtesy of Edison Lamp Works

Children get their basic qualities by inheritance. If they are to be strong, keen, efficient, and great, there must be good blood back of them

If you want your children to be well-born, choose your husband because of fine qualities in his family as well as in himself. Then add the best training

These make a square deal for the children

This poster, part of the Youth and Life exhibit of the American Social Hygiene Association in 1922, illustrates popular eugenic values about properly bred progeny. Ideas such as these influenced the discussion of artificial insemination as a means to "improve the race." (American Social Health Association Records, Social Welfare History Archives, University of Minnesota)

medical advances extending the lives of the poor were disrupting the natural processes of evolution. President Roosevelt was one of the first Progressive leaders to warn of "race suicide," and urged the "best stock" of Americans to attend to their reproductive duties so that the nation would not be overrun by the "inferior races." Other reformers, including the radical birth-control advocate Margaret Sanger, were also drawn to the concept of scientific breeding known as eugenics, because of its utopian possibilities. The different strains of Progressive reform came together in complicated ways over the issue of reproduction.

Among those who believed in the principles of planned breeding as a means to improve society was Dr. Hard. In his article in the *Medical World* in which he described the artificial impregnation of 1884, he extolled the virtues of the procedure as a way to improve the racial stock of the nation. "[A]rtificial impregnation offers valuable advantages," he wrote. "The mating of human beings must, from the nature of things, be a matter of sentiment alone. Persons of the worst possible promise of good and healthy offspring are being lawfully united in marriage every day. Marriage is a proposition which is not submitted to good judgement or even common sense, as a rule. . . . Artificial impregnation by carefully selected seed, alone will solve the problem." The problem, according to Dr. Hard, was that the wrong people would mate and create inferior offspring.

Hard argued that the seed carries the essential human qualities. But he immediately reversed himself by claiming instead that the "true father" is not he who contributes the sperm, but rather the husband of the mother who gives the child birth. "It may at first shock the delicate sensibilities of the sentimental who consider that the source of the seed indicates the true father, but when the scientific fact becomes known that the origin of the spermatozoa which generates the ovum is of no more importance than the personality of the finger which pulls the trigger of a gun, then objections will lose their forcefulness, and artificial impregnation become recognized as a race-uplifting procedure."

Dr. Hard chose a particularly vivid and violent metaphor to describe the process. A gun is a symbol of masculine prowess and force. By using the metaphor of the "personality of the finger," he downplayed the role of the father in raising the child, while underscoring the power of the man's "gun." It was an effective means of reconciling the apparent contradiction in his argument. He then extolled one of the most time-honored of all American values: motherhood. Ultimately, he argued, it matters little who contributes the sperm because "[i]t is gradually becoming well establisht [sic] that the mother is the complete builder of the child. It is her blood that gives it material for its body, and her nerve energy which is divided to supply its vital force. It is her mental ideals which go to influence, to some extent at least, the features, the tendencies, and the mental caliber of the child. 'Many a man rocks another man's child and thinks he is rocking his own,' for it looks like him. And often two children by the same parents have features entirely dissimilar. It is the predominating mental ideals prevailing with the mother that shapes [sic] the destiny of the child." In other words, the "gun" creates the child, but the mother molds it.

Hard's final comments represent the sentiment of turn-of-the-century eugenicists who believed that scientific breeding held the key to the nation's future. He exhorted his readers to heed his advice: "A scientific study of sex selection without regard to marriage conditions might result in giving some men children of wonderful mental endowments, in place of half-witted, evil-inclined, disease-disposed offspring which they are ashamed to call their own. The mechanical method of impregnation, whether it be the orthodox way, or the aseptic surgeon's skillful fingers, counts but little, except sentiment, and sentiment is fast becoming a servant instead of a master in the affairs of the human race. Few are the children who are brought intentionally into this world. As a rule they are but the incidental result of a journey in search of selfish pleasure. They are seldom sought, and often unwelcome when they put in their first appearance. The subsequent mother's love is largely a matter of growth, for affection is but an attribute of selfishness."

Recognizing that these ideas might offend his readers, Hard defended his proposition by attacking the virtue of his critics, while also articulating the widespread alarm over epidemic venereal disease prevailing at the time. "The man who may think this idea shocking, probably has millions of gonococci swarming in his seminal ducts, and probably his wife has had a laparotome which nearly cost her life itself, as a result of his infecting her with the crop reaped from his last planting of 'wild oats.' One man in every five in New York City was found to be free from the contamination of venereal disease to an extent that rendered him safe around the house in which a woman lived.

"Go ask the blind children whose eyes were saturated with gonorrheal pus as they struggled thru the birth canal to emerge into this world of darkness to endure a living death; ask them what is the most shocking thing in this whole world. Ask Helen Keller what is the most shocking thing in this sin-soaked ball of selfish pursuits. They will tell you it is the idea that man, wonderful man, is infecting 80 percent of all womankind with the satanic germs collected by him as his youthful steps wandered in the 'bad lands.' "

Dr. Hard must have been familiar with a report of a committee of New York physicians that estimated that as many as 80 percent of the men in the city had been infected with gonorrhea. Whatever the actual incidence, such reports fueled concerns over an epidemic of venereal disease. There is no doubt that venereal disease was a serious problem. A Boston doctor at the time found over one-third of a sample of male hospital patients infected with gonorrhea. But it was not Dr. Hard's discussion of venereal disease that provoked his readers. It was the procedure he described.

When Dr. Hard published his account in 1909, the reaction ranged from outrage to applause. The controversy centered around the role of the medical profession in reproduction. It is important to recognize that although the procedure was identified as a medical phenomenon, it required no complicated medical technology nor specialized expertise. Artificial insemination required nothing more than a rubber syringe and a willing donor. Virtually anyone could do it. Yet, the process was claimed as a medical innovation, and the offspring born by this method were the first to acquire the misnomer of "test-tube babies." For nearly a century after Dr. Pancoast allegedly performed his experiment, artificial insemination, as it came to be called, remained under the control of the medical profession.

Because the notice of this event appeared in a medical journal, the controversy remained confined to the medical community. Most of the readers who responded in the Letters to the Editor section of the journal were horrified by Dr. Hard's account. Two questioned whether the event actually took place. Dr. C. H. Newth, for example, found the entire account unthinkable. "I wondered what [Dr. Hard] had eaten for supper, or what is his brand of drinking water. Dr. Pancoast was a gentleman, and would not countenance the raping of a patient under anesthetic. I must say that it should not have been told as a fact, but as a dream, which it probably was." Dr. Newth went on to question the very idea of a couple subjecting themselves to such indignities. "In the first place it is an impossible story that a wealthy merchant should present himself and wife for a 'private and confidential examination,' with a 'section of the class' of medical students to 'assist.' The story of taking the gentleman's seminal fluid to be examined by the students to see if it contained any 'spermatozoans' is a flight of fancy. . . . Accusing the professor of raping his patient with the semen of 'the best looking member of the class,' a preposterous crime, is certainly going a little." Dr. Newth also refuted Dr. Hard's theory of the relative insignificance of the sperm in terms of the resulting offspring. He argued that if Dr. Hard were correct that the sperm is merely the agent that triggers conception, like the "finger which pulls the trigger of a gun," then the child should resemble not the father but rather "the hard rubber syringe used after the masturbation of the best looking member of the class." He closed by railing one last time against "this chimera of a disordered brain."

Dr. N. J. Hamilton agreed with Dr. Newth that the event couldn't have really happened. In the June issue of *Medical World*, Dr. Hamilton explained that initially he was reluctant to respond because "it was so ridiculously criminal I hesitated to say anything on the subject." But then he went on to note that he actually performed a similar procedure frequently in his own practice. He noted that since his graduation in 1886, he had been in general practice and had "given the study and treatment of sterile married ladies much thought and attention." He claimed that "All cases coming under my treatment have been relieved in one of two ways: medicinally or by using the impregnator (of course, I mean all cases where the fault was the woman's). Have used the impregnator frequently. Have used these treatments for fifteen years without failure." His success record is, of course, a dubious claim, but he went on to describe using "an instrument which has a long, flexible point" to insert semen directly into a woman's uterus. The critical difference here, of course, was that the "impregnator" facilitated conception with the sperm of the woman's husband in cases where some physiological impediment existed in the woman. The purpose of Dr. Pancoast's procedure as described by Dr. Hard was exactly the opposite: to enable a woman to bear a child when her husband was sterile. Dr. Hamilton concluded by claiming that there was nothing new about the procedure itself; indeed, it had been used for decades. But as for Pancoast's use of the sperm of a donor, "I could hardly give it credence." His point, of course, was that although it was certainly possible—even simple— to perform such a procedure, it was entirely unthinkable to believe that any self-respecting physician would do such a thing.

The June issue of the *Medical World* contained additional responses. C. L. Egbert apparently believed the story, but was outraged by it. Dr. Egbert moved the debate from the realm of science to the realm of religion. He claimed that insemination was worse than rape, for it violated the laws of God, which are "good and sufficient on the subject of false intercourse. . . . [Y]ou have no right by any process of reasoning develop [sic] in your own mind or otherwise to break down the marriage laws of God. The deed of your professor was neither honest nor moral. It would have been a thousand fold better and more honorable had your professor seduced that woman while conscious; or, if you please, just as honorable had he had intercourse with her while unconscious."

The same writer also took issue with Dr. Hard's claims about the mother as the one who shapes the child. He was offended that the role of the father was considered so unimportant. He called Dr. Hard's argument "a ridiculous jumble of facts. As to his scientific (?) part, he tells us that it is the mother who is the complete builder of the child." He then pointed out Dr. Hard's contradictory arguments: "Now he has just told us that the male seed didn't amount to anything. That all the tendencies . . . were from the mother." If so, then how could inferior sperm lead to "half-witted, evil-inclined, disease disposed" offspring? Finally, Egbert defended himself against Hard's accusation that "the man who thinks this idea shocking probably has millions of gonococci swarming in his seminal ducts." He asserted that he did find the article shocking, "not only to me but to any male or female who has a proper understanding of marital relations or the laws of God. But I wish to assure [Dr. Hard] that there are no gonococci in my seminal ducts, even if this answer would imply such to his mind. And furthermore, I have as healthy and bright a child as one could wish for, and she was not begotten with a hard rubber syringe, either." James W. Graham echoed this sentiment, and wrote, "As regards the finding of the gonococci: If I were anxious to make a microscopical examination of this micro-organism, I should select the semen of the fellow with the hard rubber syringe, or the one who advocates the abolishing of the marriage bond; and would be disappointed if I couldn't find them."

Others were more enthusiastic about the reproductive experiment Dr. Hard described. J. Morse Griffin endorsed the procedure on eugenic grounds. Griffin himself had "personally used the impregnator with success on mares that were apparently steril [sic]" with good results, and claimed that if "from a commercial standpoint, it be a paying process in the animal kingdom, why would not its influence be many times greater in the human family?" Griffin went beyond the impregnation process, however, in his advocacy of efforts to eradicate the scourge of venereal disease: "Male colts that are not promising individuals are promptly castrated, and yet they are not diseased, and in this way the quality of horse flesh is looking forward; but we are standing idly by and witnessing thousands of infected young men of fine families select a pure, innocent young girl, perhaps your own, to deposit the deadly seed of his 'prodigal' reaping, resulting in the train of symptoms in women so common to the surgeon today. And further than this, the effect is carried down to posterity . . . if the unlikely colt is denied the privilege of sending down the line of his descent an inferior progeny, why tolerate the same, combined with disease, to go on unmolested in the human family. . . . Why not adopt the castration plan in the human family and save the state and Nation the responsibility of having the charge in the state institutions of these deaf, blind, insane, and criminals?"

While not going so far as to advocate castration, Dr. Ernest Barton wrote in the July issue of the *Medical World* that "it was bad taste to tell this story on a dead confrere." Still, he endorsed the procedure: "If Dr. Pancoast had permission from the woman in the first place and the husband in the second place, then whose biznes [sic] is it to find fault?" Of course, no such permission was requested or granted. Dr. Barton nevertheless denounced those who criticized Dr. Pancoast's experiment in the name of the "laws of God." He affirmed the principles of eugenic breeding in terms of science over superstition. To make his point, he noted, "Just think how Luther Burbank has violated 'God's Ways' and committed rape and promiscuousness thousands of times with his flowers, by putting pollen where it would otherwise not have fallen. . . . The result is a thornless rose, thornless cactus, new variety of fruits and berries. . . . Would to God we could, by proper selection and still other means, breed off the thorns from *our* nature, the dunghill tendencies of our habits. . . . What matters it, if the children are fine, whether the instrument is a hard rubber syringe. . . . ?" He called for scientific progress to free humankind from the shackles of the past: "How long, oh, how

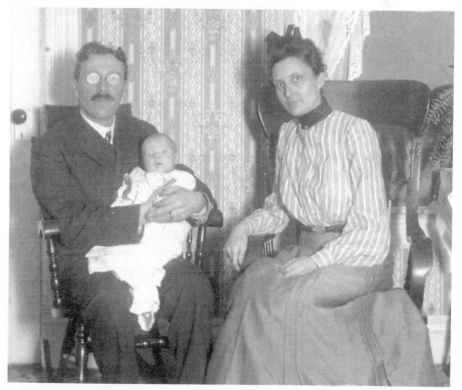

By the turn of the twentieth century, fathers became more fully identified as participants in the nurturing of children. A formal family portrait such as this, with a father holding an infant, would have been highly unusual in the nineteenth century. The controversy surrounding artificial insemination included questions about the importance of fathers in the act of conception as well as childrearing. At a time when motherhood was considered the epitome of womanhood, what was the role of men in parenting? (Minnesota Historical Society)

long shall we allow the shades of the dead, the notions of the dead, the edicts of the dead and follies of the dead to rule us, to blind us, to tyrannize over us, and to cramp us in our struggle for knowledge?" In a strong attack on the religious opposition, he asserted, "Truly the living belongs to us—the dead past belongs to God."

After months of controversy, Dr. Hard finally responded to the many letters his article had sparked. He described his delight at the debate he had provoked: "I cannot convey to you an idea of the amount of pleasure that the varied answers to my article on 'Artificial Impregnation' have given me." But then he backed away from his original claims. "In answer to all my critics and reviewers, I wish to say that while the article was based upon true facts, it was embellisht [sic] purposely with radical personal assertions calculated to set men to thinking on the subject of generativ [sic] influences and generativ [sic] evils. Bless my critics. I would not wish to own a child that was bred with a hard-rubber syringe. And I do not care to think that my child bears toward the millenium no traces of his father's personality, humble tho it be. I am a firm disciple of impregnation in the good old orthodox manner, with all its esthetic features and risks of evil." Returning to his favorite metaphor, he concluded, "Let us now pull the trigger of some other gun, and set free another explosion of cerebral action. Yours for all there is in it for good, A.D. Hard, M.D." The editor quipped in reply, "And the editorial department will hereafter realize that you are not to be taken seriously, and act accordingly."

AN INTERPRETATION

The reactions in 1909 to the news of the first alleged donor insemination reveal a great deal about the social tensions in American society at the time. Twenty-five years had passed since the event took place, yet the debate raged largely around issues of "science" versus "nature." In spite of the widespread affirmation of science in the first decade of the twentieth century (indeed, it is appropriately known as the Progressive Era because of the optimistic faith in progress that prevailed at the time), readers of Dr. Hard's article reacted vehemently to the description of such a drastic manipulation of the reproductive process. The use of the syringe, and the use of the sperm of a donor, pleased those who believed that science could and should further the goal of Progressive reformers who advocated increasing the propagation of the "best" class of people. Hard's article offended others who objected to interfering with the "natural" means of reproduction. These critics were, above all, horrified by the challenge to traditional beliefs about marriage, the family, sex, and reproduction. They found the idea of artificial insemination socially repugnant, religiously unacceptable, and morally outrageous. The debate foreshadowed many that would surround later discussions of birth control, abortion, and various other forms of artificial reproduction.

Most striking about the controversy that ensued, however, is what was not discussed. With the exception of the writer who mistakenly assumed that the couple had granted permission for the procedure, and the other who likened the event to a rape, no other respondent made reference to the enormous deception perpetrated on the woman. After the fact, the physician, the husband, and the students who witnessed the insemination all conspired to keep the woman ignorant of what happened. In the 1909 controversy, respondents paid a great deal of attention to the rubber syringe, but virtually none to the woman involved.

Several decades would pass after the publication of this article before artificial insemination by donor would become a standard treatment for infertility. It is not certain that the event reported was actually the first donor insemination; no doubt throughout history countless women have become pregnant by sperm provided by men other than those to whom they were married, with or without a rubber syringe. Within a few short years donor insemination would be a routine procedure in cases of infertility. What the article and the debate reveal are the powerful assumptions about gender, which made the woman in this story nothing more than a vessel of procreation; and the attitudes about procreation, which indicate how medical science adopted the principles of eugenics in their earliest efforts to cure infertility.

Today, rigorous standards of informed consent would prevent the deception perpetrated in this story. Yet some of the practices of today resemble those described by Dr. Hard. Abuses still occur, as in the case of a physician who inseminated dozens of women with his own sperm, or the transfer of some women's eggs to other women without their knowledge or consent. Sperm donors are still selected on the basis of eugenic criteria, such as grade point average. The medical establishment still controls most of the means of artificial reproduction, even those that require no particular medical expertise or techniques. Witness the recent controversy over surrogate motherhood, which raised many of the same issues. Infertility treatment remains a privilege of the affluent, who have the time and resources to devote to its cure. And in most cases, even if a woman is perfectly fertile and her male partner is not, she is the one likely to become the infertility patient and suffer all the indignities such treatment involves, as was the case in the first reported artificial impregnation a century ago.

Sources: Sources for this story are drawn from the medical literature, the popular press, and eugenic tracts written during the late-nineteenth and early-twentieth centuries. The original article reporting the insemination is from the April issue of the *Medical World* in 1909; the controversy that erupted is documented in letters and comments written to the journal in the following several months. I have also drawn extensively on the secondary literature written by historians, particularly the work on family history, sexuality, and Progressive reform.

7

THE LEO FRANK MURDER CASE

LEONARD DINNERSTEIN

Leonard Dinnerstein's story of the Leo Frank case has two victims: Mary Phagan, a working girl, brutally killed in an Atlanta, Georgia, pencil factory in 1913; and Leo Frank, the pencil factory's northern, Jewish manager, wrongly accused of the murder, convicted and, in 1915, dragged from prison and lynched in the town of Marietta, where Phagan had grown up. The most important testimony was provided by Jim Conley, the plant's black janitor, whose portrayal of Frank as a pervert who took sexual advantage of his female employees—and then killed one of them—was somehow persuasive for the jury. Other protagonists in the drama included Hugh Dorsey, the prosecuting attorney; Frank's defense counsel, whose errors contributed to his plight; the United States Supreme Court, which heard the appeal; Georgia Governor John M. Slaton, whose efforts to secure something resembling justice may have caused Frank's death; and some portion of Georgia's citizens, who for a variety of reasons, some of them complex, wanted Leo Frank to die.

The Leo Frank case resonates with the tensions of the American South in the Progressive Era. As usual, the problem of race was central to southern society. In Georgia, the Progressive Era produced a curious sort of progressive "reform": a literacy test and a "grandfather clause" that made it virtually impossible for blacks to exercise the right to vote. Given the intense racism of the period, it is all the more remarkable that an all-white jury found a black man's testimony credible—or was willing to act as if it had.

After the turn of the century the South had to deal with a problem, besides race, that would prove equally difficult: modernization. Led by "New South" advocates like Georgia's Henry Grady, the region encouraged industrialization and welcomed northern capital and northern managers—among them Leo Frank—to come south to participate in the area's transformation.

By 1910, the process was well under way, with results that were not to everyone's liking. Factories brought jobs, and that was good. But the jobs were often in faraway places like Atlanta, and small-town people found themselves worrying about people dear to them—friends, sons and, especially, daughters who had gone to the big city to find work. Parents were concerned that their adolescent children might be too young to deal successfully with all the challenges, including sexual ones, of an adult world.

To limit the exposure of youths to situations in which they were likely to be exploited, most northern states had laws that prohibited children under the age of 14 from working in factories. Georgia's ordinance, typical of the less restrictive regulatory legislation of the southern states, set the age limit at 12. Mary Phagan was 13. When her body was found, the search was on for a murderer who could be made to stand not only for what had happened to Mary, but also for what was happening in Atlanta, Marietta, and throughout the New South.

The Leo Frank case began with the discovery of a murdered girl in the basement of the National Pencil Factory in Atlanta, Georgia, at about 3:30 A.M. on Sunday, April 27, 1913. The night watchman had gone downstairs to use the "colored" toilet, and his flashlight shone on a human heap in the corner. It turned out to be a hefty girl with matted blood on her hair, bruises and lacerations about her face, swollen and blackened eyes, a strong cord and two strips of her underdrawers pulled tightly around her neck, a protruding tongue, distorted hands and fingers and a filthy dress. Sawdust and grime covered both the garment and the human form to such an extent that it was difficult to see immediately whether she was white or black. The night watchman called the police, who arrived within 10 minutes. The sister-in-law of one of the officers worked in the factory, and she was summoned to identify the victim. "Oh my God," she cried, "that's Mary Phagan."

Because the body was found in the basement of the factory, the police went to the home of Leo Frank, its manager, and brought him first to the mortuary to see it and then back to the scene of the crime. He did not recognize the dead girl, but after being given her name he checked his records and acknowledged that she had been paid the previous day, a Saturday. What would be revealed in the newspapers was that since it was Confederate Memorial Day, Mary had put on a fancy dress and silk stockings and had gone downtown to collect her wages. She planned to spend time afterwards watching the Memorial Day parade and having fun with her friends. She reached the factory and was paid at about noon. Thereafter no one claimed to have seen her alive.

As the police searched the basement for clues, they discovered two notes purportedly written by the girl while being murdered! They read:

> Mam that negro hire down here did this i went to make water and he push me down that hole a long tall negro black that hoo it wase long sleam tall negro i wright while play with me

> he said he wood love me land down play like the night witch did it but that long trall black negro did buy his slef

That a person being attacked would have had time to pen such things was, of course, utterly preposterous. However, more plausibly, some police thought they had been written by the murderer to push suspicion onto someone else. That was just about the only correct assumption the police made.

In addition to these scraps of paper, which would thereafter be labeled the "murder notes," observers saw a path from a ladder to where the body was found; another trail from the body to the back door, which was open; blood-stained fingerprints on that door; and a girl's hat and parasol, a ball of twine, and formed human excrement at the bottom of the elevator shaft. When the elevator was later used, it crushed everything at the bottom of the shaft and led to the spread of a foul odor. At the time no one realized how important these clues were and how significant was the crushing of everything at the bottom of the elevator shaft. Police sawed off a board in the door and took the corpse's jacket with the intent of searching for fingerprints, but no report of such tests (if they were indeed done)

Copy of notes found near Mary Phagan's body on the morning of April 27, 1913. Hugh Dorsey, the prosecuting attorney, would later argue that the note came from a pad in Frank's office. During the trial the prosecution made no comment about the location of the pad, but a later investigator suggested that the pieces of paper had to have come from the basement, where the old pads had been stored. (Courtesy, American Jewish Archives)

was ever made. A couple of days later police arrested Jim Conley, the African-American janitor, after an informant observed him washing blood off a shirt; but the police lost the shirt before analyzing the blood.

The nature of the corpse, the circumstances under which the white "little girl" was found, and the kind of work that she had been forced into—laboring in a factory with male supervisors who probably "had their way" with their female employees—aroused a city that had not been so exercised since the 1906 riot in Atlanta.

One of the reasons the populace reacted so violently to the child's death stemmed from changes caused by industrial exploitation. Mary Phagan's family was among those rural dwellers who moved to the city in search of a better life. But a "better life" meant that everyone would have to be gainfully employed; most of the opportunities for children were in the new industrial establishments.

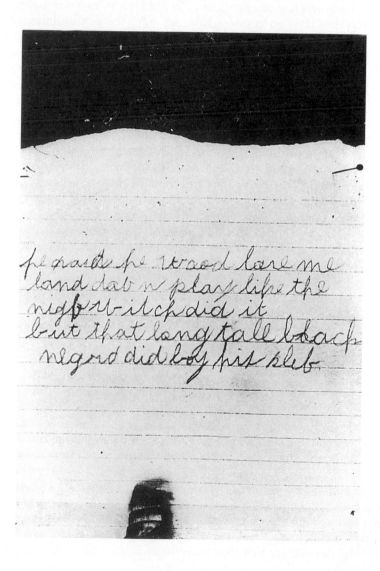

Both Baptist and Methodist preachers (an overwhelming majority of southern workers were either Baptists or Methodists) had warned their parishioners that urbanization and industrialization would sap their strength and corrupt their morals. But the industrialists who denied labor a living wage had no qualms about undermining Christian teachings.

Since the 1880s Atlanta had transformed itself from a sleepy village into an industrial metropolis. As cotton textile mills and other newly formed manufacturing enterprises proliferated, the city's population mushroomed. Census takers who counted fewer than 40,000 people in the city in 1880, found 89,000 people there in 1900. By 1913 an estimated 173,000 persons lived in Atlanta. Despite the growth of the population there were not enough laborers, and the new entrepreneurs, many from the North, hired women and children to perform menial tasks. But wages were low (Mary Phagan had earned 10 cents an hour) and hours were long. Factory workers remained at their tasks from 6 A.M. to 6 P.M. except for Saturdays, when they finished at noon. Not only were the establishments in which they spent most of their days filthy, but safety and health regulations were almost nonexistent, and many a child caught a finger or hand while operating machinery.

Atlanta proved a particularly harsh environment for workers. Thirty-five thousand families had to make do with only 30,000 dwelling units in the city; recreational facilities were inadequate and health hazards abounded. From 1904 to 1911 the number of diphtheria cases in the city increased by 347 percent, typhoid fever increased by 307 percent, and tuberculosis increased by 602 percent. Not surprisingly, Atlanta had one of the nation's highest death rates. Of 388 American cities, only 12 recorded more deaths per 1,000 people than Atlanta. The city also had an appallingly high crime rate and an inadequate police force. More children were arrested in Atlanta in 1905 than in any other city in America; 2 years later, only New York, Chicago, and Baltimore—cities with much larger populations—arrested more children than did Atlanta. That same year, 1907, the city counted 102,000 people and 17,000 arrests. It is no wonder therefore, that the 1913 president pro tem of the Southern Sociological Congress, then meeting in the city, stated, "If social conditions in Atlanta were of the best—if conditions in factories were of the best; and lastly, if children of such tender years were not forced to work, little Mary Phagan would probably never have been murdered." No doubt such thoughts crossed the minds of mourners who were present while they laid the child's body to rest.

At Mary's funeral her mother's wailings interrupted the singing of "Rock of Ages" dozens of times. "The light of my life has been taken. Oh, God," her mother sobbed, "her soul was as pure and as white as her body." Newspapers reported that before the completion of "Rock of Ages," "there was scarcely a dry eye in the whole church." The presiding minister proclaimed that he believed "in the law of forgiveness. Yet I do not see how it can be applied in this case. I pray that this wretch, this devil, be caught and punished according to the man-made, God-sanctioned laws of Georgia."

"The assault and murder of 14-year-old Mary Phagan," The *Atlanta Constitution* reported, "comprise the most revolting crime in the history of Atlanta. Homocide is bad enough. Criminal assault upon [a] woman is worse. When a mere child, a little girl in knee dresses, is the victim of both there are added elements of horror and degeneracy that defy the written word." The editorial went on to denounce the "human beast with more than jungle cruelty and less than jungle mercy" who committed the crime. "The detective force and the entire police authority of Atlanta are on probation in the detection and arrest of this criminal," the editorial warned. "All Atlanta, shocked at a crime that has no local parallel in sheer horror and barbarity," the writer continued, "expects the machinery of the law to be sufficient to meet the call made upon it. If ever the men who ferret crime and uphold the law in Atlanta are to justify their function it must be in apprehending the assailant and murderer of Mary Phagan."

The police had been sloppy in the past and there had been 18 unsolved murders in the city during the previous 2 years; the prosecutor had lost his two previous cases. This time, incompetence would not be tolerated. Law officers felt the city breathing down their necks. One day after the body's discovery newspapers headlined the hiring of Pinkerton detectives. Leo Frank did that to protect the interests of the National Pencil Factory.

With the city in a state of extreme anxiety, the police arrested five alleged culprits on scanty evidence. One was the African-American night watchman who found the body and who was tortured and encouraged to "confess" to the crime. Others included stray men who had had some contact with Mary on Confederate Memorial Day or who were known to have been in the factory on that day.

Policemen even arrested Leo Frank, the factory superintendent. Frank had asked the night watchman to come in earlier than usual on the day of the murder and then asked him to leave and return at his normal time. After Frank left the

These images of the victim, Mary Phagan, reveal something about what her death meant to many southerners. On the left is an unretouched family photo; it appeared in *Watson's Magazine* in March 1915. On the right is an idealized image that appeared in the *Atlanta Georgian* on April 28, 1913, the day after her body was found.

plant he called the night watchman to find out how things were in the factory. He had never done either of those things before. Frank also appeared nervous and "out-of-sorts" after having been awakened Sunday morning, given the news of the murder, and asked to view the body in the morgue.

Other "clues" led police to focus on Frank. He had given Mary her pay on Saturday afternoon and had been, to the best of anyone's knowledge, the last person to have seen her alive. Another factory employee, Monteen Stover, came into Frank's office around noon on the day of the murder but did not see anyone. She said that she waited for about 5 minutes and then left when no one appeared. A couple of days later what appeared to be strands of hair and "blood stains" (which after microscopic examination turned out to be chips of paint) were found in a factory workroom near Frank's office.

At the Coroner's inquest a 14-year-old boy stated that Mary had been afraid of Leo Frank, and that the factory superintendent had flirted with her and had made inappropriate advances. The statement could be neither proven nor dismissed, but it fit in with the prosecution's need, and the public's hunger, for a culprit to be identified. And relationships of the sort described—or imagined—by the boy, were not uncommon in the nation's mills and factories.

The arrest of Frank satisfied a number of inner cravings that many of Atlanta's populace probably had but did not know how to articulate. These yearnings were perhaps best expressed several decades later by the pastor of Mary Phagan's church. "My feelings, upon the arrest of the old negro nightwatchman, were to the effect that this one old negro would be poor atonement for the life of this innocent girl. But, when on the next day, the police arrested a Jew, and a Yankee Jew at that, all of the inborn prejudice against Jews rose up in a feeling of satisfaction, that here would be a victim worthy to pay for the crime." Unbeknownst to himself, Leo Frank had become a symbol.

Although born in Paris, Texas, on April 17, 1884, raised in Brooklyn, New York, and educated at Cornell University, Frank did not think of himself as an unusual person. After graduating from college in 1906 and working in the North for a time, he accepted a job offer from an uncle to come down to Atlanta, buy a share in the uncle's pencil factory, and manage it. In his new city, he met, and in 1910 married, Lucille Selig, daughter of a prominent Atlanta Jewish family; they had no children. In 1912 other lodge members elected him president of the local B'nai B'rith organization.

Although highly regarded by those who knew him well, others viewed Frank from a different light. He was well educated in a city that did not regard education as egalitarian, he was Jewish in a stronghold of Protestant fundamentalism, and he managed a factory in a city where workers were generally ill treated. Once the police fingered him, therefore, every aspect of his being came under analysis by the press and the public. He was a "small, wiry man, wearing eyeglasses of high lens power. He is nervous and apparently high-strung," the *Atlanta Constitution* informed readers. He smoked cigars, dressed neatly, spoke fluently and had a "nervous, billious temperament which at first repels rather than attracts."

Those who knew Frank were appalled as the press continued to publish items and rumors too preposterous to believe but too salacious to ignore. Reading the newspapers in Atlanta during the month following Frank's arrest, one "learned" that Jewish men were allowed to "violate" gentiles but not members of their own faith, that Frank's wife had been about to divorce him, that he had another wife and children in Brooklyn, that he had another wife in Brooklyn whom he had killed, that his wife in Atlanta believed him guilty and therefore did not visit him in jail, that he had had children out of wedlock, that he was a pervert, that he pulled girls off trolleys while they tried to resist him, and that he "was a Mason and the Masons were all for him; that he was a Catholic and they were all for him; that he was a Jew and the Jews were all for him."

The charge of "perversion" probably hurt Frank the most, but no newspaper ever explained what was "perverse" about him. During his trial, prosecutor Hugh Dorsey, who used the Frank case as a stepping-stone to the state governorship, alleged, but never stated, that Frank had had an abnormal relationship with one of the teenaged boys in his employ. Being a Jew, a northerner, and an industrialist, Frank never was able to overcome the feeling in Atlanta that the police had fingered the murderer.

Leo Frank, the defendant, in the foreground. His wife and other people are sitting behind him in the courtroom during the trial. Do you think this picture would lead people to think Frank was "perverse"? (Courtesy, American Jewish Archives)

Contributing to this belief were the assertions of Hugh Dorsey, the solicitor general, that there was no doubt that the right person had been apprehended. Why Dorsey was so keen on this thesis has never been discovered, although speculators have suggested that he believed a conviction in the case would propel his political career, while a defeat would have ended it. Had the police and the solicitor general not made up their minds too early, they could have focused upon a much more likely suspect: Jim Conley, the African-American janitor at the pencil factory, who had been arrested for having been seen washing blood off one of his shirts.

On the day that Dorsey went to the grand jury seeking an indictment against Frank, Conley was being given the third degree in the police station. The janitor had been asked to write copies of the "murder notes," but claimed that he could not write. After hearing someone remark upon this in his presence, Frank told the police that Conley certainly could write, and then the officers had the janitor rewrite the "murder notes." Conley's handwriting matched the notes more closely than that of any of the other suspects, and finally the police, with their crude methods of interrogation, obtained a confession from him.

According to Conley's tale he had been called into Frank's office the day before the murder and Frank had asked him to pen the words found on the papers. Frank allegedly mumbled something like, "Why should I hang." When Conley's account was released to the press, journalists raised two important questions. Why should Frank, or anyone else, have dictated the "murder notes" the day before the event? And why would Frank, who absolutely refused to speak with reporters during his incarceration, have made such a strange statement about hanging? The affidavit simply did not ring true.

Responding to these criticisms, the police requestioned Conley and got another affidavit from him. In this second statement he acknowledged having been in the factory on the day of the murder and claimed that he had stood guard for Frank while the factory superintendent "entertained" a young woman in his office. Then Frank allegedly whistled for Conley to come up, told the janitor he had just committed a murder, and instructed Conley to write the "murder notes." This affidavit did not satisfy the newspapers either, and so a third one had to be obtained, in which Conley claimed to have helped Frank remove the body to the elevator and take it to the basement. Subsequently there was a fourth affidavit, and thereafter the police kept Conley secluded from reporters until after the trial.

That any rational person would believe the bizarre and irreconcilable words of a person who had been brutalized by the police before giving sworn statements is difficult for modern readers to accept. But most people do not follow criminal accusations logically or put the pieces together themselves. A brutal murder had occurred, the police focused upon a Jewish, northern factory owner as the culprit, and almost everyone in Atlanta seemed to think Frank was guilty. Several newspaper reporters had pointed out inconsistencies in the janitor's successive accounts. In response, the police reexamined Conley and encouraged him to assemble a tale that would meet public acceptability.

Frank's trial opened in Atlanta on July 28, 1913. Solicitor General Hugh Dorsey and members of the police assured the public that they had no doubts that they had found the murderer and asked everyone to give them the time necessary to prove their case in court. Frank reportedly had the best southern attorneys money could buy: Luther Z. Rosser and Reuben R. Arnold. The state prosecutor, Hugh Dorsey, had at his side another well-known Georgia attorney, Frank Hooper. The prominence of these men led the *Atlanta Constitution* to speculate that observers would witness the "Greatest Legal Battle in the History of Dixie."

The prosecution began its case with familiar "facts" indicating that blood spots on the floor and strands of Mary Phagan's hair appeared in a workroom near Frank's office. Doctors had established the time of Mary Phagan's death at between 12:00 and 12:15 P.M. Frank claimed earlier that he had been in his office during that 15-minute period.

The prosecution also presented several teenaged female factory workers who swore under oath that the factory superintendent had often looked into the girls' dressing rooms, sometimes touched them, and often looked at them leeringly. Whether these things happened or not is impossible to say since many of the witnesses later changed and rechanged their testimonies. What was important, however, is that these accusations fueled public beliefs that Frank was a pervert and molested innocent females.

All of these witnesses, however, constituted a prelude to Jim Conley, upon whose shoulders rested practically all of the state's case. Conley's statements sounded "glib" and rehearsed to the reporter for the *Atlanta Journal,* but to the spectators in the courtroom and members of the jury, they rang true. The janitor recalled that he had come to the factory early on the day of the murder. Frank had allegedly then sent him on some errands and told Conley when to return because he was expecting a young lady with whom he planned to "chat," and he wanted the janitor to "watch out" for him as he had allegedly done in the past. Frank supposedly had a signal which would indicate to Conley when he should lock the downstairs door and when it should be reopened.

Conley then stated how Mary Phagan had come into the building and had gone up to the second floor office. Then he heard footsteps going back to the metal workroom and shortly thereafter a girl screamed. Right after that, Conley stated, Monteen Stover arrived and went up to Frank's office. "She stayed there a pretty good while," and then left. Soon afterwards Frank allegedly stamped his feet, a signal for Conley to come up to the office. When he got there, the sweeper related,

> Mr. Frank was standing up there at the top of the steps and shivering and trembling and rubbing his hands. He had a little rope in his hands—a long wide piece of cord. His eyes were large and they looked right funny. He looked funny out of his eyes. His face was red. Yes, he had a cord in his hands just like this here cord. After I got up to the top of the steps, he asked me, "Did you see that little girl who passed here just a while ago?" and I told him I saw one come along there and she came back again, and then I saw another one come along there and she hasn't come down, and he says, "Well, that one you say didn't come back down, she came into my office a while ago and wanted to know something about her work in my office and I went back there to see if the little girl's work had come, and I wanted to be with the little girl, and she refused me, and I struck her and I guess I struck her too hard and she fell and hit her head against something, and I don't know how bad she got hurt. Of course you know I ain't built like other men." The reason he said that was, I had

seen him in a position I haven't seen any other man that has got children. I have seen him in the office two or three times before Thanksgiving and a lady was in his office, and she was sitting down in a chair and she had her clothes up to here, and he was down on his knees, and she had her hands on Mr. Frank. I have seen him another time there in packing room with a young lady lying on the table, she was on the edge of the table when I saw her. He asked me if I wouldn't go back there and bring her up so that he could put her somewhere, and he said to hurry, that there would be money in it for me. When I came back, I found the lady lying flat on her back with a rope around her neck. The cloth was also tied around her neck and part of it was under her head like to catch blood. . . . She was dead when I went back there and I came back and told Mr. Frank the girl was dead and he said, "sh-sh!" He told me to go back there by the cotton box, get a piece of cloth, put it around her and bring her up.

Frank then allegedly asked Conley to remove the body to the basement via the elevator, which, Conley claimed, he did before returning the elevator to the second floor. After returning to Frank's office Conley was asked if he could write, and when he answered affirmatively, Frank allegedly dictated the murder notes.

A montage of newspaper drawings during the trial. The man with the cord is Hugh Dorsey, the prosecuting attorney. The man in the chair is Jim Conley, the prosecution's main witness. The three women are sitting in the courtroom. What do their expressions suggest about their interest in the trial? (Courtesy, American Jewish Archives)

Conley told his tale deliberately, and people in the courtroom hung onto his every word. He looked and sounded believable. What's more, Frank's attorneys could not break him. Nor did they comprehend the impact that allegations of Frank's alleged sexual improprieties would have upon jurors and the public. For 16 hours Rosser and Arnold questioned Conley. They were the ones who induced the janitor to talk about other occasions when he had supposedly "watched out" for Frank while the superintendent was alone with the girls and young women in his employ.

Conley made one mistake. During his testimony, he acknowledged that he had defecated at the bottom of the elevator shaft on the morning of the murder. Since police had seen formed stool (along with Mary Phagan's parasol and other personal items) at the bottom of the shaft on the day that Mary's body was found, this meant that the elevator had not been used from the morning before the murder until the next day. Inquiry along this line might have been profitable, but Frank's attorneys did not pursue it. Two years later Governor John M. Slaton would remark on this aspect of the testimony.

Frank's attorneys also erred when they tried to have Conley's testimony about other times that he had "watched out" for Frank stricken from the record. In doing so, they had not only initiated the topic, but encouraged the sweeper to tell what he knew. The prosecutors agreed that the material should not have been admitted, but they also acknowledged that once the defense attorneys had introduced the subject, encouraged Conley to make his remarks, and allowed the jurors to hear the story, it was too late to remove Conley's devastating tales. Although prosecutors never argued that Mary Phagan had been sexually assaulted, it obviously helped their case to have the defense attorneys induce witnesses to talk about other times that the accused may have behaved improperly with his female employees. The presiding judge also recognized that the defense attorneys had miscalculated. He observed that while inappropriate testimony might be expunged from the record, "it is an impossibility to withdraw [it] from the jury's mind."

Conley proved to be an extraordinarily effective witness. Those who heard him speak found the testimony mesmerizing. Bigots, who had no respect for African Americans, concluded that if Frank's allegedly brilliant attorneys, who knew "the negro character thoroughly," could not get the janitor to change his story, then he must have been telling the truth. As one reporter who witnessed the trial later observed, "a man of his mental capacity could have been broken if he was lying."

In his own defense, Leo Frank took the stand on Monday, August 11, shortly after 2 P.M. His appearance had been eagerly awaited since he had refused to speak with newspaper reporters beforehand; this would be the first time he spoke publicly. As he approached the courthouse that afternoon the usually boisterous crowd hushed; as he took the stand to speak, and for the following 4 hours, spectators in the courtroom hung on his every word. Under 1913 Georgia law, a defendant charged in a capital case could not testify under oath or be cross-examined by the prosecutor. An individual could, however, make a statement on his own behalf. Frank chose to avail himself of this opportunity and presented his case strongly, articulately, and without emotion.

Frank claimed that he had been at the factory all morning, had gone home for lunch at about 1 P.M., and had returned to the factory shortly after 3 P.M. He explained that Monteen Stover might not have seen him when she came to the office because he might have been sitting at his desk where he could neither see anyone in the front of the office or be seen if the safe door was open. Alternatively, he suggested that he might have been out of the office for a few moments because of "a call of nature."

Frank's account of his time made it impossible for him to be telling the truth and for Conley also to have been accurate. Reporters had already tried to do what Conley said he had done for Frank: observe the girl entering the building and going up to the second floor, being called up to Frank's office, being asked to remove the body, and then being asked to write the "murder notes." It took them more than an hour to reenact the alleged activities. The Atlanta *Georgian* thought Frank had defended himself well, while the *Constitution* noted that Frank's comments "carried the ring of truth in every sentence."

The jurors, however, had to contend with more than the witnesses and the evidence. The trial took place on the first floor of a building with large, and open, windows. Spectators, both inside and outside of the courtroom, were vocal in their cheers when the prosecution scored a point, and Hugh Dorsey, the prosecutor, was lionized as he entered and left the courtroom each day. Shouts came from the outside, "Hang the Jew," and others claimed that jurors had been warned, "Hang the Jew or we'll hang you."

In summation Frank's attorneys argued that their client was victimized because he was a Jew, and they claimed that he would not even have been put on trial had he been a Christian. Dorsey, in rebuttal before the jury, denied that Frank's religion had entered into consideration, but he went on to state that while some Jews such as former Prime Minister Benjamin Disraeli of England and former Confederate Cabinet member Judah P. Benjamin had praiseworthy accomplishments, other Jews "sink to the lowest depths of degradation."

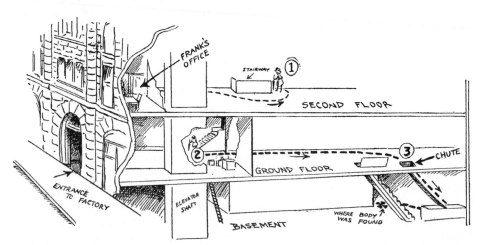

A cutaway drawing of the Atlanta, Georgia, pencil factory where Mary Phagan was murdered. The drawing was made from a model of the factory used by the defense at Leo Frank's trial. (The *Atlanta Journal*, August 10, 1913)

The trial lasted 4 weeks, yet it took the jurors less than 4 hours to find the defendant guilty. Presiding Judge Leonard Roan had anticipated a riot if Frank had been found innocent, and in the presence of the jury asked the sheriff how the crowds would be handled under such a circumstance. Georgia's governor made plans to call out the National Guard. Frank's attorneys were asked to keep their client away from the court when the jury rendered its verdict. They agreed. The judge had also decided not to sentence the convicted murderer at the time that the jury provided its decision.

After hearing the jury's finding and the judge's resolution to postpone sentencing, Hugh Dorsey left the courtroom. According to the *Atlanta Constitution*, "Three muscular men" immediately slung him "on their shoulders and passed him over the heads of the crowd across the street to his office. With hat raised and tears coursing down his cheeks, the victor in Georgia's most noted criminal battle was tumbled over a shrieking throng that wildly proclaimed its admiration. Few will live to see another such demonstration."

The next day Judge Roan secretly convened the principals in the case and sentenced Frank to hang. This had been done quietly and without fanfare because Roan feared the consequences if Frank's public appearance became known. A north Georgia newspaperman later wrote, "There is no use mincing words when a human life is at stake. If the jury in the Frank case had brought in a verdict of 'not guilty,' the defendant would have been lynched."

As soon as the trial ended, Frank's attorneys made plans for an appeal. They also sought assistance from Louis Marshall, president of the American Jewish Committee, an organization primarily dedicated to the preservation of civil rights for Jews. Marshall recognized that the matter would have to be dealt with quietly, behind the scenes, and with southerners, rather than Jews, appearing in the forefront seeking justice. Behind the scenes, Marshall and other Jews were willing to help with money, legal assistance, and careful publicity. But they were adamant in stating that whatever assistance Frank received must come from individuals; they did not want it to appear that any Jewish organization was assisting a Jew who had been convicted of criminal activity.

Although Frank's Georgian attorneys sought Marshall's assistance, they did not take his advice. He argued that in their appeal to the state's Supreme Court, they should raise federal questions about whether there had been due process of law if the defendant was forced to absent himself from the court. His attorneys did not do this. They thought they would easily win a new trial because in their first appeal the trial judge, Leonard Roan, stated that he had thought about the case more than any other he had ever tried and was not certain whether Frank was guilty. "The jury was convinced," Roan concluded, and he felt it was his duty, therefore, to deny the motion for a new trial.

By a 4 to 2 vote, the Georgia Supreme Court denied the appeal. The majority did not think that Roan's personal opinion warranted a retrial or that the demonstrations favorable to the prosecution witnessed by the jury sufficed to reverse the original decision. Subsequently new evidence was found which indicated that some of the jurors might have been antisemitic, that the "murder notes" had been written on old note pads found only in the basement, and that many of the prosecution witnesses might have been coerced into giving false testimony. But these tidbits also failed to induce the Georgia Supreme Court to order a new trial. At that point Frank's attorneys sought redress from the United States Supreme Court in Washington.

Twice Frank's attorneys petitioned the Supreme Court. Once they did so on the ground that Frank's involuntary absence from the courtroom at the time the jury rendered its verdict constituted lack of due process of law; the Supreme Court rejected that position, arguing that his attorneys should have raised the issue earlier, when petitioning for a retrial in Georgia. The second time, however, it was brought to the Supreme Court's attention that Frank had involuntarily absented himself from the courtroom *because of the fear of mob violence,* and that this constituted lack of due process. This point appealed to the Supreme Court, and the justices voted to hold hearings and render a decision.

Ultimately the Supreme Court, by a vote of 7 to 2, rejected Frank's claims. Some of the bases for the decision were technical but one was quite clear: Frank's attorneys' failure to raise the issue of his absence from the court near its end should have been noted in the first appeal. "Because it was waived by his failure to raise the objection in due season when fully cognizant of the fact," the majority rejected that argument as relevant. The members of the majority claimed that Frank had received every opportunity to defend himself that the courts could provide.

The two best-known and most highly regarded members of the Supreme Court at that time, Oliver Wendell Holmes and Charles Evans Hughes, dissented. They focused on one issue: popular influence upon the jurors. "Mob law," they wrote, "does not become due process of law by securing the assent of a terrorized jury."

With all of the judicial appeals over, Frank's attorneys presented their evidence to the Georgia Prison Commission, which would take the petition, vote on it, and make a recommendation to the governor. The Prison Commission had not only the trial record, but the records of the judicial appeals and the new data that Frank's attorneys had unearthed. But they divided 2 to 1, with the majority opposed to clemency.

Frank's final hope lay with Governor John M. Slaton, who not only reviewed the records carefully but also took the unusual step of visiting the pencil factory where the murder had been committed to inspect the building's layout. Since the prosecution had asserted that the murder had been committed in the second-floor workroom near Frank's office, and the defense had argued that the crime had taken place in the basement, the Governor wanted to familiarize himself with these areas as well as the elevator.

The governor devoted several days to this case and then, before announcing his decision, had Frank removed from the county jail in Atlanta to the state prison in Milledgeville. Slaton then announced that he was commuting Frank's sentence to life imprisonment. "Feeling as I do about this case," he wrote, "I would be a murderer if I allowed that man to hang."

The governor then elaborated upon his decree. He focused upon the human excrement found in the basement the day after the murder. If Conley were telling the truth, he would have taken the girl's body to the basement in the elevator on Saturday. But items belonging to Mary Phagan and formed feces were seen in the shaft on Sunday morning. Because Conley had acknowledged defecating in the elevator shaft on Saturday morning, his tale about the use of the elevator on Saturday afternoon had to be false. If the elevator had not been used, the governor concluded, then Conley's entire account had to be discounted. And without Conley's testimony there was insufficient evidence to convict Frank.

The governor also noted that Mary Phagan had been smashed in the head. But no blood appeared in the workroom, on the floor nearby, in the elevator, or on the steps leading from the second to the first floors. Blood had been found, however, along with sawdust and grime, in Mary's nostrils, which meant that she had met her doom in the basement, where those ingredients appeared in abundance. Slaton also accepted Frank's attorneys' argument that because the date listed at the top of the "murder notes" read "190__," the pages had to have been ripped from old records stored in the basement. The governor concluded that he could not allow Frank to hang on the basis of the evidence that he had seen. Elaborating upon his actions a few days later Governor Slaton observed:

> Two thousand years ago another Governor washed his hands of a case and turned over a Jew to a mob. For two thousand years that Governor's name has been accursed. If today another Jew were lying in his grave because I had failed to do my duty I would all through life find his blood on my hands and would consider myself an assassin through cowardice.

Privately, Slaton confided to friends that he thought Frank innocent. He assumed that once tempers in Atlanta calmed down, one of his successors would be asked to review the case again, would recognize that Frank was innocent, and would probably give Frank a full pardon. Slaton thought that if he had pardoned Frank, there would have been a lynching. The governor was probably right. What he did not realize at the time, however, was that his own life would also be in jeopardy.

The popular reaction to Slaton's decision was explosive. Mobs attacked Jewish homes and stores in several Georgia towns and cities. The governor was hanged in effigy and denounced as "King of the Jews and Georgia's traitor forever." A lynching party tried to storm the governor's mansion, but state guards held them back. Slaton's term ended 4 days after he announced his decision and during that entire time, until he was escorted to a train leaving from Atlanta on June 26, 1915, he was heavily guarded. People wondered if he would ever return to Georgia. He did—at the end of World War I—but he never again ran for public office.

Commutation and life on the prison farm may have given Frank a new sense of hope, but it was short lived. After only 1 month in Milledgeville, a fellow prisoner slit Frank's throat with a butcher knife. The culprit claimed he had been called "from on high" to slay the Jew. Frank was quickly taken to the prison hospital and was recovering nicely from the near fatal wound when, on August 15, 1915, some of the "best men" from Marietta, Georgia, Mary Phagan's hometown, drove across the state and took Frank from his bed. They drove him back the 175 miles to where they came from and hung him from a tree on the morning of August 16. The Dean of the Atlanta Theological Seminary described the lynch mob as "a sifted band of men, sober, intelligent, of established good name and character—good American citizens."

This "sifted band of . . . sober, intelligent" citizens had been planning the lynching since Governor Slaton had pardoned Frank in May. They included a clergyman, two former justices of the Georgia Supreme Court, and an ex-sheriff. These men believed that Frank had been given every legal opportunity to reverse the original sentence, and they were well aware that all of the courts had refused his appeals. They despised Slaton for commuting Frank's sentence and for allowing him to live, even though the Georgia state constitution gave the governor the power of commutation and/or pardon. In the minds of the lynchers, justice had been undermined by the governor, and they felt that they had to take the law into their own hands.

As Frank was driven back to Marietta, he convinced two of the men who rode in the same car with him that he was innocent. When all of the cars converged in Marietta, just before dawn, he convinced several others as well. But four individuals wanted the execution to take place, day was breaking, and the kidnappers felt the need to finish their task before other townspeople began their daily chores. The lynchers feared being discovered. So they quickly tied the knot around Frank's neck, flung the rope over the branch of a sturdy oak tree, and secured it in place. They then lifted Frank onto a table, saw to it that his feet barely touched the platform below, and then removed the table. As they left, they saw Frank swaying in the wind.

Men standing around the body of Leo Frank after lynching. They are from Marietta, Georgia. Notice Frank's hands and neck. (Courtesy, American Jewish Archives)

The lynching met with the approval of most Georgians. The local newspaper editorialized, "We regard the hanging of Leo M. Frank . . . an act of law abiding citizens." Two years later Lucian Lamar Knight, one of the most prominent of the state's historians, wrote, "There is something inherently fine in the passionate desire of a people to keep inviolate the honor of womanhood and to visit swift punishment upon a wretch who dares to stain the purity of a child's life."

After the lynching the men who committed the evil deed lost their sense of purpose. But soon Colonel William J. Simmons stepped into the vacuum as he sought to revive what he regarded as a hallowed southern institution dedicated to preserving women's honor, exalting Anglo-Saxon superiority, and reaffirming the Protestant fundamentalist faith. The nucleus for this new group was Frank's lynching party, then known as the "Knights of Mary Phagan." One night in the fall of 1915, they joined Simmons at Stone Mountain, just east of Atlanta, where together they proclaimed a revived Ku Klux Klan.

AN INTERPRETATION

In retrospect, what can we say about Leo Frank? That he was innocent there can be no doubt. He was in the wrong place at the wrong time and thus became a victim of circumstances, because someone "important" or "prominent" was needed to pay for the death of Mary Phagan. The few bits of evidence used to connect him to the crime were clearly insufficient to either arrest or convict him.

What motivated Hugh Dorsey and the police is impossible to say. They could have focused upon Jim Conley, for whom there were much better reasons to convict. Why they failed to do so is not clear. Perhaps they truly believed Frank guilty; perhaps Dorsey and the police were too committed to Frank's guilt to alter their original positions; perhaps a black janitor would not have sufficed as the perpetrator of such a vicious crime. Who knows?

Had Frank been a Protestant southerner from a prominent family he would not have been a serious suspect. But as an alien Jew he emerged as a symbol of the exploitative industrialist who "ruined" the South and took unfair advantage of its workers. He could be made to pay for all the perceived crimes against southern society. When Frank emerged as the prosecution's prime suspect, he had few defenders in Atlanta outside of his immediate circle of friends and family. People were too quick to believe rumors, police assertions, and Conley's frequently changed affidavits.

Once the community made up its mind about Frank's guilt, no jury could have rendered a verdict of not guilty. The jurors had to live with their neighbors long after the trial ended. Lawyers and others familiar with the judicial system know that juries almost never go against the sentiments of the communities with which they identify. Frank was convicted in the eyes of Atlantans long before the trial began. Conley's testimony, and the defense attorneys' inability to break his story, sealed Frank's fate. Evidence to the contrary of the will of the majority was simply not considered seriously by members of the jury.

In 1982 an elderly man came forward and told a Tennessee reporter that he had witnessed Conley carrying Mary Phagan's body to the cellar on the day of the murder. Conley allegedly told him, "If you tell anyone about this, I'll kill you." The 13-year-old boy ran home and told his mother of the incident. She advised him to keep his mouth shut and not to get involved. Coming as it did in his 82nd year, the man's tale, although it reinforced the views of those who had always thought Frank to be innocent, failed to convince those who thought him guilty. This is not surprising because studies have shown that whereas there is a negative correlation between evidence and belief (−.03), there is a significant correlation between desire and belief (+.88). In other words, people believe what they want to believe and rarely allow factual evidence to disturb firmly held convictions. Therefore, we might safely conclude that no amount of new information suffices to change people's long-held views on an emotionally charged topic.

Leo Frank was murdered in 1915, more than three-quarters of a century ago. But his trial and lynching stand as a reminder that anyone, however honest and sincere, can be caught up and victimized by a swirl of events well beyond an individual's control. Frank was the culprit that the prosecution and the police needed. He was also a scapegoat for the ills that beset an emerging and troubled industrial society.

Sources: The Leo Frank case involved broader issues and greater complexities than could be dealt with in a short narrative. For more detail, and other interpretations, see Leonard Dinnerstein, *The Leo Frank Case* (Athens: University of Georgia Press, 1987), Harry Golden, *A Little Girl Is Dead* (Cleveland: The World Publishing Co., 1967), C. Vann Woodward, *Tom Watson: Agrarian Rebel* (New York: Rinehart & Co., 1938), Charles and Louise Samuels, *Night Fell on Georgia* (New York: Dell, 1956), and Albert S. Lindeman, *The Jew Accused* (Cambridge: Cambridge University Press, 1991). An essay focusing on the city of Atlanta and its problems at the turn of the century is Leonard Dinnerstein, "Atlanta in the Progressive Era: A Dreyfus Affair in Georgia," in Frederick Cople Jaher, ed., *The Age of Industrialism: Essays in Social Structure and Cultural Values* (New York: The Free Press, 1968), pp. 127–157. Steve Oney wrote a brief article summarizing the Frank case, "The Lynching of Leo Frank," *Esquire* 104 (September, 1985): 90–104, whereas Nancy MacLean wrote a gender-based analysis of the case, "The Leo Frank Case Reconsidered: Gender and Sexual Politics in the Making of Reactionary Populism," *The Journal of American History* 78 (December, 1991): 917–948.

8

THE BLACK SOX SCANDAL

RONALD STORY

In the fall of 1919, key members of the pennant-winning Chicago White Sox conspired with gamblers to throw the World Series to the Cincinnati Reds. Two years later, following a trial in which the players were found innocent, a stunned nation learned from baseball czar Kenesaw Mountain Landis that eight members of the team, including Shoeless Joe Jackson, one of the greatest natural hitters ever to play the game, were banned from organized baseball for life.

As harsh as the Commissioner's decision seemed, there were many who found it justified. After all, most of the eight were clearly guilty—in fact, several had signed confessions—and many Americans no doubt believed that the national pastime could be maintained in its pastoral purity only by expunging the offending players. That interpretation of the "Black Sox" scandal seems logical enough, and it certainly accords with professional baseball's current image as an impeccably "clean" game, played on artificial turf rather than grass, and under domes that shelter fans and players from the weather itself.

But, as Ronald Story's vivid narrative suggests, baseball wasn't like that at all—not in 1919, anyway. The sport had a pastoral quality, to be sure; but the men who played it—and the men who watched it—were an unruly bunch that drank, swore, and, fatefully, gambled. Against this background, Landis's ruling takes on a different meaning. Far from being an attempt to reclaim for baseball its own lost virtue, the ruling was part of a larger process through which the game was "modernized" and made compatible with the developing consumer society. Through advertising, public relations, lavish department stores, Hollywood movies, and sports spectacles, Americans were being encouraged to think of themselves less as employees, with bonds to their workplaces and other workers, and more as consumers, dependent for identity and happiness on the quality and quantity of their purchases.

While Landis presented his decision as if it were a neutral and moral one, the ruling was, in fact, highly political. It could not touch the gamblers who paid the athletes. Moreover, it did not acknowledge the responsibilities of White Sox owner Charles Comiskey, who, like other owners of baseball teams, dominated and controlled his players just as factory owners of the day dominated and controlled the lives of wage earners. In retrospect, Landis might be understood as sport's version of Woodrow Wilson, whose two-term presidency was ending just as the scandal was breaking: puritanical, moralistic, and convinced of his own rectitude, yet pursuing policies that were very much those of a particular economic class.

*Conflicts between classes and ethnic groups are central to the American
historical experience, and never more so than they were in the extraordinary year of
1919. A militant labor movement, emboldened by the Russian Revolution of 1917,
launched dramatic strikes in the Seattle shipyards, among Boston policemen, and—
only days before the World Series opened—in the steel mills. Apparently convinced
that the nation was about to be overrun by Bolsheviks, Wilson's Attorney General
arrested thousands of immigrant aliens and Communists in a series of dramatic raids
undertaken in total disregard of elemental civil liberties. In late October, Congress
passed the Volstead Act, providing the enforcement apparatus for the Eighteenth
Amendment on prohibition—a measure that came down especially hard on the urban
working class. When the baseball season opened the following April, fans had to go
without their usual beer.*

*The Black Sox scandal took place in a climate broadly shaped by these events.
Like the nation, the White Sox players were polarized by class and ethnicity. In the
intensely political atmosphere of 1919, some of them decided that they had been
victimized by an unfair employer, just like other workers. Landis would have none
of this. His decision not only ignored the baseball player's claim to the status of
worker, but also accelerated baseball's evolution from a rowdy representation of male,
working-class culture to the respectable, middle-class, family game that modern
Americans know so well. By the fall of 1921, Landis had put baseball back on the
straight-and-narrow and Congress had passed an important law severely restricting
immigration. Baseball, and the nation, were headed full speed into the homogenized
world of the mid-twentieth century.*

C incinnati was astir on October 1st, 1919, as seldom before. The Cincinnati
Reds, champions of the National League, winners of their first pennant since
joining the fledgling league back in 1876, were getting ready to play game one of
the World Series. It would be their first Series ever, and therefore their first Series game at home, so that even though it was Wednesday and a workday, people
began streaming toward Redland Park long before noon to cheer the boys on to
victory that afternoon.

The Reds faced a formidable foe: the Chicago White Sox, winners of the
American League flag 2 of the last 3 years. The White Sox sported a fearsome attack—leftfielder Joe Jackson batted .351, Happy Felsch in center field slammed
52 extra-base hits, second baseman Eddie Collins hit .319 with 33 stolen bases;
and a balanced attack—seven of the eight regulars hit .275 or better, seven stole
10 or more bases, five scored or drove in at least 80 runs. In the field the Sox featured the flashy Collins at second base, a strong-armed Felsch in the outfield, fiery
catcher Ray Schalk, tough third baseman Buck Weaver, and the remarkable Chick
Gandil, who led American League (AL) first basemen by making just three errors
all season! As for pitching, future Hall-of-Famer Red Faber had a sore arm. But
that still left Eddie Cicotte at 29 wins and 7 losses, Lefty Williams at 23-11, and
rookie Dickie Kerr, 13-7 in two-thirds of a season, and a manager in feisty Kid
Gleason who knew (or thought he knew) how to use them.

But the Reds were plenty good. They had won the pennant by nine full games
over John McGraw's tough New York Giants, and they considered themselves the

probable winners of this Series. And so did the 31,000 ticketholders for game one and the tens of thousands of others who crammed every Cincinnati hotel lobby, cigar store, barbershop, and saloon to talk baseball and bet on the hometown favorites.

Cincinnati's backers, to be sure, were not getting the odds they might have expected, given Chicago's reputation. As of the morning of October 1, in fact, the odds were downright bad, only 5-6 on the Reds to take the nine-game Series, down from 2-1 a few days earlier and even money only yesterday. Lots of Reds backers bet anyway, despite the odds. More should have. Because what they did not know, and what underlay the shifting odds, was that eight Chicago players had agreed to "throw" the 1919 World Series.

It began in early September when Chick Gandil, the fancy-fielding White Sox first baseman, telephoned Joseph "Sport" Sullivan, a Boston bookie and gambler, to set up a meeting at the Hotel Buckminster, where the Chicago players were staying during their series with the Red Sox. A flashy operator with good connections, Sullivan earned a fair living making book on sports events, especially ball games. Gandil had fed him tips on how various games might go since Chick's Washington Senators days before 1916. He knew Chick was a rough customer who lived on the edge of honesty. But that hardly prepared him for Gandil's current proposition—that for $80,000, the White Sox would "bag" the upcoming World Series. Initially incredulous, then excited, Sullivan hastily closed the deal with Gandil in principle and started to scout around for the money.

Betting on baseball had been common enough since baseball became the most popular American spectator sport after the Civil War. One reason for the standardization of playing rules was to make games easier to handicap. With gambling, however, often went corruption. Gamblers sometimes paid players to lose particular games; sometimes promoters or saloonkeepers paid players to divide a series of games in order to keep interest, and therefore attendance, high. In 1877 four major league players were expelled for throwing games, but gambling accusations and investigations remained commonplace throughout the nineteenth century. Because baseball retained more than a few traces of the brawling, sensual, hard-drinking nineteenth-century male subculture from which it originally grew, there was undoubtedly much fire behind the smoke.

The actual fixing of games supposedly declined after 1900, but baseball betting pools thrived, particularly after the closing of the nation's racetracks during World War I, and players were still suspected of "lying down" in exchange for money, whiskey, or women, or under the threat of violence. "Prince" Hal Chase, a graceful first baseman with five big-league teams, was supposedly behind countless thrown games. But league investigations of Chase and others were little more than perfunctory whitewashes. After all, accusations against one player might lead to accusations—and penalties— against many others and to the wreckage of valuable big-league franchises. So reporters, players, and owners, whatever they might think, kept quiet in public.

Nevertheless, Gandil's proposition was startling. First, it involved the World Series. There would be big money around but also much publicity; and therefore, much risk of detection. And because sports fans, and Americans generally, were so passionate about the Series, if things went awry the penalties might involve more than whitewash. Also, here the players, not the gamblers, seemed to be taking the initiative—and not just players, but members of the best and most famous team in baseball.

There were reasons, to be sure. For one thing, the owner of the White Sox, Charles Comiskey—"Commy" himself, the famous "Old Roman"—paid his ballplayers poorly. A son of Irish Chicago, an outstanding player-manager with the fabled St. Louis Browns of the 1880s, the only ex-player to become sole owner of a big-league team, a popular hero of South Chicago where Comiskey Park was located, Comiskey's substantial fortune came entirely from his ownership of the White Sox club, which he had established in 1900 at the time he was helping found the American League. In the process of becoming rich Comiskey had gained two reputations: one for generosity with fans and reporters, many of whom touted him for mayor, and one for tight-fistedness with his players. After a war-shortened 1918 season, Comiskey had capped salaries unusually tightly, except for players like Eddie Collins who were on multiyear contracts. He then added insult to injury by distributing only $3 per day in meal money when the team was on the road, the lowest stipend in the league, and deducting the cost of laundering the players' uniforms from the players' paychecks. When attendance unexpectedly boomed in 1919, the White Sox players nearly struck in July to protest continued low pay in the midst of sky-high revenues.

There was also a festering factionalism on this ball club. One clique centered around Eddie Collins, a college graduate whose $14,500 salary was twice that of any other player, creating much resentment. Near Collins could usually be found catcher Ray Schalk, an intense competitor; pitchers Red Faber, a college man like Collins, and Dickie Kerr, the rookie; and a part-time outfielder and leadoff batter, Shano Collins. The chief antagonists of this Collins faction were Gandil, a rough ex-copper miner and boxer from California; Swede Risberg, the shortstop, another Californian and even tougher, reputedly, than Gandil; and Risberg's buddy, utility infielder Fred McMullin. Around this trio were ranged at various times the club's two Southerners, Jackson and Williams; plus Felsch and Weaver, good-time Charlies who enjoyed an occasional drink and roll of the dice; plus the team elder, Cicotte.

There may have been a class factor in this factionalism. The Collins group and others on the club came mostly from small-town America and had a secondary education or better. Jackson, by contrast, was an illiterate Carolina millhand, Felsch a Milwaukee carpenter, Weaver a mechanic from the Pennsylvania coal country, Cicotte a copper miner like Gandil. There may also have been an ethnic and regional factor. The Collins group included no one who was not of English, German, or Irish extraction or from the Northeast or Midwest; their adversaries included two French-Canadians and a Scandinavian as well as two Southerners. Perhaps reflecting this divergent background, several members of the Gandil clique had supported an unsuccessful effort in the early 1910s to organize a players union.

This gang of eight was probably less a tight clique than a coalition of "hard livers" shaped by grudges against Comiskey off the field and Eddie Collins on it. To be sure, the faction's hard living—drinking, gambling, fighting, flashy clothes—would have been less distinctive a generation earlier when baseball was closer to its roughhouse roots than it was in 1919, or at least less than the Collins group was. At any rate the factions existed—for one 2-week period Risberg actually refused to throw the ball to Collins even to start a double play! And Gandil knew it.

Chick Gandil's first recruit was Eddie Cicotte. Gandil had to have Cicotte, who would pitch game one and start at least two additional games in a long Series. Cicotte listened. He'd just had a great season, but at 35 years of age he was nearing the end of his career, and he faced stiff mortgage payments on a new Michigan farm with no financial cushion beneath him. Cicotte agreed, for $10,000 in advance. Next came Lefty Williams, certain to start game two and another likely three-game pitcher if the Series dragged on. Lefty hesitated, then agreed because Cicotte was in, again for the going rate of $10,000. There was also Swede Ris-

Charles Comiskey, owner and president of the Chicago White Sox, with his crosstown counterpart, William Veeck of the Chicago Cubs, 1920. A wealthy man who affected, like Veeck, the expensive hats and three-piece suits favored by tycoons of the day, Comiskey was never comfortable among Chicago's established families, preferring the rougher company of journalists, politicians, and baseball magnates such as Veeck, an ex-sportswriter as well as Cubs president. At one time the most powerful owner in the American League, Comiskey seemed to be on the verge of founding a baseball dynasty until the Black Sox scandal destroyed his team. (Chicago Historical Society)

berg, whose glove at short would be a Series key; Comiskey paid Risberg under $4,000, one of the lowest salaries of any starting American Leaguer. The Swede not only came in but insisted that his pal McMullin be included, too. Gandil agreed. Finally, with pitching and defense in tow, Gandil went after Buck Weaver, Joe Jackson, and Hap Felsch, the three-four-five hitters in the lineup. Jackson, nick-named "Shoeless" from an incident early in his career when he removed his spikes during a game because they were new and hurt his feet, came in for the money and because his friend and fellow Southerner, Williams, was in. When Felsch and Weaver finally agreed, the scheme was complete. Chick had worked not only the grudges against Comiskey but the team factionalism—and in doing so had the play-ers he needed to work the fix.

Because the players never discussed just who would do what to lose which Series games, this crucial part of the scheme remained murky to the last. Things were equally murky, for now, on the gamblers' end. Not only had Sport Sullivan failed as yet to line up the $80,000, another "operator"—a former big-league pitcher named Sleepy Bill Burns—had rolled into New York fresh from a suc-cessful speculation in Texas oil leases. When Burns heard rumors of a Series fix, he contacted Eddie Cicotte, an old baseball friend, who confirmed the rumor but said no money had changed hands. Burns now determined, with the help of a cou-ple of cronies, to raise the money himself, only to discover that Gandil was now demanding $100,000 rather than $80,000.

In 1919, $100,000 was a considerable sum, especially for a small-time plunger like Sleepy Bill Burns. So for help Burns turned to the one man sure to have that kind of money on hand: Arnold Rothstein—known as "AR," the "Big Bankroll"—a New York sports gambler and hoodlum with intimate ties to New York City politicians and police and a luxurious gambling establishment in Saratoga, New York. AR discussed the fix with Burns, then, on reflection, in-formed Burns that he would not underwrite so risky a scheme. In actual fact, he had decided to do precisely that—except that he would work through Sport Sul-livan, whom he knew and respected, rather than through Burns, whom he did not. Rothstein gave Sullivan $40,000 to give to the players prior to the Series opener, and had another $40,000 placed in a safe in Chicago for distribution when the Series was over. Sport found the $40,000 advance money (which was all he had access to) a grievous temptation—so much so that, thinking he had the play-ers on a string anyway, he bet $30,000 of it, on the Reds to win, for himself. He then gave the remaining $10,000 to Chick Gandil, with a promise of "more later."

This was far less than Gandil expected or than he had promised the players, who were getting jittery. With the Series mere hours away, Cicotte still refused to throw game one without cash in hand; so Sullivan's $10,000 had to go to him. But Williams now told Gandil he wanted out, and so did Weaver. Jackson told him he wanted $20,000 instead of $10,000, then told Kid Gleason, the Sox manager, that he didn't feel like playing at all. Obviously no one was happy. For-tunately for Gandil (or so it seemed) Bill Burns had decided, even without Roth-stein's participation, that he, too, would try to play the fix by promising to pay the players money after each game they lost from the profits he would make by bet-ting on that game. With money coming from two directions, from Sullivan and from Burns, Gandil and the others believed they would still get something significant. In any case, several of them had placed bets of their own on the Cincinnati Reds. By now Cincinnati was alive with rumors of a Series fix, and a swarm of gamblers was now in evidence, including a St. Louis syndicate and a gaggle of Chicagoans that numbered the likes of Nick "The Greek" Dandalos, songster George M. Cohan, and Big Tim O'Leary, owner of the biggest speakeasy in the stockyards district. The odds had swung so far toward the Reds that gamblers were trying to "fix" the Reds, too! The Black Sox were in deep, maybe over their heads—maybe too deep to get out.

As for the Series, it was an insiders' game all the way. In the bottom of the first inning, Eddie Cicotte hit the Cincinnati leadoff man squarely in the back with his second pitch—a prearranged sign to Arnold Rothstein, who was watching the game's progress on an electric scoreboard in a New York hotel lobby, that the fix was on. Rothstein promptly added another $100,000 to the $200,000 he already had down on the Reds to win the Series. In the fourth inning, with the score tied 1-1, Cicotte booted a double play ball and started grooving his pitches, and by the time the inning was over the Reds had a 6-1 lead that would lengthen to 9-1

The most famous practitioner of the slash-and-run "inside baseball" favored by the White Sox of 1919 was the great Ty Cobb, seen here hook-sliding into third base. It was a game well-suited for old-fashioned rough-cut men such as Buck Weaver and Chick Gandil (who fought Cobb twice on the field) and for old-fashioned ballparks where fans sat close enough to the action to respond to its nuances and intensity. (National Baseball Library, Cooperstown, NY)

by game's end. Game two was tighter. Lefty Williams allowed just four hits while Chicago got ten. But the Reds combined two of their hits with three Williams bases on balls for a three-run fourth inning. Final score: 4-2. Arnold Rothstein by now had another $85,000 on the Reds.

The teams headed for Chicago and games three through five under thick clouds of suspicion, not only from the press corps—Ring Lardner of the *Chicago Tribune* strolled through the train singing "I'm Forever Blowing Ballgames"—but from Ray Schalk, who jumped Lefty Williams under the stands after game two; from Kid Gleason, who publicly tongue-lashed Cicotte and Risberg and swung at Chick Gandil; and from Charles Comiskey himself, who was tipped by a Chicago gambling acquaintance about what might be happening. Not that much money had materialized. Sleepy Bill Burns managed to come up with a measly $10,000, which he passed on to an enraged Gandil (who stuffed it in the lining of his suitcase) along with the brazen suggestion that maybe the Sox should win game three to improve the odds! Gandil, incensed, told Burns the fix was still in all the way. That afternoon he handled 15 chances without an error and drove in two runs while Swede Risberg made 10 flawless plays, stroked a long triple, and scored. Little Dickie Kerr tossed a three-hit shutout. Chicago won 3-0. Sleepy Bill lost his shirt betting on the Reds and bowed out of the Series doings.

This Chicago victory and the roles that Chick Gandil and Swede Risberg had played in it disturbed Sport Sullivan enough to prompt a call to Gandil, who told him that the group of eight was no longer bought. Sullivan panicked, quickly scraped together $20,000, which he wired to Gandil. Chick split it evenly among Risberg, Felsch, Williams, and Jackson. Gandil and Cicotte had their $10,000 already. McMullin would have to wait. Weaver, who in Chick's view was playing to win, was asking for, and would get, nothing.

Game four was a near-repeat of game two. Cicotte allowed only five hits, but two came in the fifth inning along with two errors by Cicotte to allow two runs. The White Sox collected a meager three hits. Final score: Cincinnati 2, Chicago 0. And so with game five, the third straight before standing-room-only Comiskey Park crowds. Lefty Williams gave up four hits, but three came in the sixth inning along with errors by Felsch and Risberg, enabling the Reds to score four times. The Sox again had just three hits. Final score: Cincinnati 5, Chicago 0.

Gandil expected another $20,000 from Sport Sullivan to be waiting when the clubs arrived back in Cincinnati on October 7 for game six. When it wasn't, there was more rage and yet another change of heart. Dickie Kerr did not sparkle the way he had in game three, but Weaver, Jackson, and Felsch went 7-for-14 with three doubles, and Gandil drove in a run in the ninth for a 5-4 victory. The next day Jackson and Felsch drove in two runs each, and Cicotte held the Reds to a lone tally. Chicago pulled within a game of Cincinnati in the Series with two possible games remaining, both in Chicago where the White Sox, apparently back on track and with Lefty Williams up, would have a home field advantage.

Arnold Rothstein had seen enough. With nearly $400,000 riding on this Series, he was in no mood to take chances. AR summoned Sport Sullivan to New York and told him to make absolutely certain that Chicago lost game eight, preferably in the early innings. There could be no mistake; matters were critical. Sullivan, duly frightened, put a call into one "Harry F." of Chicago, a hired gunman.

Sport told Harry F. to make sure Lefty Williams threw tomorrow's game in the first inning, even if it meant threatening to murder his wife, and sent him $500 advance money.

Harry F. did what he was paid to do. Kid Gleason sent Williams to the mound after delivering a clubhouse harangue in which he threatened all sellouts with "iron"—meaning a gun. But the Kid's words were just words; the gunman's iron was real. Buck Weaver singled and doubled, Shoeless Joe Jackson homered and doubled, Chick Gandil tripled, and Ray Schalk made the only error, all before another big Comiskey Park crowd. But Lefty had made his decision. Disregarding Schalk's signals, he threw batting-practice fastballs down the heart of the plate to the Reds batters, who feasted on them, then feasted some more on Gleason's parade of journeyman relievers. Final score: Cincinnati 10, Chicago 5. Arnold Rothstein's money was safe. So was Sport Sullivan's—along with Lefty Williams and his wife.

One bit of unfinished business remained. Sullivan went out to Chicago to give Chick Gandil the $40,000 that Rothstein had had sequestered in the safe. Of this amount, Gandil gave $10,000 to Risberg and $5,000 to McMullin. The remainder he kept, unbeknownst to his accomplices, for himself.

For Charles Comiskey, the Series had been a dismal affair. He strongly suspected seven players of throwing games; he even named them (omitting only Buck Weaver) to a friend. Understandably, Commy felt betrayed by his players and desperately wanted to punish the guilty parties. But there was much to consider, as talks with his lawyer, the urbane Alfred Austrian, made clear. If Comiskey acknowledged that there had been a fix and released the guilty players, he would weaken his team and damage his franchise, while the very players he released might sign with other clubs and play against him. On the other hand, if he did nothing, he ran the risk of exposure at some later date, with possibly the same consequences, except that he would look guilty along with the players. Austrian advised him to do nothing because there seemed to be more hearsay than hard evidence in the case. Comiskey could cover himself by announcing a "private" investigation with a reward for information on Series corruption.

Comiskey took Austrian's advice. Informants seeking reward money did emerge. One said Risberg bet on the Reds; another mentioned the St. Louis syndicate. Austrian considered both leads flimsy because neither described money changing hands. Joe Jackson wrote offering to discuss "crooked" plays; he received no answer. Comiskey hired a private detective to investigate the players, then not only shelved the report but urged the Illinois State's Attorney, a friend of his, not to inquire into Series corruption in view of the "insubstantial" nature of the evidence. Comiskey had initially withheld the World Series checks (losers' shares amounting to $3,254) of his seven suspects. Now, with talk of a fix smothered, he mailed them.

The 1920 season began on a sour note. Chick Gandil did not report for spring training. Swede Risberg reported just 2 days before the opening game. Jackson and Buck Weaver held out before signing 3-year contracts. Once set, however, the team played excellent baseball, settling into a summer-long three-way pennant race with the Cleveland Indians and the New York Yankees. With Jackson and Collins leading the way, the Sox topped the league in batting average, stolen bases, and runs scored, while Cicotte and Williams won 20 games again. So did Red Faber, back from arm trouble, and Dickie Kerr, who proved that 1919 was no fluke. Attendance at Comiskey Park—and revenues into Charles Comiskey's pocket—rose by 50 percent.

If the White Sox were so good, why didn't they run away with the pennant in 1920? Partly because the Indians and Yankees were also good. Tris Speaker hit .388 at Cleveland; Babe Ruth walloped an incredible 54 home runs for New York. But there was another, less visible reason: Midwestern gamblers were threatening the Series fixers with exposure if they did not throw additional games from time to time. And throw games they did, all through the summer—not many, but enough. Eddie Collins went to Comiskey about suspicious play in August, to no avail.

Ban Johnson, president of the American League, now quietly began an investigation of his own that turned up not only enticing, if circumstantial, evidence about suspicious activity during the 1920 season but leads to possible Series corruption the previous fall. Johnson, a respected baseball man, had co-founded the American League with Charles Comiskey, then his close friend. For obscure personal reasons, by 1920 Johnson had become Comiskey's mortal foe, eager to see the White Sox shattered. He therefore pressed his investigation hard. By midsummer, stories about possible crooked play were peppering the nation's sports pages.

The result was exactly what Charles Comiskey had feared and Ban Johnson had hoped for: the empanelling in early September of an Illinois Grand Jury to probe reports of corruption in major-league baseball. Comiskey loudly proclaimed his loyalty to the national pastime and his willingness to suspend any Chicago player proven to have thrown games and accused Ban Johnson of pursuing a personal vendetta against him. The Grand Jury, undeterred, began its work.

Initial testimony was more tantalizing than conclusive. Gamblers and baseball officials reported various, sometimes contradictory, rumors of payoffs to various players, including White Sox players. Rube Benton, a pitcher for the New York Giants, said he heard about a Series fix from none other than Hal Chase, recently retired as a player but long reputed to be on the take. Chase (said Benton) had heard from Sleepy Bill Burns that gamblers gave Chick Gandil, Happy Felsch, Lefty Williams, and Eddie Cicotte $100,000 to throw Series games, and that they had done it. Much of this testimony leaked out to the newspapers, producing sensational headlines concerning baseball—and World Series—corruption and the need, as the Chicago Tribune put it, to "SAVE BASEBALL FROM GAMBLERS."

Then on September 27 a Philadelphia newspaper published a story, based on interviews with anonymous gamblers, entitled "THE MOST GIGANTIC SPORTING SWINDLE IN THE HISTORY OF AMERICA." The story described how a group of White Sox players headed by Eddie Cicotte had thrown games one, two, and eight of the Series for a promise of $100,000. The players, said the paper, saw only $10,000 of the promised payoff money because the gamblers who started the whole thing lost everything when Chicago won game three. The story was only partially accurate in its account of the Bill Burns initiative and mostly inaccurate in its omission, save for the game eight loss, of the far more significant Rothstein-Sullivan initiative. But it rang true enough to panic Eddie Cicotte, who went that morning to see Alfred Austrian, Comiskey's lawyer, who got him to sign a confession, together with a waiver of immunity that would show the confession to have been uncoerced. Austrian then took Cicotte to the Grand Jury. "Yeah," said Eddie, "we were crooked. Gandil was the mastermind. I did it for the wife and kids and a farm. I'm through with baseball."

The floodgates were open. Joe Jackson, hearing that Cicotte had talked, went to see Felsch and Risberg. Swede, recounted Jackson, threatened "to kill you if you squawk." Jackson went to the Grand Jury judge's chambers anyway. There he met Alfred Austrian, who had Jackson, like Cicotte, sign an immunity waiver and a confession and advised him that the authorities were after the gamblers, not the players, and that he should tell everything. What he told the Grand Jury that afternoon was that although he had gotten his $5,000 from Williams, the ring leaders were Gandil and Risberg. He then asked for bailiff protection because "the Swede is a hard guy." Lefty Williams also met with Austrian, to whom he gave a signed statement confirming the Series fix and his part in it and fingering Gandil as the organizer. Later that day Felsch said much the same thing to a Chicago reporter. Weaver spoke briefly to Austrian and the State's Attorney but refused to confess. When Charles Comiskey informed the suspected players of their "indefinite" suspension by cable that evening, he sent eight cables. One went to Weaver.

The White Sox lost their last season series, and therefore the pennant, to Cleveland. According to Chicago novelist James T. Farrell, when Shoeless Joe Jackson and Happy Felsch emerged from the locker room after the final Cleveland loss, a fan shouted "It ain't true, Joe!" The surrounding crowd (which included the young Jimmy Farrell) took up the call, "It ain't true, Joe!" Both men walked silently away through the crowd. In late October the Grand Jury, its work completed, announced 13 indictments. Five were from the gambling fraternity: Bill Burns, Hal Chase, Sport Sullivan, and two other minions of Arnold Rothstein. From the baseball fraternity came Gandil, Risberg, Jackson, Felsch, Williams, Cicotte, McMullin, and Weaver—thereafter to be known as "the Black Sox."

Arnold Rothstein did not like the looks of the indictment list because it included men whose testimony could drag him deeply into the proceedings. This he proposed to avoid, even if it cost him a significant amount of money to do so. First, he would ensure that Sullivan and his other gambling contacts could not be extradicted to Chicago for trial. He would—and did—pay Sullivan to go to Mexico until the trial ended; he would—and did—pay to ensure "errors" in the extradition proceedings against Hal Chase and the rest. Secondly, Rothstein himself went to Chicago in early October, where he testified that he was entirely innocent, that the Series tampering had all been the doing of Sport Sullivan (now safely in Canada) and the rest, and (most outrageously of all) that he personally had bet "not a cent" on the World Series. While in Chicago, AR also met with Alfred Austrian about the Grand Jury testimony and the players' confessions and immunity waivers. Was there a way to obtain these documents and thus avoid the possible incrimination of Rothstein and also, if Charles Comiskey was interested, the conviction and likely disbarment of these valuable ballplayers? Apparently there was. The documents turned up missing shortly thereafter. Austrian meanwhile declared, for the record, that he believed Arnold Rothstein to be "entirely innocent"—just as he claimed.

Amidst the storm of corruption charges sweeping the nation and the prospect of widespread public disaffection and anger with the "grand old game," organized baseball, too, was moving to shore up its interests. The high tribunal of baseball at this time was a three-man national commission comprised of the presidents of the National and American Leagues plus a third member selected by the other two. But many people had no faith in this commission, including its most influential member, Ban Johnson himself. The Commission had already proven ineffectual in dealing with baseball corruption, and given current circumstances this ineffectualness simply could not continue if the game were to remain financially and also morally healthy. Albert Lasker, an advertising executive and Chicago Cubs stockholder, proposed a simple solution: Abolish the national commission and replace it with a single commissioner of uncompromising rectitude from outside professional baseball, who would be paid enough to place him above temptation and have enough power to make decisions stick. All eight National League owners liked the Lasker Plan because it would undercut the influence of American Leaguer Ban Johnson; three American League clubs—the White Sox together with the New York Yankees and Boston Red Sox, both under new ownership—also supported it. Two meetings of the 16 major league clubs failed to reach consensus because five American League clubs remained loyal to Johnson, who naturally opposed the new plan. Only after the "reformers" threatened to establish a new 12-team major league did the Johnsonites relent. And so in November, 1920, not long after the Grand Jury handed down its indictments, organized baseball got its new commissioner, a flamboyant federal judge named Kenesaw Mountain Landis. His salary: $50,000 a year—$42,500 more than he had made as a mere judge. No one knew quite what Landis would do. But everyone, Charles Comiskey included, hoped for the best.

Comiskey, after all, had big interests at stake, bigger perhaps than anyone (save possibly the ballplayers), and he was maneuvering hard to protect them. The Lasker Plan, which undercut Johnson, Comiskey's nemesis in this as in every other affair, was a part of that maneuvering. So was the pilfering from the State's Attorney's office of the ballplayers' signed confessions and immunity waivers. Copies existed, but the copies were unsigned and therefore might not be admitted as evidence, and without them neither guilty verdicts nor disbarment were likely. In addition, as the July 1921 trial date approached, the indicted players were approached by prosperous-looking lawyers offering to help with the players' defense. These lawyers were prominent in the Chicago bar—"fancy operators" and "lawyerin' birds," in the players' parlance, including one who started the case working for the prosecution only to switch, for no apparent reason, to the defense. Not only that, they were offering their services for little or no money. Charles Comiskey's telegram suspending the Black Sox had said that they would be reinstated if they were "innocent of any wrong-doing." Clearly, he was pulling out all stops to ensure that at least in the eyes of the law, innocent they would be.

As the long-awaited trial began in the summer of 1921, the prosecution sought to prove five charges of conspiracy against the defendants: conspiracy to defraud the public, to defraud Ray Schalk, to commit a confidence game, to injure the American League, and to injure Charles Comiskey. Because no gamblers ever materialized, thanks to Rothstein's machinations, the only defendants were the Black Sox. Bill Burns, whom Ban Johnson's agents had found hiding in the backcountry of Mexico, was the State's chief witness because Burns could testify that he attended meetings at which the defendants discussed throwing the Series and, more important, that he himself gave money to some of them. Burns also testified that, according to Cicotte, it was the players, not the gamblers, who instigated the scheme. The prosecution persuaded the judge to admit copies of the confessions and immunity waivers of Cicotte, Jackson, and Williams as evidence, even though they bore no signatures. The ballplayers themselves were never called to the witness stand, presumably because they would have denied having thrown any games. The prosecution concluded, in what was probably a tactical mistake, by demanding 5 years imprisonment and a $2,000 fine for each defendant.

The defense lawyers attempted to undermine Burns as a witness by showing that Ban Johnson had paid him to come to Chicago and that his testimony could not be corroborated. Because only the players could have corroborated it, the defense, too, avoided calling them to the stand. The defense also labored to prevent testimony as to whether the Black Sox had played beneath their abilities. When the prosecution questioned Kid Gleason and Ray Schalk on this point, the defense successfully objected on the grounds that the witnesses could not answer the question reliably.

The Black Sox seated in court, summer 1921 (L to R beginning second from left): Joe Jackson, Buck Weaver, Eddie Cicotte, Swede Risberg, Lefty Williams, Chick Gandil. Standing behind them (and seated to far left) are their attorneys. Normally gaudily attired with spats and diamond stickpins, the players are wearing subdued suits for their court appearances. Their relaxed good humor suggests that they knew the trial was going their way. Weaver and Jackson later sued Comiskey for the salary from the years remaining on their 3-year contracts. Comiskey eventually settled both cases out of court—although not before the missing confessions showed up in his lawyer's briefcase. (Chicago Historical Society)

The main defense strategy, however, was to portray the players not as perpetrators but as victims. The players had agreed to throw ballgames, argued the defense, not to defraud anybody but for the money, which they needed because Charles Comiskey (who was hopping mad at this line of reasoning by lawyers that he was paying) paid them such miserable salaries. The real culprits, claimed the defense, were not these poor ballplayers but big-time gamblers who were not even on trial, especially the "Big Bankroll" himself, Arnold Rothstein. It was an argument designed to appeal to the jury, which consisted of blue-collar and clerical workers who might identify with players depicted in this light. It was also an argument designed to appeal to the judge, who might construe the charges literally by requiring the jury to find premeditated malice on the part of the players rather than simply injurious effect.

The defense strategy worked. On August 2, after a trial of almost 6 weeks, the judge instructed the jury that the State's charges required a finding of malicious intent to injure particular parties, not simply the throwing of games. Two hours later the jury returned a verdict of "not guilty," and the courtroom erupted in cheers and congratulations. The players retired to a nearby Italian restaurant to celebrate. When they found the jury doing likewise, the two groups celebrated together. Charles Comiskey's gambit appeared to have succeeded. The players had been found "innocent," if not of "any wrongdoing," at least of any legal crime, and would presumably not only avoid the penitentiary but be reinstated—and in the nick of time, too, as the decimated White Sox were mired deep in the second division.

The celebration was premature. Legal innocence was not the same as moral innocence, at least to Kenesaw Mountain Landis, the new commissioner of baseball. The following morning Landis issued this statement: "Regardless of the verdict of juries, no player who throws a ball game, no player that undertakes or promises to throw a ballgame, no player that sits in conference with a bunch of crooked players and gamblers where the ways and means of throwing a game are discussed and does not promptly tell his club about it, will ever play professional baseball!" The Black Sox might be free from prison, but they were not reinstated, whatever Comiskey might think. On the contrary, they were barred from all professional baseball everywhere—for life.

Not everyone accepted this decision. A group of Chicago citizens circulated a petition urging reinstatement; Kid Gleason signed it. Some American League owners expressed outrage, as did a few editorial writers. Landis, however, was unyielding, and for the most part he was hailed in the national press as a hero whose "reassuring dictum" earned him "the nation's confidence and respect" for returning sports to "decent sporting circles." The Illinois State's Attorney meanwhile declared the case closed—meaning that there would be no inquiry into either the stolen Grand Jury documents or the role in the affair of one Arnold Rothstein.

The Black Sox scandal ended the careers of the eight indicted players, who tried to play semipro ball, then drifted into other work unconnected with baseball. It also shattered Charles Comiskey, who increasingly withdrew from active club management or league participation and lived more and more at his summer retreat in upstate Wisconsin. He did spend freely in an effort to rebuild his shattered franchise and, like other owners of the 1920s, to expand Comiskey Park's seating capacity. But few of the gaudy purchases worked out, and in any case the Old Roman reverted to form. After Dickie Kerr won 19 games in 1921, Comiskey cut his pay because his earned run average was too high. When Kerr returned the contract unsigned, Comiskey refused to tender him another, and Kerr sat out the 1922 season in protest. Then because he played for pocket money in a semipro game against expelled players, Landis suspended him for 1923 as well. So Comiskey's stinginess cost him a good pitcher for 2 years instead of one. The White Sox finished in the second division every year from 1921 until Comiskey's death in 1931 and in 16 of the next 20 years. The franchise was still valuable—Comiskey left his son $3,000,000—but nothing like what it might have been with no scandal.

Arnold Rothstein, the only big winner to emerge from the Black Sox scandal, was shot dead a few years later in a high-stakes New York poker game. Sometimes you win, sometimes you don't.

The Black Sox episode had both less and more influence on the history of baseball than people expected. The public revulsion against money-grubbing and corruption that many feared never really materialized. Attendance was as strong in early 1921, months after the fix had hit the newspapers, as in early 1920, and the fans, reassured perhaps by Commissioner Landis's hard line against the Black Sox, remained enthusiastic throughout the decade.

There was smaller, less obvious influence, however. When the story of the fix hit the papers in September of 1920, the Chicago White Sox were about to win their third pennant in 4 years, and as only Eddie Cicotte was close to retiring they looked good for more years of American League dominance during baseball's most lucrative decade to date. Kenesaw Mountain Landis's accession to power changed that. Landis not only ruined the White Sox franchise by barring its best players, he permitted practices that led to striking long-term imbalances within major-league baseball. He showed extraordinary leniency toward the New York ballclubs in particular, refusing, for example, to press inquiries into the widely known gambling affairs of John McGraw, manager of the Giants and, more important, failing to prevent the establishment, following the purchase of Babe Ruth, of a long-term sweetheart relationship whereby the New York Yankees acquired outstanding players from the Boston Red Sox for modest remuneration, including five 20-game winners who went a collective 541-346 while wearing a New York uniform. Baseball supremacy passed from the White Sox to the Yankees for the next 40 years in part because Landis tolerated this dubious relationship. By supporting the new commissioner system, Comiskey may have gotten rid of Ban Johnson, but it cost him and the rest of the league dearly. In this respect, they were perhaps the final victims of the Black Sox scandal of 1919.

AN INTERPRETATION

American baseball and American culture crossed a great divide with the advent of Babe Ruth and Kenesaw Mountain Landis. Baseball was, most notably, both effect and cause of the consumerism that was so defining a force in the culture of the 1920s. Even casual fans, after all—even men who had never played baseball

or women and small children—could appreciate Babe Ruth's exploits and Yankee prowess and would buy tickets to see them. Seeing the money to be made,
other clubs, too, cultivated powerful offenses; batting averages and power hitting
jumped sharply everywhere. Baseball's potential audience, already large, thus became larger. And because a significant part of this new audience consisted of girl-
friends and wives and families, management labored to make the game and the
parks more decorous and respectable. Grandstands became better policed. There
was less open gambling, rowdiness, swearing, and bottle-throwing. Spittoons vanished, as did hard liquor. Umpires, backed by Commissioner Landis, reduced
fighting among players and arguing among managers. Spitballs were banned because they were distasteful not only to power hitters but to fans. Landis and the
great owners with their big, cleaned-up stadiums thus wrenched baseball farther
from the drinking, brawling, gambling, ramshackle nineteenth-century subculture
of sensuality where it was born, and planted it solidly at the center of twentieth-
century consumer society, a fit companion to the great department stores on the
one hand and the giant movie palaces on the other.

The comparison with the motion picture industry is instructive in another
way, too. When the movie studios faced criticism of Hollywood immorality in the
1920s, they drew on the example of baseball to appoint an "outside commissioner," Will Hays, to review film content. Progressives had long urged the use of
central administrators—city managers, a federal trade commissioner—to control
unruly areas of life. The appointment of baseball and movie "czars" merely extended this control mechanism to the world of leisure and entertainment. Moreover, the illusion of control, of "somebody in charge," was nearly as important as
the control itself. Image mattered. Albert Lasker, whose plan made Landis commissioner of baseball, had made his money in advertising. His most memorable
slogan was for Ivory Soap: "99 and 44/100 percent pure—and it floats!" Banishing the Black Sox was a step toward a pure image for baseball. Not surprisingly,
when other professional sports came looking for ways to deal with instability and
image, they imitated baseball, too.

Landis's expulsion of the Black Sox also corresponded to major efforts—
prohibition in 1919, the arrest and deportation of radicals in 1919 and 1920, restrictive immigration laws in 1921 and 1924—to impose greater homogeneity and
conformity on American society. Until the Black Sox scandal, professional ballplayers had conducted themselves pretty much as they pleased while they were not playing. Many of them drank, fought, ran pool halls, played dominoes, chased fire engines, hung out at vaudeville houses, and patronized prostitutes the same way most
young urban males did when they had the chance, and club owners paid little attention as long as they showed up to play ball the next day. Landis's ruling against
the crooked players began to change that. The ruling sent a signal to professional
ballplayers that from now on their behavior off the field and out of season would
be subject to unprecedented scrutiny from the commissioner's Office.

And this level of control involved more than homogenization. It also involved
hard-nosed economics. The 1920s witnessed sweeping triumphs not only by consumer culture and commission politics but also by industrial corporations over their
labor adversaries, who lost three big strikes—by police in Boston, steelworkers in
Illinois, and workers generally in Seattle—in 1919 alone, then virtually every big

conflict for the next 15 years. As the defense attorneys claimed, the Black Sox scandal was in part a quarrel between a profit-maximizing capitalist, Charles Comiskey, and his underpaid workers, the players. Chick Gandil and the others threw ballgames, it is clear, in order to increase their income. In banishing them, Commissioner Landis announced, in effect, that the subversion of the integrity of the game by the players in this way was an unfair labor practice that would not be tolerated. What's more, Landis ruled repeatedly over the next decade that because players were bound by contract to play ball exclusively for their owners, they could not participate, except by permission, in unauthorized barnstorming or semiprofessional games during the off-season. Landis defended this ruling on the grounds that appearances in the off-season might dilute the value to the owners of regular-season play, which may have been true in some cases. What he did not say, al-

The most famous practitioner of the new "power game" favored by the New York Yankees, who dominated the American League after 1921, was Babe Ruth, pictured here during batting practice at Yankee Stadium in the mid-1920s. There was nothing subtle about Ruth, who held his bat at the end and swung for the fences. When he connected, the ball flew—much to the delight of fans everywhere in the giant park. Comiskey expanded his own park in the 1920s not so that Chicagoans could see the White Sox, who by now were no good, but so they could see the Yankees and Babe Ruth. (National Baseball Library, Cooperstown, NY)

though it was equally true, was that off-season income from playing ball might strengthen the negotiating leverage of the players at contract time, thereby raising salaries and reducing profits.

In other words, not only would the ballparks be well policed in the 1920s, so would the players, and not in the interests of public image and homogeneity alone. Indeed, one implication of Landis's stance was that if players wanted to improve their lot, they would have to do so not through gambling or organizing their own teams but through forming a real labor union. In the 1930s industrial workers finally stopped losing. A generation later, ballplayers did, too.

Sources: The standard account of the 1919 World Series and the Grand Jury investigation and trial that followed is Eliot Asinof's novelistic *Eight Men Out* (1963). Asinof should be supplemented by the summer 1920–1921 issues of the *Chicago Tribune* and *New York Times,* and by "Harry's Diary" in Bill Veeck and Ed Linn, *The Hustler's Handbook* (1965). Useful for leading personalities are G. W. Axelson, *"Commy": The Life Story of Charles A. Comiskey* (1919); Donald Gropman, *Say It Ain't So, Joe!: The Story of Shoeless Joe Jackson* (1979); Leo Katcher, *The Big Bankroll: The Life and Times of Arnold Rothstein* (1959); Marshall Smelser, *The Life That Ruth Built* (1975); and J. G. Taylor Spink, *Judge Landis and 25 Years of Baseball* (1947). The most helpful interpretive study of the American sporting scene is Benjamin G. Rader, *American Sports from the Age of Folk Games to the Age of Spectators* (1983).

9

DEADLY FUEL: AUTOS, LEADED GAS, AND THE POLITICS OF SCIENCE

DAVID ROSNER
GERALD MARKOWITZ

When workers began dying at a Standard Oil of New Jersey plant in late October of 1924, the newspaper headlines were vague and frightening: "Another Man Dies from Insanity Gas"/"Gas Madness Stalks Plant." It was soon clear that the killer was tetraethyl lead, a recently discovered compound that was being manufactured as a gasoline additive. For the next 2 years, scientists, public health officials, government agencies, social reformers, the press, representatives of organized labor, and the nation's largest and most powerful corporations studied the potentially lethal substance, debated its merits and liabilities, and determined a course of action—one that allowed the unfettered use of tetraethyl lead for more than a half century.

The almost hysterical response to the deaths at the Elizabeth, New Jersey, facility was unprecedented. Disasters of much greater magnitude had occurred during the Progressive Era—in December 1907 a single explosion killed 361 West Virginia coal miners—but aroused nothing like the level of public anxiety and even paranoia that followed the Standard Oil tragedy.

Two factors were responsible for the heightened response to tetraethyl lead. One was the nature of the hazard. Death in a coal mine was horrible, to be sure, but it was also understandable and, statistically, at least, predictable; to work underground in the presence of methane gas was to take a certain obvious risk. In contrast, tetraethyl lead did its damage gradually and virtually imperceptibly, attacking the nervous system in ways that ordinary people found almost incomprehensible.

The second factor was even more important. While an earlier generation of reformers had been almost entirely concerned with occupational hazards, tetraethyl lead posed a potential environmental problem, as the substance in question was to be used in automobiles, and automobiles were everywhere. In general, occupational hazards affected only workers. Environmental hazards affected members of every economic and social class.

Had the crisis over tetraethyl lead occurred in the Progressive Era, it no doubt would have been resolved differently—probably with federal or state legislation. But it occurred in the 1920s, only a few days before the voters would enthusiastically elect a

143

conservative Republican, Calvin Coolidge, to the presidency. Of course, Progressive-
Era reformers like Alice Hamilton were still around. But the imperatives of the 1920s
were far removed from the moral concerns that had helped humanize the industrial
and business system only a few years before. The climate of deregulation in the 1920s
might be likened to that of the last decades of the twentieth century, when federal
regulatory and welfare functions were turned back to relatively ineffectual state
governments, or eliminated altogether.

The world described by David Rosner and Gerald Markowitz was driven by the
imperatives of technology, consumerism, profit, and what was labeled "progress." At
the Washington conference that determined the fate of tetraethyl lead—and that of
millions of Americans who were condemned to inhale its fumes—the most powerful
voice was not Hamilton's but that of the Ethyl Corporation's Frank Howard,
trumpeting the virtues of growth and progress while glorifying tetraethyl lead as an
"apparent 'gift of God.' " In a society given over to such values, science was inevitably
corrupted and "regulatory" agencies proved incapable of regulating. Worst of all, the
decision was made to sacrifice the future to the god of the present.

Ernest Oelgert of Elizabeth, New Jersey, a laboratory worker in the Standard
Oil Company's plant in Elizabeth, New Jersey, died strangely on Sunday, October 26, 1924. Witnesses declared that he had been hallucinating on Thursday,
had become severely paranoid and, by Friday, was running around the plant "in
terror, shouting that there were 'three coming at me at once.' " On Saturday, he
was forcibly restrained and taken to Reconstruction Hospital in New York City,
where he died the next day. Although company officials at first denied any responsibility, claiming that Ernie "probably worked too hard," the workers at the
plant were not surprised. They all knew that Ernie worked in what was called "the
looney gas building," an experimental station secretly established the previous year.
Only 45 workers were employed in the laboratory and their fellow laborers had
already made them the object of "undertaker jokes and farewell greetings." Standard Oil spokesmen suggested that "nothing ought to be said about this matter
in the public interest."

By Monday, another worker had died and 12 others were hospitalized from
what everyone at the plant called "insanity gas." Terror-stricken workers were
being carted away to New York City in straight jackets, hallucinating, convulsing,
and screaming about the visions that were coming before their eyes. Yandell Henderson, professor of applied physiology at Yale University, said that the victims
had been poisoned by a gasoline additive called tetraethyl lead, which he regarded
as one of the "greatest menaces to life and health." At first, Standard Oil said that
Henderson's charge was itself a paranoid fantasy, and, in fact, "bunk." But, as the
workers continued to be hospitalized and as the New York newspapers began to
pick up the story, it became more and more difficult to deny its significance. Without naming the gas, Standard Oil issued a statement that claimed that the company had done everything possible to "make the work safe." They maintained that
every new product carried with it certain inherent risks, but that these risks were
necessary for the nation's progress: "This newly invented gasoline combination
made it possible for automobile engineers to produce a more powerful engine than

any yet in use . . . plans for putting this new engine on the market have advanced simultaneously with the experiment on lead gasoline."

By Friday, as the fifth victim of "looney gas" died—and as three-quarters of the laboratory's workers lay sick—the New York City Board of Health, the City of Philadelphia, and various municipalities in New Jersey banned the sale of leaded gasoline. The *New York Times*, the *New York World*, and all the regional newspapers were by this time blaring out front-page headlines like, " 'Mania Gas' May Kill Through a Dual Poison," "Odd Gas Kills One," "Tetraethyl Lead in Victim's Brain," and "Gas Madness Stalks Plant."

The story really begins with the emergence of the American auto industry in the early 1900s. Throughout the country, scores of local bicycle and buggy companies began to attach to their vehicles motors powered by steam, electricity, and gasoline. One producer, Henry Ford, broke away from the pack by revolutionizing the production system through the development of the assembly line to produce an affordable automobile. Suddenly the car was not a luxury and thousands upon thousands of Americans could think for the first time of owning their own cars. By 1919, there was one automobile for every 16 Americans.

This enormous expansion of the market for cars whetted the appetite of other industrialists eager to cash in on a potential bonanza. E. I. DuPont, for example, patriarch of the famous chemical conglomerate, invested heavily in the General Motors Corporation (GM). In contrast to Ford's famous Model T that looked the same year after year, GM offered powerful cars whose appearance and engineering changed constantly. No longer would a 6-month-old car look the same as one that was 4 years old. It was now possible to tell who had the latest, the most powerful, and most fashionable automobile. Built-in obsolescence and the consumer society were born. GM's fortunes took off and, by the end of the 1920s, it replaced Ford as the nation's leading car manufacturer, producing 40 percent of all the cars in the country. By 1929, there was one car for every six Americans and President Herbert Hoover predicted that there would soon be a "car in every garage."

But to provide the power required by the new generation of automobiles, the manufacturers needed a more efficient fuel than plain gasoline, which burned far too quickly and unevenly in larger engines. In 1922, Thomas Midgley and his co-workers at the General Motors Research Laboratory in Dayton, Ohio, discovered an answer. Gasoline mixed with tetraethyl lead—a viscous, dark-brown, foul smelling liquid composed of lead molecules embedded in a compound of hydrogen and carbon—would burn evenly in a car engine. That would eliminate engine "knock," enabling the car to get more power from every gallon of gas. GM, which had an interlocking directorship* with the DuPont Chemical Company, quickly contracted with DuPont and Standard Oil of New Jersey to produce leaded gasoline. It was placed on sale in several markets on February 1, 1923. The "no-knock" product was popular, and the following year DuPont and General Motors created the Ethyl Corporation to market the substance. A few years later, the new com-

---

*DuPont owned more than 20 percent of General Motors' stock and had several members of its board of directors on GM's board.

pany took over the manufacture of tetraethyl lead, which it still makes today. (In 1985, its plant near New Orleans produced millions of barrels of the additive.)

In the very year that Midgley and his team made their find, however, several scientists warned that the use of tetraethyl lead could expose large numbers of people to the dangers already associated with simple lead—neurological problems, kidney damage, even madness—or to other hazards that could not be predicted. DuPont and GM recognized that they would have to respond to scientists' apprehension. They also knew that such fear would not be assuaged in a study conducted by a corporation with an interest in tetraethyl lead. So the companies struck an agreement, in September, 1923, with the U.S. Bureau of Mines. The agreement called for the General Motors Research Corporation to provide funding for an investigation of the dangers of tetraethyl lead. The Bureau of Mines would provide the facilities and do the work. And the U.S. Government would certify the results. The Bureau, which had authority to regulate and stockpile fuels and other resources that would be needed in wartime, was considered to have the greatest familiarity with the occupational hazards posed by gasoline.

The contract was the first in a series of agreements that would develop between the Bureau of Mines and the corporations. It allowed the government agency considerable freedom to report its conclusions. But the contracts also indicated the subservience of government to the commercial interests of the corporations. S. C. Lind, the chief chemist of the Bureau of Mines, wrote to the superintendent of the Bureau's Pittsburgh field station where the investigation was being carried out, objecting to the government's use of the trade name "ethyl" when referring to tetraethyl lead: "of course, their [GM's] object in doing so [is] fairly clear, and among other things they are not particularly desirous of having the name 'lead' appear in this case. That is alright from the standpoint of the General Motors Company but it is quite a question in my mind as to whether the Bureau of Mines would be justified in adopting this name so early in the game before it has the support of popular usage." The superintendent replied that the avoidance of "the use of 'lead' in the interbureau correspondence" was intentional because of fears of leaks to the newspapers. As the Bureau had agreed to a blackout of information, he asserted that "if it should happen to get some publicity accidentally, it would not be so bad if the word 'lead' were omitted as this term is apt to prejudice somewhat against its use." The willingness of the Bureau of Mines to avoid publicity and even the use of accurate scientific terminology reflected the Bureau's weak position vis-à-vis the giant corporations, GM and DuPont.

By June, 1924, GM wanted much more control over the results of the research. It rewrote the contract to require that the popular press not be informed of the research results and added a new stipulation that "all manuscripts, before publication, will be submitted to the Company for comment and criticism." Two months after the Bureau acquiesced to this new stipulation, the newly created Ethyl Corporation took over the contract from GM and asked for an important change. A new clause providing for corporate review of findings, read, ". . . before publication of any papers or articles by your Bureau, they should be submitted to [Ethyl] for comment, criticism, and approval."

The Bureau of Mines, which had always been sympathetic to the industries it regulated, agreed. Not surprisingly, its decision was widely interpreted as a sign of apparent collusion with GM, DuPont, Standard Oil, and Ethyl to certify the safety of tetraethyl lead. On September 27, 1924, Yale Professor Henderson, who was to become an important opponent of tetraethyl lead's manufacture, wrote an angry letter to R. R. Sayers, the Public Health Service researcher who was conducting the studies for the Bureau of Mines. "It seems to me," Henderson wrote, "extremely unfortunate that the experts of the United States government should be carrying out this investigation on a grant from General Motors." He called for "an absolutely unbiased investigation." C. W. Deppe, the owner of a competing motor car company, was much blunter in his criticism of the government's relationship to GM: "May I be pardoned if I ask you frankly now, does the Bureau of Mines exist for the benefit of Ford and the GM Corporation and the Standard Oil Company of New Jersey, and other oil companies parties to the distribution of Ethyl Lead Dopes, or is the Bureau supposed to be for the public benefit and in protection of life and health?"

Soon, however, tetraethyl lead's opponents found that they had much of the public on their side—thanks to the disaster in late October, in Elizabeth, New Jersey (the site of Standard Oil's Bayway chemical plant) and to the growing skepticism of government and industry fostered by the exposure of massive corruption during the administration of President Warren G. Harding. After Harding died in August, 1923, the public gradually learned that major industries had bribed high government officials. It became apparent that there was a pattern of officials being manipulated by private industries in violation of the law and the public's trust. Significantly, the most famous scandal—called "Teapot Dome"—involved the oil industry and the Department of Interior, home of the Bureau of Mines. In 1924, a Congressional investigation revealed that Secretary of Interior Albert Fall had leased vast oil reserves owned by the government to a private oil company in exchange for hundreds of thousands of dollars delivered to him as cash in "little black bags." Fall was the first member of any presidential cabinet to go to jail.

In the midst of these revelations, and on the day after the fifth victim from Standard Oil's Elizabeth plant disaster died, the Bureau of Mines released its preliminary findings. Not surprisingly, its report exonerated tetraethyl lead. Also, not surprisingly, public officials did not trust the integrity of its conclusions. New York City banned the sale of leaded gasoline and New Jersey quickly followed suit.

While public health officials largely ignored the report, many labor activists and scientists agreed with Dr. Alice Hamilton, the Harvard professor and reformer who was a noted expert on the hazards of lead poisoning, when she called for "an investigation by a public body which will be beyond suspicion."

Perhaps the strongest criticism of the Bureau of Mines' report came from the Workers' Health Bureau, an organization of labor activists who investigated hazards to workers' safety and health. The group's advisor, Professor Henderson, voiced the concern of the public health profession—a loose fellowship of sanitarians, toxicologists, health educators, and bench scientists—over the fact that "the investigators in the Bureau of Mines have used experimental conditions which are fundamentally unsuited to afford information on the real issues." The Bureau's researchers had examined gas-station attendants and truck drivers. But they looked neither for the subtle motor problems that signal organic lead poisoning nor even for gross coordination trouble; the only sign of poisoning that their studies were designed to detect was raving lunacy or death. Further, the research on humans focused on workers in plants and gas stations—there was no inquiry into the effects of exposure on those who did not work with the substance, but simply lived in a city where it was used. Henderson was the most persistent critic of the Bureau's report and his critique went farther than mere criticism of its technique. Charging that the introduction of tetraethyl lead into the environment was "probably the greatest single question in the field of public health that has ever faced the American public," Henderson warned that the use of lead in gasoline "would cause vast numbers of the population to suffer from slow lead poisoning with hardening of the arteries, rapidly decaying teeth, weakening of certain muscles and other symptoms."

Not all public health professionals sided with the opponents of lead, however. In the months after the Bureau of Mines report, as the corporations involved sought to win back a skeptical public, a leading figure in their efforts was Emery Hayhurst, a respected and ostensibly independent industrial hygienist who worked for the Ohio Department of Health. Even before the Bureau of Mines issued its report, Hayhurst had decided that tetraethyl lead was not an environmental toxin. He had advised the Bureau of Mines to include a statement that "the finished product, Ethyl Gasoline, as marketed and used both pure or diluted in gasoline retains none of the poisonous characteristics of the ingredients concerned in its manufacture and blending." No one knew that throughout the months of public controversy over tetraethyl lead, while Hayhurst was advising the Workers' Health Bureau and other labor groups about industrial hygiene, he was also working for the Ethyl Corporation as a consultant. In fact, Hayhurst was supplying advocates of tetraethyl lead with information regarding the tactics to be used by their opponents. After the Bureau of Mines report had been released, Hayhurst secretly sent to the Public Health Service a copy of the criticisms developed by the Workers' Health Bureau (which that group had decided not to send to the Government) so that the Public Health Service and Bureau of Mines could frame a detailed reply.

Hayhurst and Sayers also worked together to build public and professional support for the Bureau of Mines' and the Ethyl Corporation's position that tetraethyl lead was not a public health danger. After the Bureau of Mines' report had been criticized, Sayers urged Hayhurst to use his position as an editor of the prestigious and ostensibly neutral *American Journal of Public Health* to lend "scientific" credence to industry's position. Hayhurst obliged, and his statement ran as an unsigned editorial that proclaimed, "Observational evidence and reports to various health officials over the country . . . so far as we have been able to find out, corroborated the statement of 'complete safety' so far as the public has been concerned."

While Hayhurst and the public health officials sought to quell professional doubts about the safety of tetraethyl lead, Midgley, now vice-president of General Motors and known as "the father of ethyl gas," called a press conference to quiet popular fears. In an effort to show the harmlessness of tetraethyl lead, he asserted that workers could have it spilled on them without ill effect. To prove his point, Midgley called for an attendant to bring a container of tetraethyl lead to him and he "washed his hands thoroughly in the fluid and dried them on his handkerchief." He told the reporters, "I'm not taking any chance whatever. Nor would I take any chance doing that every day." What he did not reveal was that only a year before he had taken a prolonged vacation in Florida to cure himself of lead poisoning.

This public relations effort was incapable of quashing the doubts about the safety of leaded gasoline or the integrity of the Bureau of Mines report. After the incident at Standard Oil's Elizabeth facility, newspapers around the country began printing accounts of death, illnesses, and cover-ups occurring at other tetraethyl plants, including the DuPont facility in Deepwater, New Jersey, and the General Motors Research Division site in Dayton, Ohio. The *New York Times* revealed that there were over 300 cases of lead poisoning among workers at the Deepwater plant during the past 2 years. Workers at the DuPont facility dubbed the plant "the house of the butterflies" because so many of their colleagues had hallucinations of insects hovering around their heads during bouts of lead poisoning: "The victim pauses, perhaps while at work or in a rational conversation, gazes intently at space, and snatches at something not there." The *Times* reported that "about 80 percent of all who worked in 'the house of the butterflies' or who went into it to make repairs, were poisoned, some repeatedly."

The local papers, on the other hand, printed very little news about what was happening at the plants. They said nothing about the death of Frank W. (Happy) Durr, who had worked in Deepwater for DuPont for 25 years. Durr had literally given his life to the company. He had begun working for DuPont as a 12-year-old child and died from exposure to tetraethyl lead at the age of 37 years. The editor of the local paper told the *Times*, "I guess the reason we didn't print anything about Durr's death was because we couldn't get it. They [DuPont] suppress things about the lead plant at Deepwater. Whatever we print, we pick up from the workers." DuPont's control even extended to the local hospital, where it was almost impossible to get information about the source of workers' illnesses.

Throughout April and May of 1925, *The New York World* ran nearly daily front-page headlines. The *World* proclaimed leaded gasoline a "Menace." Elsewhere, it warned that even "Columbia [University] Experts Assert[ed] Ethyl Gas is Public Menace." The *Times* tried to get in on the action by asserting that leaded gasoline was a "Deadly Peril In The Streets." The *World*, known nationally as a leading muckraking paper, sought to use the Bureau of Mines' Report against the industry by asserting that "Tetraethyl Peril To All Motorists Indicated in Tests by Mines Bureau." These and other three-column front-page headlines dwarfed other stories on the fall of the German economy and "red scares" throughout the world. As a result of this publicity and the continuing public disquiet over the Bureau of Mines Report, the head of the Public Health Service, the Surgeon General, called a national conference to assess the tetraethyl lead situation.

On May 20, 1925, the conference convened in Washington, D.C., with every major party to the controversy in attendance. Each corporation and organization had prepared a statement, which its representative read to the assembly and then defended during a question and answer session. In the words of one participant, the conference gathered together in one room "two diametrically opposed conceptions. The men engaged in industry, chemists, and engineers, take it as a matter of course that a little thing like industrial poisoning should not be allowed to stand in the way of a great industrial advance. On the other hand, the sanitary experts take it as a matter of course that the first consideration is the health of the people."

The companies—General Motors, DuPont, Standard Oil, and the Ethyl Corporation—went first. Their speakers outlined the history of leaded gasoline and the reasons its continued production was essential to the nation. The Chairman of GM, Charles F. Kettering, and a lead researcher from GM's Kettering Laboratories, Robert Kehoe, both invoked one of the industry's most common arguments—that oil supplies were limited, and that tetraethyl lead would help stretch them out. (Industry spokesmen claimed that the world's petroleum supplies would run out in the 1940s if lead was not added to gasoline. With leaded gas, studies said, supplies might last until the 1950s.) Frank Howard, the Ethyl Corporation representative, stressed the broader point that, whatever the health risks, the entire controversy had to be seen from the economic and political perspective, as well as the environmental one. "You have but one problem," he remarked rhetorically, "Is this a public health hazard?" He answered that "unfortunately, our problem is not that simple." Rather he posited that automobiles and oil were central to the industrial progress of the nation, if not the world. "Our continued development of motor fuels is essential in our civilization," he proclaimed. Noting that at least a decade of research had preceded the discovery of tetraethyl lead, he called it an "apparent 'gift of God.' . . . Because some animals died and some do not die in some experiments, shall we give this thing up entirely?"

These remarks proved to be the recurrent themes for the industry: The nation's progress depended on gasoline, and the risks involved were worth it. Dr. H. C. Parmelee, editor of the industry trade magazine *Chemical and Metallurgical Engineering* stated, "The research and development that produced tetraethyl lead were conceived in a fine spirit of industrial progress looking toward the conservation of gasoline and increased efficiency of internal combustion motors." Parmelee believed that the companies did their best to safeguard the workers. In the end, he said, "its casualties were negligible compared to human sacrifice in the development of many other industrial enterprises." The company representatives blamed workers' carelessness for the deaths and illnesses in tetraethyl lead plants.

For their part, the labor activists and public health specialists who were fighting leaded gas pointed out that lead compounds were already known to be slow, cumulative poisons. They believed that the federal government had to assume responsibility for protecting the health of the nation, and they rejected the notion that the workers were the ones responsible for their own poisoning. Finally, they asked the conferees to consider not just lead's potential for causing occupational diseases, but also its effects on the environment as a whole. As the country's foremost authority on lead, Alice Hamilton, put it, "You may control conditions within a factory, but how are you going to control the whole country?"

Henderson, the Yale physiologist, compared tetraethyl lead to a serious infectious disease like the influenza and diphtheria that periodically swept the country. He was horrified at the thought that hundreds of thousands of pounds of lead were going to be deposited in the streets of every major city of America. The problem was not that more people would die like those in the laboratory in New Jersey, but that "the conditions would grow worse so gradually and the development of lead poisoning will come on so insidiously . . . that leaded gasoline will be in nearly universal use and large numbers of cars will have been sold . . . before the public and the government awaken to the situation." In a private letter to R. R. Sayers of the Bureau of Mines, Henderson wrote: "In the past, the position taken by the authorities has been that nothing could be prohibited until it was proved to have killed a number of people. I trust that in the future, especially in a matter

Be the Judge and Jury
..then Render Your Own Verdict
on
BLUE **SUNOCO**

Follow the Sun Sign

BLUE SUNOCO *is a pure petroleum product, non-poisonous and harmless. Its high knockless qualities are obtained by exclusive methods of manufacture and not by the addition of foreign substances.*

IT is not what WE say about this powerful, knockless motor fuel. It is what YOU find out about it that really matters.

No gasoline has ever before shown such tremendous gains in sales. This is due to its own qualities which prove themselves in your own car.

Use BLUE SUNOCO for a few weeks, then go back to the gasoline you formerly used.

We will rest our case right there.

BLUE SUNOCO
THE ONLY TRUE BLUE

HIGH-POWERED, QUICK-STARTING MOTOR FUEL AT NO EXTRA PRICE

By 1929, Sunoco was appealing to the public rather than to the experts, who had by then deemed tetraethyl lead "safe." Here, Sunoco asked consumers to "be the judge and jury" and "render your own verdict." In another advertisement that same year, Sunoco claimed that "the verdict of the jury" was in and that unleaded Sunoco had triumphed. (Courtesy of Hagley Museum and Library)

of this sort, the position will be that substances like tetraethyl lead can not be introduced for general use until it is proved harmless."

Opponents were most concerned, however, about the industry propaganda that equated the use of lead with industrial progress and the survival of civilization itself. Reacting to the Ethyl Corporation representative's statement that tetraethyl lead was a "gift of God," Grace Burnham of the Workers' Health Bureau said it "was not a gift of God when those eleven men were killed or those 149 were poisoned." She denounced the priorities of "this age of speed and rush and efficiency and mechanics" and said, "the thing we are interested in [in] the long run is not mechanics or machinery, but men." A. L. Berres, secretary of the metal trades department of the American Federation of Labor, also rejected the prevalent conception of the 1920s that "the business of America is business." He told the conference that the American Federation of Labor opposed the use of tetraethyl lead, saying, "We feel that where the health and general welfare of humanity is concerned, we ought to step slowly."

Of course, the public health experts listening to the two camps hoped that scientific research would prove one position correct and the other wrong. Yet a final, scientific answer was impossible for two reasons. In the first place, scientists at that time did not adequately understand what they were studying. All previous experience with lead poisoning had involved inorganic molecules, which do not create symptoms until large amounts have been absorbed in the bones. Tetraethyl lead is what we would now call an organic compound, which creates symptoms very soon after entering the body. So while inorganic lead in the body tends to appear in blood or excretions before symptoms appear, traces of organic lead compounds may not be found until after severe symptoms have occurred. Naturally, the first cases of poisoning by organic lead compounds did not fit well into models created to explain the action of inorganic lead compounds, and so evidence of poisonings by tetraethyl lead was regarded as perplexing and ambiguous. Even the medical director of Reconstruction Hospital in New York, probably the only facility devoted exclusively to the study and treatment of occupational disease and accidents, could not explain the strange manifestations of chronic tetraethyl lead poisoning. Of the 39 patients he treated after the Elizabeth disaster, he said, "some . . . gave no physical evidence and no symptoms or any evidence that could be found by a physical examination that would indicate that they were ill, but at the same time showed lead in the stools."

The second reason that public health officials could not look to science was political. Pressured by industry's desire to market ethyl gasoline and the public's desire for speedy, definitive answers, scientists were designing studies that could be finished in a few months—simple research on worker health records, or a few tests on humans or animals with no follow-up after the initial work was done. These were not sufficient to provide the definitive proof of harm that the public wanted and the companies said did not exist. Many public health officials agreed with the industry that it would be unfair to ban the new gasoline additive until there was proof it was dangerous. Suggestive studies and possible problems were not enough to keep the product off the market, because of vigorous industry opposition. Pure science would not provide the answer. In the face of industry arguments that oil supplies were limited, and that there was an extraordinary need to conserve fuel by making combustion more efficient, most public health workers believed that there should be overwhelming evidence that leaded gasoline actually harmed people before it was banned.

In private, even the advocates of tetraethyl lead were ambivalent about the scientific issues. Hayhurst, for example, wrote Sayers that he accepted the argument that "lead has no business in the human body . . . everyone agrees lead is an undesirable hazard and the only way to control it is to stop its use by the general public." But, he went on, "I am afraid human progress cannot go on under such restrictions. Where things can be handled safely by proper supervision and regulation they must be allowed to proceed if we are to survive among the nations." Another investigator, Frederick Flinn of Columbia University, voiced similar reservations in private: "The more I work with the material [TEL], the more I am confused as to whether it is a real public health hazard." In the end, however, he was "convinced that there is some hazard —the extent of which must be studied around garages and filling stations over a period of time and by unprejudiced persons." As Flinn was a consultant for the Ethyl Corporation, it is not surprising that he ended his letter by saying, "Of course, you must understand that my remarks are confidential."

The public was not so philosophical. People were still alarmed by the previous year's accident and continuing reports of other deaths caused by tetraethyl lead. The *New York Times,* for example, continued reports of poisonings and deaths from tetraethyl lead: "Tetraethyl Lead Fatal to Makers," one headline announced in an article that claimed that 8 had died and 300 were poisoned in one DuPont plant in Deepwater, New Jersey.

At the end of the Surgeon General's conference, the Ethyl Corporation announced that it was suspending the production and distribution of leaded gasoline until the scientific and public health issues involved in its manufacture could be resolved. Furthermore, the conference called on the Surgeon General to organize a Blue Ribbon Committee of the nation's foremost public health scientists to conduct the unbiased study of leaded gas that the Bureau of Mines had failed to produce.

But this apparent triumph for scientific inquiry over economic interests was ephemeral. The conference decided that the new committee had to report definitive findings by the end of the year—only 7 months away. To meet the deadline, the committee members designed a short-term, and in retrospect, very limited, study of garagemen, filling station attendants, and chauffeurs in two cities in which lab equipment was available, Dayton and Cincinnati. The brief inquiry naturally missed the most significant aspects of possible lead poisoning from car fumes—the slow accumulation of the compound in the body over many years of exposure.

After its 7 months were up, the committee duly found that "in its opinion there are at present no good grounds for prohibiting the use of ethyl gasoline . . . provided that its distribution and use are controlled by proper regulations." The report suggested the Surgeon General formulate specific regulations for the product's use, to be enforced by the states. Although it appears that the committee rushed to judgment, it must be pointed out that this group saw their study as only interim, to be followed by longer range follow-up studies in the coming years. Indeed, the committee had warned that

> Longer experience may show that even such slight storage of lead as was observed in these studies may lead eventually in susceptible individuals to recognizable or to chronic degenerative diseases of a less obvious character.

Recognizing that their short-term retrospective investigation was incapable of detecting such danger, the committee concluded that further study by the government was essential. Noting a "vast increase in the number of automobiles throughout the country," the committee remarked that this was "a matter of real importance from the standpoint of public health." It strongly suggested that studies be continued and that Congress appropriate funds for long-term investigations to be carried out by the Surgeon General.

These suggestions were never carried out. Instead, the Public Health Service dropped the issue and allowed all following studies on tetraethyl lead to be conducted by the Ethyl Corporation and scientists employed by it. The man who conducted those studies was Kehoe, who, in direct contradiction of the committee, interpreted its report to mean that there was no need to waste public money studying tetraethyl lead: "as it appeared from their investigation that there was no evidence of immediate danger to the public health, it was thought that these necessarily extensive studies should not be repeated at present, at public expense, but that they should be continued at the expense of the industry most concerned, sub-

The Organic Chemicals Department, DuPont Deepwater Chambers Work, Deepwater Point, New Jersey, 1951: the site of the Deepwater disaster, where tetraethyl lead production workers were poisoned in 1924. (Courtesy of Hagley Museum and Library)

ject, however, to the supervision of the Public Health Service." It should not be surprising that Kehoe concluded that his research "fails to show any evidence for the existence of such hazards." Over the next 40 years, other studies came to the same conclusion. That too is not surprising, because between 1927 and 1967, there was no research conducted on tetraethyl lead that was not funded by either the Kettering Laboratories or by General Motors.

AN INTERPRETATION

The history of public policy regarding leaded gasoline must be understood as part of the history of the American chemical and auto industries. During the 1920s these industries emerged as the corporate backbone of the United States. Because leaded gasoline was critical to the development of these industries, a

An advertisement from the British journal *Punch,* October 19, 1932, shows one way in which producers of leaded fuel overcame doubts about the safety of the tetraethyl lead additive. (Courtesy of Hagley Museum and Library)

heated controversy arose regarding its possibly unhealthful effects. Public health professionals found themselves under intense pressure to sanction and minimize the hazards associated with the manufacture and use of this new potentially toxic substance.

Yet this controversy arose at a very particular moment in American history. The 1920s were marked by the almost unrestrained growth of corporate power and an ideology in government that, in Coolidge's words, the "Business of America is business." In the 1920s the federal government was small and weak in comparison with such giant corporations as General Motors and DuPont. Unlike the first two decades of the 1900s, when many groups were pressuring the federal government to expand its powers and assume responsibility for regulating big business, the 1920s saw unrestrained corporate aggrandizement as a part of the "Age of Normalcy." Hence, the protests that led to the initial ban of tetraethyl lead represented, in part, the older Progressive Era vision of government's role as regulator of business. During the 1920s, however, the country abandoned its older faith in public regulation and allowed voluntary agreements to replace legislative action.

The questions and issues raised in the 1920s continue to haunt us in the 1990s. How should society regulate private interests that threaten the public health and safety? Should public officials or private organizations have responsibility for establishing standards? How does one study potentially toxic substances while protecting the right to health of human subjects? Does industry have to prove a new substance safe or do public health experts have to prove it dangerous? In the face of scientific uncertainty concerning the safety or dangers posed by leaded gasoline, and the perceived need for this substance by the auto industry, the broader question became, What was the level of acceptable risk that society should be willing to assume for industrial progress? At every stage of the debate, the political, economic, and scientific issues were inextricably intertwined.

Every year thousands of new chemical agents are developed by industry and introduced into the workplace and environment. All too often, the threat these agents pose to the health and well-being of the community is only discovered after an environmental or occupational disaster. Bhopal, Three Mile Island, and Love Canal* have all come to symbolize the hazards of our modern industrial and chemical society. Although most people assume that toxic chemicals are introduced into the environment through ignorance or error, the actual history is usually more complicated. Lead's presence in our air, lungs, and bones was a product of political, economic, and public policy decisions, not simply a scientific mistake.

Forty years after the Surgeon General's conference, in the late 1960s, doctors in inner-city hospitals began reporting instances of lead poisoning among children living in tenements—coats of leaded paint, which had been applied to buildings before it was banned in the 1940s, and sometimes after, were peeling and

---

*Bhopal, India, was the site of a massive disaster in which thousands of people were poisoned by the release of highly toxic gas from a Union Carbide Chemical plant. Three Mile Island was the site of the nation's worst nuclear reactor accident, and Love Canal is a community in upper New York State that was found to be contaminated by chemicals dumped by the Hooker Chemical Company.

being eaten by the children. By the early 1970s, studies of children's exposure were turning up the fact that people on lower floors had more of the metal in their systems than their upstairs neighbors. This led a new generation of researchers to look into automobile emissions. They found what their predecessors could not: evidence of lead's insidious and pervasive effects on the development of children. Thanks to the research, and the burgeoning environmental movement of the era, the federal government ordered the phasing out of leaded gasoline. The amount of lead permitted in gasoline is steadily shrinking. In the meantime, the political and scientific battles focus on how much lead can be put into "unleaded" gas. The issue of tetraethyl lead is still with us but no one thinks of it as "a gift of God."

As we look back on the controversy today from the era of nitrites, PCBs, and asbestos, we may be tempted to disapprove of a public health profession that failed to stop the introduction of ethyl gasoline. After all, prominent experts such as Alice Hamilton and Yandell Henderson warned about the dangers and strongly advocated an impartial government-sponsored scientific study, and opponents did manage to win a temporary moratorium on the manufacture of the substance until the scientists' results became available. What went wrong? Why is tetraethyl lead still a prime source of lead in the environment? Of course, there were those who had such an ideological commitment to industrial progress that they were willing to put their science aside to meet the demands of corporate greed. But more important, we should look at those who considered themselves honorable scientific investigators for, ultimately, they could not distinguish their "science" from the demands of an economy and society that was being built around the automobile. Any boundaries between science and society, if they ever really exist, broke down as they agreed to conduct a short-term study that would provide quick answers— answers guaranteed, in retrospect, not to disrupt this vital industry. The symptoms of lead accumulation due to exhaust emissions would be unlike anything they had previously encountered in industrial populations. But because of compromises in their experimental design they could not possibly understand what we now know today: that those most affected would not be adults, but children, slowly accumulating lead. Their suffering is all the more tragic because of the amorphous and still poorly understood effects of lead on the nervous system of children. The best of the public health scientists of the 1920s were working from an inadequate model of disease causation. But their inability to draw conclusions valid from modern standards speaks more to the interlocking relationships between science and society than to the absence of a link between lead and disease.

Sources: A wide variety of different types of material was used to unravel the complex history of leaded gasoline. We began by looking at the newspapers and magazines of the period. This material gave us a good sense of the controversies that accompanied the introduction of lead into gasoline in the 1920s. The *New York World*, the *New York Times*, the *American Journal of Public Health*, *The Survey*, and various industry journals provided a sense of how the public, professionals and industry viewed the issue. But this public literature provided only part of the story. Private correspondence and memos between industry spokesmen, government officials in the U.S. Bureau of Mines, and the Public Health Service were invaluable for understanding the interlocking relationships between government and industry during the period. The National Archives in Washington preserved this material, but other material in the hands of the industry is unavailable to scholars.

10

THE TOWNSEND MOVEMENT AND SOCIAL SECURITY

WILLIAM GRAEBNER

He was an old man and not much of a public speaker. He held no political office and, like millions of older Americans, he had no money. Despite these handicaps, in the midst of the Great Depression of the 1930s Francis Townsend became one of the most popular and influential men in America. The source of his strength was a plan— indeed, a very simple plan—for providing federal pensions to all retired people over the age of 60 years. In less than 2 years, Townsend parlayed his idea for old-age pensions into hundreds of Townsend Clubs and millions of devoted followers—the Townsend movement—with the strength to bully Franklin D. Roosevelt's New Deal into the landmark Social Security Act of 1935.

When Townsend first made his proposal in the fall of 1933, a small number of Americans already had some kind of claim to an old-age pension. Federal civil service employees were minimally covered under a law passed in 1920. Some military veterans and state and municipal employees could look forward to future benefits. And about 10 percent of employees in the private sector had some kind of coverage. But otherwise, most people had to depend on personal savings in their old age or count on their children to take care of them. If these sources of security proved inadequate, older people had only two options: In some states, the indigent aged could apply for public assistance; or they could seek room and board in the county almshouse. Although Germany, Great Britain, and most of the other industrialized nations of the world had had comprehensive national programs of old-age pensions and assistance in place for many years, the United States had nothing of the kind.

Even in ordinary times, the worsening condition of the nation's elderly would probably have brought forth an advocate such as Townsend. But these were no ordinary times. Across the country, young and old struggled to make ends meet, even to survive, in the most severe depression in the nation's history. The trauma was symbolized by Detroit, a city whose automobile assembly lines had represented the boom of the 1920s and that now found itself devastated by the Great Depression: By 1933, more than half of the city's workers were unemployed, and once-proud citizens dug homes in the ground, rummaged for food in alley garbage cans, or stole dog biscuits from the city pound. Conditions in other American cities, and in the small towns and countryside, were only marginally better.

Into this chaos stepped Townsend, full of hopes and high expectations, tempting the nation's aged with the promise of a better life. To Roosevelt, an economic conservative whose primary goal was to save the capitalist system, Townsend's spectacular promises made him a dangerous radical, a demagogue whose politics threatened the comfortable two-party system and whose economics endangered the fragile and partial recovery from the trough of the Great Depression that the New Deal had begun to piece together in 1934 and 1935.

There was, to be sure, a core of truth in this assessment of Townsend and his movement. But if Townsend was a radical, his was an odd sort of radicalism that came packaged as the American dream. To proud older people who valued their independence, Townsend stood for the prospect of a dignified retirement. To younger people, he offered the jobs that had been vacated by the recently retired. To young and old, he proposed a new kind of national economy, driven not by production but by consumer purchases. This mixture of security and social engineering was hardly revolutionary. In its own, more oblique way, Roosevelt's New Deal was moving in similar directions. And a half century later, Townsend's ideas —if not his plan—were national policy.

I t was 1936. For 6 years, all of them years of the Great Depression that had begun with the crash of the stock market in the fall of 1929, Charles Lewis had struggled to make ends meet while working a 260-acre, rented dairy farm in the foothills of Chautauqua County, New York, not far from Lake Erie and only a few miles from the Pennsylvania line. Since 1898, Lewis had kept a day book—a brief daily record—of weather and work. For the most part, the entries chronicle the year-around drudgery of cutting "poles" for fencing and drawing manure. But they also reveal Lewis's interest in the major spectacles of the day. During the year 1936, Lewis noted the death of the King of England; the electrocution of Bruno Richard Hauptmann, kidnapper and murderer of Charles Lindbergh's infant son; and Joe Louis's victory in a prize fight ("nigger Lewis & dakota farmer only 1 blow/struck and the nigger did it"). For June 28, Lewis wrote:

> Cold wind clowdy [sic] I picked some berries P.M.
> We all went over to Lily Dale to a big
> Townsen [sic] meeting awful crowd

Lily Dale was an established spiritualist community—the sort of place where one could find help in contacting the soul of a dead relative. But on this particular Sunday, the grounds had been given over to an all-day political rally. According to the *Jamestown Evening Journal,* an estimated 8000 people, most of them representing Townsend clubs in Buffalo, Niagara Falls, Lockport, and other Western New York communities, showed up for the day's events, which included a morning concert by the Falconer Townsend Club band, a noon "picnic basket," and an evening softball game.

Although Franklin D. Roosevelt had only the day before accepted the nomination of the Democratic Party for a second term as president, most of those who attended the Lily Dale rally had little interest in Roosevelt or, for that matter, in the more conservative Republican candidate, Kansas governor Alfred M. Landon. Many were considering voting for William Lemke, a North Dakota Republican who was running for president on the new Union Party ticket. But even Lemke's candidacy was suspect. As the day wore on, the Lily Dale delegates passed a resolution urging fellow Townsend followers to withhold support from the Union Party until Lemke had pledged his unequivocal support for the single-issue platform of the Townsend movement: the old-age revolving pension (OARP), otherwise known as the Townsend Plan.

At its core, the Townsend Plan was simple: Give every retired person over 60 years of age a "pension" of $200 per month, provided only that the pensioner agree to retire from the work place and spend the money before the next check arrived. With the presidential election only months away, it seemed possible that millions of Americans would forsake the major parties to cast their ballots for nothing more than an old-age pension plan.

The cause of this bizarre situation was Francis E. Townsend, a gaunt, energetic, white-haired man 69 years of age. Born in a log cabin near Fairbury, Illinois, in 1867, Townsend was one of seven children reared in a poor, religious, and hard-working farm family. "We knew poverty in those days," he recalled in *New Horizons,* his 1943 autobiography,

> but it seems to have been a different sort of poverty. There were many years of my childhood when I am sure my father handled less than $100 a year in actual cash, but I have no recollection of ever being hungry after I was grown up. . . . As neighborhoods and as families, we were self-sufficient. We made our things or did without.

Participating in the same sort of unending round of labor that would characterize Charles Lewis's life in the 1930s, Townsend acquired a "distaste" for what he described as "this toilsome existence in which men were conscripted by life into an endless battle with nature and in which women grew old before their time." In contrast, Townsend fondly recalled the entrepreneurial energy of his brother-in-law, who in the serious depression of the 1890s had bought up Kansas lands that had been seeded and then, under conditions of drought, abandoned:

> The snows melted and soaked the good ground and the volunteer wheat came on from the dormant seed. . . . Crops grew and matured amazingly and these far-seeing men were ready with their great machinery [the enormous harvesting "combines" of the day] when the harvest time came on. They reaped and they reaped until all bins and granaries and barns that could be rented were full and overflowing. Such a harvest! At such an insignificant cost!

Following the family's move to Nebraska in the mid-1880s, Townsend spent more than a decade as a virtual transient. In 1887, he tried—and failed—to make his fortune during an early California land boom. A series of odd jobs in Spokane and Seattle were no more productive. Returning to Nebraska, Townsend taught school, worked a tract of land in northwestern Kansas, and completed a college preparatory course at Franklin (Nebraska) Academy. In 1899, having lost his farm, he enrolled at Omaha Medical College. Graduating in 1903, he practiced medicine among the miners and cowhands of Belle Fourche, South Dakota, and, in 1906, married "Minnie" Brogue.

After the Great War (World War I), when health problems made life in the Black Hills intolerable, Townsend took his family to Long Beach, California. Despite the city's rapidly growing population of older people, Townsend's medical practice remained a marginal one. Perhaps for this reason, in 1927 he put his ever scarcer resources into Midway City, a Southern California real estate venture—again without success. Most of his remaining savings were lost in the first year or two of the Great Depression.

Townsend's luck seemed to have turned in 1930, when a former medical school classmate hired him for the staff of the county hospital to provide in-home care for the "needy ill" of Long Beach. "We were besieged incessantly with calls for help," Townsend wrote. But in the summer of 1933, in the depths of the Great Depression, the county program under which Townsend was employed was discontinued, and the job was gone. The stage was set for the Townsend Plan.

Just how Townsend emerged from the despondency of unemployment to advocate a celebrated "plan" is a matter of some dispute. One analysis, written in 1936, emphasized that Townsend's rise to "the position of national political dictator" was undeserved, the product of a "series of fortuitous incidents"—the last one a Long Beach election that had resulted in a political decision to discontinue the county's health programs. In *New Horizons*, Townsend preferred to represent his personal experience—indeed, the plan itself—as a typical product of twentieth-century life. "Here were mother and I," he wrote referring to his wife,

> both past 60, both intelligent and experienced but not active enough to compete in the world of commerce and economics. Or was that true? Economics in America is something controlled by politics—and politics is votes. We might be too old to work, but we were not too old to vote. And there were millions of others like us. . . An idea came to me which might alleviate the hopelessness of the aged people of our community.

The Townsend Plan logo. The letters OARP stand for Old Age Revolving Pension, the plan's formal name, while LTD (for limited liability) was perhaps intended to emphasize that the plan was as solidly grounded as any other business organization. The slogan highlighted the plan's goal of redistributing by age a finite amount of work.

According to the most frequently repeated explanation of Townsend's politicization—and, curiously, one that is not repeated in his autobiography—Townsend conceived of the plan one day in 1933, when he happened to observe three old women rummaging in garbage cans for something to eat. As Townsend later told the story: "A torrent of invectives tore out of me, the big blast of all the bitterness that had been building in me for years." Minnie's efforts to calm her husband were to no avail. "I want all the neighbors to hear me!" Townsend purportedly said. "I want God Almighty to hear me! I'm going to shout until the whole country hears!"

On September 30, 1933, the first version of the Townsend Plan appeared in the Long Beach *Press-Telegram* as a letter to the editor:

> Because of man's inventiveness less and less productive effort is going to be required to supply the needs of the race. This being the case, it is just as necessary to make some disposal of our surplus workers, as it is to dispose of our surplus wheat or corn or cotton.

Referring to an infamous New Deal program that had resulted in the slaughtering of 6 million little pigs to head off a glut in the hog market, Townsend wrote:

> But we cannot kill off the surplus workers as we are doing with our hogs. . . . We must retire them from business activities and eliminate them from the field of competitive effort.

Estimating the population of Americans over 60 years of age at between 9 and 12 million, Townsend proceeded to the heart of his plan:

> I suggest that the national government retire all who reach that age on a monthly pension of $150 a month or more, on condition that they spend the money as they get it. This will insure an even distribution throughout the nation of two or three billions of fresh money each month. Thereby insuring a healthy and brisk state of business, comparable to that we enjoyed during war times.

Townsend was just as frank about financing the plan. New taxes—substantial taxes—would be necessary. The proper tax, he argued, was a sales tax—"sufficiently high to insure the pensions at a figure adequate to maintain the business of the country in a healthy condition." Finally, Townsend called on readers to understand the growing role that the national government must take in stimulating economic activity when private businesses were too cautious. "This function of the Government," he concluded, "could be easily established and maintained through the pension system for the aged."

In the years that followed, there were changes in certain details and emphases of the Townsend Plan. The $150 would soon become $200—a lot of money at a time when only about 10 percent of all American families earned more than $2500 in a year—and in legislation introduced in Congress in April 1935, the $200 would become a maximum rather than a guaranteed sum. It was not long, either, before Townsend dumped the sales tax for a "transaction" tax of 2 percent on all commercial and business transactions. "A sales tax would hit the little man," he told a Senate committee. "A transactions tax will make the rich fellow pay. The Townsend tax is in no way a sales tax." In addition, the movement's most widely used slogan—"Youth for Work/Age for Leisure"—reflected Townsend's growing inclination to present his pension movement as a boon to workers in their 20s and

30s, who in the absence of his pensions might have trouble finding employment. Referring to the Civilian Conservation Corps, a New Deal program that employed some 500,000 young men in forestry projects, a Townsend Plan ready-reference book said, "[Youth] do not want a mountain camp, segregated from society, under military dictatorship and martial law. THEY WANT A HOME and a place in the civil life of the nation." By and large, the Townsend Plan that soon became familiar to Americans closely resembled Townsend's first letter to the editor.

Within months, Townsend's simple idea was transformed into a social movement. By the end of October, the *Press-Telegram* carried a regular page of reader reactions to Townsend's proposal. By early November, in response to a 1-inch newspaper ad, a platoon of Long Beach elderly were accumulating thousands of signatures on the first of many Townsend petitions. From an 8- by 10-foot room in the rear of a real estate office, the Townsend organization moved to larger quarters. On New Year's Day, 1934, Townsend and his new partner, 40-year-old real estate promoter Robert "Earl" Clements, hung a large sign: "Old-Age Revolving Pension Headquarters." A few days later, the organization was incorporated as a non-profit corporation; Clements, Townsend, and Townsend's brother, a Los Angeles hotel porter, were the organization's only directors.

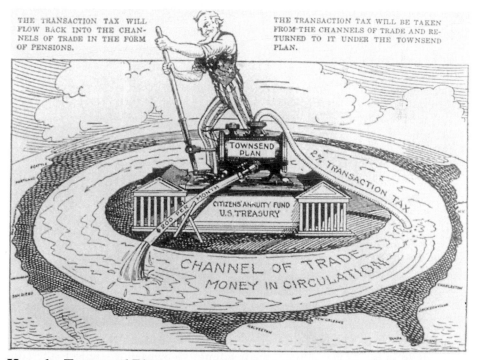

How the Townsend Plan was supposed to work: a closed system, with the government at its center, helping things along. The cartoon also reflects the Plan's reliance on theories of the circulation of money as well as the confidence that American economic recovery could be achieved independent of the rest of the world. This illustration appeared in a Townsend publication in 1936.

Using direct-mail techniques, voluntary and paid organizers, and a news-paper, *The Modern Crusader* (later renamed *The Townsend National Weekly*), Townsend and Clements rapidly expanded the organization beyond Long Beach. San Diego, a city of 180,000 people with the nation's largest percentage of older people, was an obvious target. By early 1935, the city had some 30,000 dues-paying members and was able to produce 105,000 signatures on a petition endorsing the Townsend Plan. Stimulated by "Townsend budgets" that showed precisely how $200 per month might be spent (monthly payments on a refrigerator, an electric washer, a radio, and a vacuum cleaner totaled $30), many residents of San Diego and other cities acted as if payment of the pension were imminent. One San Diego couple, convinced that the November, 1934, congressional elections would lead immediately to passage of a Townsend measure in Congress, insisted that a furniture dealer allow payments to be deferred until January, when the first Townsend Plan checks would arrive.

The movement registered similar successes in cities and towns throughout the Far West and the Midwest; among other communities, Los Angeles, Seattle, Portland, Chicago, Toledo, and Cleveland were bastions of Townsendism. By 1936, Townsend was claiming 3,500,000 supporters and a circulation for *The Townsend National Weekly* of some 2,000,000. The Northeast, and especially the South, where employers feared that the movement would threaten the supply of black labor, proved more resistant to the Townsend message.

A sign in Saw Pit, Colorado, September 1940. Although the sign describes what it means to be a "Townsendite," the heading—"Townsend"—reflects the continued importance of Townsend's personal leadership within the movement. Russell Lee, who took the photograph for the Farm Security Administration, probably also intended to emphasize that Townsend was no less a "product" of advertising than Bubble Up and Chesterfields. (Library of Congress)

As the movement grew, it was sustained by a network of locally organized but nationally administered Townsend Clubs. The first club was chartered in Huntington Park, California, in August, 1934; by January of 1935, there were 3,000 clubs, each with from 100 to 1,000 dues-paying members. Reporting on the Townsend movement in the election year of 1936 for the *Twentieth-Century Fund,* a committee of prominent citizens expressed concern over the growth and power of the clubs. "If there are 7,000 Townsend Clubs with a membership of 3,500,000 organized by congressional districts, as Dr. Townsend claims, the organizations give him the balance of power between the two parties. That is, if one candidate of either party endorses the Plan and his opponent does not, the Townsend sentiment may decide the election."

The typical Townsend Club gathering of the mid-1930s drew a middle-class membership of farmers, clerks, clergymen, skilled workers, insurance agents, and small businessmen, many of them already retired and others thinking about retirement, to a small-town church or public school building. On the walls of the auditorium are the slogan "The Townsend Plan is religion in action" and card-

Real estate and insurance salesman and Townsend Club member John W. Dillard, reading the *Townsend National Weekly* in his Washington, Indiana, office, June 1941. Like Dillard, many Townsendites were thoughtful, respected—and elderly—members of their communities. Photo by John Vachon for the Farm Security Administration. (Library of Congress)

board pictures of the founder. Following the salute to the flag, a patriotic song or two, and a prayer led by a minister (amens echo through the hall), the local president reads a message "direct from Dr. Townsend and Mr. Clements in Washington" and exhorts the faithful to pay their dues—no doubt emphasizing, as a Townsend pamphlet did, that the plan was "an organization of the masses, the common people, supported by their nickels, dimes, and quarters." Addressing the throng as "You dear old folks," the evening's speaker—perhaps a candidate for Congress in the district—lavishes praise on the plan, lauds Townsend as a David slaying the Goliaths of "Wall Street" and "Moscow," and enjoins those assembled to "take up the cross of this crusade." The speech over, plans are made for selling official literature, collecting signatures on petitions, and securing new members—all with the goal of electing congressmen and senators pledged to vote for the Townsend Plan. The meeting closes with the audience on its feet, repeating after its leader: "The Townsend Plan must succeed. I therefore pledge my allegiance to its principles, its founders, its leaders, and to all loyal co-workers; and re-dedicate myself to maintain the democratic spirit and form of government in America."

In the first 6 months of 1934, as Townsend was building the strength of his organization in southern California, the President of the United States was laying the groundwork for his own program of old-age insurance (i.e., pensions), putting his administration on a collision course with the Townsend movement. In early March, Roosevelt discussed the problem over lunch with General Electric president Gerard Swope, a reform-minded businessman whose company had a "contributory" pension plan to which employees contributed a portion of their earnings. Like many executives of the nation's largest corporations, Swope believed that only contributory plans would allow employees the freedom to leave one job, and one geographical location, for another. He also favored a pension system run by the federal government rather than individual states, as only then would the costs of doing business be equalized across state lines and industries.

On June 8, Roosevelt outlined for Congress a comprehensive program of federal-state cooperation "to provide at once security against several of the great disturbing factors in life—especially those which relate to unemployment and old age." And he made clear that unlike Townsend, he favored a system funded by contributions, not by "an increase in general taxation." To produce the administration's package of legislation, Roosevelt appointed a special cabinet-level committee—the Committee on Economic Security (CES). The CES was headed by executive director Edwin Witte, a University of Wisconsin professor of economics. At Roosevelt's urging, Witte left Washington to consult with Swope, Walter Teagle of Standard Oil, and John Raskob of General Motors. Witte also met with Henry Harriman, president of the United States Chamber of Commerce, whose "general attitude," Witte reported, "was that some legislation on social security was inevitable and that business should not put itself in the position of attempting to block this legislation, but should concentrate its efforts upon getting it into acceptable form."

Although the Raskobs and Harrimans had their say, the administration's old-age legislation was actually conceptualized and written by four people who were not exactly household names: Barbara Armstrong, professor of law at the University of California at Berkeley and author of a book, *Insuring the Essentials,* that advocated contributory old-age pensions; Murray Latimer, for years an employee of Industrial Relations Counselors, a private firm involved in pension consulting for Standard Oil of New Jersey and other large corporations; J. Douglas Brown, a young economist from the Industrial Relations Section at Princeton University; and Otto Richter, a pension actuary employed by American Telephone and Telegraph.

Armstrong and her colleagues in the old-age section of the CES did their important work—and wrote one of the most important bills in American history—under a variety of constraints and pressures. Although Roosevelt had given them a great task to do, his instructions—the June 8 address—were remarkably vague. Indeed, for a time even his commitment to old-age security legislation was in doubt. In her 1946 memoir, Secretary of Labor Frances Perkins presents the President as an early and firm advocate of a "cradle to the grave" system of social insurance. "There is no reason why just the industrial workers should get the benefit of this," Roosevelt told his cabinet. "Everybody ought to be in on it—the farmer and his wife and his family." But Roosevelt was giving the CES other, more negative signals. In fact, in a November 14 public statement, Roosevelt appeared to set aside a good portion of the CES agenda: "I do not know whether this is the time for any federal legislation on old age security." According to Douglas Brown, a deeply distressed CES staff now took "desperate measures." Armstrong used her contacts at the Scripps–Howard chain of newspapers to generate an editorial questioning Roosevelt's commitment to old-age legislation. Upset and exasperated, the President got on the phone to Perkins, who in turn sounded out Witte. As Brown tells the story, a "much excited" Witte rushed to the office that he and Armstrong shared. "He asked us if we knew how and why the speech had received such a bad press. From then on, the President seemed to take a greater interest in old age insurance."

Throughout the fall of 1934, the CES functioned under the shadow of the growing Townsend movement. As Perkins recalled, "The pressure from its [the Townsend Plan's] advocates was intense. The President began telling people he was in favor of adding old-age insurance clauses to the bill and putting it through as one package." Within weeks of his arrival in Washington, D.C., in late July, Witte had asked the Postmaster General to investigate the Townsend movement to determine if funds sent through the U.S. mails were being used for illegitimate purposes. (By late September he had his answer: the Townsend Plan was clean.) The heat was turned up a notch in November, when the election of a number of pro-Townsend representatives, including the eloquent and personable poet laureate of California, John S. McGroarty, made the introduction of a Townsend measure imminent. By December, when Townsend opened an office in the nation's capital to begin the lobbying process and sought a meeting with the President, Roosevelt refused to grant him an audience—an act described by the *Townsend Weekly* as "an insult that the masses of the people should resent."

At the Committee on Economic Security, an anxious Witte wrote a colleague of the growing danger:

> In the last three months I have become more concerned than ever with the Townsend Plan. There is no doubt that this movement has made tremendous headway. The battle against the Townsend movement has been lost, I think, in pretty nearly every

state west of the Mississippi, and the entire Middle Western area is likewise badly infected. At this time the Republican party organization is at least flirting with the Townsendites. . . . The Townsend movement has become a terrific menace which is likely to engulf our entire economic system.

When the 74th Congress convened in January, the two sides were prepared for combat. The comprehensive administration package included a plan for unemployment insurance and two old-age measures. One of the old-age bills was a welfare measure, designed to provide joint state and federal relief for the elderly poor and for those who were too old to make sufficient contributions to an insurance plan. The other—in its essentials the future program of Social Security—provided for a national system of old-age insurance, to be funded by contributions from employers and employees. The Townsend bill, introduced by Rep. McGroarty, sought to do everything the administration measure did, but through the mechanism of the Old Age Revolving Pension Plan.

The issue was joined in the House Committee on Ways and Means, where the administration bill was the only one being formally considered, and where advocates of the administration measure—Democrats, all—were in control. Labor Secretary Perkins offered lengthy testimony. In language that sounded very much like Townsend's, she emphasized that "new and labor-saving machinery" and "new methods of work" on the one hand raised the standard of living "of the whole community" and, on the other hand, produced "transition periods" that were "extremely difficult for the individuals put out of work."

When asked about the Townsend Plan, however, Perkins was brutally critical. It was not "insurance," but a "dole," and an expensive dole at that. According to her estimates, payments under the plan would amount to "something considerably more than half of the total national income of the U.S.A. . . ." Perkins also challenged the claim that appropriations under the Townsend Plan would immediately and dramatically increase purchasing power and create a market for consumer goods. The plan, she concluded, was "in the realm of fancy rather than in the realm of practical statesmanship."

The next to testify was Murray Latimer. As head of the agency charged with administering the recently passed Railroad Retirement Act, Latimer could explain to the committee how that law had been openly designed to relieve crowded labor markets and increase efficiency by forcing the retirement of railroad workers over age 65. Latimer believed that the administration's proposal for old-age insurance could provide a similar service for the larger economy. If payments were large enough, they would induce considerable numbers of people to "withdraw from the labor market." "Nor," he added, "should the advantages of the maintenance of a large and continuing stream of purchasing power directed almost entirely to consumers' goods be overlooked."

Still another administration spokesperson, J. Douglas Brown, offered a rationale for the joint worker–employer contributions called for under the old-age insurance proposal. He emphasized that by contributing, workers would establish an "earned contractual right" to their annuities. And because employee contributions would result in larger payments in old age, they would "encourage the displacement of superannuated workers and of minor children and women supporting dependent old persons from the labor market."

Although the Committee on Ways and Means was not officially considering the McGroarty bill, it agreed to allow Townsend to testify; to have done otherwise would been politically unwise. Townsend appeared on a Friday morning, February 1, 1935, as the Committee was concluding its second week of testimony. In a prepared statement, he set the stage for the presentation of his plan. "For the past 5 years," Townsend said,

> the people of the United States . . . have been starving in the midst of plenty. They have seen experiment after experiment tried out; experiments which bore the recommendation and hearty approval of men we call "economists." Experiment after experiment has failed. . . . The rich are growing richer and the poor are growing poorer.

Townsend called for a "new experiment," one that had not had "the blessing of the so-called 'economists.' " Describing his plan as "only incidentally a pension plan," he claimed it would solve the unemployment problem and, by restoring purchasing power to the people, bring back prosperity. "The old people," he added, "are simply to be used as a means by which prosperity will be restored to all of us."

As much as Townsend disliked economists, he knew the politicians would want evidence of how his plan would work economically. He told the committee that because he was "simply a country practitioner of medicine," he had arranged for Glen Hudson, an actuary, to appear before the committee. On the following Monday, Townsend and Hudson testified together.

Almost immediately, the committee's inquiries became pointed and aggressive. Representative Samuel Hill, a Washington state Democrat, questioned Townsend about who was eligible under his plan:

DR. TOWNSEND: We agree that the plan shall be nondiscriminatory and applied to all citizens equally.

MR. HILL: In other words, it would apply to John D. Rockefeller, Sr., to Henry Ford, to J. P. Morgan, as well as to a man who has no means of income at all?

DR. TOWNSEND: If they wish to acquire the pension under the provisions of the act.

When Hill inquired about the "revolving" concept claimed for the plan, Townsend appeared unsure and even confused. He could not clearly explain just how his plan "revolved," or how its revolving feature differed from any other dispersement of tax monies by the government. Townsend also had trouble fielding simple questions about the inner workings of the Townsend movement. Concerned about the size and strength of the Townsend organization, committee Chairman Robert Doughton (D-N.C.) asked Townsend to describe the plan's salaried sales force and explain the commission system used to compensate other employees.

DR. TOWNSEND: Mr. R. E. Clements is vice president and secretary, and he has all of that data.

THE CHAIRMAN: You ought to know. You are the head of the organization, and you should have such data before you.

Fortunately for Townsend, Hudson held forth through most of Monday afternoon, defending the plan with intelligence and enthusiasm. One congressman charged that the transaction tax would dramatically inflate the economy by adding 9 percent to consumer prices; another attacked the McGroarty bill for its failure to meet the needs of workers between ages 45 and 60, many of whom had trouble getting or holding jobs; and another claimed that at best, the Townsend Plan would retire only 3 million persons, far less than the 10 million retirements needed to eliminate unemployment altogether. Time and again, Hudson answered the critics by emphasizing that the plan depended for its success on the velocity of money. Because, he claimed, the average dollar turned over 34 times in 1 year, the economic stimulus provided by the Townsend pensions would be many times that of the money taken in through the transaction tax. Yet even Hudson was not thoroughly committed to every aspect of the McGroarty bill. Sensing Hudson's distance from the very measure he was there to support, Rep. Jere Cooper, a Tennessee Democrat, asked a revealing question:

MR. COOPER: Suppose you sat in the seats that we occupy at this table. As the [Townsend] bill now stands in its present form, do you think you would be safe in voting to report it and support it, as a representative of the people?

MR. HUDSON: No; I do not.

Not long after the hearings concluded, an amended version of the administration bill passed the House on April 19 by a vote of 371 to 33. Most of the opposition came from Republicans. An earlier effort to substitute the McGroarty bill—the Townsend measure—received only about 50 votes. Nonetheless, the Senate Finance Committee seemed ready to reject compulsory old-age insurance—

Francis Townsend, addressing a newly organized club in Washington, D.C., March 6, 1937. The original caption for this photo noted that Townsend had been recently found guilty of contempt of the House of Representatives yet was "not the least apprehensive" that he might be sent to jail. (Library of Congress)

that is, until Witte told committee members in closed session that "the probable alternative was a modified Townsend plan." In mid-June, the Senate passed the bill, 77 to 6. When Roosevelt signed the measure on August 14, 1935, the Social Security Act became law.

Even then, the Townsend movement would not go away. Indeed, it gained strength as the provisions of the Social Security Act became known. Over 9 million Americans—domestic servants, government employees, farm workers like Charles Lewis, and everyone over age 65—were not eligible for old-age insurance benefits—what Americans today refer to as "social security." In contrast, even the very rich were entitled to benefits. Those who qualified were to begin paying into the system immediately, but they would not see their first check until 1942. Until then, those over age 65 could apply to their respective states for old-age assistance payments that averaged $19.21 per month ($3.92 in Mississippi). Eleanor Roosevelt, who continued to speak out against the Townsend Plan even when her husband would not, received thousands of letters from irate Townsendites, many of them women. "Security Bill is a joke so far as assisting the old people is concerned," wrote one woman. Another described the "so-called 'social security' act" as "niggardly and inadequate."

In October 1935, less than 3 months after the passage of the Social Security Act, some 7000 inspired Townsendites assembled in Chicago for the organization's first annual convention. They seemed ready to launch a movement rather than end it. A delegate from Texas took the floor to explain his hope

> to see erected in Washington, D.C. a statue with arms and legs made of strongest steel . . . adorned with a crown and priceless pearl . . . on his brow the word "Liberator," and under it all the name *TOWNSEND*. [applause, amens]

Although not a powerful speaker, Townsend rose to the occasion. To thunderous applause he described his movement as "an avalanche of political power that no derision, no ridicule, no conspiracy of silence can stem." Reaching for an analogy, he found one:

> Where Christianity numbered in hundreds in its beginning years, our cause numbers in millions. And without sacrilege we can say that we believe that the effects of our movement will make as deep and mighty changes in civilization as Christianity itself.

Later, when some delegates asked for clarification during the reading of the financial report, the convention burst into song:

> Onward Townsend soldiers
> Marching as to war,
> With the Townsend banner
> Going on before.

Flushed with the triumphal meeting at Chicago, Townsend increasingly attacked the major parties. Looking ahead to the fall, 1936, congressional elections, he predicted that politicians of both parties would have to renounce their Republican and Democratic affiliations and support the Townsend Plan in order to get elected. Against Clements's advice, he pressed for a third party. In doing so, he may have attracted some additional followers—among them, perhaps, Charles

Lewis—but he had also threatened the existing distribution of political power. In mid-February, 1936, the House of Representatives voted to initiate a bipartisan investigation of the Townsend movement. In late May, after 3 days of grueling testimony before a hostile committee, Townsend denounced the inquiry and walked out. A contempt citation was not issued until late in the year. In the meantime, Roosevelt had been elected to a second term in office with 27,751,612 votes; the Republican Landon, who had denounced the Social Security Act, received 16,681,913; running on the Union Party ticket and carrying the banner of the Townsend Plan, Lemke received only 891,858.

AN INTERPRETATION

The story of Francis Townsend and the Townsend movement is in part the story of how a significant and organized minority was kept on the margins of American political life. Roosevelt played a major role in this process of marginalization by refusing to meet with Townsend or to comment publicly on the Townsend Plan. At the Committee on Economic Security, Witte tried to use the U.S. Post Office to sabotage the movement. The Congress did its part, denying to the Townsend bill the primary status that was granted to the administration measure. The major parties, fearful that an attack launched by either the Republicans or the Democrats would injure the party taking the initiative, joined forces to investigate the Townsend movement, then, when Townsend walked away from what he rightly called an "inquisition," made sure that the 1936 elections were over before issuing a citation for contempt of Congress.

One could argue that this effort to purge Townsend and his movement from American political life was justifiable, in that Townsend was a demagogue—that is, he made irrational and irresponsible appeals to a mass audience incapable of separating truth from falsehood. As events at the 1935 national convention reveal, there is no doubt that he had a devoted and even fanatical following; that he was enamored of his own movement and perhaps, even, eventually attracted to his movement as a sort of modern-day Christianity. In addition, the movement utilized a variety of up-to-date promotional techniques that contributed to Townsend's personal success and to the movement's rapid growth. Charles Lewis, whose diary reveals an attraction to spectacle, might be interpreted as a typical Townsend victim. On the other hand, Townsend makes an unlikely demagogue: an old man, a boring speaker, incapable of controlling critical information. Hardly a man driven by the desire for adulation, Townsend emerged as a prominent political figure almost by accident. The most disturbing aspect of the Townsend movement's appeal was its reliance on religion, probably because this gave the cause a foundation exterior to traditional politics.

What makes Townsend's marginalization so remarkable is that many aspects of the man and his movement seem quite conservative. Although Townsend often couched his appeals in a familiar populist rhetoric of rich and poor, the Townsend Plan itself promised no significant distribution of income from one social class to another. As opponents pointed out, the sales tax, and the transaction tax that replaced it, were both harshly regressive. Furthermore, Townsend's desire to make his plan "nondiscriminatory" meant that even extremely rich people would be receiving checks for $200 per month that they did not need and probably would not spend. As Townsend's account of his life experiences reveals, the founder embraced and applied many aspects of capitalism, including speculation, promotion, entrepreneurship, and mechanical efficiency. His sharp criticism of the Civilian Conservation Corps confirms that Townsend did not wish to ameliorate suffering by creating agencies and bureaucracies; on the contrary, the thrust of the Townsend Plan was toward decentralization; it was a way of distributing money downward, in order to reinforce home and family. If anything, Townsend valued individual independence too highly. Overall, Townsend's conservatism explains his appeal to the rural middle class. But it may also account for the movement's failure—and it was a critical one— to attract significant support from industrial workers.

His radical-sounding rhetoric aside, perhaps Townsend was just another of those "economists" he regularly denounced. Indeed, Townsend's ideas about the economy and economic recovery resembled those of his New Deal adversaries. During the hearings before the House Committee on Ways and Means, Perkins expressed Townsend-like anxieties about the long-term impact of technology. She and Latimer echoed the Townsend Plan's position on the importance of stimulating consumer spending; Latimer and Brown shared Townsend's enthusiasm for reducing unemployment by using old-age insurance to encourage the retirement of older workers from the labor force. While Perkins lambasted the Townsend Plan as a "dole," the Social Security Act was not strictly an insurance plan, as payments to the elderly were funded largely by the current contributions of those still working. The Townsend Plan probably was more than the nation could afford in 1935; its scope may even have been fanciful, as Perkins claimed. But its assumptions and mechanisms were in many respects part of the mainstream. In fact, Townsend's idea of turning the elderly into what historian Abraham Holtzman has called "distributor custodians" foreshadows the prominent role of consumerism in the post-World War II economy of affluence, and Townsend's emphasis on retirement anticipates the rising social security rates and private pension plans that would fuel the postwar retirement boom. Although the plan might well have damaged the economy had the McGroarty bill become law, Townsend's point —that the economy had been severely harmed while being managed by the same economic establishment that now attacked his plan as unworthy—was not unreasonable.

One could argue, in fact, that Townsend was anathema to politics not because his ideas were unfamiliar, but because he so blatantly articulated and presented the assumptions on which mainstream policy was based. When Roosevelt spoke about social insurance, he used the language of altruism, talking about a "cradle-to-the-grave" system of "security." Townsend, in contrast, spoke the language of the hard-nosed realists at the Committee on Economic Security. Although he was not without an altruistic side, he could also be very frank in explaining his goal of using the elderly to redistribute available work and to revive the economy.

By being so open, Townsend succeeded for a time in revealing the sources of the welfare state. One view of the origins of the welfare state, suggested by Roosevelt's rhetoric, locates the origins of measures like the Social Security Act in a benign response to the long-term insecurities produced by industrialization and urbanization. Even Townsend's life—a mobile life that began in the security of a large farm family and ended in the isolation of a city on the edge of the continent—supports this interpretation. Townsend's claim that the idea for the Townsend Plan came to him as he observed elderly women searching the garbage for food also sustains this view, although the fact that the story is not repeated in Townsend's autobiography suggests that the event may never have happened, and that Townsend concocted the incident only because he knew it coincided with what people expected to hear. Another interpretation of the emergence of the national welfare state emphasizes the growing power of organized labor. But as the story implies, organized labor did not play much of a role in the events leading to the passage of the Social Security Act.

The Townsend movement came under attack in part because it put in bold relief two other important explanations of the welfare state. Roosevelt's flacid leadership and lack of commitment to old-age insurance, as well as the Senate Finance Committee's rapid turnaround on the issue, are evidence that the New Deal was moved to create a national welfare state partly by the ongoing challenge of a movement that lay beyond the regular party system. Once goaded into action by Townsend, Roosevelt, Perkins, Witte, and other New Deal liberals turned to the big business community—to Swope and Teagle, and to Latimer, Richter, and other experts who had advised the nation's largest corporations. Townsend's forthrightness in describing the operations of the welfare state stripped the welfare state of its ideological protections, revealing the prominent role played by big business in its evolution. In the process, Townsend became a marked man.

Sources: Francis E. Townsend's autobiographical *New Horizons* (Chicago: J.L. Stewart 1943) remains an important source on the pension advocate's personal background. On the Townsend movement, see Richard L. Neuberger and Kelley Loe, *An Army of the Aged: A History and Analysis of the Townsend Old Age Pension Plan* (1936; New York: Da Capo Press, 1973); Abraham Holtzman, *The Townsend Movement: A Political Study* (New York: Bookman Associates, 1963); and David H. Bennetts, *Demagogues in the Depression: American Radicals and the Union Party, 1932–1936* (New Brunswick, NJ: Rutgers University Press, 1969); and the Twentieth Century Fund's indictment, *The Townsend Crusade* (New York: Twentieth Century Fund, 1936). Differing perspectives on the Social Security Act of 1935 can be found in W. Andrew Achenbaum, *Social Security* (Cambridge, MA: Cambridge University Press, 1986); Edwin E. Witte, *The Development of the Social Security Act* (Madison: University of Wisconsin Press, 1963); William Graebner, *A History of Retirement* (New Haven: Yale University Press, 1980); and Jill Quadagno, *The Transformation of Old Age Security: Class and Politics in the American Welfare State* (Chicago: University of Chicago Press, 1988). Frances Perkins's memoir, *The Roosevelt I Knew* (New York: Viking, 1946), is an important source, and there is much to be learned from Congressional hearings on old age measures (see U.S. Congress, House Committee on Ways and Means, *Economic Security Act: Hearings on H.R. 4120. . . . 1935* (Washington, DC: GPO, 1935).

11

HARLEM HELLFIGHTERS: THE 369th IN WORLD WAR II HAWAII

BETH BAILEY AND DAVID FARBER

In the summer of 1942, members of the 369th Coast Artillery Regiment—skilled, proud, well-led, committed to its duty, and African American to a man—arrived in the territory of Hawaii, prepared to man the antiaircraft guns that would protect the islands from another Japanese attack. Expecting a mythic paradise of sand and sunshine, they found uniformed rednecks who wanted them off the sidewalks, brothels that refused their business, and a local population that was at once fearful, curious, and accepting. As Beth Bailey and David Farber explain, they also found in World War II Hawaii a set of conditions and circumstances that would change their lives: a mixture of peoples and colors that defied the rigid racial categories of the mainland; a national commitment to victory in war; a code of military rules and regulations to which everyone had to conform; and their own burgeoning self-confidence, rooted in the community of Harlem and nurtured in the palpable meritocracy of war.

If Hawaii seemed to open up possibilities for racial change, it was partly because conditions on the mainland were so unsatisfactory. On the eve of American entry into World War II, the United States was in most respects a segregated and racist society. Conditions were worst in the South, where at least six lynchings took place in the first 6 months of 1940, and where a great majority of African Americans could not or dared not vote. North and South, blacks and whites existed in separate worlds. Supported by decisions of state and federal courts, they went to separate schools, lived in separate neighborhoods, and went to the movies at separate theaters. As laughable as it now seems, in 1940 President Franklin D. Roosevelt helped celebrate a Chicago exposition that was described as "the first real Negro World's Fair in history." When Roosevelt's New Deal built some of the first public housing projects, they were intentionally segregated.

Conditions did not change overnight. Indeed, African Americans in many southern states did not vote in significant numbers until the mid-1960s, and most schools remained segregated—in fact, if not by law—decades after the historic decision in Brown v. Board of Education *(1954). Even so, the war was responsible for a near revolution in American economic and social relations. Using the leverage of wartime, A. Philip Randolph and his all-black union, the Brotherhood of Sleeping Car Porters, forced the Roosevelt administration to commit itself to opposing racial discrimination in employment, initiating a process that would turn that commitment into the law of the land. Drawn from the Deep South to northern cities by the demand for labor, hundreds of thousands of African Americans found industrial work at high wages, developed skills, and joined unions. The armed forces remained segregated, but military exigencies and black anger created a field of opportunity that made possible the 99th (Negro) Pursuit Squadron of Tuskegee, Alabama, and brought the 369th to Hawaii. Of more symbolic importance was a change in the tone of certain public gatherings, as Americans tried to live up to the democratic creed that sanctioned their participation in the war. Having been refused the right to sing in Constitution Hall in 1939 by the Daughters of the American Revolution, Marian Anderson performed there in 1943 before an integrated audience.*

Wartime changes in the racial status quo were inevitably accompanied by tension, conflict, and violence. In the South, the Ku Klux Klan added thousands of new members, and the number of lynchings and beatings of blacks rose alarmingly. Race riots or riots with racial overtones rocked Detroit; El Paso; Los Angeles; Springfield, Massachusetts—and Harlem. The 369th had missed the riot in their hometown, but the Harlem Hellfighters had surely lived some version of it—on the streets of Honolulu.

Every year on Veteran's Day, dozens of African-American men gather at the Regimental Armory in Harlem. These men, who served with the 369th Coast Artillery (AA) Regiment during World War II, have been meeting every year since 1953, when one-time Chief Warrant Officer William De Fossett (by then a detective in the New York City Police Department) and some of his friends founded the 369th Veterans' Association. The strong young men in the WWII Regimental photos are old now, retired from their jobs, ever fewer in number. But on Veteran's Day they meet, pass around family photos, plan community activities, laugh at each other's jokes, and remember the history of the 369th.

During these gatherings, the Armory echoes with the voices of young soldiers. There are uniformed Americans of all races and both sexes: the current members of the 369th. But during World War II, when these men served, the United States fought its battles for freedom and liberty with a segregated armed forces. Every member of the 369th Regiment—known as the "Harlem Hellfighters"—was black.

William De Fossett, president of the 369th Veteran's Association for 26 years, joined the regiment when he was 16, almost 5 years before the Japanese bombed Pearl Harbor on December 7, 1941. He was supposed to be 18 to join, but he was big for his age and already playing as a fill-in for the professional Negro Baseball League during the summer. His parents had no objections, so Bill found a sponsor in the regiment and, along with several of his ball-playing buddies, became a private in the 369th Regiment of the New York National Guard.

For De Fossett, like many of the young men who lived in Harlem, becoming a member of the 369th was a rite of passage, a statement that he was somebody special in the neighborhood, a young man with a future. For in the years preceding World War II, the 369th was a symbol of black pride throughout the nation and a badge of honor for New York City.

The 369th's fame had been won during the waning days of World War I when the regiment, attached to the French Army, had fought in the Meuse-Argone offensive in the siege of Sechault. They fought under the French flag, as the United States government refused to have white and black Americans, even in segregated units, fighting alongside one another. The courage of the 369th had been exemplary under fire, and the French government awarded the Croix de Guerre to the 369th regimental colors and individually to more than 150 of the men. When they returned from "over there" at war's end, all of New York, white and black, had turned out to pay their respects as the regiment marched down Fifth Avenue.

The demonstrated courage of the 369th was highly publicized in the independent black press and in progressive northern magazines and newspapers, and stood in contrast to much being written and said about the performance of black troops in World War I. An article in *The Outlook* argued that the performance of the 369th Infantry, "characterized by some as 'possessing black skins, white souls and red blood,' ought to silence for all time the slanderous charge that Negroes are cowards and will not fight. . . ." In an era in which the President of the United States, Woodrow Wilson, could publicly celebrate a movie, *Birth of a Nation*, which depicted

William and Joe De Fossett of the 369th Coast Artillery. Over a million servicemen and war workers came to Hawaii during the conflict. (Courtesy William K. De Fossett)

the Ku Klux Klan as heroic and the lynching of a black man as justice, the honors and accolades earned by the African-American men of the 369th stood in sharp contrast to the treatment usually accorded black Americans by white America.

William De Fossett was a natural for the highly selective and demanding 369th Regiment. At 16, he was best known in his Harlem neighborhood (just uptown from the Armory) for his athletic prowess. He could hit the long ball, and people had begun to call him "Babe," as in the great Babe Ruth. While still in his teens, he would play for the New York Black Yankees, the Pittsburgh Crawfords, the Baltimore Elite Giants, and with Alex Pompez's Cuban Stars. But De Fossett was more than just a standout ballplayer.

Bill De Fossett's parents had raised him and his older brother, Joe, to be hardworking, responsible, and studious. His mother was a college graduate, and though her skin color barred her from a job commensurate with her education (like most black working women in the North, she worked as a domestic for a white family), she emphasized the importance of education. William's father, too, set his boys an example. At night, home from his job at the Southern Pacific Steamship Company, he'd take out the *New York Times* crossword puzzle, begin inking in the answers, and ask his sons what new word they had learned that day. "Not a day should go by," their father told William and Joe more than once, "without learning a new word."

De Fossett also had the advantage of growing up in one of the must culturally rich neighborhoods of Harlem. His immediate neighbors in Harlem's Paul Dunbar Apartments included the singer and actor Paul Robeson, the dancer Bill "Bojangles" Robinson, the intellectual and civil rights activist W. E. B. DuBois, the labor leader and civil rights organizer A. Philip Randolph, and the explorer Mat Henson. As a kid, De Fossett and his friends played in Henson's apartment, trying on the Eskimo garb Henson had worn when he—and not Commander Perry, Henson told them—had become the first American to reach the North Pole. Paul Robeson, who was just "the singer on the third floor" to young Bill, taught him how to throw a football. Though Harlem had been disproportionally hard hit by the Great Depression of the 1930s, with black unemployment in New York City approaching 50 percent during the worst times, De Fossett came of age in one of the most vibrant communities in the nation.

As a child and then young man, William De Fossett was well aware of the illustrious history of the 369th, but at 16 his main reasons for joining were more in keeping with his age. On weekends the men of the 369th, in sharp uniforms, drilled outside the armory. They were often accompanied by what was generally acknowledged as the best regimental band in the United States, and the neighborhood turned out to watch. Every summer the 369th spent 2 weeks in the mountains, training—or as De Fossett and his friends saw it, "playing soldier." They loved the idea that the state of New York would pay them for this "duty."

But in January 1941, in an early phase of the war buildup, the 369th was federalized. Hardly any of the men knew it, but the question of what duty to assign this black regiment in the segregated U.S. armed forces was an extremely controversial and much debated question in the higher circles of Washington, D.C.

The issue of what to do with black troops emerged directly from World War I and the heightened antiblack racism of the early twentieth century. Despite the superb records of the 369th and some other black troops during WWI, they were overshadowed by powerful criticisms. These criticisms had some basis in reality. In general, black troops had not performed especially well. They had been insufficiently trained and often badly led by unsympathetic or hostile white officers (one southern white officer thought it appropriate to introduce himself to his men with the information that he had "suckled black mammies' breasts"). They lacked basic equipment, and morale suffered from discriminatory policies (unlike the white troops, for example, they were prohibited from most contact with French civilians). Due to widespread school discrimination in both the North and the South, a higher percentage of black soldiers than white were uneducated or illiterate. The explanations for failures abound; in that light the successes are more remarkable.

Many white army officers were, however, perfectly willing to attribute the failures to racial inferiority: Negroes would never make good combat soldiers, they argued, for blacks lacked both the necessary intelligence and the discipline. Major General Robert Bullard, the World War I commander of the Second Army (in which blacks had served as the 92nd Division), wrote in his memoirs, which he published in 1925: "Poor Negroes! They are hopelessly inferior." There was, however, an even more challenging message for those who sought equality. Drawing on diary entries from the war, Bullard mused: "If you need combat soldiers, especially if you need them in a hurry, don't put your time upon Negroes. . . . If racial uplift or racial equality is your purpose, that is another matter."

Going into World War II, the Army's policy toward the employment of black troops was predicated on the "lessons" learned in World War I. The goal of the Army, or of any other branch of the armed forces, was not racial uplift—it was mounting a successful fighting force as quickly and efficiently as possible. And coming into World War II, using black troops clearly presented problems. Racial tensions tended to flare when blacks and whites were in close proximity. Moreover, Army intelligence, G-2, argued against sending black troops just about anywhere beyond the U.S. mainland, for fear that the presence of blacks might create or exacerbate local racial tensions. The United States was not the only Allied nation with a race problem. Throughout the colonized world of America's allies, black troops might create political trouble.

Perhaps most important, the Army found blacks ill-prepared for military life. Black men, in aggregate, scored very badly on the Army General Classification Test (AGCT) and the Mechanical Aptitude Test, which were devised to use in assigning men to units; the AGCT was intended to measure the level of skill and ability the inductee already possessed and to evaluate "how ready [he is] to pick up soldiering—how likely [he is] to learn easily the facts, skills and techniques necessary for carrying out Army duties." Scores were closely related to educational and cultural background, so it is perhaps not surprising that 49.2 percent of black inductees fell into the lowest quintile of the AGCT (compared to 8.5 percent of whites), and that 83.9 percent of blacks scored in the bottom two quintiles. (Test scores were meant to form a bell curve, and they did for white troops.) The vast majority of blacks inducted into the Army were unskilled, many illiterate. Officers found that it generally took two times as long to train a "black unit" as a "white unit."

Proponents of black combat forces during the World War II mobilization had a hard argument to make. Given the potential for disruptive racial tensions, even violence, given the poor promise indicated by AGCT scores—what evidence could they offer? Here, the 369th's actions in World War I were compelling evidence against charges that blacks were *constitutionally,* inherently, racially, poor soldiers.

One of the most outspoken champions of black soldiers during the World War II mobilization was Hamilton Fish, Jr., the fiercely anti-New Deal conservative white Republican congressman from New York, who had been a company commander with the 369th during the Great War. Fish had stood shoulder to shoulder with his black troops while under enemy fire and shell; he had seen his men bleed and die. In honor of their courage and as sign of his own, he tenaciously lobbied the indifferent and even hostile Secretary of War, Henry Stimson, to give black Americans a fair chance and an honorable role in the armed forces.

Other powerful voices, too, spoke up on behalf of blacks in the armed forces. Eleanor Roosevelt, Walter White of the National Association for the Advancement of Colored People (NAACP), A. Philip Randolph (leader of the Brotherhood of Sleeping Car Porters and William De Fossett's neighbor), the editors of black-run newspapers such as the *Pittsburgh Courier,* and many others argued that the United States must not go to war against the Axis powers blighted by the shame of officially mandated racism and discrimination.

As a sign of his concern, and in recognition of the pressures mounted by and on behalf of black Americans, Franklin Roosevelt did appoint a black civil rights activist as a special civilian aide to the Secretary of War. But Roosevelt knew this appointment was more sop than solution. Because racism was so ingrained in American life, President Roosevelt decided that the free and democratic country he led, notwithstanding its claims to equality and world leadership, would fight its enemies with segregated armed forces. And it would not be a "separate but equal" military force but one in which African Americans would be overwhelmingly restricted to a lowly caste of mess boys, stevedores, and common laborers.

The Secretary of War's office clearly stated the rationale for such segregation: "The War Department administers the laws affecting the military establishment; it cannot act outside the law, nor contrary to the will of the majority of the citizens of the Nation." Secretary of War Stimson and President Roosevelt were in accord with political reality; in overwhelming numbers, white Americans opposed integrating the armed forces. A wartime survey of five major American cities, north and south, showed that nine out of ten white Americans supported a segregated army. Not surprisingly, most black Americans felt differently; the same survey showed that eight out of ten African Americans opposed segregation in the armed forces.

In Harlem, the decision to continue government-sponsored segregation of the armed forces added fuel to the fire for those who opposed black participation in the American war effort. The black playwright Loften Mitchell reported: "Irritated black people argued that when colored Ethiopia was attacked [by fascist Italy], Uncle Sam hadn't raced to her defense, but when white Europe was in trouble Uncle was right there. . . . Others declared openly they were not going to fight for colonial England, colonial France, and Jim Crow America." But those openly opposed to black participation in the war were a tiny minority. Many more Harlemites subscribed to the position advocated by the editors of the *Pittsburgh Courier,* the largest circulation black-oriented newspaper in the country during the World War II era.

The *Courier* called for a "Double V" campaign: "Victory over our enemies at home and victory over our enemies on the battlefields abroad." The editor and publisher of the paper, Robert Vann, wrote: "We call upon the President and Congress to declare war on Japan and against racial prejudice in our country. Certainly we should be strong enough to whip both." Even though President Roosevelt made it clear that only one of those wars would be fought, most African Americans in Harlem and throughout the United States chose to support the national effort and to do what they could in ways small and large, private and public, to win that second "V" against racial prejudice.

William De Fossett, early in 1941 when the 369th was federalized, like most of the young men of the regiment, thought little about the larger political questions raging around Army racial policies that would so affect his life. Twenty-year-old De Fossett was much more concerned with practical and immediate questions: Where was the unit going? How long would they be gone? Would the United States get involved in the war spreading across the globe?

At first all De Fossett and the troops were told was that they had been called up to serve a 1-year tour of duty and that they were to be trained for antiaircraft artillery (AA) duty. Some of the men, including those in the regiment's all-black officer corps, understood that the call-up of the 369th meant that the United States was beginning to seriously mobilize for the war that had already been raging in Europe for 3 years and in Asia for more than 10. Federalizing National Guard units like the 369th represented a major step in preparing the undermanned, poorly equipped and trained American Army for the looming war.

A few of the more politically sophisticated men recognized that the training for which the 369th was slotted represented a complex compromise between opponents and proponents of African Americans in the armed forces. The highly visible and well-championed 369th, along with the four other black regiments that had been assigned to antiaircraft artillery training, had done far better than most of the segregated African-American units. In the segregated American military, black troops were given low status duties, regardless of the specific abilities or experiences of the men. In the Army, they served most often as cargo loaders, truck drivers, and common laborers. In the Navy it was worse: at best, black men could become messmen or bandsmen.

Antiaircraft duty, in contrast, was genuinely high-status and required arduous and demanding training. Army command was showing good faith in the "Negro" units selected. But as William Hastie, the special civilian aide in the War Department, wrote in protest to his boss, Secretary of War Stimson, AA units were "in a special category" of combat units:

> Such a unit could be given a separate and more or less permanent defensive station in the theater of operations. It need not be integrated with other combat forces. So the utilization of Negro antiaircraft units in the theater of operations was adopted as a device best calculated to confound the critics of any policy as to Negro combat troops without basically changing that policy.

As Hastie protested to no avail, Army command had cunningly slotted the 369th for the kind of combat training that would satisfy all but its most zealous champions, but which would minimize its integration into combat operations with white soldiers.

The War Department's racial motivations in assigning the 369th to AA duty were not publicized or publicly debated, and were not considered by most men in the 369th. In general, while most of the men had mixed feelings about being called up for active duty in early 1941, they were pleased about their duty assignment and particularly pleased when they found out where their training was to take place. The 369th were being sent to Camp Ontario in upstate New York. They would not have to endure the racist hell of a training camp in the Jim Crow South.

Racism was common throughout the United States, and none of the black men in the 369th escaped its reach. De Fossett, remember, was playing in the Negro Baseball League; blacks were not accepted in the National or American leagues until 1947, when Jackie Robinson broke the color barrier. The armed forces in which they served was segregated—by federal mandate. But conditions were much worse for blacks in the rural South, and northern blacks sent to the South for military training confronted a more aggressive and demeaning racism than was commonly practiced in northern cities.

When a reporter for one of the black newspapers visited the 369th at their training camp in Oswego, New York, he told stories about the camp at Fort Bragg, North Carolina, that shocked the young men from Harlem. The day they were sent south, some of them told the reporter, they would go "prepared for any and all emergencies." In fact, a few months later cadres from the 369th were sent to

369th Coast Artillery, 1943. (George Strock; *Life Magazine*© Time, Inc.)

Camp Stewart in Georgia for special duty. After constant racist provocations and command indifference to their protests of on-base discrimination, they loaded their rifles and proceeded to level the Jim Crow facilities. The "Harlem Hellfighters," as one of the men later told William De Fossett, "do not go by this stuff."

Over the next year in Oswego the men worked hard. The snow was so deep at Camp Ontario that first winter that they had to form human snowplows, pushing through the waist-high snow eight men abreast. But they became expert in handling the antiaircraft weaponry they had been assigned, and Lieutenant Woodruff was able to tell the white press: "They're dead eyes . . . and I don't mean with the galloping dominoes." In less than a year's time the 369th, under black officers' command (with two white artillery officers serving as advisers in weapons training), had been transformed from young men playing soldier on the weekends to professional, highly trained soldiers.

Outside Harlem, in an area one of the men called "lily white," race became a more immediate issue for the men. They were dependent upon the town of Oswego for all their nonmilitary needs, and some of Oswego's white citizens were

369th in Training, Oswego, New York, 1943. (George Strock, *Life Magazine*© Time, Inc.)

concerned about the presence of so many black men. But relations between the military and civilian populations were smooth overall until, in that first winter, a white woman brought charges of rape against one of the 369th.

The whole unit was lined up; each man was inspected for "evidence." The men believed the charges unfounded—the desperate act of a white woman caught breaking the taboo against interracial sex. But in any case, they believed their rights had been violated in the blanket lineup. These men read the *Amsterdam News* and knew about the treatment of other black troops. They were highly conscious that they were a special combat unit, and they meant to be treated with respect.

Angry and outraged at what they saw as racial politics, the 369th staged a boycott of Oswego. Many of the men remembered the "don't shop where you can't work" campaigns that Reverend Adam Clayton Powell had led in Harlem in the mid-thirties, and resolved to try similar tactics. The officers supported the men, and provided vehicles so they could take their business to other towns. Eventually Governor Lehman, partly in response to concerns of the Oswego business community, mediated the conflict. The charges were dropped. The 369th had won.

The remainder of the time at Camp Ontario was spent without incident, and the men were looking forward to completing their year's training and returning home in January 1942. But on December 7, 1941, their plans were changed.

Their first wartime assignment was to guard Cape Cod from air attack. A few months later, they were sent to defend the southern California coast, near the big Lockheed defense plant. Here, American race relations took another odd turn.

The military command worked out the coordinates and issued the orders, and the 369th did as they were told. But someone in the command hierarchy must have realized that they were sending the 369th into the backyards—literally—of some of the wealthiest white people in America, including a few major Hollywood stars. Each landscaped lawn hosted 12 men and their antiaircraft guns.

Bill De Fossett, by then a regimental sergeant major, heard some complaints: "We've never had Negroes living here and now they're in our backyards with those horrible guns." But most of the residents welcomed their defenders. Humphrey Bogart told the men on his lawn they were welcome to use his house, and gave them keys to show he meant it. And black celebrities like Lena Horne, Hattie McDaniel, Eddie "Rochester" Anderson, and Leigh Whipper came out to visit the troops.

The southern California assignment lasted only a few weeks. The 369th had trained in Oswego for cold-weather duty. They had been issued cold-weather gear, including snow boots and heavy woolen union suits. So, as Army logic would have it, after a few weeks in sunny southern California, the men boarded a troop ship and set out for . . . Hawaii.

None of the men in the 369th had been to Hawaii. Back in the days before affordable air travel, Hawaii was the vacation spot of the rich. The only other men from the mainland likely to have spent time there were regular army—"the pineapple army," they called themselves. But like most Americans with any access to popular culture, these men had images of Hawaii. Some had heard the popular radio program, "Hawaii Calls," with live music broadcast from the terrace of the Royal

Hawaiian hotel. Others had seen some of the movies that played up exotic Hawaiian locales—so many were produced in the 1930s that a *New York Times* film review referred sarcastically to "the well-known Hollywood suburb of Wacky-ki." The hula had even enjoyed a brief popularity in Harlem clubs and cabarets in the late 1920s.

But the soldiers who traveled to Hawaii from the mainland during WWII had quite a different experience from the wealthy tourists who made the 4-day trip on the Matson cruise ships. Troop ships were crowded. The men slept on canvas bunks that were laced to steel frames and stacked five high. The tables in the mess hall were at waist level; men stood to eat their two meals a day. Many of the men, of course, did not eat. They were much too seasick. Because it took 2 to 3 minutes for a submarine to sight and fire a torpedo with any degree of accuracy, the ships changed course every 2 or 3 minutes. They zigzagged all the way from San Diego to Honolulu, exacerbating whatever seasickness was normal for men who had never been on the open sea before.

The 369th came to Hawaii with a strong sense of purpose and good morale. They were well prepared for their assignment to defend the islands from air attack.

Ironically, however, as the troops of the 369th were transported on the small sugar-cane railroad from the harbor to their initial base camp, people reacted to them as if *they* were the invading force. Grown men and women ran away, frightened of the trainload of black men.

It did not take long to find out what had happened. Hawaii had almost no black residents before the war, and white southerners—soldiers, sailors, and war workers—had spread rumors among the local people. They said blacks were dangerous, not fully human. They said blacks were animal-like. Some said that black men had tails, and if a local woman and a black man had a baby, the baby would have a tail like a monkey.

By the time the men of the 369th arrived in Hawaii in the summer of 1942, the tail story had gained great credibility. One story, perhaps apocryphal but widely circulated among the black men on Oahu, shows the power of the rumor. A small group of men were invited to a social gathering with a group of local people. It was very pleasant, but some of the men thought it odd that they were consistently steered to chairs with pillows on them. When one of the men began to sit down on a chair without a pillow, the host ran over and flung a pillow under the soldier's descending posterior. The punch line, of course, was that the hosts believed black men had tails. The chairs were hard. They were trying to be nice.

All over the island, in those first few weeks, men of the 369th explained that the tail business was a racist lie. How could it be true, they asked, that black men made monkey babies? But too often their explanations left a residue of uncertainty, and the men "dropped drawers" all over the island to prove, as Bill De Fossett (drawing on his father's passion for vocabulary) put it, that they "were an anurous biological species."

The Hawaii to which the 369th came was a complicated place. The terror of the Japanese attack hung over the islands for a long time, and Hawaii felt the presence of war more than any other part of the United States. The territory was under martial law until late 1944. Every night there was a total blackout; absolutely no light could show anywhere on the islands. The newspapers were censored and so was civilian correspondence. The beaches were strung with barbed wire. There were curfews and shortages, and at first gas masks were carried everywhere, even to weddings.

Over a million men came to Hawaii with the war. These were men from all walks of life, from all regions of the states. In most ways, though all Americans, they saw themselves as quite different from one another: the Italian kid from Brooklyn, the farm boy from Iowa, the one from Mississippi who called them both Yankees, the soldier with the "Harlem Hellfighters," and the sharecropper's son. Men from very different cultures were jammed together with little regard for the differences that loomed so large to them. There were tensions. And the tensions were made more complicated because of the nature of the society to which they came.

Unlike most of the places these men came from, Hawaii was not racially or culturally homogenous, nor was it organized as a bipolar racial society. A minority of wealthy whites exerted much disproportionate economic and political power in the islands, but the majority of the population were drawn from Asia and the Pacific. Fully a third of the islands' population were of Japanese descent. What that meant, for the men who came to Hawaii from the mainland (white or black), was that their notions of racial normality were upset. One could not be in wartime Hawaii and not confront the issue of race.

Some whites were angry and appalled; others saw possibilities for a new, better society. Some blacks wrote home of living "in a part of the world where one can be respected and live as a free man should"; others wrote of the suspicion evidenced by local people, especially the women, and of the rising racial tensions in overcrowded Honolulu. But because of the juxtaposition of so many different sorts of men from the mainland, in a context of unfamiliar racial composition and relations, the issue of race was explosive.

The men of the 369th had excellent relations with local residents. Bill De Fossett and his brother Joe hooked up with a semipro baseball team that played in the small town of Aiea. The manager was Hawaiian, the owner haole (the Hawaiian word used for whites), the coach of Japanese-American descent, and the players all of the above plus the De Fossett brothers. This integrated ball club was, to De Fossett, a symbol of hope for better days to come.

But on the streets of Honolulu, with other men in uniform, the old racial struggles persisted. The American armed forces understood, quite clearly, that racist practices were incompatible with military procedures, and that is one reason that African-American troops were either kept separate from white troops or confined completely to the lowest ranks of the service. Once black men became officers in an integrated armed forces, they would have command over white men. Military hierarchy would—must—take precedence over racial hierarchy. That inversion, most believed, would cause problems. And it did. On the overcrowded streets of Honolulu, most especially in the charged atmosphere of the vice district, known throughout the Pacific theater simply as "Hotel Street," white and black men clashed over issues of race.

From their first days of liberty in Honolulu, the men of the 369th faced racial harassment from white men in uniform, mostly southerners. The setting was usually the densely packed streets of the Hotel Street district, where thousands of men in uniform, many of them drunk, wandered past the lines for bars and brothels, avoiding the street hustlers and shoeshine boys and sidewalk concessionaires. The black men would see, from a distance, a group of white soldiers or sailors coming down the street toward them. And then, right in their faces, there would be the words, the same words every time. "Nigger, get off the street!" And when the black men did not move, again: "Nigger, don't you know you're supposed to get off the street!" In the first few months in Hawaii, the men from Harlem faced this set piece again and again—southern street protocol played out in the middle of the Pacific Ocean. But there were some very important differences.

The first difference was the 369th. These men claimed equality and respect, and meant to see that they got it. De Fossett saw it happen over and over. The white soldier or sailor would say those words: "Nigger, get off the street," and the black soldier would punch him. Hard. "We were raised in New York," De Fossett says. "We were not strangers to street fighting."

At least two white servicemen died in these confrontations. One struck his head as he dropped from the punch; another collapsed during a fist fight from an aneurism or other natural cause. Here, though, was the second difference between the deep South and wartime Hawaii. In the Deep South in the 1940s, a black man who killed a white man over issues of racial protocol would be lucky to see the in-

While the armed forces remained segregated in Hawaii, the semiprofessional Aiea baseball team had a Hawaiian manager, a Japanese-American coach, and players from across the racial spectrum, including the De Fossett brothers of the 369th. (Courtesy William K. De Fossett)

side of a jail cell. But in these cases, both Preston Daniels and Wentworth Morris, the black servicemen involved, were cleared of all charges. The decisions sent a message as powerful as the individual street fights. A black man's right to self-defense was formally endorsed by the standards of military justice. The 369th made sure the word got around.

Street incidents were never completely banished, but the 369th had made a point. And the military police supported the men, acknowledging that they "did not seek trouble but . . . never backed up from trouble." Some of the other black troops on the island, members of the quartermaster's corps, for example, tried to borrow some of the 369th's respect. On pass, they'd replace their blue-trimmed caps with the red-trimmed caps worn by the 369th AA Regiment.

The southern servicemen in Hawaii who had tried to enforce their racial hierarchy had lost. They could try to save face by ignoring the black men in uniform. But there was a problem with that tactic. Rank had to be observed. In the United States Army, enlisted men saluted officers; lower-ranking officers saluted their superiors. It wasn't simply custom; it was required.

Many of the white servicemen did not intend for their version of racial hierarchy to be overruled by the hierarchy of rank. As one young white private in a southern training camp told a black lieutenant: "If you would take your clothes off and lay them on the ground I would salute them but I won't salute anything that looks like you."

The solution adopted in Hawaii was equally novel, if a bit more practicable. No one knew whether it was a plan, or just a spontaneous act that inspired a group of white junior-grade officers, but the scene was repeated many times.

A lower-ranking white officer saw a black officer of superior rank. He began running—not away from the black officer, but toward him. He'd run right up to the man and begin shaking the officer's hand, "Hello, hello, how are you," as if the men were old acquaintances, even friends. Then he'd walk smartly away.

The white men were mocking the system. Perhaps they assumed that the black men would be pleased by the friendliness and would forget the breach of regulation. The white men were willing to feign intimacy, even to make physical contact, rather than to salute black men as their superiors. The tactic was so bizarre that it did, briefly, work.

It worked until a junior-grade lieutenant tried the routine on Major Edward I. Marshall, the Battalion Adjutant of the 369th. Major Marshall was a stern, commanding, even intimidating presence. He was not amused. He certainly was not flattered.

Military style, in full fury, he called upon the authority of rank and the force of the U.S. Army: "Do not shake my hand. I don't like you and you don't like me. But I am a Major!!! You are a lieutenant!!! Salute me!!!" The lieutenant complied in silence, and scuttled off, shaken. Regimental Sergeant Major De Fossett watched the whole thing with barely suppressed laughter. There were no more such incidents.

Major Marshall had commanded respect and he got it. Military protocol had been enforced by a black man answering to his own confident sense of twinned duty. But in Hawaii, Marshall and the men of the 369th were not operating in isolation. In these confrontations, the men of the 369th drew on their upbringing in

Harlem and on their identity as elite combat troops. They had sources of strength that many other black troops in Hawaii and elsewhere lacked. But without the willingness of the military to enforce its own rules (a willingness markedly absent in many training camps and bases, especially in the South), these struggles might have turned out very differently.

To this end, their location in Hawaii was very important. In Hawaii race was defined and managed differently than anywhere on the mainland. Local customs were different, and somewhat more flexible. And—crucially—Hawaii was America's border of war.

The military governor of Hawaii, Lt. General Emmons, was an ally in their struggles. Emmons believed that racism was, in Hawaii, an inefficient system for maintaining the order he saw as critical to the war effort. Significantly, civilian government officials and the local elite raised no objections to Emmon's antiracist efforts.

On November 6, 1942, a few months after the 369th arrived in Hawaii, Emmons issued a confidential memo to each commanding general and to all commanding officers of every post, camp, station, depot, district, and service command in the Hawaiian Islands. Emmons was angry over the increasing number of "instances of interracial conflict in the city of Honolulu." He wanted the incidents stopped, and he laid the blame squarely on white shoulders.

"The fact that such incidents have occurred indicates a lack of proper training, instruction, and discipline on the part of the personnel involved, and of the officers under whom they are serving," Emmons wrote. He ordered all commissioned officers to "adopt every possible means to eliminate the causes for any racial discord" and, by example, to "inculcate a spirit of harmony and unity" among the men under their command. "It is of the utmost importance that our ranks present a united front in the present emergency and that racial prejudice, jealousies, and discord be not permitted to create or foster internal friction. The reasons for the total elimination of such friction are so apparent and so compelling that they require no reiteration."

Emmons' "compelling" reasons were not principles of equality or visions of social reform. They were the practical matter of winning the war. America's Pacific war was not going well; Hawaii was key to the Pacific campaign. There was no room for racial strife that, in any way, compromised the war effort.

In 1944 the 369th Coast Artillery Regiment was ordered to join the forces invading Okinawa, and these men, like so many who'd passed through Hawaii during the war, moved forward to war. The struggles over race would continue in Hawaii, for they were not the only black men in the islands, and the black-white dimension of racial struggle was only one in a complex panoply of racial difference. But the presence of the 369th on Oahu set an example of resolve and courage, and the men of the regiment took away lessons that would serve them well for the rest of their lives.

William De Fossett had, by the time the 369th departed for Okinawa, been reassigned to Task Force 58, an interservice unit that would fight in Saipan. He was battalion supply officer in an all-black unit. Here, De Fossett would confront the kind of direct and degrading racism that he had so far avoided in the armed forces.

Almost all the other men in his unit were southerners, and this, unlike the 369th, was not a highly trained combat unit. De Fossett found the differences disturbing. The other men in the unit observed the protocol of racial hierarchy that he and his comrades had battled on the streets of Honolulu. When a white officer came into their area, the men would take off their hats. De Fossett argued with them. Salute an officer, he said, but your hat stays on. The other men said that was just how they'd been raised, and the white men expected it. De Fossett said he didn't care; they had to stop. The men did not like the order.

De Fossett was upset by their submissiveness. But he also understood the practical implications. If the other men took off their hats to whites and he did not, there was going to be trouble. De Fossett, however, did not intend to play that game.

Some of the men complained to a white officer about De Fossett's order. The battalion colonel called on De Fossett and, in a strong southern accent, asked him what was going on. De Fossett replied: "Sir, I am following Army regulations." The colonel called him an "uppity nigger"—but he did not tell De Fossett to rescind his order. Henceforth, De Fossett's men kept their hats on. It was a small victory, but a sweet one.

After the war ended, some of the black men who had been stationed in Hawaii chose to stay. At least two men from the 369th demobilized there and married local women. While in 1940 the census of Hawaii recorded only 255 Negro residents, in 1950 there were 2,651 black men and women living in the islands.

De Fossett, however, chose to return to his native New York. Back in Harlem, he, like so many other returning servicemen, used the bonus points all veterans received on civil service exams to secure a good government job. Within a couple of years he was working for the New York City Police Department, and in 1963 he became the first black State Department Security Officer in the United States. William De Fossett raised his family in Harlem, and worked hard for the good of his community and its youth. He and the other men who returned from war became part of the force that transformed American race relations in the postwar era.

Like many of his comrades-in-arms from the 369th, William De Fossett saw the seeds of social change in his wartime experience. He was proud to have been part of the 369th, proud of his regiment and its war record. He was proud of how the men stood up to racism, and believed it significant that, if not always, at least *sometimes* the U.S. government had backed them up. But of all his memories of the war, and of Hawaii, he treasures the memory of playing ball in Aiea, he and his brother Joe, and their Japanese-American, Hawaiian, and white teammates. It still seems to him a hopeful vision.

AN INTERPRETATION

By the mid-1950s, African Americans and their white allies, openly and in large numbers, had begun to fight the racist system of injustice and inequality that had governed American race relations throughout the twentieth century. In the 1950s and 1960s, the civil rights movement, led by people like Martin Luther King, Jr.,

Thurgood Marshall, Ella Baker, Diane Nash, Medgar Evers, Stokely Carmichael, John Lewis, and Robert Moses, would defeat *legal* racial segregation and discrimination. The successes of the civil rights movement depended on the heroic efforts of hundreds of thousands of grassroots protesters and demonstrators. But large-scale changes begun earlier in the twentieth century set the stage for the civil rights movement of the 1950s and 1960s, and were critically important in making it possible.

One of the most significant changes affecting race relations was the growing power and authority of the federal government. In both the Great Depression of the 1930s and World War II, the federal government dramatically increased its role in the lives of the American people. New Deal policies implemented during the Roosevelt presidency created a national system of social provision and economic regulation. And while African Americans were greatly frustrated by the New Dealers' failure to confront racism and racial inequality, increasingly, many Americans looked to the federal government to tackle the nation's most vexing problems.

During World War II, the federal government (partly in the guise of the War Department) greatly expanded its power. In practice, this meant that the federal government exercised control over all matters deemed pertinent to winning the war, reaching into individual lives and into local communities in an unprecedented manner. The possibility for uniform national policy was greater than before.

But government agents, military or civilian, did not enforce laws and policies in a completely standard fashion. On particular issues, they often bowed to the weight of local or regional custom and tradition. Race was one of those issues. During World War II the policies affecting black Americans were shaped by competing, overlapping, and uncertain lines of political power and social authority. As a result, America fought WWII with a segregated and racially discriminatory armed forces.

Still, as the men of the 369th learned, the federal government had an agenda quite different than, say, the state of Mississippi. Sometimes, if pushed hard enough, the federal government would support limited racial progress. If African-American soldiers took the rights and freedoms that rank, regulation, and law seemed to guarantee, federal authorities might well support them. And the support of the federal government, because of its power and authority, meant victory over local racist practices.

While the story of the 369th during World War II is a complicated one, it pointedly reveals the changing nature of racial struggle in the United States. The 369th received combat unit designation because the federal government, in wartime, needed to show its African-American citizens that the United States was not an unremittingly racist nation. The men of the 369th received justice in New York, California, Hawaii, and overseas because the federal government—specifically, the War Department—had a set of rules and regulations that put military needs and protocol ahead of traditional racist practices. Though it was not easy, during World War II African Americans were learning to use the federal government to challenge and change racist policies and practices.

In the immediate postwar years, under pressure from African Americans and because of Cold War politics that made legal racism an international embarrassment, President Harry Truman would desegregate the armed forces. And by 1954, the Supreme Court would side with the legal arguments of the NAACP in *Brown v. Board of Education* and declare that state laws mandating racially "separate but equal" schools were inherently discriminatory and unconstitutional. While national politicians and federal officials would rarely take the initiative in confronting racial discrimination, African-American activists, building on WWII experiences such as those of the 369th Regiment, learned that if pushed hard enough the federal government could be made an ally in the fight for racial justice and equality for all Americans.

Sources: This story is adapted from Beth Bailey and David Farber, "The 'Double-V' Campaign in World War II Hawaii: African Americans, Racial Ideology, and Federal Power," *Journal of Social History* 26:4, 817–843. Interviews with members of the 369th were an important source for this account. For more on Hawaii during World War II, see Beth Bailey and David Farber, *The First Strange Place: Race and Sex in World War II Hawaii* (Baltimore: Johns Hopkins University Press, 1994). The most comprehensive book on African-American soldiers during World War II is Ulysses Lee, *The Employment of Negro Troops*, Vol. 8, *The United States Army in World War II* (Washington, D.C.: Government Printing Office, 1966). Other excellent sources on African Americans and World War II include Merl Reed, *Seedtime for the Modern Civil Rights Movement* (Baton Rouge: Lousiana State University Press, 1991); Graham Smith, *When Jim Crow Met John Bull* (New York: St. Martin's Press, 1987); Jervis Anderson, *This Was Harlem* (New York: Farrar, Straus, Giroux, 1988); and Morris J. MacGregor, Jr., *Integration of the Armed Forces, 1940–1965*, Defense Studies Series (Washington, D.C.: Government Printing Office, 1981).

12

THE MAKING OF DISNEYLAND

GEORGE LIPSITZ

The decade of the 1950s has a special place in Americans' collective memory. It is fondly recalled as the last "good" decade: an innocent, affluent, peaceful, and secure time, before the riots and protests of the 1960s set Americans against one another, and before the defeat in Vietnam, the Arab oil boycott, Watergate, and other events of the 1970s forced the American people to begin the painful process of reevaluating the nation's position and role in the world. God's country. Hula Hoops and Pat Boone. A two-bedroom ranch house in the suburbs. Television. Disneyland.

Many Americans actually lived this idealized version of the fifties—enough so that it could be fashioned into a believable myth. After the Korean War ended in early 1953, the nation was at peace. Beginning in 1946, an unanticipated baby boom helped sustain high rates of economic growth while fostering a new family-based domesticity in the rapidly expanding suburbs. By mid-decade, living standards were at an all-time high, and Americans were buying consumer goods in unprecedented quantities. In a story entitled "Everybody Rich in the U.S.?" U.S. News and World Report claimed that poverty had virtually disappeared, and that it was an "unusual family that does not own a home, a car, a TV, many luxuries. Nothing like it has ever been seen before." Holding this "new economic order" together was the intrepid consumer, whose purchases would presumably prevent the economy from reverting to the depression conditions of the 1930s. There were, to be sure, anxieties about the "affluent society," even in the 1950s: Consumers were heavily in debt; automation was threatening to eliminate skilled work; and to some social critics the homogeneity of the suburbs seemed boring and even threatening. But by and large, Americans wanted to believe that their worries were over—and they did.

When it opened in 1955, Disneyland represented this collective dream. As George Lipsitz's account reveals, all of Disneyland was fantasyland, an imaginary world of universal experience where poverty didn't exist, where slavery had never happened, and where no real work was ever done. Like the postwar suburbs, which generally excluded blacks and other minorities, Disneyland was designed not for all families, but for those—mostly white and middle-class—that could afford the admission charge and desired the isolating experience that the park provided. And in the shops on Main Street, park patrons lined Walt Disney's pockets and did what in the fifties seemed very much an act of social benevolence: They consumed.

If at times Disney's perspective seems narrow and provincial, it is well to consider that Disneyland was the success it was in part because the founder's fantasy so closely resembled the shared desires of millions of Americans. To what extent, then, does the Disneyland experience merely reflect American values? Were the white, middle-class Americans who patronized Disneyland in search of uniformity, homogeneity, and passivity? Were Americans responsible for Disney's pioneering multimedia promotions, or for the ugly heritage they have yielded: hour-long commercials that masquerade as entertainment; news "documentaries" that dramatically recreate past events; and feature films that relentlessly promote particular products? Did Americans seek to be constituted as consumers rather than producers? When youngsters bought Davy Crockett coonskin caps and spent their weekly allowances on Mickey Mouse ears, were they exercising free choice, or were they being prepared—like millions of visitors to Disneyland—for advanced consumer capitalism?

On July 17, 1955, a nationwide television audience watched the opening of the Disneyland amusement park on that evening's broadcast of the Disneyland television program. Before what was then the largest concentration of television equipment and personnel assembled for any one event (63 engineers and 24 live cameras) hosts Bob Cummings, Art Linkletter, and Ronald Reagan presided over ceremonies that one critic likened to "the dedication of a national shrine."

Despite 3 months of rehearsal for the program and an $11 million investment in the park, all did not go smoothly on opening day. Audio and video portions of the program went dead intermittently, and the hosts had considerable difficulty synchronizing their reporting with the pictures on the screen. The park's drinking fountains did not work, leading to long lines at the concession stands. Hot weather melted the freshly laid asphalt on streets and walkways, causing women in high-heeled shoes to sink into the pavement and providing small children with the opportunity to track footprints and leave rude messages on the sidewalks. In an emblematic indignity, the dramatic appearance of actor Fess Parker (dressed as his television character Davy Crockett) riding on horseback through Frontierland lost some of its intended drama when someone accidentally turned on lawn sprinklers, soaking Parker and his horse. One disappointed critic described Disneyland as being "like a giant cash register, clicking and clanging, as creatures of Disney magic came tumbling down from their lofty places in my daydreams to peddle and perish their charms with the aggressiveness of so many curbside barkers."

If everything seemed to go wrong for Disneyland on opening day, everything seems to have gone right for it ever since. By 1958, the annual attendance at Disneyland surpassed the number of patrons at Yellowstone, Yosemite, and the Grand Canyon combined. After 10 years of operation, one-quarter of the U.S. population had visited the park and Disneyland had earned $273 million for the Disney Corporation. In the early 1970s Disney Enterprises joined the list of the 500 largest corporations in America, and by the late 1980s California's Disneyland and Walt Disney World in Florida accounted for 62 percent of the sales and 70 percent of the operating earnings for a corporation the annual revenues of which approached $3 billion each year.

Disneyland has been more than just a financial success story. It has exercised an influence on American culture that can scarcely be measured in dollars. Film maker George Lucas (the producer of *Star Wars*) says that Disneyland was his favorite playground when he was growing up. The pop singer Michael Jackson visits Disneyland frequently, and astronaut Sally Ride borrowed from the park's terminology when she described her first trip into space as "a real E ticket ride." Harry S. Truman ceremonially received the Disneyland flag bearing the image of Mickey Mouse when the former president visited the park in 1957, and every U.S. president since has put in a personal appearance at the park, as have numerous visiting heads of foreign countries. Security concerns prevented the Soviet Union's Nikita Khrushchev from visiting Disneyland in 1959, but newspaper photographs over the years have captured Egypt's Anwar Sadat shaking hands with Goofy and India's Jawaharlal Nehru piloting the jungle boat in Adventureland. "Oh, this is so much fun, father is having such a good time," enthused Indira Gandhi, Nehru's daughter and herself a future Prime Minister of India. "We looked forward to Disneyland as much as anything on our trip."

Walt Disney dons a straw hat and picks up a fishing pole as he poses for a photograph designed to provide publicity for the opening of Disneyland. Child actors pose as Mark Twain's characters Tom Sawyer and Becky Thatcher in a picture that presents Disney at the center of America's storytelling traditions. (Department of Special Collections, University Research Library, UCLA)

As the creator of Mickey Mouse and numerous other popular cartoon characters, Walt Disney Studios had become an American institution by the 1930s. But Disney's personal wealth never equaled his enormous prestige, and by the late 1940s both he and the studio he headed faced serious financial problems. These financial pressures encouraged Disney to diversify into the amusement park business. At that time, amusement parks were not doing well financially, and few investors thought of them as places with a potential for profit making. He borrowed as much as he could from the Bank of America in California and the Bankers Trust Company in New York, but their skepticism about his chances of building a financially successful amusement park limited the amount of money they would make available to him. When Disney exhausted his credit with the bankers, he sold his second home at Smoke Tree Ranch in Palm Springs, California, and cashed in his life insurance policy in order to finance the amusement park. He took on a personal debt of over $100,000, confounding the bankers who expressed understandable skepticism about the likelihood of an amusement park repaying that kind of investment. Even Disney's brother Roy limited the financial investment of the studio in Disneyland to $10,000 because he considered the park to be just another of "Walt's screwy ideas."

Disney wanted to build a new kind of amusement park, one that broke with the traditions of the past. While planning his own park he inspected fairs and amusement parks all across the country to see what worked and what didn't. He was particularly depressed by the conditions at New York's Coney Island, which had been the first successful amusement park in the 1890s. One journalist reports that Disney found Coney Island "so battered and tawdry and the ride operators were so hostile that Walt felt a momentary urge to abandon the idea of an amusement park. But when he visited Copenhagen [Denmark] and saw that city's Tivoli Gardens, he proclaimed 'Now *this* is what an amusement park should be.' " He felt that most amusement parks had become unsavory places, that they placed too much emphasis on risk taking, danger, "thrill rides," games of chance, barkers, and concession stands.

Disney vowed to establish a park that replaced those sensations with "educational and patriotic values" transmitted through wholesome family fun. As a publicity brochure for Disneyland explains, "As a pioneer in the motion picture industry, Walt developed an intuitive ability to know what was universally entertaining. When his daughters were very young, Walt would take them on what he later called "very unsatisfying visits" to local amusement parks. He felt he could build a park at which parents and children could have fun together. He wanted Disneyland to be a place where "people can experience some of the wonders of life, of adventure, and feel better because of it."

Walt Disney wanted his amusement park to operate by the same principles as his motion pictures. "I hate to see a down-beat picture," he once explained, "so that when I come out [of the theater], it makes me feel that everything's dirty around me. I know it isn't that way, and I don't want anybody telling me that it is." That commitment to a wholesome and upbeat view of the world led Disney to take great pains with his creations. In the case of Disneyland, he wanted a park that would physically block out any view of the outside world, so that visitors could concentrate on the pleasant fantasies within its walls. He wanted to create a forum for fun, a public space free of danger, dirt, and depravity. To millions of Americans he succeeded magnificently, and they have repaid Disney and his heirs many times over with their patronage. But in order to accomplish all this he needed to raise large sums of money in a fairly short time.

It was Walt Disney's understanding of television that not only won him the financing necessary to build Disneyland, but also the resources to make it a success after it opened. Disney had produced a successful Christmas special in 1950, and he knew that the new medium of television was hungry for the sort of product that he could provide. He offered to produce a weekly series for television, but only if one of the networks would help finance Disneyland. ABC network officials agreed to invest $500,000 directly and to guarantee loans of up to $4.5 mil-

Vice President Richard M. Nixon, his wife Pat Nixon, and their daughters Tricia and Julie visit Disneyland in 1955. This staged photo displays one function of the park—its role as a site for adult celebrities to show their "personal" sides. The smiles and postures of Mr. and Mrs. Nixon in this photo indicate that they understand this role very well, but their identically dressed daughters seem less at ease with their day at Disneyland turning into an opportunity for publicizing their father's career. (Department of Special Collections, University Research Library, UCLA)

lion for the amusement park in return for one-third ownership in the park and a weekly series titled "Disneyland."

Armed with this new infusion of funds, Disney commenced construction of the park. He commissioned the Stanford Research Institute (SRI) to identify a centrally located tract of land available at a reasonable price. Harrison "Buzz" Price, director of the Los Angeles branch of the Institute, recommended building the park in the vicinity of the main railroad station in downtown Los Angeles, but the cost of land in that location proved too high for Disney's budget. Disney rejected a proposed ocean-front location because he felt that the beach attracted unsavory individuals. Price and his fellow researchers noticed that residential growth in the Los Angeles area tended to follow the paths of new freeways heading east and south from the central city. They recommended several sites in suburban areas, but eventually settled on an Anaheim location because it received five fewer inches of rain

During the construction of the park, Disney Corporation engineers transformed fields of orange groves and palm trees into an environment with many identities including the terrain along the Mississippi River. This photograph shows what Disney tried so hard to hide about the park—people doing actual labor in a real workplace. (Department of Special Collections, University Research Library, UCLA)

per year than alternate locations in San Gabriel and in the San Fernando Valley. The SRI advised Disney to buy 65 acres of orange groves in Anaheim for $4,500 an acre; 10 years later the land was worth $80,000 an acre.

Disney cleared the orange groves and relandscaped them, sending his staff on scouting missions throughout Southern California to find "interesting" trees and shrubs for the park. He deliberately reshaped the terrain so that once inside Disneyland, visitors would lose visual contact with the surrounding area. "I don't want the public to see the world they live in while they're in the park," he explained to his design staff. "I want them to feel they are in another world." Yet financial considerations led Disney to include at least one part of the outside world in the park: advertising. As part of his efforts to raise money, Disney got 32 major corporations to lease concessions in the park, in effect paying him for the opportunity to sell their products and advertise their brands. The Bank of America opened up a small branch in the "Main Street" section of the park, and the Continental Baking Corporation paid for the privilege of having "Wonder Bread" designated as the "official white bread" of Disneyland.

Financial rather than aesthetic considerations dictated the connection between television and Disneyland. In his heart, Disney felt that television (then largely a black and white medium) was actually a poor vehicle for displaying the vivid colors and high production values of his cartoons and nature films. But he needed money for the amusement park, and he thought that the new medium could be very important as a marketing device, not just for Disneyland, but for all of his studio's other ventures. "We wanted to start off running," Disney later told *Business Week* magazine in regard to his decision to tie the amusement park to a television series. "The investment was going to be too big to wait for a slow buildup. We needed terrific initial impact and television seemed the answer." The Disneyland television program went on the air on October 27, 1954, with a full hour program previewing the opening of the Disneyland amusement park the following summer. Two other programs later in the season gave progress reports on the park.

The success of the Disneyland television series, and consequently the success of Disneyland itself, stemmed in large measure from a three-part episode broadcast during the 1954 to 1955 season about the frontiersman Davy Crockett. At first glance, the likelihood for success of such a series seemed slight. Popular tastes at the time in film and television had been moving away from western and frontier stories. Furthermore, Crockett himself was, at best, an ambiguous historical figure—a man celebrated as a hero for his part in clearing the wilderness, fighting Indians, serving in Congress, and dying in battle at the Alamo, but one equally reviled as a villain for his destructive hunting practices (killing 105 bears in one season, shooting six deer in a day and leaving five of them to hang in the woods), the betrayal of his political supporters when he turned against Andrew Jackson and joined the Whig Party, and his crude antisocial behavior. To further complicate matters for Disney, the actor selected to play Crockett, Fess Parker, was allergic to horses and hated the costumes his role required him to wear. According to one account, Disney personnel had to teach Parker how to ride a horse, and he disliked the leather breeches that he had to wear so much that when out of camera range "he shied away from them as if they were a bunch of poison ivy, swearing they would give him 'crotch rot.'"

Whatever shortcomings the story of Davy Crockett presented for purposes of history or drama, it nonetheless offered an ideal marketing opportunity for Disney executives. While the show was still in the planning stages, Disney merchandisers explored the possibilities for manufacturing and distributing coonskin caps like the ones Crockett would wear on television. Even though almost no American homes had color television sets at that time, Disney producers shot the episodes in color in anticipation of stringing them together and releasing them to theaters as a feature film.

Vince Jefferds, Disney's head of promotion boasted, "I could make a good case that licensing of an article is more profitable than manufacturing it. I often made money out of movies that were a loss at the box office." Shortly before the first episode of the Davy Crockett trilogy was scheduled to air, producers realized that they did not have enough film footage to fill their entire program. They asked the creative staff at the studio to write a song that would enable them to bridge over some gaps in the story, and their creation, "The Ballad of Davy Crockett," went to number 1 on the hit parade and stayed at the top of the charts for 13 weeks. Merchandisers sold more than 10 million coonskin caps, making them out of rabbits and squirrels when they ran out of raccoon fur.

The filmed portions of the Davy Crockett series cost $700,000 to make with only $300,000 in advertising revenue guaranteed for their dates on the air. But when the episodes were spliced together for theatrical release, they made a profit of almost $2.5 million even though they had already been seen by an estimated 90 million viewers on television. The Davy Crockett phenomenon was perfectly timed for the opening of Disneyland the following summer. The episodes not only enhanced the royalties from record sales and coonskin caps, but they also served as advertising for the "Frontierland" section of the amusement park.

Television provided Disney with the money to finish building Disneyland, and the shows he made for ABC in return worked to advertise his films and amusement park. The second program of the 1954 to 1955 season was a promotional film about the making of the motion picture *20,000 Leagues Under the Sea,* which was soon to be released by Disney Studios. Bolstered by the program-length commercial on the second Disneyland show, *20,000 Leagues Under the Sea* became the biggest grossing live-action Disney film up to that time, earning over $6 million in its first release. "The amazing thing is that nobody complained that we were doing publicity movies," recalls Disney executive Bill Walsh. "Far from it. Our '20,000 League[s]' documentary even won us an Emmy. *And* it brought in sponsorship for our programs, first from Coca-Cola and then from Johnson and Johnson." The deal benefited ABC as well. The network received one-third of the profits generated by Disneyland until Walt Disney Productions exercised its option to buy back the network's one-third share of ownership of Disneyland in 1960 for $7.5 million, a sum 15 times the size of ABC's investment. In addition, the Disneyland television program established ABC as a competitive network for the first time, attracting a flood of national advertisers to its entire schedule.

Television gave Walt Disney the financial resources essential for the construction of Disneyland, and it also served as a marketing device crucial to the success of the park. The rides in the park advertised Disney comic books, cartoons, films, and television programs, and all of Disney's other entertainment and marketing efforts functioned as a commercial for the park. Customers paid money to enter Disneyland and to go on rides that advertised Disney entertainment. They bought souvenir merchandise that further advertised the characters and stories copyrighted by Disney Productions. Furthermore, they bought concessions from corporations that had paid money to Disney for the privilege of associating their products with the fun and frolic at Disneyland.

Walt Disney presided over every decision about Disneyland with an attention to detail that staggers the imagination. He often slept overnight in a small apartment above the fire station on Main Street, and he insisted on training sessions at what he called "the University of Disneyland" for all employees about how to treat the park's visitors. "Always smile," he ordered his staff. "Turn the other cheek to everybody, even the nasty ones. And above everything, always give them full value for their money. If a boat ride is supposed to last 12 minutes and they only get 11 minutes 30 seconds, they've a right to feel cheated. Thirty seconds shy, and they hate us for selling them short. Thirty seconds extra, and they feel they've gotten away with something. That's the way we want them to feel. Contented, even smug." Disney insisted that his staff completely clean the streets with high pressure hoses every night, and he ordered the installation of more than 45,000 signs to communicate with the public.

Most emphatically, Disney pursued uniformity and predictability in the Disneyland experience. He wanted everyone to enter at the same place and to see the same things. As one admiring journalist observed, "He saw the need for Disneyland to flow, as did a movie, from scene to scene." To maintain the "flow" of the Disneyland experience, Disney made sure that all visitors entered by the same gate and started their day with a view of Sleeping Beauty's Castle that served as a visual lure to pull them through the Main Street shops and into the rest of the park. Visual concerns dominated the aesthetics of a day at Disneyland. A corporate publicity brochure boasted about the park's visual clarity, its ability to present visual stimuli in a unified and coordinated manner: "Disneyland was the first to use visually compatible elements working as a coordinating theme avoiding the contradictory 'hodge-podge' of World's Fairs and amusement parks." To preserve the clean visual line of the park and to ensure that maintenance could take place outside the vision of park customers, Disney buried all water, power, and sewer lines beneath the street level. Each theme land (Fantasyland, Adventureland, Frontierland, and Tomorrowland) appeared completely self-contained and could not be seen from any of the other sections of the park. Costumed "characters" in each theme section traveled to their destinations in underground tunnels so they would never be seen in "inappropriate settings." Even on the jungle ride, Disney insisted on mechanical rather than real animals, "so that every boatload of people will see the same thing."

Disney also thought of the park in transitory terms, like a television series that could undergo revisions over time. He complained about the permanence of films, about how they could no longer be changed once they had been released, and he talked longingly of making Disneyland a place that would change constantly. "The park means a lot to me," Disney explained to a reporter. "It's something that will never be finished, something I can keep developing, keep 'plussing' and adding to. It's alive. It will be a live breathing thing that will need changes."

No section of Disneyland carried as much of the burden of Walt Disney's ideals as did Main Street. In that part of the park, Disney drew on his youthful memories of Marceline, Missouri, as well as on the nostalgia for the Gilded Age evident in 1940s films like *Meet Me in St. Louis*. Disney scaled Main Street's buildings slightly smaller at the rear and top to give the illusion that they were bigger than they actually were, creating a perspective that enabled an adult to see the buildings through the eyes of a child.

In a press release, Disneyland's publicists described Main Street as "Walt's and anyone else's home town—the way it should have been." But unlike the real town squares of turn-of-the-century small towns, Disneyland's Main Street offered little space for leisure and none for work. Despite occasional parades by the Disneyland band and scattered benches in public spaces, Main Street's real social life

Opened at a time when human space flight had not yet taken place, Disneyland presented images of space travel in its Tomorrowland section. Yet the rapid pace of technological change has made this the part of the park most subject to obsolescence, as its futuristic fantasies sometimes came true in the present. (Department of Special Collections, University Research Library, UCLA)

depended on shopping, on funnelling (as rapidly as possible) enormous numbers of consumers into a "comfortable" environment for making purchases. Although buildings appeared to be distinct and separate on the outside, inner passages made it easy to walk from store to store (and difficult to walk back out into the noncommercial space of the street). The meaning of this was not lost on developer and retailer Mel Kaufman who observed that "Main's Street's purpose is exactly the same as Korvette's [a major department store] in the Bronx, but it manages to make shopping wonderful and pleasant at the same time. I'm sure people buy more when they're happy."

Although its prominence on commercial network television made Disneyland a national phenomenon, its success also stemmed from its strategic role in the cultural life of Los Angeles. Disneyland was most often described as a site specially designed for children, but most surveys showed that adults outnumbered children at the park by ratios of 3 to 1 or 4 to 1. Architect Charles Moore attributed Disneyland's success to its ability to provide Californians with a "public environment" in the midst of a region dominated by the private spaces of suburban subdivisions and automobile interiors. Just as Main Street functioned as the town square of Disneyland, Moore described Disneyland itself as the "town square of Los Angeles."

If there was ever a city in need of a town square it was Los Angeles in the 1950s. Home to the first and largest automobile-oriented highway program in the country, Los Angeles developed into a major metropolis as a scattered city with many well dispersed focal points. The city had experienced longer and more sustained population growth than any American city since the 1850s, and it enjoyed particularly enormous population growth during the 1930s, with 200,000 new migrants between 1936 and 1939 alone. Defense spending during and after World War II propelled an even greater expansion. Los Angeles became the second largest industrial center in America during the war (trailing only Detroit), and between 1940 and 1944 over 780,000 new immigrants entered southern California. This extraordinarily rapid growth continued after World War II. Between 1945 and 1955 more than a million and a half people moved to Los Angeles, a total then equal to the *combined* total populations of Pittsburgh and Baltimore. Figures from the 1950 census reveal that more than 50 percent of the residents of Los Angeles in that year had lived in the city for less than 5 years.

Workers came west to secure employment in Los Angeles's shipyard and aircraft industries during World War II, and massive defense spending for the Cold War in the postwar era fueled even further growth. During the war, blacks, whites, Chicanos, Native Americans, and Asian Americans worked side by side in the defense plants and traveled together on the city's efficient and effective streetcar and bus network.

Cultural interactions enlivened urban life. The city's vibrant popular music mixed Afro-American, Chicano, and Anglo forms in reflection of the increasingly heterogeneous culture of the city. Dances and concerts at El Monte Legion Stadium on the eastern border of the city attracted youths from diverse backgrounds who combined their styles of dress, dance, and speech to form an exciting multicultural youth culture. On the playgrounds and streets of inner-city neighborhoods, in public parks, and at commercial amusement centers at the Long Beach and Santa Monica piers the city's heterogeneous population enjoyed the fun of participating in public play.

But the growth of the postwar suburbs (largely subsidized by tax spending on new highways and the extension of city services including water, gas, electric, and sewer lines), encouraged new forms of isolation and segregation. Racial discrimination by private realtors and developers denied most African Americans and Mexican Americans access to the new suburbs, while the federal government's discriminatory home loan policies effectively subsidized the creation of all-white neighborhoods in the San Fernando Valley and Orange County. The newly dispersed population made public transit less efficient per mile and the numbers of automobiles driven by commuters further slowed the speed of trolleys and buses, thereby providing central city dwellers with even more reasons to move to the suburbs. In less than a decade, Los Angeles's diverse urban space became more segregated than ever, its effective rapid transit system collapsed, and the success of suburbs and freeways only contributed to ever increasing fragmentation, segregation, and dispersal of the city's population.

Disneyland's emergence corresponded with the increasing suburbanization of Los Angeles. Even though a majority of the park's visitors came from out of town, Disneyland firmly established itself as an important public space in Los Angeles—as the place one took visitors from out of town, as a site for special celebrations like high school proms, and as an emblem of a whole way of life built around suburbanization and the automobile in Southern California. The park provided an alternative to the beaches, dance halls, parks, and streets of the city, and it powerfully projected its image of middle-class suburban consumer culture as a norm to which other groups should aspire. Massive in-migration and the city's dispersed physical form left Los Angeles without the kinds of geographic and focal points common to other cities. In addition, dependence on the automobile produced unhealthy and unpleasant smog and brought about traffic jams that inhibited access to the beaches, deserts, and mountains once within easy reach of most local residents. Disneyland came into existence as an easily reachable attraction conveniently located near new freeways in the midst of the region's largest locus of population growth. It redefined the nature of public gathering places, with its location and admission costs making it much more accessible to suburban white families than to ethnic minority residents of the inner city. But its appeal depended on more than accessibility; as a new kind of public space Disneyland contrasted sharply with alternative experiences in the Los Angeles area.

Visitors left their cars in parking lots with more acreage than the park itself, and entered a world with comfortable walkways and efficient rail public transit. The high price of admission and tickets attracted an economically homogeneous crowd and encouraged patrons to devote the entire day or evening to leisurely utilization of the park's facilities. The efficient movement of people through the park and the careful timing of rides and attractions worked against any feeling of overcrowding or stagnation, and the Disney philosophy of viewing visitors as an audience and park personnel as entertainers worked to effectively inculcate passivity in park patrons. A revealing phrase in a Disneyland promotional brochure identifies the kind of social space constructed in the park with startling precision:

Up until now audience participation in entertainment was almost non-existent. In live theater, motion pictures and television the audience is always separate and apart from the actual show environment . . . Walt Disney took the audience out of their seats and placed them right in the middle of the action for a total, themed, controlled experience.

Disneyland also spoke to the break with the past that formed an important part of the lives of Los Angeles residents. In a city made up of migrants from all over the country, no common heritage served to underpin individual or collective identity. But by presenting images of familiar figures from television and motion pictures, Disneyland spoke to the commonality of experience made possible by popular culture. People came to Disneyland with a variety of experiences and beliefs, but the reach and scope of electronic mass media guaranteed that they all shared familiarity and knowledge about Disney stories and products.

Disneyland self-consciously promoted itself as an educational institution, as a place, among other things, for learning about the past. Many people admired its successes in that regard. The Freedoms Foundation at Valley Forge awarded Walt Disney its George Washington Medal, and California State Superintendent of Education Max Rafferty lauded Disney as "the greatest educator of this century, greater than John Dewey or James Conant or all the rest of us put together." When Disney died in 1966, California Senator George Murphy claimed that he knew of no individual "who has contributed more to the general welfare of mankind" than Disney did. But Disney himself explained his goals more modestly. "I've always wanted to do American history," Disney explained to an interviewer shortly before the opening of the park. "It's due. We have taken too many things for granted. I'm not really telling history, though. I'm telling about people; history happens to be going on at the time."

Disneyland showed Abraham Lincoln agonizing over the Civil War, but not over slavery. Its "authentic" Frontierland Indians came from reservations in the desert southwest, and had to learn how to handle the "real Indian canoes" from non-Indian park personnel whose knowledge came from their experiences at summer camp. All of its "adventures" replicated the history of white Euro-Americans as they conquered the American or African frontiers. It looked at the conquests of the frontier and the jungle as the spread of European civilization rather than as the plunder of the possessions of indigenous peoples.

In some places, Disneyland's liberties with the past went beyond mere insensitivity. One restaurant featured an "Aunt Jemima" theme echoing the vicious "Mammy" stereotypes of black women that became a staple of popular culture after the Civil War, showing black women invariably as fat, nurturing, child-like, and totally devoted to their white masters. For years the jungle cruise encountered a "humorous trapped safari," which depicted "four red-capped porters, all blacks, who cling bug-eyed to a tree with their white client above them as a menacing rhinoceros stands below." These may seem like innocent errors, mere manifestations of the racism extant in the larger culture of which Disneyland was a part. But Disney's personal prejudices often guided his business practices. He never employed African Americans as studio technicians, and did not allow them to work in Disneyland in *any* capacity until pressured to do so in 1963 by civil rights protests.

Disney's anti-semitism was equally intense; as one writer well acquainted with the details of Disney's life notes, "disappointment and resentment seemed to bring out his latent anti-semitism. He was often heard making snide comments about the Jews, whose success seemed to infuriate him." Disney tried to cloak himself in the American flag and to appropriate for his own purposes the patriotism of his customers. Yet his version of the national narrative was highly selective, prejudiced, and distorted. If his amusement park united its customers in a shared fantasy, it was one tailored to the economic and social interests of a small group of people and not one reflective of the larger shared experience of unity and disunity out of which the complex American nation and society have been forged.

Disneyland management has always tried to present the park as a world apart, as an island of fun in a serious world. Yet no multimillion dollar marketing effort

"Mouseketeers" from the syndicated "Mickey Mouse Club" television program visit Los Angeles City Hall. As a 5-day-a-week afterschool show, "The Mickey Mouse Club" extended the Disney Corporation's popular and commercial influence to the everyday experiences of children. The uniformity of the Mouseketeers' outfits (and ears) hides the symbols of youthful rebellion incorporated into adolescent dress and styles of the day. Adolescence itself disappears as the Mickey Mouse Club appears as a children's "gang" under wholesome adult supervision. (Department of Special Collections, University Research Library, UCLA)

is really cut off from the real world, much less one with the commercial and cultural power of Disneyland. Whether one looks at the lone individual who commented that his first trip to the Mississippi River reminded him of the first part of the Pirates of the Caribbean ride, or to the five high ranking members of the Nixon Administration who received their public relations training handling both the Disneyland and the Richard Nixon accounts for the J. Walter Thompson advertising agency, evidence of Disneyland's influence over American life and culture during the past 40 years has not been hard to find.

Over the years Disneyland has faced strikes ("Disneyland is a kingdom all right, and we're the serfs," complained a worker in a Br'er Bear costume during a 1970 work stoppage), lawsuits over a ban on members of the same sex dancing together, and repeated arguments over what constitutes appropriate attire at the park. One particularly vivid example of the links between Disneyland and the "real world" came on August 6, 1970, when 300 "yippies" marked the twenty-fifth anniversary of the dropping of the first atomic bomb on Hiroshima by staging a demonstration in Disneyland. The youths chanted anti-war slogans on the drawbridge to Sleeping Beauty's Castle, followed the Disneyland band down Main Street, and raised a Viet Cong flag over the fort on Tom Sawyer's island. They accused Disneyland of being "a plastic world of fantasy" at odds with the realities outside its walls. Over 100 uniformed Anaheim police officers equipped with riot batons eventually cleared the youths from the park, making nine arrests. Disneyland management closed the park 6 hours early and handed out refunds to 30,000 customers. The next day a *San Diego Union* editorial condemning the disruption of business at the park advised that "smaller folk who need an explanation for what happened at Disneyland Thursday might be told they saw a lifelike reproduction of the pre-historic world—before shaggy creatures with small brains gave way to the human race as we know it today."

In order to further secure the park and to control the nature of its experience, Disney officials began a rigid policy of dress and grooming codes, denying admission to the park any individuals whose hairstyles or clothing seemed inappropriate to park guards. This policy was based on the idea that there was only one respectable way for people to look and dress, that men should not have long hair or beards, that women should not wear sandals and "love bead necklaces," that black people should not have "Afro" haircuts or be allowed to wear African "dashikis." But as popular styles changed and allowed for more diversity, park guards found themselves facing a losing battle trying to stem the tide of rapidly changing subcultural styles and fashions. Similarly, the park's administrators enforced a policy against men dancing with men or women dancing with women on the grounds that "some patrons might find partners of the same sex offensive," until a lawsuit charging the park with violating the Constitutional rights of its patrons convinced them to drop the policy.

AN INTERPRETATION

Any cultural expression advances one view of reality, and in the process runs the risks of ignoring or erasing other ways of looking at the world. Any struggle over meaning influences struggles over resources, because cultural stories, signs, and symbols help determine what is legitimate and what is illegitimate, what is permitted and what is forbidden, who is included and who is excluded, who speaks and who is silenced. Like many other sites of commercialized leisure, Disneyland provides a useful site for the examination of these larger social questions.

Disneyland initiated and refined distinct cultural practices that characterize much of American society today. It created one of the most important public spaces in our society out of the imperatives of a private profit-making corporation. It redefined public recreation as primarily spectatorship and shopping, and carried the forms and logic of commercial network television outside the home. Its multilayered opportunities for profit-making mixed marketing, merchandising, and advertising into one unified activity, and it broke down barriers between media by blending film, comic book, and television references in the shared space of a theme park. It connected the personal memories of individual childhoods with carefully crafted narratives about the "childhood" of the nation, and it injected a profit-making corporation into the shaping of family life in an unprecedented manner.

In fact, Disneyland is such a microcosm of cultural practices in our society, it is sometimes difficult to view it as a carefully created and manipulated artifact. Like any good ideological cultural work, it seems to flow naturally from the consciousness of the audience and to demand no special investigation. To think of fun as consisting of shopping and spectatorship makes sense in a world of shopping malls and television sets, but these inevitably erode our collective memory of other more sociable, active, spontaneous, and creative ways to have fun. Disney's idea of a park that would always be in flux is a perfect expression of an economic system that is constantly in the service of fashion—changing clothing styles and automobile styles regularly to create "new" needs for what are essentially the same old products. Disney's success at creating a centralized site for recreation that standardizes stories for people around the world speaks powerfully about the forces of homogenization that have undermined localized ethnic and folk traditions that keep alive creative differences among and across diverse populations. Coming into existence at the same time that commercial network television and suburbanization changed the nature of culture and social life in America, Disneyland succeeded at least in part by recognizing that its visitors were likely to watch television and live in suburbs, and that consequently they expected a park that would conform with their other experiences.

Yet asking questions about Disneyland can help us begin to think critically about the world in which we live. It can help us to inquire into the relationships between commerce and art, between labor and leisure, between citizenship and spectatorship, and between our roles as consumers and our lives as community members, gendered subjects, and world citizens.

In 1955, Walt Disney and his corporation established their phenomenally successful amusement park in the wake of the popularity generated by their television films about Davy Crockett. More than 100 years earlier the historical Davy Crockett boasted that "Fashion is a thing I care mighty little about, except when it happens to run just exactly according to my own notion. . . ." Walt Disney created an amusement park, an entertainment empire, a version of American history, and an important element in the lives of many children by getting fashion to run exactly according to his own notion. We know that Disneyland's blend of commerce and art, its exclusion of those outside of mainstream narratives, and its insertion of cash transactions into the operative realities of family life have been the profitable thing, the successful thing, and the effective thing. But we need to think again about their consequences for what we think we know about the American past and for how we live the American present and future.

Sources: The Disneyland story has been told many times from many different points of view. From the wide range of secondary sources on the establishment and development of the amusement park in relation to the larger vision of the Disney Corporation, I have drawn repeatedly on the valuable information and insights presented by Herbert Schiller in *The Mind Managers* (Boston: Beacon, 1973), Michael Real, *Mass Mediated Culture* (Englewood Cliffs: Prentice-Hall, 1977), Richard Schickel, *The Disney Version* (New York: Simon and Schuster, 1968), and Leonard Mosely, *Disney's World* (New York: Stein and Day, 1985). Also useful for descriptions and quotes were Randy Bright, *Disneyland: The Inside Story* (New York: Harry N. Abrams, Inc., 1987), and Bob Thomas, *Walt Disney, An American Original* (New York: Simon and Schuster, 1976). In journals and periodicals, the articles I found most useful were Richard Francaiglia, "Main Street USA," *Journal of Popular Culture* 15 (September 1981), Mark Gottdiener, "Disneyland: A Utopian Urban Space," *Urban Life* 11 (July 1982), and Paul Goldberger, "Mickey Mouse Teaches the Architects," *New York Times Magazine*, October 20, 1972.

13

WOODSTOCK AND ALTAMONT

MICHAEL FRISCH

When people today, especially young people, are asked what they know or remember about the 1960s, Woodstock and Altamont are always among the most frequently mentioned events: Woodstock—the monster rock festival in New York that verged on catastrophe but ended up demonstrating the youth culture's ideas of harmony and peace; and Altamont, its dark star opposite—the Rolling Stones concert near San Francisco that collapsed into violence between young rock fans and the Hell's Angels motorcycle gang, culminating in a brutal murder in front of the stage, an ugly, depressing event that seemed to belie the naive hopes of the "love generation" of sixties "flower children."

Occurring in the closing months of the 1960s, Woodstock and Altamont came together in one story that presumably gave meaning to each festival, and to a decade of cultural change in the United States. That the story has not seemed to alter very much in the more than 20 years since the concerts suggests there may be more here than meets the eye. After all, interpretations of the 1960s have diverged widely, some viewing the decade as a lost dream and others as a happily forgotten nightmare. But the stories of Woodstock and Altamont have remained a shared legacy, perhaps because they combine both dream and nightmare images so neatly and conveniently.

Michael Frisch's recasting of these events evokes the older parable of Woodstock and Altamont as a tale of good and evil. But it does so in order to frame a very different perspective that at once uncouples the events from each other and yet provides ways of linking them that does not depend on a moralistic mythology of innocence and corruption. Setting aside the powerful dream-nightmare images that have so neatly "explained" the concerts after the fact, Frisch draws on the complex, individual histories of Woodstock and Altamont to tell a very different story. In this new version, Woodstock emerges not as symbol of pastoral simplicity and retreat, but as a veritable city, sustained by technology and engaged in a complex game of survival and collective, political experimentation.

Altamont receives less attention in the narrative, but it, too, is reinterpreted. Although hardly cleansed of the horrific violence that occurred there, Altamont becomes a more sympathetic and understandable event—even, in an odd way, a more intimate one—than the hallowed Woodstock. And for the vast majority of those who

210

attended the concerts, the events that now seem polar opposites must have appeared to be very similar expressions of the musical culture of sixties youth.

At issue in this new interpretation of Woodstock and Altamont is more than a new set and arrangement of facts. The story asks us to think about important questions that have to do with stories themselves. Is the older version just an older story, a kind of instant history with enormous slaying power? Or is it a myth? If it is a myth, is the myth any less real than "history," or any less useful in reconstructing the fascinating and tumultuous years of the late 1960s? If, as hindsight reveals, the optimism and exuberance of the "sixties" were fast eroding under the influence of an ongoing Vietnam war and a Richard Nixon presidency, were Americans so wrong in interpreting the tragic events in front of the Altamont stage as another harbinger of the end of an era?

O n March 22, 1967, a small ad appeared in both the *New York Times* and the "Business Opportunities" column of the *Wall Street Journal:*

> Young men with unlimited capital looking for interesting legitimate investment opportunities and business propositions.

The unlimited capital came mostly from John Roberts, 21, whose family owned a major pharmaceutical firm and who was then an indifferent graduate student at the University of Pennsylvania. His partner was Joel Rosenman, 23, son of a wealthy orthodontist, recent graduate of the Yale law school, and bored junior attorney. The two had decided that life could be more interesting than graduate school or an uncle's law firm: They knew they had the money, connections, and talent to do something—but what? The advertisement was one way to ask the question. The Woodstock Music and Arts Fair ended up being the answer.

Two years later, a circuitous route had led the partners through some 7000 ad responses to a meeting with two young men seeking funds for a state-of-the art recording studio in Woodstock, New York, a town north of New York City that had become home base for folk and rock musicians like the already legendary Bob Dylan. Roberts and Rosenman sat down with the two, both also in their early twenties: Artie Kornfeld, a hard-driving hip young rock executive with Capitol Records, and Michael Lang, a counterculture figure with bell bottom pants, fringed leather vests, and a huge halo of long curly hair who had recently been the proprietor of a "head shop" and an active figure on the rock music scene near Miami Beach, Florida. When Lang and Kornfeld suggested that a promotional concert in Woodstock could inaugurate the planned studio, the two investors jumped on the idea, reversing the priorities—we'll finance the concert, they decided, and use the profits from that to build your studio. Woodstock Ventures, Inc. was born.

This was in February, 1969, and within weeks the four partners had assembled an impressive team to mount a 2- or 3-day festival. The key individuals were Mel Lawrence and Stanley Goldstein, friends who had worked with Lang on the big Miami Pop Festival and had extensive experiences in recording, festivals, and project management. Lawrence was put in charge of all site and facility preparations; Goldstein, a recording engineer, ended up handling anything and everything. "I had taken the position of Holy Ghost," he joked later, "no one knew what I did, but you knew you had to have one."

Each new recruit seemed to bring in others who had needed skills or experience. There was E. H. Beresford "Chip" Monck, later known to the Woodstock audience and to millions of movie viewers as the unflappable stage MC passing on calming messages about lost children and bad drug trips. But in rock circles he was "pretty much the best-known lighting tech around at the time . . . unflustered by anything." There was John Morris, former manager of the Fillmore East rock auditorium in New York, who was to handle artists, agents, bookings, and stage managing. Morris brought in Chris Langhart, who in his early twenties was already head of the theater tech department at New York University (NYU). The sound man, Bill Hanley, headed a company that was the best in the country at delivering quality music systems for large outdoor audiences. Jean Ward, one of the few women at the center of things, brought her husband Bill and a large group of art students from the University of Miami to literally sculpt the grounds and environment, as they had done at other major festivals. Other women had supportive roles at first, but some soon assumed leadership positions at command center, women like Penny Stallings, a recent Southern Methodist University (SMU) graduate, and all-around executive assistant Lee Blumer, who had worked for famed rock promoter Bill Graham at the Fillmore East.

And so it went—a team of experienced young professionals, most in their mid-to-late twenties, solidly grounded in the emerging rock music business. There was one striking exception: a tough ex-cop named Wes Pomeroy, placed in charge of security. In his late forties, Pomeroy had recently left a top policy position at the Department of Justice in Washington; he was one of the few law enforcement and crowd control experts in the country with both credibility among police and sensitivity to the culture of the young people who would be coming to the Festival.

For all the experience, energy, and expertise, it still would have taken a minor miracle to pull off such a complex operation in just a few months, with no wiggle room for unexpected problems. And there turned out to be plenty of problems, especially involving site and security.

The intended site, close to the actual town of Woodstock, vanished as soon as the landowner learned what was planned. John Roberts then found 600 acres in the town of Walkill, not too far away, a site that had good road and electricity access. The technical wizards and art students plunged into the challenge of bulldozing this ugly industrial park site into bucolic hills, trucking in old farm equipment for atmosphere. But the real problems were not so much physical as political, even spiritual.

In the late 1960s, it was a given that rural or small town America would not take kindly to an invasion of hippies. It didn't help that the recent hit movie *Easy Rider* had told a story of motorcycle-riding pot-smoking hippie dropouts in violent collision with rural culture and straight America. The promoters obtained early zoning board approval for the project, but only by soft-pedaling what was planned. As a small army of longhaired young people drifted in to work on the site, Joel Rosenman remembers, the local citizens "started to think, 'Maybe that's what was coming.' In fact it *was* what was coming."

A group called Concerned Citizens sprang up to block the Festival, and the opposition snowballed. Finally, the town of Walkill set up deliberately prohibitive conditions and requirements. In the middle of July, the promoters found themselves with most of the bands contracted, with commitments for everything from an elaborate stage to 2000 portable toilets, and with nearly $750,000 spent and $600,000 in advance ticket sales—all for a festival to be held within the month that now had no site.

Frantically, Bill Ward and Michael Lang searched for usable land, helicoptering around the hills with a Texaco road map and swooping down to read the highway signs so they could know where they were. Finally, with no time to spare, the answer came to them, in the improbable form of a successful Jewish dairy farmer named Max Yasgur of the Catskill mountain town of Bethel. Mel Lawrence and Lang rushed out to see the farm, steeled for another disappointment. But this was different. Yasgur drove them to the top of a broad hill. "And there it is," Lawrence recalled:

> It's like a lake and a natural amphitheater and roads and woods. So we say, like, "Oh, and how much of this land is yours?" "It's all mine," he says, "all mine except the lake's not mine, but I know the guy . . ." *Whew.* And Michael and I looked at each other and said, "This is it."

Indeed, as Stanley Goldstein noted, "it would be very hard to have found a more ideal site than that."

Yasgur proved a tough negotiator when it came to money and contract details, but the key, Goldstein recalled, was that "he felt we had been mistreated, that people deserved to have their say and their moment, that we were entitled to that as folks." His determination and commitment only increased when one of his neighbors put up a sign saying "Don't buy Yasgur's milk, he loves the hippies."

There were some other last minute problems raising the specter of another Walkill, including a threatened holdup on building permits and a self-inflicted PR disaster: A week before the Festival, the promoters invited local citizens to an "open house" to show the careful preparations being made. They asked a "street theatre" group working a nearby hotel to give a sort of "demonstration" of what the festival would be like. With everyone on best behavior, the troupe (whom nobody had actually seen perform) proceeded to strip naked and simulate an orgy, chanting something on the order of "Repressed Rednecks, Provincial Prudes, Loosen your Chains and Live!" It didn't help.

But this was not Walkill. Yasgur's support counted for a lot, and the setting was really very different—located close to the substantial "borscht belt" hotels of the Catskills, Bethel had a declining economy based on a few run-down bungalow colonies and struggling hotels, and farms run by exurbanites like Yasgur. There were quite a few people around who shared his principles, and others who could see how much the area needed the economic boost the Festival could obviously bring.

With only weeks to go, the pace became frenzied. At the site, wells were dug and water systems laid out, hundreds of phone lines installed, garbage and carting service arranged, and electricity run in. "It was like wiring a city up, actually," one worker remembered. "We probably put in a couple of hundred poles, strung wires. Then all of a sudden they realized they had to have a heliport." The stage was 76 feet across and deep, with a 60-foot turntable, 11 feet off the ground and served by an elevator, behind two tall barrier fences, and connected by a bridge to an imposing performer's pavilion. The bridge and pavilion were designed by the brilliant Chris Langhart, whose combination of counterculture daffiness and professional competence seemed characteristic of the overall effort:

> Well, I figured if Jimi Hendrix was running across that bridge and then chased by as many groupies as he could get on that bridge and they were all coming down on one foot at one time, what was the weight load for that bridge? Then I doubled it.

Indeed, the work spanned the cultural spectrum. "A lot of Woodstock was planned from U.S. Army field manuals," John Morris recalled. "Try to find out how many toilets you have to have for how many thousand people and how you set up food and how you do the rest of it—the only data was little brown U.S.

Farmer Max Yasgur delights his 500,000 guests by greeting them from the stage with a "peace" symbol. Yasgur became a counterculture hero not only for agreeing to lease his fields for the site of the Woodstock Festival despite great local opposition, but also for regarding the young people with respect despite vast cultural differences. His appearance on the stage was a welcome sign that communication was possible across the "generation gap." Note, in contrast to the setting at Altamont, how the barrier fence and the height of the stage keep the Woodstock crowd at a safe distance. (Elliott Landy, Magnum Photos)

Army field manuals." Meanwhile, Michael Lang was riding romantically through the fields on a horse, inspecting the work. If to some this suggested the offensive image of a hippie plantation overseer, to others Lang seemed a charismatic guarantee that the countercultural heart of the festival was still beating. "He just seemed to glow. He had this cosmic aura about him," one remembered, "this little smile on his face like he knew something that none of us knew. . . . He managed to glow a lot of things into existence."

One thing that could not quite be glowed was security, the other major problem area. Everyone understood the problems a large crowd camped for several days might present, especially with the expected widespread use of pot and LSD. The potential for confusion, panic, and violence was all too real. But these very circumstances made it just as clear that order could not be imposed by force without catastrophic consequences.

Nobody felt this more strongly than Wes Pomeroy, who used all his savvy to assemble a professional public safety force whose objective would not be law enforcement but community self-help. Early in the summer, Lee Blumer spent several days in a New York City armory interviewing over a thousand police officers, trying to select the several hundred who could maintain professional competence and cool while floating in a sea of pot-smoking hippies.

A secondary approach was more daring, and led Stanley Goldstein to the Hog Farm commune, a large and already legendary hippie group then based in New Mexico. Goldstein arrived attaché case in hand so there would be no misunderstanding that he represented a business venture needing solid commitments on clear terms. He more than met his match. The hippie dreamers agreed to run a free kitchen, to manage the camping areas and cleanup, and to provide overall coordinating and security assistance, for all of which they cut a hard bargain that included a free charter flight from Sante Fe for nearly 90 members with room for tepee poles and with free goat's milk provided en route.

Not a bad combination of straight professionalism and countercultural imagination, or so it seemed until the police commissioner of New York, just days before, barred his off-duty officers from working at the Festival. On the eve of the event Pomeroy and his crew found themselves almost fully dependent on the Hog Farmers, who had created quite a stir when their goat's-milk express landed in New York on the way to Bethel. "My God, we're the cops! I can't believe it!" exclaimed their leader, Hugh Romney, a.k.a. Wavy Gravy. When a reporter asked him what he intended to use for crowd control, he replied "Chocolate cream pies and seltzer bottles," recalling later "and then I noticed they were all writing it down!"

Put-ons can be deceiving. Behind the scenes the Hog Farmers, with Roberts' funds, were trucking in tons of rolled oats, barrels of wheat germ, honey, onions, soy sauce, and 1500 pounds of bulgur wheat, chosen because it would cook faster than the brown rice then a symbol of counterculture cuisine. And the communards had their own approach to security, whimsical on the surface and deeply serious underneath. Offered a hundred arm bands decorated with cheerful flying pigs to identify members of the commune, Wavy Gravy asked how many people were actually expected. "They say they're expecting a couple of hundred thousand," he recalled, "And we say, 'we'd like to have that many arm bands.' We just thought if everybody was a cop there couldn't possibly be a problem." He called this the "Please Force," rather than the police force; the idea, his wife Bonnie explained, was

> when we saw somebody who was taking responsibility in a really excellent way that we would have an extra arm-band in our pocket and would say, "You are part of the Please Force, help out where you can.

The last week or two was a race between things coming together and time running out. One focus was the great bowl itself, where the stage, pavilion, sound system, and medical areas were pretty much ready. Another was near the Hog Farm's encampment in the woods, where a 5-acre Aquarian shopping mall had been set up with hippies selling leather goods and tie-died shirts and incense, and with tot lots, sandboxes, and even a small children's zoo complete with lambs, chicks, and piglets. The campgrounds were more or less ready, as were the adjacent fields and farms rented for parking lots. Huge banks of pay phones and Port-O-San toilets stood waiting.

But this still left hundreds of checklist items incomplete. When Joel Rosenman arrived at the site on Monday of the last week, he recalls, "everything was in a state of preparation roughly on target for a festival to be thrown sometime in November. But not for one that was supposed to begin within four days." Priority had to be given to the primary human support systems, and other things just had to be abandoned. Some didn't matter much—like plans for elaborate light-show screens. But others did, certainly from a business point of view, especially the detailed but unexecuted plans for fencing and 20 turnstiled gates through which ticket-holders could be admitted and the grounds cleared between each of the 3 days' shows. By Wednesday, some 50,000 people were already sitting in front of the stage; with the stream rising to a torrent by the hour, the promoters confronted the fact that they could never clear the bowl to collect tickets, that in fact they never would get the turnstiles or fences in place. They decided that one of the first announcements from the stage would have to be to declare Woodstock a free festival.

At this point, the crowds were so far beyond anyone's imagination as to make the distinction between completed and incomplete preparations almost beside the point. Rosenman and Roberts frantically tried to get the State Police to put into effect a traffic control system slated for Saturday, but they could not convince the authorities of the emergency. The result was that Route 17B leading to Bethel quickly became a 13-mile-long parking lot, and Route 17, the "Quickway" bisecting the Catskills, was rapidly backing up toward the New York Thruway. "The situation is hopeless," one trooper reported, "and getting worse." Too late, the police began to close roads and broadcast appeals to people to turn back. Although the 500,000 or so who eventually arrived at Woodstock dazzled the world and made this probably the largest mass entertainment event in history, some authorities estimate that as many as 2 million may have been trying to get to the Festival.

Who were all these young people, and why were so many on the road to Woodstock? One thing they weren't was a gathering of the flower-children tribes seeking a kind of hippie theme park, as the conventional image has come to suggest. What they were was a representative cross-section of largely middle-class white American youth, a broad spectrum that the promoters, succeeding beyond their wildest dreams, had explicitly sought to reach. Rosenman and Roberts sensed that by 1969 most young people were feeling the strain of a decade of diverse conflicts with parents, teachers, and politicians about hair, drugs, sex, race relations, urban crisis, and the war in Vietnam. And so their Woodstock ads barely mentioned the star musicians or the counterculture, speaking instead of "three days of peace and music." "Walk around for three days without seeing a skyscraper or a traffic light," the copy went on, "Fly a kite, sun yourself, breathe unspoiled air." Paintings would hang on trees, and "artists will be glad to discuss their work, or the unspoiled splendor of the surroundings, or anything else that might be on your mind."

But imagery explains only so much, and like most advertisers the Woodstock promoters exaggerated its importance. Deep down, products matter; consumers buy because there's something that they want. And if the newspaper and magazine ads were projecting an image, rock music radio stations and record stores and head shops across the country were trumpeting the news that Woodstock would bring together the most sensational constellation of top musicians and bands ever

Route 17B, the road to and from the Woodstock Festival. For most of the weekend, the highway was jammed like this for some 13 miles. This photo, taken on Saturday, shows some disillusioned young people heading home after an uncomfortable, rainy Friday night, while in the background others are still moving toward the Festival. (Associated Press/Wide World Photos)

seen at any festival. To understand why this massing of talent sent so many young people careening toward Woodstock requires a bit of attention to what rock music was and what it had become.

In the early 1960s, most American high schools were still complex quilts of visibly divergent subcultures—"hoods" who dressed in blue jeans and danced to rockabilly music, for instance, and "bohemians" who favored black clothes, coffeehouses, jazz, and folk music. The divide between rock music and the folk music revival of the early 1960s was particularly sharp, with fans of each seeming to have very distinct social and cultural roots: In 1965, concert fistfights broke out between Bob Dylan's folk followers and fans of his first great electric rock hits, neither group having previously been very aware of the other. For most kids the music that mattered most was music that helped signal and solidify social differences rather than music that reached across them—music that told you who you were by distinguishing your group from others among your peers.

By the late 1960s, however, old divisions were breaking down. Musical influences were flowing across every category in every direction. The numerous hit records of Creedence Clearwater Revival had the simplicity and heavy beat of 1950's rockabilly—but the lyrics were often countercultural. Iron Butterfly was a favorite counterculture group whose sound anticipated later heavy metal. The brooding music of the Doors fused black blues, the drug experimenting of the counterculture, and Jim Morrison's philosophical poetry. And the Beatles' epic album "Sgt. Pepper" brought together rock, popular balladry, traditions of music hall and theater, and experiments on the outer limits of studio production. These movements across borders of style suggest that rock music was beginning to define a new, inclusive youth culture very different from the fragmented "teenage" cultures of previous years, which had never pretended to be more than a stage on the road to conventional adulthood.

In 1969, this emerging new rock music culture was by and large a private and small group experience. Young people shared albums, danced at parties, listened to "underground" FM radio, and indulged in the illicit marijuana and hallucinogenic drugs that were embraced as the doors to a new consciousness and a higher reality—and a sharp generational divider. Public concerts and festivals attracted small and specialized audiences. But the musical lineup for the Woodstock festival promised a very different sort of public experience, on a new scale. It was spectacular not because it represented the great mega-stars of the rock revolution (neither the Beatles, nor the Rolling Stones, nor Bob Dylan were to be there) but because it so embodied just about every tendency and dimension of rock creativity, from folk to avant garde. Indeed, it was not until August 15, 1969, as those two million young people struggled to get to the Woodstock Festival, that it began to become apparent what the music of the previous few years was beginning to add up to for this generation.

For most of the young people at or on the road to Woodstock, the mood on that Friday was less one of exhilaration than of surprise, frustration, and annoyance. They found themselves in what one student recalled as a stream of initially frightening diversity, from "real hippies" to "teeny boppers" to clean-cut suburban college types, to bikers and rockers and even Hell's Angels, all bumping into each other with the frayed tempers sure to be found in any mammoth traffic jam.

At the concert site, there was some excitement at discovering the fallen fences and the absence of gates, rules, regulations, police, or supervisors. But the realization that the situation was by that token beyond control contributed a dark undertone of anxiety for many, who wondered exactly what they had gotten themselves into.

Spirits lifted when the music got off to a good, if unplanned, start around 6 P.M. Among the first performers was Country Joe McDonald, who brought the crowd together with his famous "Fixin' to Die Rag," an anti-Vietnam War singalong, preceded by his even more famous call and response "Gimme an F . . . U . . . C . . . K" cheer—imposing when shouted by several hundred thousand kids realizing that there were no grownups around to disapprove or even be shocked.

But as night came on the mood darkened: Everything was so uncertain, from food to safety to shelter, and the parade of folksingers programmed for the evening, headed by Joan Baez, and curiosities like Indian sitar master Ravi Shankar, left much of the audience distracted and unmoved. Persistent rain dampened spirits further. As one youngster recalled,

> It seemed more like a war zone that happened to be peaceful at the moment. It was real strange and I didn't care for it. There was no question about the fact that I wanted to leave the next morning. And so we ended up hitchhiking out of the area back into New York City.

Saturday was a different story. Many spent the morning wandering around the fields, discovering the crafts area and Hog Farm compounds in the woods, and skinny dipping in the ponds. Meanwhile, streams of people were still arriving, and as the hillside bowl filled for the afternoon concert, the enormity of the crowd became visible and tangible for the first time, an immense human spectacle. One youth remembers that

> we walked from where we were in the woods to the stage and looked out and all of a sudden what had been what seemed to me a few thousand people had become this half million people and it all seemed to have happened on Friday night in the middle of the night . . . I was standing and thinking, "Oh my God, this is unbelievable."

This individual response quickly grew into a collectively shared sense that something momentous was happening, a realization assisted by commentary from the stage. A stream of announcements—by Mel Lawrence, John Morris, Wavy Gravy of the Hog Farm, and especially the calm-voiced Chip Monck—crystallized everyone's feelings and broadcast them back, amplified, to the crowd.

In this electronic dialogue, the pastoral vision of nature and rural harmony in the now irrelevant Woodstock advertisements gave way to an urban frame of reference. "Welcome to one of the biggest cities in the United States," Mel Lawrence boomed into the mike on Saturday morning. The image indeed fit: The density and variety of the immense crowd was generating the infectious excitement associated with city life at its best. But there was another side to the image: The environment was swiftly coming to seem a vast free-form museum of modern urban problems at their worst—litter and garbage, disintegrating communications, water and food shortages, and inadequate sewage and health care facilities. And looming in the shadows was the possibility of violence or chaotic rioting, with which urban America was all too familiar after the "long hot summers" of the 1960s.

In real cities, problems are handled bureaucratically, through administrative authority. But at Woodstock, administration did not survive the first day, and authority was nonexistent. In this situation, the promoters had no choice but to turn to the crowd. From the stage, spokesmen began telling vacationing kids, most of whom would have cheered the sixties slogan "Power to the People," that in fact they had the power—or rather, there was no power except what they, the people, chose to exercise. The genuine accomplishment of these voices was to help generate a sense of collective urban adventure, making everyone realize that they were a city not because of the exciting size or the real problems, but simply because they were so fully dependent on each other.

One motif epitomized the uniqueness and potential of this situation. Surrounding the stage were a number of huge scaffold towers for lights and cameras. During every set, some kids would climb up to enjoy the unsurpassed view from the towers' platforms, and invariably someone, usually Chip Monck, would patiently plead over the PA for them to come down. He would acknowledge politely that nobody could make them come down, but that they should anyway, because each person on a tower blocked the view of tens of thousands of others looking down from the hill. "There's a half a million people here," he said at one point, "and if we don't help each other we'll die. Come on, up there, join us!" The towers would usually clear after each of these sermons, although during the next set the kids, or different ones, would climb up again, producing another appeal and another sheepish retreat. It was almost as if some kids wanted the scolding, as a way to reestablish parental authority where none really existed and thus to decline the responsibility the situation was demanding that they assume.

There was even more at stake in the handling of other problems, particularly drugs. Widespread use of marijuana and experimenting with hallucinogenic drugs was a hallmark of the generation, viewed less as an escape than as an adventurous reaching to an alternative reality and a higher consciousness. But for most this was usually done with friends under familiar circumstances with known substances of reliable quality, precisely the opposite of conditions prevailing at Woodstock. The result was a great many unexpected reactions that could suddenly turn into terrifying "bad trips." Rumors that bad LSD was circulating made things worse—and presented organizers with a desperate dilemma. As Chip Monck said, "How do you keep them from taking it without freaking out those who already have?" His answer was a cool, hip voice that struck just the right note of reassurance and concern:

> You may take it with however many grains of salt you wish that the brown acid that's circulating around is not specifically too good. It's suggested that you do stay away from that. Of course, it's your own trip, so be my guest. But please be advised that there's a warning on that one.

In another risky stage decision, it was decided to share with the crowd the horror stories filling the national press and airwaves about the catastrophe taking shape at Woodstock—images of a drug-ridden anarchy careening out of control, and calls for the National Guard to step in. Sharing this news, a strategy Joel Rosenman called "reverse information dissemination," challenged everyone to pull together and prove the authorities wrong.

Like the drug warnings, the images of crisis might themselves have provoked anxiety and panic. But the tactic worked: A remarkable ethic of mutuality and co-operation began to spread throughout the entire Festival area. People willingly shared scarce food with strangers, helped those who were lost, shepherded those freaking out on bad drug trips to the medical aid stations, did what they could to gather in the rising tide of garbage, and linked into the chains of volunteer work-ers spiraling out of the Hog Farm. Throughout it all, the calm, encouraging voices from the stage, the public face of the community, magnified these efforts and made the instant city of half a million youngsters seem a tight knit community.

The other thing that made a difference on Saturday was the music itself—an incredible concert that began at 1 o'clock in the afternoon and did not end until well after dawn the next morning. For the first time it seemed as if all of rock's various streams were coming together, fusing diverse groups of fans into a single, public generational audience. The performers included the hard driving Creedence Clearwater Revival; the queen of acid rock blues, Janis Joplin; the experimental,

Climbers on the light and camera towers at the Woodstock Festival. All the climbers appear to be young men—perhaps it seemed at first a macho chal-lenge to scale these heights for a better view, regardless of how many thousands of others were thereby prevented from seeing the stage. (From the film *Woodstock*, Michael Wadleigh, Warner Brothers/Courtesy, Museum of Modern Art Film Still Archive)

theatrical British group The Who; the then virtually unknown Santana, antici-
pating the infusion of Latin rhythms into rock; and the quintessential San Francisco groups—the classic folk–rock–blues band the Grateful Dead and, closing out
the long event after sunrise, the Jefferson Airplane, wellspring of a harder acid rock
sound. But for most people, the peak came somewhere in the middle of the long
night, with the black group Sly and the Family Stone, psychedelic rock grafted
onto R&B (rhythm and blues) and gospel. As Sly Stone led the crowd in an ec-
static, almost religious call and response on the song "Higher," it seemed that rock
music had finally become a kind of communal binding force.

It was not ecstasy, however, that kept music going all night—this was a decision of the organizers who knew that chaos was still a danger if the crowd were
not kept focused and occupied. All day and night long, while the musicians played,
they had been battling a ceaseless barrage of emergencies. Artists had to be heli-
coptered in, not to mention emergency medical and food supplies. Outside officials had to be persuaded that calling in the National Guard would be catastrophic. Outraged locals arrived waving lawsuits. Frantic parents were trying to
call their children and desperate messages had to be passed on about lost friends
who had needed medicine. And then some of the musicians refused to go on until
paid up front: While the hillside was soaring on sound, John Roberts was frantically arranging to helicopter the local bank manager, in his pajamas in the middle
of the night, to retrieve the needed cashier checks.

There were also problems with the more political activists from New York's
East Village, especially Yippie leader Abbie Hoffman, who saw the festival as a
plot to exploit the alternative culture for profit with nothing given in return. Early
on, Hoffman had flatly threatened sabotage unless given $10,000 for community
organizing and political work at the Festival. A sort of deal was struck, and at the
scene Hoffman threw all his formidable talents into organizing everything from a
camp newspaper to emergency field hospitals. But he remained frustrated that political issues were so suppressed in the Festival's public voice and presence. Finally, he tried to seize the microphone while The Who was playing, to rally support for John Sinclair, an activist who had recently begun serving a 10-year jail
term for possession of two joints of marijuana. A whack from Peter Townshend's
guitar sent Hoffman running, and seemed to announce that his "political" approach to the Festival was not welcome.

But what was happening at Woodstock *was* political. The counterculture was
demonstrating its capacity to solve problems in its own terms, and in ways that
advanced a broader vision of change. In the organization of the free kitchen that
fed tens of thousands and in dealing with the medical emergencies, the Hog Farmers' "armband" approach reached its most inspiring heights, as Wavy Gravy recalled:

> So there were these five doctors in white coats and shirts and ties and me. And this
> guy comes in screaming, "Miami Beach, 1944! Joyce! Joyce!" And this psychiatrist
> leans in and says, "Just think of your third eye, man." So I figured it was time
> for me to make my move. And the guy says, "Miami Beach, 1944!" And I said,
> "What's your name, man?" He says, "Joyce!" I said, "What's your name, man?"
> He says, "1944." I said, "WHAT'S YOUR NAME, MAN?" He says, "Bob!" I

said, "Your name is Bob! Your name is Bob. Your name is Bob." And he is getting it, and he's getting it, and he's getting it. And when he's got it I say, "Guess what?" He says, "What?" I said, "You took a little acid and it's going to wear off." He says, "Thank God." They don't want to know about third eyes. They just want to know they're going to come down.

And then—which is what made Woodstock unique—when he was near normal and ready to go back to rock 'n' roll, we said "Hold it. You see that sister coming through the door with her toes in her nose? That was you three hours ago. Now you're the doctor. Take over." And they'd take turns.

Sunday tested and deepened the intensity of Saturday's experience. It began easily enough, someone reading the Sunday comics to the crowd and Wavy Gravy announcing "breakfast in bed for 400,000," with the Hog Farmers and hundreds of volunteers passing out paper cups of granola across the hillside. But soon after the music began in the afternoon, the skies suddenly darkened and a monster thunderstorm of near-tornado intensity broke over the unprotected hills and fields. "It was Dante's Inferno," John Morris recalled, "it was all hell breaking loose, it was everything you could ever have possibly wrong at one situation at one given moment."

He and the staff had good reason to be terrified. The crowd pressure had exposed electrical cables; the whole stage complex was sliding slowly into the mud; the electrified light towers were swaying in the gale like pendulums. Mass electrocution was a real possibility, as was a tower collapse that could kill scores and panic thousands more. It was imperative that the power be turned off—yet the music and the medium of the stage PA were the lifeline keeping the huge crowd from panic. In another desperate gamble, one mike was kept alive while everything else was shut down. John Morris, alone on the huge stage, helped the crowd ride it through, talking kids down from the swaying towers in a voice calm enough to avoid panicking those huddled underneath.

Although the tension soon gave way to mudslide frolicking as the worst of the storm passed over, the emergency had been a dramatic reminder that Woodstock Nation was subject to larger forces, still enmeshed in a world beyond its own control. This was acknowledged ironically when the hillside multitudes chanted the demand "no rain, no rain" just as the immense thunderstorm was so obviously about to break. It was acknowledged respectfully in the way the young volunteers and organizers accepted the outside aid that began to make such a difference. One of the biggest cheers of the weekend came when a green helicopter swung in ominously over a crowd fearing a National Guard takeover, and John Morris announced with excitement, "Ladies and Gentlemen, the U.S. Army . . . Medical Corps!"

In the aftermath of the storm, kids skinny-dipped off the mud and thousands of others began to drift homeward. There was a growing sense of fulfillment and completion, a mood helped along by the final concert, also an all night affair that ended early Monday morning. This session featured the English singer Joe Cocker, launched to stardom by his Woodstock performance of "With a Little Help from My Friends," a Beatles song especially appropriate to the situation; the new folk-rock based combo of Crosby, Stills, and Nash; the Band, Dylan's former backup group; and Blood, Sweat, and Tears, pointing mainstream rock toward a newer, broader 1970s sound.

But it was the closing of the festival early Monday morning, when a good part of the huge crowd had already left, that best brought the music and the meaning of the whole event together. The last performer was Jimi Hendrix, the enigmatic black superstar who was more a figure of the counterculture than of the black musical scene, his wild electric guitar style having propelled him to the frontier of experimental rock sounds. Hendrix closed the festival not with rock but with a long, meditative, almost tortured solo version of the Star Spangled Banner. The moment was very special, as one witness recalled:

> There was a sort of stillness and it really looked like those old photos you see
> of old Civil War battlefields, where you see a dead horse and these mounds of
> things that have been left. And there was Jimi Hendrix up there playing "The Star
> Spangled Banner" . . . I mean it was like a very strange, eerie close to the whole
> thing, you know. I just remember those two images together: him playing that
> song, and everything being so still while he played . . .

The image has become one of the lasting symbols of Woodstock—to some a flag-desecrating emblem of the counterculture's alienation, to others a more complex gesture of both respect and defiant pride.

Indeed, as it closed and even before, Woodstock was becoming a series of contested images. The process had begun in the first often-hysterical reactions to the crisis in Bethel, when a *New York Times* editorial called the whole thing "a nightmare of mud and stagnation" with "freakish looking intruders" who "had little more sanity than the impulses that drive the lemmings to march to their deaths in the sea. . . . What kind of culture is it," asked the *Times,* "that can produce so colossal a mess?"

Almost immediately, this posture gave way to grudging acknowledgments that the young people had been generally well behaved, cooperating with each other and with those who rushed food and medical help to their rescue. The *Times*'s next day's editorial, "Morning After at Bethel," generously pronounced Woodstock "essentially a phenomenon of innocence." But something more was going on in this shift of imagery: Woodstock's diverse cultural mix and complexity of interdependence was coming to be replaced, after the fact, by an image of a dreamy youth culture straight out of the "flowers in your hair/gentle people there" hippie stereotype born in San Francisco's Haight Ashbury district in the mid 1960s. And this was not just a response of the mainstream media. In the song that became a kind of "Woodstock Nation" national anthem Joni Mitchell sang, "We've Got to Get Ourselves Back to the Garden." But the song was written after the Festival; Mitchell, in fact, had not even been there. In the fall of 1969, this Garden of Eden imagery seemed to be recapturing and transforming the meaning of Woodstock. And it also set the stage, in a kind of biblical drama, for the entrance of the serpent—at Altamont Speedway.

The great free Rolling Stones concert near San Francisco on December 6, 1969, would never have occurred had not Woodstock preceded it. The Stones and lead singer Mick Jagger were then at the height of their popularity, and somewhat jealous of the shadow that the August festival threw over their upcoming fall American tour. Knowing that a major documentary about Woodstock was being readied, they decided to have one made about their own tour, and began to toy with the idea of a huge free concert to provide its climax.

But it was not simply their idea, or even their choice. The tour had been grossing millions of dollars for the Stones in sellout appearances across the country. In New York City alone, a single advertisement brought requests for over 500,000 tickets. In the glow of the Woodstock spirit, the alternative community placed increasing pressure on the Stones to rise above profit, to return something to the community in the form of a free, public concert, especially considering the climax of the tour in San Francisco, the heart of the counterculture.

The Stones finally agreed, and the details began to be thrown together while their tour crisscrossed the country. If Woodstock needed years and only had months to prepare, this 1 day event needed months and had only weeks, and then only days. There was some of the same professionalism, including many of the same individuals behind the scenes—Chip Monck, for example, was in charge of the stage facilities—but no time or resources with which to work. After false starts and dashed hopes paralleling the Woodstock site location fiasco, land for this concert finally materialized with only 1 day to prepare. The grossly inadequate site was Altamont Speedway, a seedy drag strip 50 miles east of San Francisco offered by an owner hoping to put himself and his facility on the map. ("Please call it Dick Carter's Altamont Speedway," he kept insisting to the press, to no avail.) And where emergency security provisions at Woodstock had come to depend on the Hog Farm commune, the Stones and their agents were persuaded to deputize a very different group: the Hell's Angels motorcycle gang. Given how catastrophically this turned out, it is hard now to appreciate how appropriate it seemed.

The Stones occupied then (and still do) an unusual place in the evolution of rock, encompassing within their own music and persona the kind of broad synthesis it took many different groups at Woodstock to represent. They had begun as blues purists, alienated middle-class English boys reaching beyond their backgrounds for what seemed a music of authenticity and power. In contrast to the genial Beatles, the Stones had fashioned themselves into the bad boys of rock, projecting an insolence, rebellion, and raw sexuality that flaunted their contempt for society's conventional values and institutions. Where the Beatles moved forward into experimental song forms and eclectic stylizing, the Stones deepened their hold on a hard-driving, R&B based sound that brought the full energy and spirit of black music into rock and roll. As they turned from performing their own versions ("covers") of black songs to writing their own material, the insolence became more culturally rebellious and even political. The Stones' music seemed increasingly to embrace violence and evil; their blatant sexuality became more excessive, taunting the mainstream with what appeared to be a kind of countercultural perversion. All these tendencies were at a peak in 1969, embodied in hit songs like "Sympathy for the Devil," "Street Fighting Man," and "Honky Tonk Woman."

As for the Angels, they had been a minor gang on the edge of dissolution when, in 1965, an incident or two led to a newsmagazine media blitz. Suddenly they were an overnight national phenomenon and began to live up to the image that had been created for them, roaring down the highway in huge convoys on a "run" to this or that location where locals cowered in fear. Said one of the Angels, almost as if he were speaking to an expectant public, "We're the one percenters, man—the one percent that don't fit and don't care. We've punched our way out of a hundred rumbles, stayed alive with our boots and our fists. We're royalty among motorcycle outlaws, baby."

The motorcycle outlaw motif held particular fascination for a San Francisco counterculture eager, in 1965, to identify with others who opposed authority. "We're in the same business," LSD missionary Ken Kesey told the Angels when he met them, "You break people's bones. I break people's heads." Soon he had turned them on to acid and drawn them into the "love generation" scene, where they were embraced by poet Allen Ginsberg and other hip intellectuals.

The Angels themselves never quite knew what to make of all this—love, said their leader, Ralph "Sonny" Barger, is "the feeling you get when you like something as much as your motorcycle." And the hip romance burned off quickly; in October of 1965 the Angels beat up antiwar demonstrators trying to march from Berkeley to Oakland to shut down the Army Terminal there, a ship-out point for Vietnam troops. By 1969 there were few remaining illusions about the Angels and the violent threat their hostility could pose.

Mick Jagger and the Rolling Stones in performance, earlier in the tour that was to culminate in the concert at the Altamont Speedway. Note how Jagger's costume and gestures seem to combine both masculine and feminine sexual imagery—one of the things that made him seem so outrageous to "straight" society. Also note how close the crowd is to the stage and the performers, a pattern that was to prove so disastrous at Altamont. (From the film *Gimme Shelter,* David Maysles, Albert Maysles, Charlotte Zwerin; Maysles Films, Inc./Courtesy, Museum of Modern Art Film Still Archive)

But it was this very realism that led to the request that the Angels serve at Altamont. The organizers were not thinking of general peacekeeping in a large temporary community on the order of Woodstock; they faced the narrower, classic challenge of rock concert security: protecting stars from overexcited fans. On previous tours, there had been repeated clashes between fans and police protecting the Stones, often ending in tear gas and indiscriminant beatings by police. And in San Francisco, pressure was guaranteed to be intense: Where the elaborate Woodstock stage had stood 11 feet off the ground and was protected by high barrier fences, the stage set up hastily at Altamont was at eye level, with the crowd able to press right up against it.

The Stones' managers and their San Francisco contacts thus knew that some sort of physical, visible, formidable protection would be needed at a huge free concert. But they feared, correctly, the provocation that uniformed police, armed or unarmed, would present. And so the Stones agreed to invite the Angels to protect them in exchange for the now legendary $500 in free beer.

On Saturday, December 6, the mood at Altamont seemed uneasy from the start, although not particularly because of the Angels, whom most of those attending never even saw. Perhaps it was the unpleasant, uncomfortable site, littered with junked cars, or the edge of counterculture violence in the air. (The previous week had seen the arrest of Charles Manson, a charismatic figure on the fringe of the hippie rock scene, for the horrific Tate–La Bianca murders, which themselves had taken place just before Woodstock.)

The concert got underway in early afternoon to the rhythms of Santana, the huge crowd of nearly 500,000 settling in for the long wait before the appearance of the Stones. Down in front were the Angels—sitting on the edge of the stage with their bikes parked nearby, hefting chains and cut-off, weighted pool cues, "dangling their legs over the side," Stones biographer Stanley Booth recalled with pointed irony, "like little boys fishing at a creek in the nineteenth century."

It might have worked, if so many of the Angels had not been so drunk or so hopelessly stoned. But with the crowd pressed tightly against the stage, the Angels, and their beloved bikes, the situation proved volatile almost from the start. Fights broke out again and again, brief flurries of violence that would erupt and then subside—defenseless, often stoned young people beaten with pool cues and stomped by crowds of Angels, in full view of the stage and the documentary movie cameras. Carlos Santana stopped playing and tried without effect to calm things down. A while later Marty Balin of the Jefferson Airplane tried to break up a fight and was knocked unconscious by one of the Angels. Beyond the area in front of the stage, most people couldn't know quite what was happening, but a fitful mood of fear and anxiety began to spread back through the throng. On stage Stones assistant Sam Cutler was proving no Chip Monck at the microphone: Exhausted and frustrated, he scolded the Angels and the crowd like an unpleasant schoolmaster.

Finally the Stones took the stage, Jagger in his outrageous silver tights, black shirt, orange cape, and Uncle Sam hat. For the first few tunes it almost seemed as if the music would carry the mood beyond the reach of the Angels now massed at the front of the stage. But as the band launched into "Sympathy for the Devil," the Angels resumed the savage pool cue beatings, enraged by what seemed to have been an attack on one of their motorcycles. The Stones stopped playing, trying to quiet things down: "Hey people—I mean, who's fighting, and what for? Why are we fighting?" a puzzled Jagger asked.

The Stones retreated to some "cool out" tunes, and Jagger continued to try to sooth the crowd between songs. But then the violence erupted again, as he began "Under My Thumb." In full view of the stage, a tall, black boy in an iridescent suit suddenly leaped up and was as suddenly set upon by a frenzied gang of Angels, stomped to the ground, and stabbed repeatedly with a long knife. The incident was over in a flash. Nobody beyond the immediate circle could see the blood from the youth's massive wounds or realize that indeed a murder had taken place in their midst, but the violence was still traumatic—including the fact that many *had* seen the young man, Meredith Hunter, 19, brandishing a pistol just before the Angels descended on him.

Cutler appealed for a doctor, and ineffectively tried to calm the crowd, as did another backstage figure who took the microphone—Michael Lang, the hippie promoter of Woodstock. Finally, announced Jagger, "It seems to be stuck down to me":

Hells Angels beating concertgoers with pool cues in front of the stage at Altamont. Most onlookers show no emotion, not because they are indifferent but because the events are unfolding so quickly and unexpectedly at a concert intended as a celebration of countercultural harmony. A few faces begin to register the horror of what is happening. (From the film *Gimme Shelter*, David Maysles, Albert Maysles, Charlotte Zwerin; Maysles Films, Inc./Courtesy, Museum of Modern Art Film Still Archive)

> All I can ask you, San Francisco, is . . . this could be the most beautiful evening
> we've had this winter, let's get it together, everyone, come *on* now. . . . You know,
> if we *are* all one, let's fucking well *show* we're all one. Everyone just sit down.
> Keep cool. Let's just *relax*, let's get into a groove. Come on, we can get it together,
> come on.

The emotional appeal was perplexing to most of the 500,000 who couldn't see
what was happening down front. Meanwhile, with crazed intensity, the Angels
continued to fulfill their assigned mission to protect the stage, mercilessly beating
a stoned, naked girl trying to clamber up toward Jagger.

But in fact the groove did take hold. Perhaps Jagger's impotence in his spo-
ken role inspired greater intensity in his singing. Many still say that what followed
was one of the Stones' greatest performances ever; in the final analysis, its sheer
power may well have made the crucial difference in preventing the horror up front
from spreading and escalating into a catastrophic crowd panic. But the Stones were
numbed by the effort and what they had seen. "I thought the scene here was supposed to be so groovy," Jagger commented soon after. "I don't know what happened, it was terrible, if Jesus had been there he would have been crucified."

AN INTERPRETATION

For most of those present, Woodstock involved struggle, process, and challenge.
For 3 days, individuals were forced to relate to each other under great pressure,
and to rise above circumstances that had somehow—to everyone's surprise—
placed their destiny in their own hands. What made Woodstock exciting was how
the emergency, the music, and the linking of strangers in long voluntary chains of
collective self-help all served to create a community—a political, cultural, and musical community where none had quite existed before. If those who kept climbing
up the towers seemed almost nostalgic for a missing parental authority to challenge, the vast majority underneath were creating their own authority, discovering their capacity to take responsibility for the situation, and each other.

In all these ways, Woodstock epitomized the values of culture, politics, and
community at the core of generational change in the 1960s. Abbie Hoffman may
have wanted to provoke the assembled Woodstock Nation into a political confrontation. The promoters may have imagined an apolitical, purely cultural celebration. But the real meaning of the experience—and of much of the sixties—was
how these were merging. Political and cultural change were becoming entwined
in the experience of an increasingly unified, self-conscious generation.

To be sure, Woodstock also revealed how incomplete this community was,
and how dependent it was on extraordinary circumstances—how hard it was for the
same sense of unity, struggle, and spirit to survive for very long without confrontation, whether that confrontation involved the emergency of food and health care at
Woodstock or the confrontation with the government over the war in Vietnam.

And it revealed something more as well: the power of cultural images in political, cultural, and generational conflicts. It showed how these can transform the
meaning of experience—even becoming, after the fact, what is remembered as the
reality of that experience.

Woodstock, as advertised, had promised a pastoral garden, an opportunity for people to come into harmony with nature and each other. At the end of the rebellious sixties, with conflict and violence spiraling out of control even within the counterculture, this dream evidently had enormous appeal. And as we have seen, it is to this theme of gentle innocence and simple harmony that images of Woodstock quickly and permanently returned. In so doing, these images obscured, after the fact, the deeper political and cultural experience of those who had been there.

Altamont played an important, even crucial role in this process—a process, at its heart, that involved a struggle to define the meaning of the sixties. "Altamont was the killer of the dream," wrote one observer from inside the counterculture; said another: "On this day, hip jargon, flower power, and the Age of Aquarius were finished. The great sixties dream was washed up . . . all the beautiful fantasies of the sixties withered and died." Ralph Gleason, a mainstream San Francisco journalist who had done much to explain the rock world to his readers, wrote, "Is this the new community? Is this what Woodstock promised? Gathered here as a tribe, what happened? Brutality, murder, despoilation." Many concluded, as Vincent Canby was to say a bit later in the *New York Times,* that "Everything that the people feared would happen (but didn't) at Woodstock happened at Altamont."

Such statements say little about history and much about myth-making. There were four deaths at Altamont, true, but three were in accidents much like the one death that occurred at Woodstock. In either event, what is remarkable is how minimal was the conflict or disorder. The violence at Altamont remained restricted to a handful of Angels in a circle of several hundred people around the stage; horrific as this was, what needs to be explained is why the incidents became such powerful symbols of the experience not just of 500,000 concertgoers, but of the entire counterculture.

The explanation lies in the relationship between the two events—or, more precisely, in what the events at Altamont supposedly revealed about Woodstock. For Altamont was almost immediately embraced as proof of the fatal fragility of the Woodstock vision. If Altamont is the face of evil, then Woodstock must have been its opposite—the face of innocence. With the help of Altamont, Woodstock became remembered not for struggle, process, or community, but rather as a temporary Garden of Eden, inhabited by a naive generation. And—so the story goes—the Woodstock generation came to be (deserved to be?) expelled from the Garden for the dark, countercultural sins of Altamont. The story is an old one, of course, with proven appeal.

This dichotomy of blissful innocence and cruel, violent reality is all too convenient, deflecting us from the more challenging complexities of the 1960s. Indeed, the images might well be reversed, with Altamont understood as the more innocent, Woodstock the more real event. It was at Altamont, after all, that old-fashioned face-to-face confrontations led to violence, unprevented by desperate microphone messages from the stage that left a dazed Mick Jagger pleading for peace like a little boy. And so much of what was taken for innocence at Max Yasgur's farm was the product of those hallmarks of modern society, electronics and mediated communication: The blasts of music and the electronically amplified voices of folksy stage spokesmen combined to draw hundreds of thousands of distrustful strangers into sustained interaction with each other—into meaningful community and mutual responsibility.

Indeed, in broader cultural and political senses as well, it is Woodstock that offers the more complex testimony on young people in America at the end of the 1960s. This was, after all, a moment when for many young people the challenges of the festival were just beginning to harden into wider confrontations with the policies and institutions of American society. Tom Law, a friend of the Hog Farm who gave the yoga demonstrations that seem so apolitical in the movie *Woodstock,* put it this way:

> The thing I kept thinking when I look back on those times is, yes, you can say we were naive, but we were naive with a vengeance. What we were trying to avenge was the nastiness of what America had become in the Vietnam era. And I think that was the prevailing motivator: to do something different and to do something right. . . . Everybody was really pouring their time and energy into trying to heal this gaping wound, which, as you know, got worse and worse for the next three years . . .

> The question is not "What happened to those of us who went to Woodstock?" It's "Where's the Woodstock for today's generation?" That's more important, because out of that sense of community comes the energy to go out there and actually participate in the process so that social change occurs.

Sources: The most valuable primary source for Woodstock is Joel Makower, *Woodstock: The Oral History* (New York: Doubleday, 1989). Most of this chapter's direct quotations from Festival participants are taken, with appreciation, from the extensive interviews in this well-edited collection. Also useful are the recollections of the Festival promoters, wittily crafted by a professional writer: Robert Pilpel, Joel Rosenman, and John Roberts: *Young Men with Unlimited Capital* (New York: Bantam, 1989 [original edition 1974]); Abbie Hoffman's *Woodstock Nation: A Talk–Rock Album* (New York: Vintage, 1969) a spirited memoir–manifesto that Hoffman claims he wrote in a drugged frenzy immediately after the Festival; and a history based on many recent interviews with those who had been at Woodstock: Jack Curry, *Woodstock: The Summer of Our Lives* (New York: Weidenfeld and Nicolson, 1989).

There has been less written about Altamont, but I found Stanley Booth's participant–observer memoir of the Rolling Stones 1969 tour (at once a primary and a secondary source) the most helpful: *Dance with the Devil: The Rolling Stones and Their Times* (New York: Random House, 1984). The best documentation of the Altamont event is in the periodical press at the time, particularly *Rolling Stone.* A good example of mainstream reportage, with rich detail, is Ralph J. Gleason, " 'Aquarius Wept': After Woodstock and Love Came Altamont and Disaster," *Esquire* 74/2 (August, 1970).

Finally, of course, there are the major documentary films of each event released in 1970 and still widely available in libraries and video rental stores: Michael Wadleigh's *Woodstock* (Warner Brothers) and *Gimme Shelter* by David Maysles, Albert Maysles, and Charlotte Zwerin (Maysles Films, Inc.). These include primary documentary footage of each event, but each film is also a highly crafted interpretation—a version perhaps more valuable as a primary source for tracing cultural imagery than as a secondary source version of the event as history.

For broader background on the history of popular culture and music in the 1960s, the following were especially helpful in developing the interpretation I offer in this chapter: Jim Curtis, *Rock Eras: Interpretations of Music and Society, 1954–1984* (Bowling Green, OH: Bowling Green State University Popular Press, 1987); Morris Dickstein, *The Gates of Eden: American Culture in the Sixties* (New York: Basic Books, 1977); Simon Frith, *Sound Effects: Youth, Leisure, and the Politics of Rock 'n Roll* (New York: Pantheon, 1981); David P. Szatmary, *Rockin' in Time: A Social History of Rock and Roll* (Englewood Cliffs, N.J.: Prentice-Hall, 1987); and Hunter S. Thompson, *Hell's Angels: A Strange and Terrible Saga* (New York: Ballantine, 1967).

14

THE IRANIAN HOSTAGE CRISIS

WALTER LAFEBER

During the 444 days in 1979 to 1981 that Americans waited for the return of 76 American hostages, held by Iranian militants, they were entertained by a song by country artist Kenny Rogers. It was called "Coward of the County," and it told the story of a young man named Tommy and his efforts to deal with a menacing trio of local punks called the Gatlin boys. Raised by his father to believe that one could achieve manhood without fighting, Tommy had always walked away from trouble—and, in the process, had become known as the "coward of the county." But when the Gatlin boys gang-rape Tommy's girlfriend, Becky, Tommy takes his father's picture down from above the fireplace, finds the Gatlin boys in a bar, and avenges Becky's rape with a fury born of righteous indignation and "twenty years of crawling." Of course, from then on no one called Tommy the "coward of the county."

It was a good song, and no doubt would have been popular under any circumstances. But it had special appeal in 1980 because its parable seemed so closely to parallel the American experience with the Iranian hostage crisis. To many Americans, the conduct of the Iranian militants seemed no less barbaric and no more explicable than that of the Gatlin boys; indeed, the holding of American hostages seemed a violation as complete and horrifying as that Becky had experienced. According to Rogers's story, Tommy's problem—and the American nation's—was fundamentally one of the spirit, something inside Tommy, rather than a matter of some exterior condition that Tommy was helpless to deal with. In his July 15, 1979, television address, President Jimmy Carter had interpreted the American condition in much the same terms: as a "moral and spiritual crisis," a crisis of the "national will." And like Tommy, Carter and his advisers attempted to resolve this spiritual crisis through action—the rescue mission of April 1980—only to discover that the world no longer yielded to the brawling barroom tactics of the wild west.

Walter LaFeber's narrative confirms this view of the Iranian hostage crisis as a moment in which an ignorant American people acted badly. But it also tells another, more encouraging story, a story of a nation's first, begrudging adjustment to the changing distribution of economic, political, and military power in the world. The Carter administration was, of course, in charge of this process of adjustment, and the conflicts and disagreements over foreign policy that are apparent in LaFeber's account

232

are indicative of the nation's divided sensibilities at a difficult moment in its history. To open a dialogue with the Ayatollah Khomeini or prop up the Iranian shah; to allow or refuse the shah access to the United States; to let the hostage crisis take its course or intervene militarily—at every turn, policy makers disagreed over what ought to be done. Carter, too—Carter, especially—appeared unsure and even confused, a champion of human rights toasting the leadership of one of the world's great tyrants.

Hoping to find a way out of its confusion, the nation turned in 1980 to Ronald Reagan. His foreign policy—a reinvigorated Cold War—seemed to give Americans a welcome sense of direction. But many of Reagan's initiatives, including the invasion of the tiny Marxist country of Grenada in 1983, failed to measure up to the Berlin airlift, the naval blockade of offensive weapons into Cuba, or other compelling moments in the epic of the Cold War. As Carter and then Reagan would discover, the post-Vietnam era of the 1970s and 1980s was no longer what Time magazine publisher Henry Luce had described in 1941 as "The American Century."

O n November 4, 1979, 400 screaming Iranian youths stormed the stone walls surrounding the United States Embassy in Iran's capital city of Tehran. They then invaded the embassy itself, captured 100 people, including 66 Americans, and declared that the Americans would be held hostage for the crimes of "The Great Satan"—the United States—against the Iranian people. Elizabeth Montagne, an American working as an embassy secretary, soon faced an Iranian holding a gun. He put a single bullet into the pistol's chamber, pointed it at Montagne's temple, and demanded the combination to an embassy safe. When she replied she did not know the combination, he began pulling the trigger on the empty chambers one-by-one. There was one more click to go. "Do you think I'll pull the trigger?" he asked her. "We stared at each other," Montagne recalled, and then he put the gun down. "He said: 'OK, so you don't know the combination.' I just kind of collapsed."

Montagne's horror was relived in other ways by the American hostages during the 444 days they endured captivity. The world, especially tens-of-millions of Americans who followed the hostages' fortunes almost hourly on television, watched the ordeal with wonder and fear. Americans soon learned, however, that the story did not actually begin that rainy November afternoon in Tehran. Like all historic events, it had deep, tangled roots. In this case the story went back to 1941 at least, when a thin 22-year-old, Muhammad Reza Pahlavi, became shah, or king, of Iran. He was made shah by the United States, Great Britain, and the Soviet Union. These nations removed his father from power because the old dictator had moved his strategically located, rich oil-producing nation too close to the Nazis. From the beginning, therefore, the young shah owed his kingdom to foreign powers. By 1946 he especially owed his throne to the United States, which that year forced the Soviets to leave Iran. The Americans then replaced the British as the dominant foreign power. When the shah's rule was threatened by a nationalist, antiforeign movement in 1953, the U.S. Central Intelligence Agency (CIA) played a key role in overthrowing the threatening movement. In partial thanks, the next year the shah allowed American oil companies to begin extracting the black gold for the first time.

By the mid-1950s the world and especially the Iranians, who had the best view, saw the young shah and the powerful Americans as political bedfellows. In 1964, the relationship was almost stretched too far. The shah agreed to a Washington request that U.S. troops stationed in Iran be liable only to U.S. law, not Iranian law—even if they committed a crime against an Iranian. The 62-year-old, bearded Ayatollah (or Islamic religious leader) Ruhollah Khomeini bitterly attacked the deal. The shah and the Americans, Khomeini declared, "have reduced the Iranian people to a level lower than that of an American dog." "The dignity of Iran," he concluded, "has been destroyed." Khomeini's influence, already immense in this nation that had followed the Shi'ite Muslims since the sixteenth-century, became even greater—so great that the shah's police threw the Ayatollah out of the country. Khomeini spent 15 years of exile in Turkey, Iraq, and finally France. But whatever the distance, his influence continued to grow in Iran.

That was proven in 1970 when the shah announced that a group of visiting American investors, led by David Rockefeller of Chase Manhattan Bank, would receive large investment opportunities. Anti-American riots erupted as Khomeini condemned the deal from exile in Iraq. One of his students, Muhammad Reza Sa'idi, publicly condemned the American group. Shortly after, the shah's dreaded secret police, SAVAK, tortured the young student to death. When other Islamic leaders mounted protests, the shah cracked down with arrests, more torture, and imprisonment of the protesters and their religious leaders. In 1974 the head of Amnesty International (a London-based organization that later won the Nobel Prize for Peace for its work on behalf of human rights around the world), announced that Iran had the globe's worst human rights record.

This announcement did not cool the United States relationship with the shah. By 1974 it grew even warmer because President Richard Nixon concluded he desperately needed Iran. Because of overspending (especially in Vietnam) and too many overseas commitments, the United States no longer had the resources to defend its allies everywhere. Nixon begged the shah to help protect vital U.S. interests in the Middle East. Americans' need for Iran, moreover, grew dramatically in 1973 and 1974, when Arab oil producers protested Israel's invasion of their ally, Egypt, by cutting off petroleum shipments to Israel's closest ally, the United States. The shah was willing to help Nixon, but for a price: almost unlimited access to the non-nuclear U.S. military arsenal. Nixon happily obliged.

With his immense oil wealth generating revenues that jumped five times to $20 billion in only a matter of months, the shah increased his defense spending seven times to nearly $10 billion between 1973 and 1977. He bought military goods, as one historian phrased it, "with the abandon of an alcoholic using a credit card in a liquor store." Thus at the very moment the shah used force against his country's powerful religious leaders, the United States was publicly sending him all the weapons he could buy. Then, in 1975 and 1976, Iran's oil revenues flattened out. The economy began to decline. The already wide gap between poor rural and well-off urban incomes greatly widened. As many Iranians resorted to criminal activities to make a living, corruption became so rampant that the shah was advised not to begin an anticorruption campaign because, as one adviser suggested, "people will laugh."

Conditions were ripening for revolution. The first small revolutionary bands had actually appeared in 1971. Between 1972 and 1975 the country endured more than 400 bombing acts of terrorism. Americans soon became targets. Three U.S. military officers and three American civilians had been murdered by late 1976. Even the U.S. Peace Corps office, as well as the U.S. Embassy, had been blasted by bombs.

When President Carter assumed power in January of 1977, he was determined to restore American moral authority at home and abroad by emphasizing human rights—supporting, in his words, "the idealism of Jefferson" instead of the right-wing monarchs and military dictators the United States had too long supported just as long as they were anti-communist. In Iran's case, however, Carter was trapped. If he demanded that the shah stop the arrests and torture, the Iranian ruler might be overthrown and the cornerstone of U.S. military policy in the Persian Gulf region removed. The president tried to escape the trap by continuing to talk publicly about human rights, but at the same time sending over half of all American arms sales to the shah. The king was too important, revenue from the $5.7 billion in arms sales too vital for the U.S. economy, to anger the occupant of Iran's Peacock Throne.

When the shah again cracked down brutally on protesters in 1977 and 1978, Iranians believed (wrongly) that it happened with Carter's consent, if not on United States orders. Their belief seemed confirmed when President Carter visited Iran on New Year's Eve of 1977, and delivered one of the most stunning, and unfortunate, banquet toasts in recorded history. "Iran, because of the great leadership of the shah," Carter began, "is an island of stability in one of the more troubled areas of the world. This is a great tribute to you, Your Majesty, and to your leadership and to the respect and the admiration and love which your people give to you. . . . We have no other nation with whom we have closer consultations on regional problems that concern us both. And there is no leader with whom I have a deeper sense of personal gratitude and personal friendship."

Within 10 days after Carter spoke those words, massive anti-shah riots, led by Islamic clergy and religious students, erupted in the holy city of Qum. The police killed at least 24 people, including religious leaders. The shootings ignited a chain-reaction of protests. By November and December, 1978, literally thousands of demonstrations were erupting. The death toll reached 10,000. Nearly all the dead were unarmed protesters whose only strengths were in numbers and the hot conviction that the shah had to be overthrown. "For more than a year," two close observers wrote, "literally millions of Iranians faced [the shah's] tanks and machine guns with little more than moral outrage."

Islamic religious leaders guided the demonstrators, but those leaders were divided. On one side was a small fundamentalist group that hated the shah's western friends. This group wanted to turn Iran into a fully religious state shorn of all possible western influence. A much larger and more powerful group of clergy wished to modernize Iran and bring it fully into the late twentieth-century, but under religious direction. These moderates were less opposed to the shah's vast plans to modernize (the "White Revolution" as it became known) than to driving peasants off their land and destroying communities; the changes that only made the rich much richer and the poor desperate; and the shah's ideas that seemed to be turning the country over to nonreligious, non-Iranian developers from the West, especially from the United States. These critics pointed out that even when the shah tried to meet some of their demands by reorganizing his government in 1977, his new advisers were Iranians who suspiciously held degrees from universities in California, Colorado, Nebraska, Kentucky, Utah, and New York.

This growing fear of western control even brought many educated Iranian women over to the anti-shah side. Their decision seemed especially remarkable because Islam required that they wear veils (*chadurs*) in public, and have a traditional, and inferior, role in society. But these women were first of all Iranian and aware of the shah's devastating policies. They were also young: Half the country's population was under 16 years of age, and two-thirds was under 30 years of age. As unemployment and educational problems increased, the young, both men and women, became more radical. As the protests grew, however, they cut across age, geographical area, and class. The Islamic clergy became the steering wheel but not the engine of the revolution. As one Western expert on Iran explained: "The causes of the revolution, and its timing, were economic and political; the form of the revolution, and its pacing, owed much to the tradition of religious protest."

Americans understood none of this. Most read little or nothing about Iran or other foreign policy problems. They received their view of world events from easily digested television programs. But in the 6 years of growing revolution between 1971 and 1977, the three United States television networks spent an average of only 5 minutes per year on events in Iran. The most respected national newspaper, the *New York Times,* closed its Tehran office in 1977. Not one regular U.S. reporter remained in Iran. American experts on Iran were few, and those few were either overlooked or ignored when they tried to explain the deep economic, religious, and anti-U.S. roots of the revolution.

The upheaval confused even some observant Americans. Throughout much of the twentieth-century, they had judged the anti-American sentiment of most revolutionaries by their communist ties. But Islamic fundamentalists hated atheistic communism. The revolutionaries' rallying cry was "Neither East Nor West!" Soviet leaders, sharing a 1600-mile border with Iran, and nervously watching millions of Muslims inside their own country, were nearly as fearful of the revolution as were Americans. The U.S. media, however, had long viewed the shah as a close anti-communist ally, so it began to characterize his opponents with other stereotypes—"religious fanatics," "Muslim fundamentalists," even "Islamic Marxists"—in order to discredit the revolutionaries. Columnist Meg Greenfield of *Newsweek* was one of the few exceptions. "No part of the world is more important to our well-being at the moment," she wrote in early 1979, "and no part of the world is more hopelessly and systematically and stubbornly misunderstood by us." She compared American ignorance of the Islamic Middle East with Columbus's ignorance when he landed in the New World and thought he was in India.

Greenfield and other close observers of President Carter also realized that confusion and ignorance paralyzed United States official policy. Carter's administration divided sharply between his secretary of state, Cyrus Vance, and the national security adviser in the White House, Zbigniew Brzezinski. Vance believed the problem was wholly Iranian and that the shah had to come to terms with the revolutionaries. His position would lead him to favor contact with Ayatollah Khomeini, who was now orchestrating the revolution from exile in Paris where he put his instructions on audio tapes that secretly circulated throughout Iran. Brzezinski, on the other hand, feared the shah's fall would have ramifications far beyond Iran: It could lead to a pro-Soviet Iran and a major U.S. defeat in the Cold War. Brzezinski urged that the shah establish a military regime that would ruthlessly crush the uprising. Carter could not make up his mind whether to follow Vance or Brzezinski.

By January of 1979, the shah himself could not make up his mind. Increasingly weakened by cancer of the lymph glands, which had been discovered several years earlier, and unable to destroy the revolution through either mass killings or political reforms, the king waited for advice and help from his longtime friends in Washington. But little of either advice or help appeared. Brzezinski continued to push a military solution. He even wanted to use force to prevent the plane carrying Khomeini back to Tehran from landing. But it was too late. The Iranian military, with its Muslim soldiers and its ranks infiltrated with Islamic leaders, simply disintegrated as a thousand and more troops defected each day.

On January 16, 1979, the shah and his family climbed aboard a blue-and-silver Boeing 707 and flew into exile in Egypt. Celebrations erupted on Iranian streets. On February 1, Khomeini landed in Tehran to be welcomed by two million followers. The United States, American Ambassador William Sullivan reported, was now linked in Iranian minds with "evaporating institutions." A new Iran was arising. On February 2, 45,000 U.S. citizens began to leave. Despite crowds that surrounded the U.S. Embassy shouting "Death to the Great Satan," Carter ordered 75 American diplomats to remain at their posts. Rumors spread through Tehran that the Americans were harboring hated agents of SAVAK. On February 14, Iranians, some armed, broke into the Embassy, seized 70 Americans, and demanded that Carter return the shah for punishment. The Americans, however, were quickly released.

Khomeini's role in all this was not clear. He seemed to hold ultimate power, although he did not occupy a government post. Khomeini despised the United States for its long friendship with the shah, but he did not want an immediate, possibly armed, confrontation with the world's most powerful nation. It was not clear whether Khomeini controlled the mob, many of whom were political leftists and not devout followers of the Islamic clergy. He also worked with a badly divided government. Several top officials, including the new Iranian president and prime minister, were moderates. They hoped to restore some relations with Washington because they believed Iran especially needed American spare parts and other help for the nation's wrecked economy. Other Iranian leaders, however, notably those among the clergy and in the streets, hated the United States. They hoped to use the Iranian fear of "The Great Satan" to gain control over the revolution and the country. In May of 1979, 50,000 marched to the U.S. Embassy shouting "Death to Carter!"

The United States had no contact with either the radical left or the religious right-wing in Iran. Americans talked only with the relative moderates at the top of the government, but these officials obviously did not control the street mobs. Washington knew too little about what was occurring. "We simply do not have the bios [biographies], inventory of political groups, or current levels of daily life as it evolves at various levels in Iran," the top State Department expert on the country, Henry Precht, wrote in July 1979. "Ignorance here of Iran's events is massive. The U.S. press does not do a good job but in the absence of [U.S.] Embassy reporting, we have to rely on inexperienced newsmen" for information.

Amid this "ignorance," Carter was touching a low point in his presidency during the autumn of 1979. The American economy was slipping badly, the victim of inflation and the loss of six million barrels of Iranian oil that were no longer available each day on the international market. Americans suddenly paid nearly twice the regular price for gasoline—or they did after sitting for hours in lines at the pumps. Carter's relations with both the Soviet Union and his own allies, as well as with Iran, steadily worsened. As prices jumped and gasoline supplies slumped, and both angry Democrats and Republicans circled Carter to wait for a political kill in the 1980 elections, the president escaped to his Camp David mountaintop retreat to ponder the American, and his own, decline.

He emerged to give a nationally televised address on July 15, 1979, that is unsurpassed in presidential messages for its pleading and pessimism. "It's clear that the true problems of our nation are much deeper—deeper than gasoline lines or energy shortages, deeper even than inflation or recession," he declared. "And I realize more than ever that as President I need your help." He spoke of "a moral and a spiritual crisis," a "fundamental threat to American democracy" that "strikes at the very heart and soul and spirit of our national will." The president became specific: "There is a growing disrespect for government and for churches and for schools, the news media, and other institutions." He noted the murders of John F. Kennedy, Robert Kennedy, and Martin Luther King, Jr., and how peoples' confidence in their economy had been shattered by "10 years of inflation" and the post-1973 years "when we had to face a growing dependence on foreign oil." Americans, Carter lamented, looked to the Federal Government for help but "found it isolated. . . . Washington, D. C. has become an island." After this litany of sadness, the president had few solutions to offer except a vague national energy plan and the hope that Americans would overcome their "crisis of confidence." Critics quickly responded that the problem was less in the American people than in their leader's confusion.

Amid this bleakest time of Carter's presidency, the shah urgently asked that he be allowed to enter the United States for treatment of his cancer. Brzezinski, supported by two close friends of the shah—former Secretary of State Henry Kissinger and Chase Manhattan Bank President David Rockefeller—pressured Carter to grant the request. At first the president refused and, as Brzezinski recalled, "made the prophetic comment that he did not wish the shah to be here playing tennis while Americans in Tehran were being kidnapped or even killed" by mobs tearing down the U.S. Embassy. Brzezinski noted that when he objected that "we should not be influenced by threats from a third-rate regime [like Iran], and that at stake were our traditions and national honor, both Vance and Carter . . . became quite angry" with him. Three months later Vance and Carter changed their minds.

The Brzezinski–Kissinger–Rockefeller pressure, and the realization that the shah's life depended on quick medical help, led the president to reverse himself. On October 22, 1979, the shah's Gulfstream aircraft roared to a stop in the darkness of New York's LaGuardia Airport. Carter had given in, however, only after high Iranian officials had guaranteed the safety of the U.S. Embassy in Tehran during the shah's temporary stay in New York. Brzezinski then went much further. He tried to open talks with the Iranian moderates. Flying to North Africa, he met secretly with top officials, including Prime Minister Mehdi Bazargan. The secret quickly leaked. Iranian mobs (and perhaps Khomeini), concluded that Bazargan was trying to make deals with "The Great Satan." On November 1, 1979, Khomeini issued a statement: "It is therefore up to the dear pupils, students and theological students to expand their attacks against the United States and Israel, so that they may force the U.S. to return the deposed and criminal shah."

At 3:00 A.M. Washington time (10:30 A.M. Tehran time) on Sunday, November 4, 1979, the Department of State's Operations Center's telephone rang. Voices in the U.S. Embassy in Tehran reported that a large mob of youths was storming the building. The mob was later estimated at about 400. The embassy

The beginning of an ordeal. Within hours after Iranian militants stormed and occupied the U.S. Embassy in Tehran on November 4, 1979, American hostages are blindfolded and paraded by the mob outside the embassy. (UPI/Bettman Newsphotos)

was unprotected. The Iranian government had pulled its guard from around the building, but Carter was not concerned because he had been assured by Bazargan's government that the building would be safe during the shah's stay in the United States. Sixty-six Americans found themselves held hostage. Six others managed to escape and secretly lived in the Canadian Embassy until courageous Canadian officials helped sneak them out of Iran in January 1980. The mobs fell upon top-secret documents that the embassy staff had not had time to destroy. Other documents were found in small pieces in shredding machines. The Iranians painstakingly began to fit these together. Ultimately they had enough formerly secret U.S. documents to fill 60 published volumes.

More immediately, the documents revealed that since the shah had fled, the CIA had developed two operations in which it planned to work closely with the moderates. Within 48 hours after the storming of the embassy, Bazargan and other moderate leaders were driven from power. The new Iranian regime was more militant and anti-American, but neither it nor its spiritual leader, Khomeini, could fully control the youths who now occupied the embassy. Khomeini did convince them to release eight African-Americans and five women (including Elizabeth Montagne) because of Iran's professed respect for "oppressed" blacks and women. Otherwise, Khomeini—who apparently had at first quietly disapproved of the occupation and then changed his mind when he discovered the widespread support for it—found that the occupiers included different leaders of competing political factions. They had few common goals except to humiliate both the United States and the Iranian moderates.

The militants succeeded far more than they had hoped. Television cameras quickly showed the world graphic pictures of triumphant Iranians leading blindfolded, apparently confused Americans through the streets as crowds shouted insults. When the militants discovered that a global audience, and especially the United States, seemed to be hanging on their every word, their every burning of a U.S. flag, and their every success at putting thousands into the streets shouting anti-shah and anti-American slogans, they also discovered how valuable the hostages had become for their cause. Americans who could not have located Iran on a map before November 4 now became addicted to watching such daily programs as ABC-TV's *America Held Hostage* (later to become the popular *Nightline*), with Ted Koppel, an influential late-night news show created to follow the crisis in the embassy.

Carter at first profited politically. As is usual during foreign policy crises, Americans rallied around their leader as they expressed fury and frustration. In Denver three teenagers hurled a rock at a window of an Iranian; he fired a shot in return and killed one of them. The International Longshoremen's union ordered all members not to load vessels bound for Iran. A Kansas wheat farmer declared, "I'm beginning to think we should either seize [Iranian] oilfields or destroy them if we can." A New York truck driver concluded, "We might as well write off the hostages; they're going to be killed no matter what we do. We should bomb the hell out of the country so it will be a long time before anyone else does the same thing." Even the president's mother, Lillian Carter, was quoted as telling a New Hampshire men's club: "If I had a million dollars to spare, I'd look for someone to kill [Khomeini]." The men cheered. Carter's approval rating shot up from a lowly 32 percent just before the hostage seizure to 61 percent in December.

The president understood, however, that both his nation's honor and his own political future depended on freeing the hostages quickly, and certainly before the presidential elections only 11 months away. A Palo Alto, California, resident expressed the views of many Americans: "The political booby prize of 1979 should be shared by President Carter and Secretary Vance for giving a visa to the shah of Iran. . . . The United States cannot afford to have a president with such poor judgment." As one of his top aides later told the Phil Donahue television show, Carter developed an "emotional obsession" about the hostages, especially as he feared the Iranians might begin to execute one hostage each day until Carter met their demands. Those demands included the shah's return to stand trial, and the return of the shah's fortune that was variously estimated at $50 million to $250 million. The president had no intention of meeting either demand. He instead retaliated by cutting off imports of Iranian oil, froze Iran's assets (estimated at $18 billion) in U.S. banks, and ordered the aircraft carrier *Kitty Hawk* and five other warships to steam from their station in the Philippines to the Arabian Sea close by Iran.

As it became clear that the militants did not intend to surrender the hostages, American anger grew even more passionate. The *Wall Street Journal* urged a military solution that would use paratroopers and a helicopter attack to rescue the captives. Inside the privacy of the White House, Brzezinski also pushed again for military action. On December 27, 1979, however, he changed his mind when the Soviets suddenly invaded their neighbor, Afghanistan, to prop up a wobbly Communist regime. Carter was astounded and deeply angered by the invasion. He and many Americans believed it meant the Soviets were willing to use force to establish their dominance over Afghanistan and perhaps neighboring Iran. Brzezinski understood that using U.S. troops in Iran could possibly lead to a confrontation with the Soviet Union, so he reconsidered. But he and Carter, and to a lesser extent Secretary of State Vance, were now prepared to warn Moscow leaders that if the Red Army moved toward Iran and the oil-rich Persian Gulf, the United States was ready to respond with force. The president announced this "Carter Doctrine" in a nationally televised speech before Congress. Critics quickly claimed correctly that the United States did not have enough conventional power to stop any Soviet drive toward Iran. That realization led many to fear that the turmoil in Iran and the invasion of Afghanistan were setting the two superpowers on a dead-end course to nuclear war.

As tension grew, Iranian moderates recaptured some of their lost power when Abolhassan Bani Sadr was elected president. Determined to end the hostage crisis, on February 11, 1980, Bani Sadr set conditions for the captives' release: The United States must admit its "past crimes" against Iran and promise never to "interfere" again, while also recognizing Iran's right to seize the shah and recover his fortune. Carter continued to refuse to negotiate the fate of the shah, who by now had flown off to refuge in Panama. In any case, the militants were refusing to surrender the hostages to the moderate government. The Tehran power struggle became more heated. A United Nations Commission arrived in January of 1980 with the hope of negotiating the hostages' release. It was forced instead to view crippled and maimed Iranians tortured by SAVAK, was told by Bani Sadr that he sided with the militants, was threatened by street mobs, and finally decided to give up the mission.

Carter continued to seek a peaceful solution. His frustration, however, was becoming a torment. "What choices do we have," he blurted out to his close advisers in late January. "Those bastards have held our people for two months now. Nothing we have tried diplomatically has worked. The UN can't do anything, our allies have tried and struck out, everything imaginable has been attempted. We've got to take some risks." His popularity began to sink as the presidential primaries opened for the 1980 elections. "I say one thing," Carter bitterly remarked privately in March, 1980, "Khomeini says another—and who does the American press believe? Khomeini!" But by trying to use the crisis for his own political gain, he gravely wounded his own credibility. On April Fool's Day, 1980, the day of a key primary in Wisconsin, Carter faced powerful opposition for the Democratic Party nomination from Senator Edward Kennedy of Massachusetts. Early that morning, Carter called an unusual early morning press conference to announce that

An American perspective on Ayatollah Khomeini. This poster, with the Iranian leader serving as a bull's-eye, became a best-seller in the United States as frustration grew after the Iranian seizure of the U.S. Embassy and hostages in November 1979. (UPI/Bettman Newsphotos)

the hostages were about to be transferred from the militants to the more moderate Bani Sadr government. He implied this could lead to their release. Actually the prisoners' situation did not change, and Carter knew nothing about any possible release, but he scored a victory over Kennedy in Wisconsin. The president soon learned that the transfer of the captives to Bani Sadr's care had been vetoed by Khomeini. As one White House insider observed, now "there was a sense that the diplomatic route was closed." Carter angrily broke diplomatic relations with Iran. He vowed not to leave the White House to campaign until the hostages were released.

On April 11, the beleaguered president summoned his National Security Council to discuss a rescue plan. It had begun to be developed by Brzezinski and U.S. military leaders just 48 hours after the hostages had been seized. Vance condemned the plan. He believed that Khomeini, for his own interests, would not allow the hostages to be killed, but that they could be shot during a rescue attempt. Vance also feared that the use of U.S. military power would not only endanger American interests throughout the Islamic world, but anger close allies in Western Europe and Japan who were now willing to squeeze Iran economically, but wanted no use of military force.

At the decisive April 11 meeting, Vance was absent. He had flown off for several days of rest in Florida. His top aide, Deputy Secretary of State Warren Christopher, did attend. As Brzezinski viewed it, only three options existed: Continuing "negotiating ad infinitum, even if the Iranians gave no indication of a willingness or ability to accommodate"; undertake a major military operation to punish Iran severely—a strike that could, however, lead the Iranians to kill the hostages or perhaps even ask the Soviets for help; or, finally, try a quick but highly risky rescue mission. Christopher outlined possible nonmilitary options. He was quickly overruled by Defense Secretary Harold Brown and Vice President Walter Mondale. Both of them favored the rescue mission. Brzezinski himself argued that it was time "to lance the boil." After a discussion lasting 1 hour and 50 minutes, the president announced, "We ought to go ahead without delay." Convinced the plan would not work, and that the attempted use of force could deeply injure relations with allies, Vance believed he had to resign. He became the first secretary of state to resign on an issue of principle in 65 years. Brzezinski, however, privately concluded simply that Vance "is the ultimate example of a good man who has been traumatized by his Vietnam experience." (During the mid-1960s Vance had been involved in policy-making that expanded the tragic conflict with Vietnam.)

At a press conference a week later, Carter indirectly revealed one reason for his secret decision. He announced that reports had been received that Khomeini would not release the hostages until after the U.S. presidential election. Carter would not elaborate on the reports, but he reemphasized his determination not to apologize to Iran for U.S. relations with the shah.

The president had triggered a rescue plan that was as dramatic as it was dangerous. Six giant C-130 transport planes were to carry 130 army Green Berets, Rangers, drivers, and Iranian translators, along with 50 air crewmen, from an Egyptian air base to a secret landing strip in Iran—"Desert One"—260 miles from Tehran. At Desert One this force would be joined by eight Sea Stallion helicopters that had left 3 hours earlier from the U.S. aircraft carrier *Nimitz* sailing in the Arabian Sea. The troops were to transfer to the helicopters, fly to "Desert Two," a secluded mountain 50 miles from Tehran, then board trucks for a ride into the capital. Just before midnight, some would storm the compound where the hostages were held, while others would break into the Iranian Foreign Ministry where three other Americans were hostages. Forty minutes later they were all to board helicopters flown into the embassy compound or, if the compound was insecure, into a nearby soccer stadium. If mobs threatened the operation, two C-130H Spectre gunships, circling overhead, were to use any necessary force. The helicopters would then rendezvous with transport planes south of Tehran, the helicopters were to be destroyed, and everyone would fly off to safety in Egypt.

The Delta Force, as the special troops were called, had undergone special training since 1977 to combat terrorists. Colonel Charles A. Beckwith, better known to his military colleagues as "Chargin' Charlie," would lead Delta Force. Fifty-one years old, former University of Georgia football player, a veteran of the wars in Korea and Vietnam, Beckwith had become a legend among his fellow soldiers. In Vietnam he had survived a supposedly fatal chest wound. On his desk was a sign: "Kill 'em all. Let God sort 'em out."

Carter had emphasized that he wanted to "avoid wanton killings" in the rescue. The president lost sleep over the possibility of hostages dying. Beckwith held a different view: "When we went into that embassy, it was our aim to kill all Iranian guards . . . and we weren't going in there to arrest them; we were going in there to shoot them right between the eyes, and to do it with vigor!" As a military expert later observed, Beckwith's men were trained to kill anyone with a weapon, and "there would be no time for recognition of any hapless American holding a gun in the shadows." Carter wanted the hostages' lives saved, this expert continued, but "he had authorized a raid in which there was a good possibility that some of them might die."

The president's caution vividly appeared 24 hours before the attack was to begin on April 24, 1980. Brzezinski had urged that the rescue be accompanied by an air force strike against Tehran. The strike would either help the mission or, if the rescue failed, the United States would at least have punished the Iranians. Carter, however, pulled back the air attack because he wanted no needless killings and feared it would severely hurt U.S. relations with other Middle East states. Brzezinski nevertheless wrote in his journal at the last minute: "I feel good about [the mission]. I realize that if it fails I will probably be blamed more than anybody else, but I am quite prepared to accept that. If it is a success, it will give the United States a shot in the arm, which it has badly needed for twenty years."

During early dawn of April 24, Delta Force reached Desert One. But two of the eight helicopters from the *Nimitz* never made it. One suffered mechanical problems. The others ran into a dust storm that one pilot likened to "flying into a bowl of milk." A helicopter used too much gas avoiding the dust, had mechanical difficulties, and returned to the *Nimitz*. Only six helicopters remained, the minimum number Beckwith demanded for the mission. Then, after they landed at Desert One, another helicopter was disabled by a hydraulic system failure. With only five choppers left, Beckwith radioed that the mission had to be aborted. His words were relayed to Carter, who was monitoring the operation minute-by-minute in the White House. He approved Beckwith's decision. Now, Beckwith

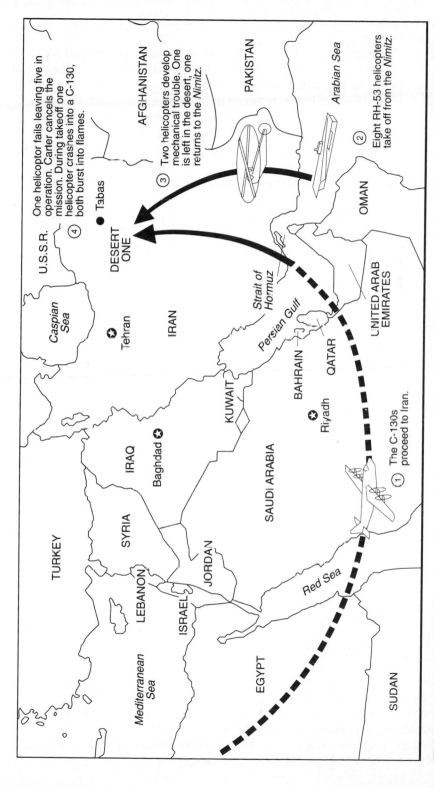

This map of the Middle East shows Iran and the routes of the attempted U.S. rescue mission in April 1980. Note the proximity of the Soviet Union and also of Afghanistan, which Soviet troops had invaded 4 months earlier.

The map contains the following labels and annotations:

TURKEY
SYRIA
LEBANON
ISRAEL
JORDAN
IRAQ
Baghdad ✪
SAUDI ARABIA
KUWAIT
EGYPT
SUDAN
Red Sea
Mediterranean Sea
Riyadh ✪
BAHRAIN
QATAR
Persian Gulf
UNITED ARAB EMIRATES
Strait of Hormuz
OMAN
IRAN
Tehran ✪
Caspian Sea
U.S.S.R.
DESERT ONE
Tabas
AFGHANISTAN
PAKISTAN
Arabian Sea

① The C-130s proceed to Iran.

② Eight RH-53 helicopters take off from the *Nimitz*.

③ Two helicopters develop mechanical trouble. One is left in the desert, one returns to the *Nimitz*.

④ One helicopter fails leaving five in operation. Carter cancels the mission. During takeoff one helicopter crashes into a C-130, both burst into flames.

recalled, "the only thing on my mind was, 'We've failed, and I've got to get my soldiers out of here.' "

As a helicopter pilot lifted away, his spinning rotor sliced through the fuselage of a C-130 loaded with troops. Beckwith "looked out to my left and a C-130 all of a sudden exploded. It was one hell of a fire. . . . The munitions went off. The heat from the [burning] aircraft forced the helicopter pilots out of their cockpits." Three Marines on the helicopter and five Air Force crewmen in the transport plane died instantly. Beckwith quickly decided that the intense heat, along with the rising sun (that made it probable the Iranians would soon discover his force), made it impossible to stay until the eight bodies could be recovered. The survivors climbed into the remaining C-130s and flew off. Beckwith put his head in his hands and cried.

Carter went on television at 7:00 A.M. to reveal the disaster. Republican presidential candidates George Bush and Ronald Reagan, as well as Edward Kennedy, quickly supported the rescue attempt and asked for national unity. By a margin of 4 to 1, Americans backed the president's decision to try the mission. But the failure helped seal Carter's political fate. Detroit Mayor Coleman Young, who led the president's campaign in Michigan, declared flatly, "Unless the hostages are rescued, it's a no-win situation for Carter." Publicly, the closest U.S. allies in Western Europe and Japan sympathized with the president. Privately some were seething. They had reluctantly gone along with U.S. demands for squeezing Iran economically in the belief that Carter would not then resort to military action. Now

The end of a failed rescue mission. At "Desert One" charred remains of Americans lie among the wreckage of C-130 transports and the destroyed U.S. helicopters on April 24, 1980. (UPI/Bettman Newsphotos)

they feared their Middle East oil supplies could be endangered by angry Arab producers. A top West German official declared privately (and was soon quoted in *Time* magazine): "The incompetence that permeates this Administration is incredible."

In Iran, Khomeini declared that the president had "lost his mind," and that the disaster proved whose side was favored by heaven. On April 26 the charred, unrecognizable bodies of the dead Americans were publicly displayed in Tehran. The government announced that the bodies would be returned to relatives, but through an organization such as the Red Cross, not through the U.S. government. The Iranians had also captured secret maps, photographs, and lists of radio frequencies that had been left behind in the abandoned helicopters. As for the hostages, the Iranians separated and moved some of them outside Tehran so another rescue mission would not be attempted.

Negotiations for their release went into a dead stall. The lack of movement was due partly to the rescue tragedy, but it was especially due to turmoil in Tehran. In what a French reporter called a "witch-hunt atmosphere," militants conducted a feverish search for moderates, "CIA agents," leftists, rightists, anyone suspected of having cooperated with the rescue plans. In early July, the hostage number dropped to 52 as Richard Queen was released because of illness; the Iranians had clearly decided they wanted no hostage to die in their hands. In late July, the shah passed away in Cairo. Tehran radio rejoiced that "the bloodsucker of the century has died," but quickly added that the hostages would nevertheless continue to be held until the United States delivered both apologies and as much as $24 billion.

Carter defeated Kennedy for the Democratic presidential nomination in August, but public opinion polls showed an astounding 77 percent of the voters giving Carter a negative rating. By 79 to 19 percent, they also condemned him for his handling of the Iranian crisis. There had been an incredible negative swing of 47 points in just 7 months over his handling of the hostages. The president, one congressman believed, "couldn't get the Pledge of Allegiance through Congress."

Republican presidential nominee Ronald Reagan declared that he would never "negotiate with terrorists," but otherwise he stressed Carter's economic failures and said little about the hostages. He did not have to say much; television kept the suffering of the hostages and their relatives in the United States before millions of viewers every night. The Republicans did worry about published reports that the Iranians and Carter were preparing an "October surprise": The hostages would supposedly be released on the eve of the election to ensure the president's victory. Republicans were especially worried about this after Carter's attempt to spring his "April Fool's Day surprise" against Kennedy during the Wisconsin primary. Nine years later, British reporters found evidence that the Republicans had sent former President Richard Nixon on a secret mission to the Iranians to prevent such a "surprise."

In April 1991, Gary Sick, who had been Carter's White House expert on Iran, dropped a bombshell. Sick announced that his investigations had turned up evidence to suggest that Reagan's campaign chair, William J. Casey, had met secretly with Iranians in July and August, 1980. Casey, so witnesses told Sick, had sent $150 million of arms to Iran in return for the Iranians' assurance that the hostages would not be freed until Reagan was safely elected. Reagan and his advisers heatedly denied Sick's allegations. (Casey could not respond. He had died of a brain tumor just as the Iran-Contra scandal broke in 1986—a scandal in which he, as director of the CIA, had secretly sold arms to Iran in 1985 in return for the release of several other hostages. Throughout the 1980s, Reagan publicly denied that he would ever deal with terrorists who held hostages.) Evidence and public outcries nevertheless built up until, in 1991, Congress had to begin investigating the possibility that 11 years before, a small group of campaign officials had seized U.S. foreign policy and kept 52 men hostage for 5 extra months so Reagan could be elected president. Whatever Nixon's and Casey's activities, the hostages were not released. Reagan won a landslide victory, taking 44 states. "The voters," Carter recalled, "expressed their disgust with our nation's apparent impotence in the face of several disturbing problems—Iran foremost."

After early November, the defeated president no longer faced a political timetable for producing a settlement. It was becoming clear to the Iranians that a deal could be struck with Carter. As the hostages were losing their political value to Tehran officials, talks became serious in December, 1980. One Iranian diplomat declared, "The hostages are like a fruit from which all the juice has been squeezed out." Another reason for the release, however, also now existed. In September, 1979, Iraq attacked Iran to begin a struggle to decide which nation would control the Persian Gulf area. The conflict turned into one of the longest and bloodiest in the post-1945 era. Iran needed at least relief from U.S. pressures and even, if possible, western help.

Tehran officials suggested, and Carter accepted, that Algeria become an intermediary to help in the talks. Deputy Secretary of State Warren Christopher flew to Algiers and on January 18, 1981, a settlement appeared. Iran had demanded $24 billion, but finally accepted Carter's offer of $5.5 billion, released out of frozen Iranian assets, in exchange for the hostages. The remaining frozen assets and the American counterclaims against Iran were to be decided through arbitration.

Throughout the night before he was to surrender the White House to Reagan, Carter remained awake in his office surrounded by his close advisers. He prayed that Iran would release the hostages during his presidency. Khomeini, however, squeezed out the last drop of "juice": The hostages became free shortly after noon on January 20, 1981, just minutes after Reagan took the oath of office.

AN INTERPRETATION

The hostage crisis was not only one of the most frustrating and embarrassing chapters in American history. It encapsulated major themes of the 1970s that mark the decade as part of a turning point in the nation's experience as a great world power. Between 1945 and the 1970s the United States controlled world affairs in a manner unmatched by any nation in history. In the 1970s, however, Americans finally lost the war in Vietnam, realized that the Soviet Union had the capacity to destroy them in a nuclear exchange, and had to tolerate the rise of a radical Sandinista government in Nicaragua (a country long considered by the United States to be in its "backyard"). They also, of course, lost the shah's cooperation, oil resources, and military intelligence listening posts in Iran. As Christopher declared in 1978, the "absolute power" of such great nations as the United States "is growing," but "the relative power of any single nation has been reduced."

Americans had to come to terms with that relative decline during the hostage crisis. In a real sense they had to understand that the 1945-to-1970 years were aberrations, an era never to be repeated because the unique conditions that made the United States so powerful after World War II would never—if human civilization is fortunate—be repeated with another such war. In the 1970s, history began to return to normal as a more multipolar world emerged, the kind of world that interestingly resembled the pre-1939 or even pre-1914 years more than 1945 to 1970.

Americans also discovered that although they had spent trillions of dollars developing weapons that could destroy all civilization, they could not negotiate a quick political settlement, or mount a successful rescue mission, to release Americans held in chains by a much weaker nation. Power other than simply military was working in the world. Indeed, the religious belief embodied in Ayatollah Khomeini's cause not only was organizing a new Iran, but neutralizing vast U.S. military and economic power. Vaunted American technology, which the nation had proudly paraded since the days of Samuel Colt's revolver and Henry Ford's Model-T, even came into question. The nation was suffering disastrous unfavorable trade balances with Japan and Western Europe because Americans were having difficulty competing in tough world markets.

The nation's most basic assumptions about how the world worked became so fundamentally questioned that its educational system, as well as its top decision-making apparatus, became suspect. Most Americans knew nothing about Iran or its neighbors, although these same Americans utterly depended on these distant nations for an energy supply. Those in the press and government who did think they knew Iran too easily assumed, as Frances FitzGerald pointed out, "that the shah was the only person who counted . . . ; that the country, being underdeveloped, had no politics in the sense that advanced countries do; and that Iranians, being apolitical, would simply accept a dictatorship as necessary and good for them. The [U.S.] foreign-policy establishment," FitzGerald emphasized, "has traditionally made similar assumptions about almost all Third World countries."

Americans' assumptions about how easily they could burn up energy were also undermined. Since 1945 they had burned or melted about 40 percent of the world's non-renewable materials. The world consumed 30,000 gallons of petroleum each second; with 6 percent of the world's population, the United States burned 33 percent of those gallons. In 1973 and 1974, and again in 1979 and 1980, severe energy shortages not only inconvenienced American motorists, but increasingly expensive petroleum made costs skyrocket until the United States found its goods less competitive on the world market and millions of its people newly out of work.

A psychological, as well as an economic, depression also set in. "For the first time in its history," influential *Business Week* magazine declared in late 1979, "the United States is no longer growing in power and influence among the nations of the world. In fact, the United States is now in steep decline." Ronald Reagan rode that pessimism into power. Three of four Americans polled in 1980 believed Reagan would ensure that the United States would be respected by other nations. The hostages were indeed released minutes into his presidency.

From 1990 to 1992 President George Bush led a U.S.-dominated coalition that waged war during another Middle East crisis. But this crisis, triggered by Iraqi dictator Saddam Hussein's invasion of oil-rich Kuwait, ended with a massive victory for Bush and the coalition's half-million troops and thousands of high-technology weapons. Republicans noted sarcastically that 11 years earlier Carter could not even get "eight helicopters across a desert." The victory of 1991, however, did not lessen the importance of learning from the events of 1978 to 1981. Saddam Hussein's threat was a more traditional military aggression that the United States and its allies could overwhelm with superior firepower. Americans did not need to understand his culture to repulse his aggression. But the Iranians had posed a more subtle threat that could not be dealt with by conventional forces and high-tech wonder weapons. The Ayatollah represented a cultural and religious force in a world increasingly shaped by cultural pluralism and non-military power. Neither the Ayatollah Khomeini's ideas nor the hostages' situation could have been dealt with successfully by military weapons, no matter how high-tech. What the United States needed was an understanding of the Iranians before 1979, the limits of U.S. military power, and the new international arena in which the United States had to act. Whether the basic conditions that led to the hostage crisis and its intense frustrations have fundamentally changed remains a central question of today's United States.

Sources: The best scholarly treatment of the background is Gaddis Smith, *Morality, Reason, and Power: American Diplomacy in the Carter Years* (New York: Hill and Wang, 1986). Especially useful for understanding the crisis and its backdrop are three revealing memoirs: Jimmy Carter, *Keeping Faith* (New York: Bantam, 1982); Cyrus R. Vance, *Hard Choices* (New York: Simon and Schuster, 1983); and, most notably, Zbigniew K. Brzezinski, *Power and Principle* (New York: Farrar, Straus and Giroux, 1983). A number of fine studies on post-1973 U.S.–Iranian relations have appeared that focus on the hostage crisis: James A. Bill, *The Eagle and the Lion: The Tragedy of American–Iranian Relations* (New Haven: Yale University Press, 1988); Gary Sick, *All Fall Down: America's Tragic Encounter With Iran* (New York: Random House, 1985); William H. Sullivan, *Mission to Iran* (New York: Norton, 1981), by the embattled U.S. Ambassador. Paul Ryan, *The Iranian Rescue Mission: Why It Failed* (Annapolis: Naval Institute Press, 1985) is a good analysis of that tragedy. The Iranian background is in R. K. Ramazani, *The United States and Iran* (New York: Praeger, 1982). The important beginnings of the relationship are traced in Mark H. Lytle, *The Origins of the Iranian–American Alliance, 1945–1953* (New York: Holmes and Meier, 1987).

15

APOCALYPSE IN WACO: DAVID KORESH AND THE BRANCH DAVIDIANS

PAUL BOYER

For almost 2 months in the winter and spring of 1993, national attention was focused on a compound of buildings on the outskirts of Waco, Texas, where members of an obscure religious cult called the Branch Davidians, led by David Koresh, had locked horns with the Federal Bureau of Investigation. Ten people had died in February, when the Bureau of Alcohol, Tobacco, and Firearms raided the compound, expecting to find a stash of illegal weapons that would justify arresting Koresh and closing down the community. When the dust cleared after a second raid (this one orchestrated by the FBI) and a series of mysterious fires inside the compound, not much was left but dead bodies, the inevitable media wrap-ups, and the sense that something had gone terribly wrong.

In the days and months that followed, most of the talk was about whether the agencies of the national government had handled the matter in the best possible way— a legitimate question, to be sure, and one taken up in the narrative that follows. Yet for the most part, Paul Boyer's story is about the history, beliefs, values, and social practices of a religious cult. The word "cult" has a couple of meanings. It means a religious community, which the Branch Davidians certainly were. But it also means inappropriately obsessive devotion to an ideal or a person. When Americans use the word "cult," it almost always has this pejorative connotation.

In the mid-1970s, two events shaped and represented Americans' anxieties about cults and their power to influence (or "brainwash") innocent people. The first involved publishing heiress Patty Hearst, kidnapped in 1974 by a cult—the Symbionese Liberation Army—and later photographed participating in a bank robbery with the SLA members. The second event was the 1978 murder and mass suicide of over 900 members of the People's Temple, a Jonestown, Guyana, religious commune led by Jim Jones. Although the members of the People's Temple were Americans, the Jonestown disaster was treated as if those involved were outsiders, with no real relationship to American society and culture. Fifteen years later, similar anxieties and attitudes would prevent many Americans from understanding the needs and concerns of Waco's Branch Davidians.

Beneath the anticult hysteria of the 1970s and the late twentieth century was the fear that America was coming apart. According to this widely held view, a society that had once been unified and cohesive was now "balkanized" and "disunited," the victim of private greed, narrow interest groups, regional conflict, religious splinter groups, and a host of movements—feminism, black nationalism, gay rights, Afrocentricity, the "cult" of ethnicity—that by the mid-1980s were grouped together under the rubric of multiculturalism. Put in the framework of religion, advocates of a unified society longed for a mid-century era when powerful, long-established religious groups— Catholics, Jews, and the Protestant denominations—were dominant.

From another perspective—the perspective, no doubt, of David Koresh and the Branch Davidians—unity and cohesiveness were simply code words for a corrupt and oppressive society and an overbearing government, and the old religious establishment was a relic of the past. All that right-thinking people could do was to remove themselves as completely as possible from the world around them. And to prepare for a battle that was sure to come.

Monday, April 19, 1993. The dawning sky is clear and blue, a brisk wind blows, and an eerie stillness hangs over the stark complex of buildings outside Waco, Texas, midway between Dallas and Austin, that is home to a religious sect known as the Branch Davidians. Encircling the compound's perimeter is a vast sea of tents, military vehicles, temporary structures, electronic communications gear, and television transmitting equipment. Cattle graze nearby; overhead, buzzards wheel and dip.

Inside the 77-acre compound, figures emerge sleepily from the spartan men's and women's dormitories and begin the day's routines. Women prepare breakfast, start laundry, or care for children. Some of the men shoulder rifles and stand guard at the windows. The leader of the community, David Koresh, has not yet emerged from his top-floor bedroom. The 17 infants and small children who live in the compound have little sense of the danger that hovers in the air. For this is no ordinary Monday. After 51 days of negotiations and inconclusive communication by telephone and television, the leaders of the small army of FBI agents and other law-enforcement officials besieging the compound have decided on action.

The plan the besiegers implemented that April morning had been carefully worked out in collaboration with Federal Bureau of Investigation officials in Washington, D.C., including FBI director William Sessions. Attorney General Janet Reno, in office only a few weeks, had approved it on Saturday. On Sunday night, Reno had briefed President Bill Clinton, who gave her a green light to proceed.

As the sky grew lighter, a final telephone exchange between FBI negotiators and Koresh's lieutenant Steve Schneider ended abruptly when Schneider contemptuously threw the telephone out the front door of the main building. At 6:05 A.M., as blaring loudspeakers called on those inside to come out peacefully, two armored combat engineer vehicles (modified M-60 tanks weighing 58 tons each) equipped with long steel barrels lumbered toward the main building and began to batter down doors and windows and to poke holes in the flimsy walls. Through the holes, the tanks shot clouds of tear gas in 15-second bursts. A hail of gunfire from the defenders inside bounced harmlessly off the heavily armored vehicles.

While the building's defenders manned their posts, other residents remained calm, soothing children, reading their Bibles, and carrying on with their chores. Donning gas masks, many retreated to the chapel and gymnasium at the rear of the complex to escape the tear gas. The standoff continued through the morning, as the large holes torn in the building, coupled with a 30-mile-per-hour wind, dissipated much of the tear gas.

But suddenly, around noon, fire broke out inside the complex. Within minutes, the entire structure had become a raging crematorium. Explosions rocked the building as stores of ammunition ignited, sending a huge fireball into the sky. Even then, FBI officials on the scene and back in Washington hoped for a peaceful outcome. After a final bravado display, they thought, Koresh would come marching out leading his ragtag band of followers. In fact, however, only a few individuals jumped from windows or escaped through the gaping holes in the building, and some of those ran back toward the inferno and certain death as FBI agents approached them. Nine Davidians escaped, but most perished. When the flames eventually flickered out, an estimated 80 Davidians lay dead, including the 17 children.

For hours afterward, superheated containers of canned fruit continued to explode, startling investigators sifting the ruins for charred remains. Whenever a body was found, investigators planted a bright orange flag to mark the spot. Eventually

April 19, 1993. As federal assault vehicles rumble in following a 51 day seige, smoke and flames envelope David Koresh's Branch Davidian compound near Waco, Texas—a compound Koresh had renamed Ranch Apocalypse. The source of the holocaust would later be disputed, but its tragic outcome was starkly clear: some 80 Davidians, including 17 children, dead amid the ruins. (Wide World)

the complex was a sea of orange flags, many clustered in little groups. On the flagpole where Koresh had flown his homemade Branch Davidian banner, the Texas and U.S. flags now fluttered at half staff.

A saga that for nearly 2 months had riveted world attention had reached a catastrophic close. Just as some Bible prophecies foretell, and as David Koresh had warned his followers, the end came in a searing holocaust of death and destruction.

Although the Branch Davidians had been in the public eye only briefly when the final showdown occurred, their story begins far in the past. Indeed, a full history of the movement would carry us back to the ancient Middle East and the emergence of a religious genre known as *apocalypse*—a Greek word meaning an unveiling of hidden mysteries. These apocalyptic works, some of which found their way into the Jewish and Christian scriptures, viewed human history as a cosmic struggle between good and evil, and foresaw a final crisis when the powers of evil would finally be vanquished by the forces of righteousness led by God himself. For more than 2 millennia, down to our own era, the apocalyptic worldview profoundly influenced Western religious thought, especially at the popular level.

A full exploration of the Branch Davidians' origins would also require a close look at America of the 1830s and 1840s, a time of great religious ferment, especially in upstate New York, which came to be known as the "burnt-over district" for its successive waves of religious revivalism and for the new religions it spawned.

One such new religion, for example, began in 1830 when young Joseph Smith of Palmyra, New York, announced that he had dug up a pair of ancient golden tablets buried on a nearby hill and, with supernatural aid, translated them. Armed with this sacred text, *The Book of Mormon,* Smith founded the Church of Jesus Christ of Latter Day Saints, or Mormons. By the end of the twentieth century, Mormonism boasted seven million members worldwide, and enjoyed broad acceptance and respect.

Another upstate New Yorker caught up in the religious and reform ferment of the day was William Miller, a self-taught Bible student and evangelist. On the basis of his reading of the prophecies in the Book of Daniel, Miller in 1831 had begun to preach the return of Jesus Christ "around the year 1843." Some of his disciples pinpointed the date even more precisely: October 22, 1844.

When the great day passed uneventfully, many disappointed Millerites drifted away. But some remained faithful, and from this remnant emerged the Seventh-Day Adventist (SDA) Church, an evangelical Protestant denomination that observed Saturday as the Sabbath, emphasized diet and health, and continued William Miller's great interest in Bible prophecy.

By the early twentieth century, the Seventh-Day Adventist Church was thriving and attracting many converts. Among the new recruits in 1919 was Victor Houteff, an immigrant from Bulgaria. Settling in Los Angeles, Houteff taught Sunday school class at the local SDA Church. Soon, however, his interpretations of the prophecies deviated from official SDA doctrine. The 144,000 saints mentioned in the fourteenth chapter of the Book of Revelation (the apocalypse that closes the Christian Bible), Houteff taught, were already being assembled by God, and would soon emigrate to Palestine to await Jesus Christ's return. Houteff explained his prophetic scheme in *The Shepherd's Rod* (1930). A second volume followed in 1932.

Though the SDA church condemned Houteff's teachings, some Seventh-Day Adventists hailed him as a prophecy interpreter with special gifts. In 1935, deep in the Great Depression, Houteff with some 30 followers established a religious commune outside Waco, Texas, they named Mount Carmel.* Calling themselves the General Association of Shepherd's Rod Seventh-Day Adventists, they soon came to be known as "Davidians," a name they officially adopted in 1942. Houteff's community in Waco soon grew to about 125 members, with other Davidians scattered throughout the country. In their early years the group maintained ties to the Seventh-Day Adventist Church, but a formal break came after World War II and SDA authorities denounced what they viewed as a dangerous heresy.

As David Koresh would do 50 years later, Victor Houteff expounded his complex prophetic system in sermons, Bible classes, pamphlets, and tracts. Houteff anticipated Koresh in another way as well: in 1937, at age 52, he married a teenage girl who lived with her parents at Mount Carmel.

Despite their unusual beliefs, the early Davidians were peaceful, hardworking, and respected by the neighboring ranchers and townspeople. A Waco attorney later recalled them as "very gentle, very soft-spoken people and very nice,

---

*In the biblical book of I Kings, Mount Carmel is the site of a contest between the prophet Elijah and 450 prophets of the false god Baal, to determine who worships the true God. Elijah wins the contest and slaughters the false prophets.

From its founding in 1935 by Victor Houteff as an offshoot of the Seventh-Day Adventist Church, the Mount Carmel community in Waco, Texas, was steeped in Bible prophecy. This 1938 publication features apocalyptic scriptures from the books of Matthew and Revelation, and a drawing of a great insect with a human head bearing a crown, based on Rev. 9:7. (Bob Darden/ The Texas Collection of Baylor University)

except that when they started talking about religious matters, they would get a kind of faraway look in their eyes."

Victor Houteff's death in 1955 triggered the first of a series of leadership struggles within the Davidian movement. His young widow Florence Houteff announced that Victor had appointed her his successor before he died. But Benjamin Roden, who had settled with his wife and son at Mount Carmel in 1953, promoted himself as the new leader.

While fending off the Roden claim, Florence Houteff devoted herself to Bible study, and soon issued a startling proclamation. The period of 1,260 days mentioned in the eleventh chapter of Revelation had actually begun on November 9, 1955, and the end would come on April 22, 1959! As the appointed day approached, several hundred Davidians poured into Waco to await the long-anticipated event, Christ's return to earth.

But again, as in 1844, the great day passed uneventfully. Disappointed believers drifted away, and by 1962 Florence Houteff and her remaining core of followers had disbanded the original Davidian organization and left Mount Carmel. Benjamin Roden now saw his opportunity. Moving with his supporters into the abandoned buildings at Mount Carmel, Roden revived the movement and proclaimed himself the new leader. He adopted the name "Branch Davidian" to suggest a restoration of the original movement supposedly betrayed by Florence Houteff.

Under Benjamin Roden's leadership, the movement revived. His complex explanations of Bible prophecy, though mystifying to outsiders, impressed his followers. New recruits arrived, including a group from Australia in 1967. With Benjamin Roden's death in 1978, his widow Lois Roden emerged as the leader, just as Florence Houteff had inherited the mantle from her husband. For a time, Lois Roden proclaimed a feminist theology, teaching that the Holy Spirit was female, and that at the Second Coming the Messiah would reappear as a woman.

But the leadership struggles continued, particularly among Davidians opposed to Lois Roden's feminist doctrines. When Lois's son George Roden challenged his mother's leadership, Lois expelled him from the community. This led to complicated legal maneuvers as rival factions struggled for dominance and for control of the Mount Carmel property. George Roden proved a tireless litigant, filing endless lawsuits against his mother and her supporters. He also became obsessed with firearms, and went about heavily armed. George Roden suffered from Tourette's Syndrome, a neurological disorder that can cause sudden bodily motions, involuntary grunts and other vocalizations, and even bursts of violence. Though controlled by medication, this condition affected his behavior and contributed to the growing climate of violence at Mount Carmel.

Amid this turmoil, a 21-year-old newcomer arrived at Mount Carmel in 1981: Vernon Howell, the future David Koresh. Howell was born in Houston, Texas, in 1959 to Bonnie Clark, a 15-year-old unwed mother. When he was 5, Bonnie married and moved to Dallas. Little Vernon apparently found this change deeply traumatic. "You're not my mother," he screamed at her.

The family led an erratic existence, and Vernon attended various schools before dropping out after the tenth grade. At an age when most boys were playing sports or joining neighborhood gangs, Vernon spent hours in agonized prayer and

Bible study, especially of the prophecies. Soon he had memorized much of the New Testament. This mastery of scripture would later deeply impress devout men and women who viewed the Bible as the literal word of God and who stood in awe of anyone who knew it so well. Howell joined a Dallas Seventh-Day Adventist Church, but was "disfellowshiped" in 1981 for disrupting the services with his own interpretations of scripture—and for telling the pastor that God had chosen the pastor's teenage daughter to be his wife.

Making his way to Mount Carmel after this rebuff, Howell was warmly welcomed by Lois Roden and her circle. Handsome, personable, and a fount of Bible knowledge, Howell adapted easily to the culture of a religious community totally absorbed with prophetic interpretation. In 1983, Lois Roden proclaimed him her chosen successor, the sect's latest Living Prophet. In January 1984, now 24, Howell married Rachel Jones, the 14-year-old daughter of Perry and Mary Bell Jones, two of Mrs. Roden's most devoted followers. Perry Jones, though not an ordained minister, performed the ceremony.

Vernon Howell quickly gained absolute dominance over the Mount Carmel community, which he reenforced with hours of Bible classes where he explained the prophecies in mind-numbing detail. A Baylor University student who interviewed Howell in the early eighties described his style:

> We didn't talk, *he* did. He went on and on about Revelation. I noticed nothing connected in anybody's mind but his. To him, all Scripture [was] prophecy for his picking and determining what it meant. He alone knew. There was something horribly wrong if you didn't agree. There was no following him; he was all over the place; [but] he clearly had stepped fully into the position of being a prophet.

Vernon Howell, the future David Koresh, at age 14, around 1973. The product of a disrupted childhood, Vernon left high school after his sophomore year, devoted himself to prayer and Bible memorization, and in 1981 joined the apocalyptic Mount Carmel sect, now called Branch Davidians, at their Waco commune. (Wide World)

Another Baylor student who also met Howell as part of a research project conveyed something of his charismatic appeal:

> He had the capacity for making you feel like you were the center of the universe when he talked to you, that you were the only thing that counted, that you were very important to him and to whatever he was pitching.

Meanwhile, however, Lois Roden's son George, angry and resentful of Vernon Howell, pursued his endless lawsuits. In 1985 George regained legal title to Mount Carmel, which he renamed "Rodenville" and protected with a stockpile of weapons. Lois Roden, Vernon Howell, and some 40 followers retreated to a remote shantytown of tents and trailers in the woods near Palestine, Texas, 180 miles east of Waco.

While Howell solidified his position among the exiles at Palestine, he also pursued his ambitions to become a rock star. He frequented the music stores in Waco, and even assembled a rock band that released a cassette tape in 1987. (One of the songs, "Mad Man in Waco," though directed at George Roden, would later seem eerily prophetic of Howell's own career.)

The conflict between the two groups turned violent in November 1987 when Howell and six male followers, fully armed and dressed in combat fatigues, raided Mount Carmel. George Roden and his well-armed followers fought back. The battle resulted in only minor injuries, but Howell and his men were arrested and briefly jailed. At his 1988 trial for attempted murder, a well-dressed Vernon Howell was at his charming best and the jury acquitted him and the other defendants. In one revealing moment at the trial, Howell's followers remained seated rather than rising when the judge entered. But when Howell gave a quiet signal, they all rose simultaneously. After the acquittal, Howell vowed to McLennan County Sheriff Jack Harwell that never again would he allow anyone to arrest or imprison him.

But George Roden also faced trouble with the law. As his debts and back taxes mounted, his lawsuits became highly abusive, not only against Vernon Howell (whom he called "Vermin" Howell) but also against the Texas judicial system and specific judges. In 1988 Roden went to jail for 6 months for contempt of court. (The following year he was committed to a Texas state mental institution for an indefinite period.)

Seizing their opportunity, Vernon Howell and his followers in 1988 returned triumphantly to Mount Carmel. Secure in his leadership at last, Howell (who in 1990 legally changed his name to David Koresh*) reigned nearly supreme over the Waco group and over Davidians elsewhere who accepted his claim to leadership.

A glib, manipulative young man, Koresh used his charm, his curly-haired good looks, and his fluency in Bible prophecy to lure new converts. He especially targeted Seventh-Day Adventists, whose vocabulary he knew well and whose interest in prophecy and the End Times he fully shared. In California, Hawaii, Canada, Australia, New Zealand, England, Israel, and elsewhere, he met with the

---

*Köreš is the Hebrew name for Cyrus II, the Persian ruler who defeated the Babylonians, befriended the Jews, and is praised in Isaiah 45:1 as one of the Lord's annointed.

Davidian faithful and courted new recruits, sometimes at Seventh-Day Adventist schools, sometimes in rock clubs. Perry Jones and other top Davidians at Waco conducted recruitment forays as well. Once in the fold, new converts turned over their assets—sometimes hundreds of thousands of dollars—to Koresh. Two wealthy California converts, Donald and Jeannine Bunds, gave him a $100,000 house in Pomona, near Los Angeles.

These successes came at a time when interest in Bible prophecy was at a high level in America and elsewhere. The message that the end was near was being proclaimed in countless evangelical churches, by radio and TV preachers like Jimmy Swaggart and Pat Robertson, and by paperback popularizers. One such popularization, Hal Lindsey's *The Late Great Planet Earth* (1970), sold many millions of copies.

As new recruits came to Waco, Koresh organized building projects, laid down rules, practiced with his rock band, and taught his Bible classes that dragged on for hours. In these rambling expositions of prophecy he embraced no consistent scheme of interpretation, but simply extemporized as he went along, quoting passages from Revelation, Isaiah, Daniel, and other Bible texts to justify whatever idea he was developing at the moment.

Soon he began to claim not only special interpretive gifts as the Living Prophet, but also actual divinity as the Lamb of God, the Messiah. "If the Bible is true, then I'm Christ," Koresh proclaimed in an audiotape distributed to his followers, adding: "But so what? Look at 2,000 years ago. What's so great about being Christ? A man nailed to the cross. A man of sorrow acquainted with grief. You know, being Christ ain't nothing."

He based his claim on the fact that he had "uncovered," or explained, the puzzling seven seals of the Book of Revelation. He alone understood the mysteries of the Last Days and could unveil them to his disciples. His Mount Carmel followers, browbeaten by his endless harangues, often under conditions of physical deprivation such as hunger or lack of sleep, and cut off from the outside world or from critical challenges to his ideas, conceded his divinity and thus his right to control every detail of their lives.

Branch Davidians followed a strict ascetic regimen, observing rules that the leader himself blithely ignored. Koresh imposed a vegetarian, alcohol-free diet at Mount Carmel, while he enjoyed roasts and beer. Sending others to bed early, he stayed up late playing amplified music or practicing with his band. While insisting that Davidian women wear modest dresses and no makeup, and haranguing Davidian males about the degrading nature of sexual desire, he pursued a vigorous and varied sex life and patronized "Sonny T's," a Waco roadhouse featuring nude dancing. To followers troubled by the contradictions between his life and his preaching, he described himself as a "sinful Messiah" who took on the burden of wrongdoing in order to lift this burden from his followers.

During this period of unrestrained power, Koresh was gripped by several obsessions: a desire for unbounded sexual access to the females of the community; a preoccupation with violence and weaponry; and paranoid suspicion of the larger society. The outside world, Koresh warned his followers, was "Babylon," the wicked power whose destruction is foretold in the Book of Revelation.

As Koresh's sexual compulsions grew, his scriptural exposition became little more than a means of coercing his befuddled followers' assent to his unbridled demands. Indeed, soon after his arrival at Mount Carmel, he had begun a sexual relationship with 67-year-old Lois Roden, justifying it by citing Isaiah 8:3 ("And I went unto the prophetess; and she conceived and bare a son"). He later claimed that Lois had, indeed, become pregnant, but miscarried because of lack of faith. He took other Davidian women into his bed as well, including 50-year-old Jeannine Bunds, again foretelling—falsely, as it turned out—that she would bear him a child.

But young girls were the special focus of his sexual obsession. In 1986, he reported to the Davidians that he had had sex with a 13-year-old girl of the community. In 1988, assuring her it was God's will, he raped his wife's 12-year-old sister. Over the next few years he added more and more young girls to the ranks of his sexual conquests. At the evening meal at Mount Carmel, he would select the girl or woman with whom he wished to spend the night. The precise number of children he fathered is unclear; Jeannine Bunds (a registered nurse who delivered many of them), placed the total at 15. Most of the children who perished in April 1993 were Koresh's own.

Koresh offered ever more convoluted biblical interpretations to justify his sexual demands. A favorite text was Song of Solomon 6:8: "There are threescore queens, and fourscore concubines, and virgins without number." God longed for grandchildren, he told his followers, and only he, as God's son, could supply this need.

In 1989, at a major assembly of Davidians in California, Koresh announced a new revelation: all married couples must henceforth refrain from sexual relations. Men and women would sleep in separate dormitories, and he alone would have sexual access to the women. Describing intercourse as a degrading practice that distorts relations between the sexes, he declared that he would free his male followers of this repulsive activity and take upon himself the duty of producing a new generation of saints to rule with him during the coming millennial age. Meanwhile, in compensation, he designated selected males of the community as his "Mighty Men," an Old Testament honorific describing King David's greatest warriors.

Most Davidians, including the parents of the girls from whom he demanded sex, accepted Koresh's erratic and self-indulgent behavior, which he invariably justified on biblical grounds. As his enemy George Roden had declared in a court deposition: "He always has a so-called prophecy from the Bible when he wants to seduce a woman." The married couples even obeyed Koresh's command to cease sexual relations while granting him total sexual freedom. As one male Davidian later explained to a baffled reporter: "You just don't *understand*. . . . We as Branch Davidians aren't *interested* in sex. Sex is so *assaultive*, so aggressive. David has shouldered that burden for us."

Intoxicated by power, Koresh increasingly lost touch with other human beings except as objects of manipulation. One disillusioned Davidian later observed:

> At first, Vernon Howell appeared to be a conservative person whose only wish
> was to reform the Seventh-Day Adventist Church. As time progressed, however,
> Howell became power-hungry and abusive, bent on obtaining and exercising
> absolute power and authority over the group. . . . [B]y 1989 he had lost all restraint.

Another of Koresh's compulsions emerged during this period of unchecked power: physical cruelty to children and infants. When babies as young as 8 months cried or fell asleep during his lessons, he would order them whipped for as long as half an hour in a "spanking room" with a paddle bearing the inscription: IT IS WRITTEN. Children who angered him were forced to sleep on the bare floor or banished to an outbuilding for the night after he had terrified them with tales of giant rats.

Gripped by apocalyptic visions, Koresh also became obsessed with firearms. In 1991–93, he spent some $200,000 amassing an arsenal that included hand grenades, over 100 M-16 assault rifles, an AK-47 automatic machine gun, an antitank rifle, and many cases of ammunition. Donald Bunds, an engineer, modified some of the guns to make them even more lethal. Koresh's "Mighty Men" stood constant guard duty, and a four-story watchtower commanded a 360-degree view. Neighbors reported frequent target practice, machine-gun fire, and even blasts of high explosives. Motorists who entered the compound by mistake quickly found bullets whizzing around their cars.

As always, Koresh justified all this biblically, citing passages that foretold a cataclysmic end-time struggle between the righteous and the wicked "Babylonians." Concluding that the cosmic struggle would begin at the Waco compound, he gave Mount Carmel an ominous new name: "Ranch Apocalypse."

In a sense, Koresh's apocalyptic fears were justified, because "Babylon"— the outside world—was indeed growing more interested in the tight-knit cult ruled by one man. That interest increased as a few dissident Davidians, led by a defector named Marc Breault, began to publicize Koresh's behavior. A Catholic convert to Seventh-Day Adventism, Breault had been lured into the Branch Davidians by Perry Jones in 1986 while attending Loma Linda University, an Adventist school in California. Initially a true believer and one of Koresh's "Mighty Men," Breault gradually rebelled at goings-on within the cult. After Koresh's 1989 claim of free sexual access to all Branch Davidian women, including Breault's Australian wife of a few months, he began to document the leader's misdeeds, on one occasion spending the night in an office beneath Koresh's bedroom to prove that Koresh had slept with a 13-year-old girl.

Breault next warned Branch Davidians in Australia (where he and his wife had settled), that Koresh, far from being the Lamb of God, was a dangerous false prophet. Koresh rushed to Australia, but his attempted reconciliation with Breault failed. In September 1990 the Australian defectors hired a private detective to gather evidence of Koresh's sexual relations with young girls and his physical abuse of children.

Meanwhile, in the summer of 1990, at a Branch Davidian house in La Verne, California, where Koresh had taken up temporary residence, 21-year-old Robyn Bunds, who with her mother Jeannine was part of Koresh's harem, told him she was leaving. In retaliation, Koresh secretly sent their young son back to Waco. Robyn contacted the La Verne police, who ordered Koresh to return the boy or face kidnapping charges. He complied, and Robyn Bunds departed. A few months later, Jeannine Bunds also abandoned the cult.

On another front, Michigan disk jockey David Jewell, having been alerted by Marc Breault, filed suit in December 1991 to gain custody of his 10-year-old daughter from his ex-wife Sherri, a high-ranking Davidian. In his suit, Jewell submitted evidence that Koresh was simultaneously sleeping with Sherri and grooming her daughter to become one of his "wives." At the trial early in 1992, Marc Breault described Koresh's pattern of dissolving marriages and his sexual and phys-ical mistreatment of juveniles. The court granted the Jewells joint custody of their daughter, but ordered Koresh to stay away from her. Shaken by all these devel-opments, in 1992, Koresh with his entourage left California permanently for the security of Waco.

But even on home ground, the outside world was pressing in, as represen-tatives of the Texas Department of Human Services began to visit, checking re-ports that Koresh was having sexual relations with girls under the age of 14, a felony under Texas law. Meanwhile, in the spring of 1992, the *Waco Tribune Her-ald* had begun to investigate the Branch Davidians; the newspaper's explosive seven-part series, "The Sinful Messiah," began in February 1993, as Koresh's world crashed around him.

But it was Koresh's obsession with weaponry, not his sex crimes, that fi-nally brought him down. In May 1992, a UPS delivery man alerted Sheriff Jack Harwell to the Davidians' heavy purchases of firearms. One package, he reported, had burst open, scattering hand grenades across the UPS loading dock! The sher-iff, in turn, informed the Federal Bureau of Alcohol, Tobacco, and Firearms (ATF). On June 4, 1992, ATF special agent Davy Aguilera met with Harwell and other local law-enforcement officials to discuss the matter. Over the next 9 months, local and federal officials documented Koresh's violation of firearms laws, in-cluding the conversion of semiautomatic weapons to automatic weapons. Robert Rodriquez, an ATF agent posing as a potential convert, spent hours with Koresh and passed along information to his superiors.

Although Koresh often visited Waco's bars, restaurants, and music shops— not to mention Sonny T's strip joint—the ATF did not arrest him on one of these trips off the compound. Before taking Koresh into custody, officials would later argue, they had to raid the compound for proof that illegal weapons were indeed stockpiled there. Once this decision was made, ATF director Stephen Higgins ap-proved plans for a full-scale raid. ATF agents from across the South were trained at nearby Fort Hood army base, using a mock-up of the Waco compound.

The raid began at 9:55 A.M. on Sunday, February 28, 1993, as three canvas-covered cattle trucks concealing 91 ATF and FBI agents rolled down the Double EE Ranch Road and into the compound grounds. As Texas National Guard he-licopters thumped overhead, agents in flak jackets and blue jumpsuits poured from the trucks and attempted to storm the main building. But a hail of grenades and rifle fire drove them back. The team assigned to storm the main building and se-cure the Davidians' weapons arsenal suffered especially heavy casualties. After a 45-minute firefight, sporadic shooting went on for more than an hour longer. Fol-lowing an afternoon of uneasy silence, another burst of shooting erupted around 5 P.M. when three Davidians emerged from the main building and fired toward the ATF positions. When the gunfire finally stopped for good, 4 ATF agents lay dead or dying, with 15 wounded, some severely.

At least 6 Davidians had been killed, included Koresh's most trusted adviser (and father-in-law) Perry Jones. A young Australian, Peter Gent, was shot as he fired at ATF agents from a water tower. His body fell into a tree, where it hung for 3 days. (Peter's twin sister Nicole was inside the compound.) Koresh claimed to have been wounded as well. After ATF officials negotiated a cease-fire by telephone, unarmed medics retrieved the ATF dead and wounded. A convoy of ambulances and private vehicles ferried the injured to Waco's Hillcrest Baptist Medical Center, swamping the hospital's emergency facilities.

As the smoke cleared, questions remained. Critics challenged the ATF's decision to raid the compound rather than arrest Koresh on a visit to town. Further, the critics asked, why did the ATF not treat more seriously the well-documented fact that Koresh's "Mighty Men" were well trained, heavily armed, and prepared to resist? And why did the raid proceed despite evidence that Koresh knew of the plan, eliminating any element of surprise? Security was so lax that local newspaper and TV reporters were waiting at the compound when the ATF convoy arrived. Early Sunday morning, undercover agent Robert Rodriquez had warned his superiors that Koresh knew of the raid and was deploying his forces. Conspiracy theorists suggested that the entire affair had been stage-managed to enhance the image of the ATF, a beleaguered federal agency facing budget cuts.

As the second-guessing began, the next phase of the story unfolded: a long, frustrating standoff between the Branch Davidians inside the compound and FBI authorities outside. Initially, the confrontation seemed likely to end quickly, without further bloodshed. Koresh, basking in the limelight, gave telephone interviews to a Texas radio station and to the Cable News Network (CNN), quoting scrip-

Bloody Sunday, February 28, 1993. Agents of the Bureau of Alcohol, Tobacco, and Firearms in full combat gear carry a dead or wounded comrade after the abortive raid and shootout. In David Koresh's apocalyptic scenario, these federal agents represented the evil power of the Antichrist, whom many prophecy believers expect to arise in the last days. (KWTX-TV/Sygma)

ture, expounding prophecy, and portraying himself as simply a misunderstood religious leader. In exchange for this media exposure, Koresh released 10 children over a 24-hour period. Over the next few weeks, some 37 Davidian adults and children left the compound. But perhaps 95 remained, and Marc Breault, who knew Koresh well, was not misled. "I think he'll go out in a blaze of glory," Breault predicted.

The seige that followed unfolded in a glare of media publicity, as more than 200 newspaper and TV reporters camped out in an area near the compound dubbed "Satellite City." Each morning at 10:30, reporters assembled in the Waco Convention Center for a briefing by FBI spokesman Bob Ricks. Not only was the story inherently dramatic, but the Davidians had followers in several countries, adding to the international interest.

In an age of global communications, the Waco story proved tailor-made for packaging and mass distribution. Indeed, the standoff became a kind of TV miniseries, *Seige in Waco,* with its own logo (usually a shot of Koresh or of the Davidian compound) and its familiar cast of characters. Representatives of the tabloid press, TV talk shows, docudramas, and made-for-television movies paid high fees for interviews with former Davidians, relatives of Davidians, and Davidians who had left the compound after the shootout. Robyn Bunds let it be known that she was considering several TV and movie offers.

In a glare of media publicity, journalists, TV crews, self-proclaimed prophets, throngs of sensation-seekers, and hawkers of T-shirts and other memorabilia descended on Waco during the 51 day seige. Here, photojournalists gather in the Waco Convention Center for the daily FBI press briefing. (Brad Bailey/The Texas Collection of Baylor University)

Hundreds of eccentrics, mystics, religious fanatics, and freelance evangelists, joined by college students on spring break and the merely curious, converged on Waco. (A few succeeded in joining the Davidians inside the compound, to the embarrassment of the FBI.) Entrepreneurs peddled buttons, bumper stickers, and T-shirts with such slogans as "David Koresh World Tour, 1993" and:

We
Ain't
Comin'
Out

David Koresh, obscure leader of an obscure movement, had become David Koresh, instant celebrity, his image emblazoned on the covers of *Time* and *Newsweek*, his interviews beamed worldwide, his pronouncements on Bible prophecy solemnly dissected on network news programs.

In Washington, President Clinton, Attorney General Reno, and the FBI's top brass followed developments closely, but delegated day-to-day operations to officials on the scene. The latter never developed a consistent strategy. At first they engaged Koresh on his own terms, conducting interminable telephone discussions of passages in Revelation or Isaiah. They consulted psychologists, psychiatrists, and theologians, and even imported prophecy experts who offered Koresh more benign interpretations of his favorite texts. A few weeks into the seige, the FBI permitted Dick DeGuerin, a lawyer hired by Koresh's mother, to confer with Koresh inside the compound. Sheriff Jack Harwell, who knew Koresh well, tried to reason with him.

The FBI's Hostage Rescue Team, by contrast, on the dubious assumption that Koresh and a few armed thugs were holding most of the Davidians against their will, viewed the standoff as a classic hostage situation. Acting on this premise, the FBI resorted to psychological-warfare techniques to disorient Koresh and induce his followers to abandon him. They cut off the compound's electricity, drove around the buildings with heavy vehicles, and buzzed the complex with helicopters. At night they turned on harsh floodlights and high-decibel amplifiers that broadcast raucous music or grating noises such as the whine of a dentist's drill.

As the weeks dragged on, and winter gave way to early spring, pressure built for a resolution of the crisis. The restless media, eager to wrap up the story and move on, added to the pressure. A few advisers, including Sheriff Harwell, argued for a pullback and a quiet waiting game. Interviewed several months later, Harwell criticized the FBI's approach:

> Those folks are trained to deal with hostage rescues. Their playbook says to apply unrelenting pressure until they crack. But the Davidians weren't hostages; they were there by choice. I urged that the agents pull back and give those people room to think and make a better choice for themselves and for those children.

But Harwell also noted the psychological dynamics on both sides that made a peaceful resolution unlikely: "When you create elite forces and train and equip them for maximum violence, they want to do what they've been trained to do. When you apply pressure to people with deeply held religious beliefs, all you do is strengthen their resolve."

Strengthening the hand of those who advocated decisive action was the ev-idence of Koresh's deteriorating mental state. On the weekend of April 10–11, Koresh transmitted to the FBI two rambling letters that revealed his deepening apocalyptic obsessions and psychotic delusions. Evidently dictated to one of his young wives, the letters were penned in a neat girlish hand on lavender notepa-per. Signed "Yahweh Koresh" in English and Hebrew, the letters declaimed in part:

> I offer to you my wisdom. I offer to you my sealed secrets. How dare you turn away My invitations of mercy. . . . The law is Mine, the Truth is Mine. . . . I AM your God and you will bow under my feet. . . . I AM your life & your death. I AM the Spirit of the prophets and the Author of their testimonies. . . . Do you think you have power to stop My will? . . . My seven thunders are to be revealed. . . . Do you want me to laugh at your pending torments? Do you want Me to pull the heavens back and show you My anger? . . . Fear Me, for I have you in my snare. . . .

On and on the hysterical, vaguely biblical phrases spilled out, thundering cosmic threats against the Babylonian enemy that was edging ever closer.

In truth, the FBI bargainers never had a strong hand. Koresh faced murder charges and a morass of legal difficulties if he came out. Within the compound, he reigned supreme among a band of followers whose faith seemed unshakable. As FBI lawyer Daniel Coulson observed in a postmortem on the disaster: "Inside, he's God. Outside, he's an inmate on trial for his life. What was he going to do?" As for negotiation, the FBI's Bob Ricks summed up the problem: "When you're God, it's very difficult to have someone come forward and prove you're not God."

And so events unfolded with the inexorability of a Greek tragedy, ending on April 19 with the clusters of orange flags fluttering over the ashes that a few hours before had been men, women, and children who had fully expected, according to their Messiah's teachings, to be the saints and rulers in a coming age of peace and righteousness.

But the climax of the siege, horrific as it was, did not end the story. A tragedy that under other circumstances would have produced an outpouring of sympathy for the victims and their families led to no such reaction. It was as though the Branch Davidians had been placed outside the pale of American society. Rather than sympathy, the Davidians became the objects of macabre curiosity and the kind of ghoulish humor reserved for shocking events that lose their emotional power as they are transmuted into media circuses. (*Q.* "What were God's first words to Koresh?" *A.* "Well done." *Q.* "How do you pick up a Branch Davidian chick?" *A.* "With a dustbuster.")

The Waco compound, now a heap of blackened rubble, remained a magnet for visitors. Some came from idle curiosity, others to mourn family and friends who had died, whether ATF agents or Davidians. But others came from different motives, transforming the compound into a shrine to imperiled American free-dom. Stories circulated of a government conspiracy to eradicate the Davidians as a first step to disarming all citizens.

Much speculation centered on the fatal fire. Some accused the FBI of de-liberately torching the compound in a cold-blooded massacre. More plausibly, oth-ers claimed that the thrusting turrets of the tanks pounding in the compound walls had burst propane canisters or flammable-liquid containers, touching off the inferno. Rejecting this theory, the FBI insisted that the fires had been deliberately set from inside. FBI surveillance devices were said to show three separate blazes erupting within 50 seconds of each other. Agreed one FBI agent:

> I saw three fires almost simultaneously. . . . [I]t was not started by the tanks in front of the building. That's ridiculous. I saw the tanks at different points from where the fires were. . . . [T]he bottom line here is that . . . [David Koresh] murdered all those people.

Strengthening the government's version, some Davidians claimed that Koresh had prepared his followers for suicide, promising them rebirth to a celestial existence. A 12-year-old girl released by Koresh after the February raid described in chilling detail on television's *Phil Donahue Show* (and later in congressional testimony) Koresh's instructions on how to position a pistol in one's mouth to assure quick death. But other Davidians vehemently denied such charges. Declared one survivor: "There was never any suicide plan and never any order to destroy the compound. We intended to come out."

Whatever the truth, it quickly became clear that many Americans rejected the official version of events. The flow of visitors to Waco increasingly included angry, alienated citizens who honored the Branch Davidians as martyrs to an out-of-control federal government.

The charred remains of the compound after the April 19 assault. The raging flames killed some 80 men, women, and children of the Branch Davidian sect, and left a smoldering residue of shock, bitterness, and controversy. David Koresh had warned his followers that the prophesied end was at hand. Few realized how quickly his predictions would be fulfilled. (Steven Reece/Sygma)

Many linked Waco to the Randall Weaver case of the year before. In 1983, Weaver, an ex-Green Beret and white separatist, had moved with his family to northern Idaho, near a settlement called Ruby Ridge, where, like Koresh, he allegedly trafficked in illegal firearms. Indicted for selling sawed-off shotguns to an FBI informant, Weaver ignored a court order to appear for trial. When U.S. marshals staked out his house in August 1992, a young man living with the Weavers, Kevin Harris, fired at them. In the ensuing shootout, Marshal William Degan and the Weavers' 14-year-old son Samuel were killed. A further exchange of gunfire the following day left Weaver's wife Vicki dead and Kevin Harris seriously wounded. Randall Weaver and three surviving daughters surrendered the next day. Again like Koresh, the Weavers viewed current events through a prism of Bible prophecy. In a 1991 letter to federal authorities, Vicki Weaver had written apocalyptically: "A long-forgotten wind is beginning to blow. Do you hear the approaching thunder?"* For many fearful citizens already deeply suspicious of government, the events in Ruby Ridge and Waco seemed compelling evidence of a coordinated attempt to destroy American freedom, beginning with the Second Amendment right to bear arms.

One of the ideologically motivated pilgrims to Waco was Timothy McVeigh, an embittered army veteran obsessed with weapons and convinced of a federal conspiracy to wipe out individual liberty. And McVeigh, it appeared, was prepared to go beyond mere protest to desperate and violent deeds. On the morning of April 19, 1995, the second anniversary of the Waco attack, a massive car bomb destroyed the Alfred Murrah Federal Building in Oklahoma City, including the offices of the Bureau of Alcohol, Tobacco, and Firearms. As rescuers risked their lives probing the rubble for survivors, the restless media once again rolled in, transforming the tragedy into images and sound bytes for the evening news. The death toll neared 170, including many children who had been playing in a day-care center at the front of the building. Within days, authorities arrested a stony-faced McVeigh. Claiming his rights as a prisoner of war, he initially gave only his name, rank, and serial number. In August 1995, as investigation of a possible larger conspiracy continued, a federal grand jury indicted McVeigh and an alleged accomplice on charges of planning and carrying out the bombing.

As the century ended, Waco cast a lengthening shadow, symbolizing for many all that is wrong in American society. Others view with apprehension the spreading climate of alienation and mistrust, the fraying of the bond between citizens and their government, that is somehow deeply enmeshed with the fate of the Branch Davidians and their sinful Messiah.

AN INTERPRETATION

Like most historical events, Waco can be viewed from a variety of perspectives to yield a variety of meanings. Most fundamentally, perhaps, it underscores the centrality of religion in American history and life. Having no established church and

---

*In 1995, faced with a lawsuit alleging the wrongful deaths of Samuel and Vicki Weaver, the Justice Department settled out of court, agreeing to pay Randall Weaver $3.1 million.

committed to religious freedom, the United States has nurtured an impressive array of self-proclaimed prophets like Joseph Smith and William Miller, and new religious movements like the Mormons and the Seventh-Day Adventists. (The Christian Science Church, founded in 1879 by Mary Baker Eddy, could be added to the list.) The Branch Davidians, though tiny by comparison to these groups, and less fortunate in their leadership, are part of this tradition of religious innovation.

To ignore this powerful strand of enthusiastic religiosity is to fail to understand much of American history—and much of contemporary U.S. culture. In an age of space travel, microcomputers, and gene splicing, religious belief, whether expressed through mainstream denominations or small sects, still saturates American life.

The Waco story also casts an interesting light on a deep desire felt by Americans—perhaps by most human beings—for history to have form and meaning. We need beginnings, and we need endings. This need helps us understand the continuing appeal of the apocalyptic outlook as found in the biblical prophecies. Despite its terrifying images of future conflict, the apocalyptic perspective exerts a powerful dramatic appeal. From this perspective, human history is unfolding according to a divine plan that we can know and understand. And history is a great moral drama, racing toward that final moment when righteousness will triumph and evil will be vanquished. As we have seen, David Koresh was far from alone in his apocalyptic outlook. Not just the Branch Davidians, but a great many Americans, find this vision of human history, with a clear moral meaning and a precise beginning and end, more appealing than the version they encounter in textbooks and public schools.

This human desire for history to have dramatic form—the need for closure, for *endings*—shaped events in Waco in more immediate ways as well. As the siege wore on, the media, along with newspaper readers and TV viewers at home, grew increasingly restless. How long would the standoff drag on? When would it *end?* The fateful decision to invade the compound, and to ignore those who counseled patience, was surely influenced by this growing pressure for a resolution of the crisis. Thus, Koresh's vision of a decisive end of human history and the media's desire for a decisive end of the siege reenforced each other, contributing to the tragic final outcome.

Along with these rather broad themes—the centrality of religion, the continuing appeal of apocalypticism, the need for endings—the Waco story illuminates some more specific features of U.S. thought and culture in the 1980s and 1990s.

For example, the rigidly hierarchical social order that Koresh imposed on his followers reflected a broader conservative reaction in these years against threatening social changes. Beginning with the civil rights movement and continuing with the women's rights campaign, the drive for gay and lesbian rights, and other movements, post-1960 America saw a succession of protest efforts by a variety of oppressed groups. In response, antidiscriminatory laws and affirmative-action plans were enacted to rectify decades of injustice against minorities and women.

For many males, the women's movement proved especially threatening, as women poured into the workplace, the professions, and the universities, and feminist ideologists challenged traditional gender assumptions that subordinated women or consigned them to the domestic realm. By the 1980s, a reaction was underway. Conservative politicians and religious groups attacked "radical feminists" and championed "traditional family values"—often a code term for male authority and a hierarchical gender order.

In the cultural realm, books like Robert Bly's *Iron John: A Book About Men* (1990) called on men to reassert their authority and rediscover their primitive powers. Muscle-bound film stars such as Sylvester Stallone and Arnold Schwarzenegger played cartoon-like macho heroes; supermarket shelves offered romance novels in which heaving-bosom heroines found fulfillment in yielding to dominant men.

In grotesquely exaggerated ways, the fantasies that David Koresh acted out at Waco mirrored this backlash. His absolutist rule, his "Mighty Men," and his debasement of women offered an extreme but recognizable prototype of the patriarchical order that feminists were challenging and conservatives were championing in these years.

The Koresh years at Waco, and their aftermath, also highlight a vein of radical individualism and suspicion of government that runs deep in American culture and that became particularly intense in the 1980s and 1990s. Rejecting the wicked society beyond the compound, the Davidians armed themselves for a final showdown with the outside world. But this hardly made them unique. The lone gunfighter, a six-shooter on each hip, confronting powerful forces arrayed against him, looms large in American popular culture. Admiration for the free individual or the independent group, coupled with hostility to society and its claims, is a fundamental theme in American ideology.

The crisis in Waco erupted at a moment when this antigovernment thinking was at flood tide. Mobilized in the 1960s by the firebreathing George Wallace, governor of Alabama, and Arizona senator Barry Goldwater, the 1964 Republican presidential candidate, and in the 1980s by President Ronald Reagan, the rhetoric of radical individualism dominated the 1994 midterm elections as scores of Republican politicians railed against government spending, government regulations, and government programs.

The libertarian mood gained strength from an army of conservative radio talk show hosts who warned darkly of a vast conspiracy to stamp out American freedom. Across the nation rolled waves of resentment against the "liberal elites" in Washington, the media, and the universities who held in contempt the freedom-loving values of all true Americans. David Koresh with his apocalyptic talk of evil "Babylon," simply translated into the idiom of biblical prophecy this larger antigovernment mood.

Waco was thus both a bizarre aberration and an event wholly in the American grain. Like the caged canaries in coal mines that once gave early warning of noxious gases seeping into the air supply, the Waco tragedy, and the response to it, offered a revealing and troubling gauge of cultural tensions and political discontents swirling across the American landscape as the twentieth century ended.

Sources: The Waco story is still so recent that the best sources are contemporary newspaper and magazine accounts. Among hundreds of articles, see, for example, *Time Magazine*, May 3, May 17, and October 11, 1993; *U.S. News and World Report*, March 15, May 3, June 7, and October 4, 1993; and *Newsweek*, May 17, 1993.

Brad Bailey and Bob Darnden, *Mad Man in Waco: The Complete Story of the Davidian Cult, David Koresh, and the Waco Massacre* (Waco: WRS Publishing, 1993) offers valuable material on the early history of the Davidians. Clifford L. Linedecker, *Massacre at Waco, Texas* (New York: St. Martin's Press, 1993), though a hastily produced "quickie" book, includes some useful material.

Analytic essays placing the Waco crisis in a larger context include Michael Barkun, "Reflections after Waco: Millennialists and the State," *Christian Century* (June 2, 1993) and Alexander Cockburn, "Waco Revisited," *The Nation* (October 18, 1993). These two essays, as well as others relating to Waco, are reprinted in Robert Emmet Long (ed.), *Religious Cults in America* 1994). In *Why Waco?* (New York: H. W. Wilson, 1995), two historians of religion, James D. Tabor and Eugene V. Gallagher, retell the story and explore its implications for our understanding of new religious movements. Stuart A. Wright (ed.), *Armegeddon in Waco: Critical Perspectives on the Branch Dividian Conflict* (Chicago: University of Chicago Press, 1995) includes perceptive interpretations by scholars in historical, sociological, media, legal, and religious-studies disciplines.

Paul Boyer, "A Brief History of the End of Time," *New Republic* (May 17, 1993) sketches the history of apocalyptic beliefs and movements, links the Davidians to the larger history of new religious movements in America, and notes the pervasiveness of apocalyptic belief in contemporary America.